Incorporating Nature-Inspired Paradigms in Computational Applications

Mehdi Khosrow-Pour
Information Resources Management Association, USA

A volume in the Advances in
Systems Analysis, Software
Engineering, and High Performance
Computing (ASASEHPC) Book Series

Published in the United States of America by
    IGI Global
    Engineering Science Reference (an imprint of IGI Global)
    701 E. Chocolate Avenue
    Hershey PA, USA 17033
    Tel: 717-533-8845
    Fax: 717-533-8661
    E-mail: cust@igi-global.com
    Web site: http://www.igi-global.com

Library of Congress Cataloging-in-Publication Data

Names: Khosrow-Pour, Mehdi, 1951- editor.
Title: Incorporating nature-inspired paradigms in computational applications
  / Mehdi Khosrow-Pour, editor.
Description: Hershey, PA : Engineering Science Reference, [2018] | Includes
  bibliographical references.
Identifiers: LCCN 2017034167| ISBN 9781522550204 (hardcover) | ISBN
  9781522550211 (ebook)
Subjects: LCSH: Natural computation. | Bionics.
Classification: LCC QA76.9.N37 I53 2018 | DDC 006.3/8--dc23 LC record available at https://lccn.
loc.gov/2017034167

This book is published in the IGI Global book series Advances in Systems Analysis, Software Engineering, and High Performance Computing (ASASEHPC) (ISSN: 2327-3453; eISSN: 2327-3461)

British Cataloguing in Publication Data
A Cataloguing in Publication record for this book is available from the British Library.

All work contributed to this book is new, previously-unpublished material.
The views expressed in this book are those of the authors, but not necessarily of the publisher.

For electronic access to this publication, please contact: eresources@igi-global.com.

Advances in Systems Analysis, Software Engineering, and High Performance Computing (ASASEHPC) Book Series

ISSN:2327-3453
EISSN:2327-3461

Editor-in-Chief: Vijayan Sugumaran, Oakland University, USA

MISSION

The theory and practice of computing applications and distributed systems has emerged as one of the key areas of research driving innovations in business, engineering, and science. The fields of software engineering, systems analysis, and high performance computing offer a wide range of applications and solutions in solving computational problems for any modern organization.

The **Advances in Systems Analysis, Software Engineering, and High Performance Computing (ASASEHPC) Book Series** brings together research in the areas of distributed computing, systems and software engineering, high performance computing, and service science. This collection of publications is useful for academics, researchers, and practitioners seeking the latest practices and knowledge in this field.

COVERAGE

- Computer Networking
- Metadata and Semantic Web
- Parallel Architectures
- Computer graphics
- Storage Systems
- Engineering Environments
- Computer System Analysis
- Distributed Cloud Computing
- Virtual Data Systems
- Software Engineering

IGI Global is currently accepting manuscripts for publication within this series. To submit a proposal for a volume in this series, please contact our Acquisition Editors at Acquisitions@igi-global.com or visit: http://www.igi-global.com/publish/.

Titles in this Series

For a list of additional titles in this series, please visit:
https://www.igi-global.com/book-series/advances-systems-analysis-software-engineering/73689

Formation Methods, Models, and Hardware Implementation of Pseudorandom Number...
Stepan Bilan (State Economy and Technology University of Transport, Ukraine)
Engineering Science Reference • ©2018 • 301pp • H/C (ISBN: 9781522527732) • US $180.00

Aligning Perceptual and Conceptual Information for Cognitive Contextual System...
Gary Kuvich (IBM, USA)
Engineering Science Reference • ©2018 • 172pp • H/C (ISBN: 9781522524311) • US $165.00

Applied Computational Intelligence and Soft Computing in Engineering
Saifullah Khalid (CCSI Airport, India)
Engineering Science Reference • ©2018 • 340pp • H/C (ISBN: 9781522531296) • US $225.00

Enhancing Software Fault Prediction With Machine Learning Emerging Research...
Ekbal Rashid (Aurora's Technological and Research Institute, India)
Engineering Science Reference • ©2018 • 129pp • H/C (ISBN: 9781522531852) • US $165.00

Solutions for Cyber-Physical Systems Ubiquity
Norbert Druml (Independent Researcher, Austria) Andreas Genser (Independent Researcher, Austria) Armin Krieg (Independent Researcher, Austria) Manuel Menghin (Independent Researcher, Austria) and Andrea Hoeller (Independent Researcher, Austria)
Engineering Science Reference • ©2018 • 482pp • H/C (ISBN: 9781522528456) • US $225.00

Large-Scale Fuzzy Interconnected Control Systems Design and Analysis
Zhixiong Zhong (Xiamen University of Technology, China) and Chih-Min Lin (Yuan Ze University, Taiwan)
Information Science Reference • ©2017 • 223pp • H/C (ISBN: 9781522523857) • US $175.00

Microcontroller System Design Using PIC18F Processors
Nicolas K. Haddad (University of Balamand, Lebanon)
Information Science Reference • ©2017 • 428pp • H/C (ISBN: 9781683180005) • US $195.00

For an entire list of titles in this series, please visit:
https://www.igi-global.com/book-series/advances-systems-analysis-software-engineering/73689

701 East Chocolate Avenue, Hershey, PA 17033, USA
Tel: 717-533-8845 x100 • Fax: 717-533-8661
E-Mail: cust@igi-global.com • www.igi-global.com

Table of Contents

Preface xi

Chapter 1
Application of Natural-Inspired Paradigms on System Identification:
Exploring the Multivariable Linear Time Variant Case 1
    Mateus Giesbrecht, Unicamp, Brazil
    Celso Pascoli Bottura, Unicamp, Brazil

Chapter 2
Comprehensive Learning Particle Swarm Optimization for Structural System
Identification 51
    Hesheng Tang, Tongji University, China
    Xueyuan Guo, Tongji University, China
    Lijun Xie, Tongji University, China
    Songtao Xue, Tohoku Institute of Technology, Japan

Chapter 3
Finding Optimal Input Values for Desired Target Output by Using Particle
Swarm Optimization Algorithm Within Probabilistic Models 76
    Goran Klepac, Raiffeisenbank Austria, Croatia

Chapter 4
Multi-Thresholded Histogram Equalization Based on Parameterless Artificial
Bee Colony...108
    Krishna Gopal Dhal, Midnapore College (Autonomous), India
    Mandira Sen, Tata Consultancy Services, India
    Swarnajit Ray, JBMatrix Technology Pvt. Ltd., India
    Sanjoy Das, University of Kalyani, India

Chapter 5

Biogeographic Computation as Information Processing in Ecosystems 127
    Rodrigo Pasti, Mackenzie University, Brazil
    Alexandre Alberto Politi, Particular, Brazil
    Fernando José Von Zuben, State University of Campinas (Unicamp),
        Brazil
    Leandro Nunes de Castro, Mackenzie University, Brazil

Chapter 6

Evolutionary Approaches to Test Data Generation for Object-Oriented
Software: Overview of Techniques and Tools 162
    Ana Filipa Nogueira, University of Coimbra, Portugal
    José Carlos Bregieiro Ribeiro, Polytechnic Institute of Leiria, Portugal
    Francisco Fernández de Vega, University of Extremadura, Spain
    Mário Alberto Zenha-Rela, University of Coimbra, Portugal

Chapter 7

Evolutionary Control Systems 195
    Jesús-Antonio Hernández-Riveros, Universidad Nacional de Colombia,
        Colombia
    Jorge Humberto Urrea-Quintero, Universidad de Antioquia, Colombia
    Cindy Vanessa Carmona-Cadavid, Universidad Pontificia Bolivariana,
        Colombia

Chapter 8

Cloud Approach for the Medical Information System: MIS on Cloud 238
    Ekaterine Kldiashvili, Georgia Telemedicine Union, Georgia

Related References 262

Compilation of References 308

About the Contributors 377

Index 384

Detailed Table of Contents

Preface..xi

Chapter 1
Application of Natural-Inspired Paradigms on System Identification:
Exploring the Multivariable Linear Time Variant Case 1
Mateus Giesbrecht, Unicamp, Brazil
Celso Pascoli Bottura, Unicamp, Brazil

In this chapter, the application of nature-inspired paradigms on system identification is discussed. A review of the recent applications of techniques such as genetic algorithms, genetic programming, immuno-inspired algorithms, and particle swarm optimization to the system identification is presented, discussing the application to linear, nonlinear, time invariant, time variant, monovariable, and multivariable cases. Then the application of an immuno-inspired algorithm to solve the linear time variant multivariable system identification problem is detailed with examples and comparisons to other methods. Finally, the future directions of the application of nature-inspired paradigms to the system identification problem are discussed, followed by the chapter conclusions.

Chapter 2
Comprehensive Learning Particle Swarm Optimization for Structural System
Identification 51
Hesheng Tang, Tongji University, China
Xueyuan Guo, Tongji University, China
Lijun Xie, Tongji University, China
Songtao Xue, Tohoku Institute of Technology, Japan

This chapter introduces a novel swarm-intelligence-based algorithm named the comprehensive learning particle swarm optimization (CLPSO) to identify parameters of structural systems, which is formulated as a high-dimensional multi-modal numerical optimization problem. With the new strategy in this variant of particle swarm optimization (PSO), historical best information for all other particles is used to update a particle's velocity. This means that the particles have more exemplars to learn from and a larger potential space to fly, avoiding premature convergence. Simulation results for identifying the parameters of a five degree-of-freedom (DOF) structural system under conditions including limited output data, noise polluted signals, and no prior knowledge of mass, damping, or stiffness are presented to demonstrate improved estimation of these parameters by CLPSO when compared with those obtained from PSO. In addition, the efficiency and applicability of the proposed method are experimentally examined by a 12-story shear building shaking table model.

Chapter 3

Finding Optimal Input Values for Desired Target Output by Using Particle Swarm Optimization Algorithm Within Probabilistic Models............................76
Goran Klepac, Raiffeisenbank Austria, Croatia

Developed predictive models, especially models based on probabilistic concept, regarding numerous potential combinatory states can be very complex. That complexity can cause uncertainty about which factors should have which values to achieve optimal value of output. An example of that problem is developed with a Bayesian network with numerous potential states and their interaction when we would like to find optimal value of nodes for achieving maximum probability on specific output node. This chapter shows a novel concept based on usage of the particle swarm optimization algorithm for finding optimal values within developed probabilistic models.

Chapter 4

Multi-Thresholded Histogram Equalization Based on Parameterless Artificial Bee Colony...108
Krishna Gopal Dhal, Midnapore College (Autonomous), India
Mandira Sen, Tata Consultancy Services, India
Swarnajit Ray, JBMatrix Technology Pvt. Ltd., India
Sanjoy Das, University of Kalyani, India

This chapter presents a novel variant of histogram equalization (HE) method called multi-thresholded histogram equalization (MTHE), depending on entropy-based multi-level thresholding-based segmentation. It is reported that proper segmentation of the histogram significantly assists the HE variants to maintain the original brightness of the image, which is one of the main criterion of the consumer electronics field. Multi-separation-based HE variants are also very effective for multi-modal histogram-based images. But, proper multi-seaparation of the histogram increases the computational time of the corresponding HE variants. In order to overcome that problem, one novel parameterless artifical bee colony (ABC) algorithm is employed to solve the multi-level thresholding problem. Experimental results prove that proposed parameterless ABC helps to reduce the computational time significantly and the proposed MTHE outperforms several existing HE varints in brightness preserving histopathological image enhancement domain.

Chapter 5

Biogeographic Computation as Information Processing in Ecosystems 127

Rodrigo Pasti, Mackenzie University, Brazil
Alexandre Alberto Politi, Particular, Brazil
Fernando José Von Zuben, State University of Campinas (Unicamp),
*   Brazil*
Leandro Nunes de Castro, Mackenzie University, Brazil

Assuming nature can be investigated and understood as an information processing system, this chapter aims to explore this hypothesis in the field of ecosystems. Therefore, based on the concepts of biogeography, it further investigates a computational approach called biogeographic computation to the study of ecosystems. The original proposal in the literature is built from fundamental concepts of ecosystems and from a framework called a metamodel that allows the understanding of how information processing occurs. This chapter reproduces part of the content of the original proposal and extends and better formalizes the metamodel, including novel experimental results, particularly exploring the role of information and causality in ecosystems, both being considered essential aspects of ecosystems' evolution.

Chapter 6

Evolutionary Approaches to Test Data Generation for Object-Oriented
Software: Overview of Techniques and Tools 162

Ana Filipa Nogueira, University of Coimbra, Portugal
José Carlos Bregieiro Ribeiro, Polytechnic Institute of Leiria, Portugal
Francisco Fernández de Vega, University of Extremadura, Spain
Mário Alberto Zenha-Rela, University of Coimbra, Portugal

In object-oriented evolutionary testing, metaheuristics are employed to select or generate test data for object-oriented software. Techniques that analyse program structures are predominant among the panoply of studies available in current literature. For object-oriented evolutionary testing, the common objective is to reach some coverage criteria, usually in the form of statement or branch coverage. This chapter explores, reviews, and contextualizes relevant literature, tools, and techniques in this area, while identifying open problems and setting ground for future work.

Chapter 7

Evolutionary Control Systems 195

Jesús-Antonio Hernández-Riveros, Universidad Nacional de Colombia, Colombia

Jorge Humberto Urrea-Quintero, Universidad de Antioquia, Colombia

Cindy Vanessa Carmona-Cadavid, Universidad Pontificia Bolivariana, Colombia

In control systems, the actual output is compared with the desired value so a corrective action maintains an established behavior. The industrial controller most widely used is the proportional integral derivative (PID). For PIDs, the process is represented in a transfer function. The linear quadratic regulator (LQR) controller needs a state space model. The process behavior depends on the setting of the controller parameters. Current trends in estimating those parameters optimize an integral performance criterion. In this chapter, a unified tuning method for controllers is presented, the evolutionary algorithm MAGO optimizes the parameters of several controllers minimizing the ITAE index, applied on benchmark plants, operating on servo and regulator modes, and representing the system in both transfer functions and differential equation systems. The evolutionary approach gets a better overall performance comparing with traditional methods. The evolutionary method is indeed better than the classical, eliminating the uncertainty in the controller parameters. Better results are yielded with MAGO algorithm than with optimal PID, optimal-robust PID, and LQR.

Chapter 8

Cloud Approach for the Medical Information System: MIS on Cloud..............238

Ekaterine Kldiashvili, Georgia Telemedicine Union, Georgia

Healthcare informatics is an important and effective field. It is characterized by the intensive development and design of the new models and protocols. The special emphasize is done on medical information system (MIS) and cloud approaches for its implementation. It is expected that this technology can improve healthcare services, benefit healthcare research, and change the face of health information technology. This chapter discusses the application of cloud computing for the medical information system practical usage.

Related References 262

Compilation of References 308

About the Contributors 377

Index 384

Preface

The complexities behind natural phenomena are profound, and yet there is still a very distinctive order to them. When combined with computing science and various other fields, the development of progressive tools and algorithms can be achieved. As modern applications of nature-inspired paradigms evolve, there is a need for knowledge resources that will empower IT professionals, computer engineers, academics, researchers, students, and industry consultants with cutting-edge techniques that have been developed to control a variety of dynamic systems.

Incorporating Nature-Inspired Paradigms in Computational Applications is a vital reference source that will meet these needs by exploring the latest coverage on areas such as natural computing, particle swarm optimization, search-based software engineering, bayesian networks, cloud computing, and the artificial bee colony algorithm.

This reference source is organized into eight chapters contributed by global experts, drawing on their experiences, observations, and research surrounding swarm intelligence, information processing, and immune-inspired algorithms. A brief description of each of the chapters can be found in the following paragraphs.

In Chapter 1, the authors explore the application of nature-inspired paradigms on system identification. A review of the recent application of techniques such as genetic algorithms, genetic programming, immune-inspired algorithms, and particle swarm optimization is presented, discussing the application to linear, nonlinear, time invariant, time variant, and multivariable cases.

In Chapter 2, the authors introduce a novel swarm intelligence based algorithm called comprehensive learning particle swarm optimization (CLPSO) to identify parameters of structural systems, which is formulated as a high-dimensional multi-modal numerical optimization problem. Simulation results for identifying the parameters of a five degree-of-freedom (DOF) structural system under conditions including limited output data, noise polluted signals, and no prior knowledge of mass, damping, or stiffness are presented to demonstrate improved estimation of these parameters by comprehensive learning particle swarm optimization.

In Chapter 3, the author explores how developing predictive models, models based on probabilistic concept, regarding numerous potential combinatory states can be very complex. That complexity can cause uncertainty about which factors should have which values to achieve optimal value of output. This paper shows the novel concept based on the usage of the particle swarm optimization algorithm for finding optimal values within developed probabilistic models.

In Chapter 4, the authors present a novel variant of the histogram equalization (HE) method called multi-thresholded histogram equalization (MTHE) that depends on entropy based multi-level thresholding based segmentation. It is reported that proper segmentation of the histogram significantly assists the HE variants to maintain the original brightness of the image which is one of the main criterion of the consumer electronics field. Multi-separation based HE variants are also very effective for multi-modal histogram based images, but proper multi-separation of the histogram increases the computational time of the corresponding HE variants. In order to overcome that problem, the authors present a parameterless artificial bee colony (ABC) algorithm which is employed to solve the multi-thresholding problem.

In Chapter 5, the authors, assuming nature can be investigated and understood as an information processing system, explore this hypothesis in the field of ecosystems. They investigate a computational approach called biogeographic computation and its relation to the study of ecosystems. This chapter also explores the role of information and causality in ecosystems, both being considered essential aspects of an ecosystem's evolution.

In Chapter 6, the authors explore how in object-oriented evolutionary testing, metaheuristics are employed to select or generate test data for object-oriented software. Techniques that analyze program structures are predominant among the panoply of studies available in current literature. This chapter explores, reviews and contextualizes relevant literature, tools and techniques in this area, while identifying open problems and setting a foundation for future work.

In Chapter 7, the authors explore how the evolutionary algorithm, multi dynamics algorithm for global optimization (MAGO), optimizes the parameters of several controllers minimizing the integral of time-weighted absolute error (ITAE) index, applied on benchmark plants, operating on servo and regulator modes, and represented in, both, transfer functions and differential equation systems. This evolutionary approach gets a better overall performance compared to traditional methods. Better results are yielded with the MAGO algorithm than with optimal proportional integral derivative (PID).

In Chapter 8, the author discusses the application of cloud computing for practical usage in medical information systems. Healthcare informatics is an important and effective field. It is characterized by the intensive development and design of new models and protocols. It is expected, that this technology can improve healthcare services, benefit healthcare research, and change the face of health information technology.

The comprehensive coverage this publication offers is sure to contribute to an enhanced understanding of all topics, research, and discoveries pertaining to nature-inspired paradigms. Furthermore, the contributions included in this publication will be instrumental to the expansion of knowledge offerings in this area. This publication will inspire its readers to further contribute to recent discoveries, progressing future innovations.

Chapter 1

Application of Natural-Inspired Paradigms on System Identification:
Exploring the Multivariable Linear Time Variant Case

Mateus Giesbrecht
Unicamp, Brazil

Celso Pascoli Bottura
Unicamp, Brazil

ABSTRACT

In this chapter, the application of nature-inspired paradigms on system identification is discussed. A review of the recent applications of techniques such as genetic algorithms, genetic programming, immuno-inspired algorithms, and particle swarm optimization to the system identification is presented, discussing the application to linear, nonlinear, time invariant, time variant, monovariable, and multivariable cases. Then the application of an immuno-inspired algorithm to solve the linear time variant multivariable system identification problem is detailed with examples and comparisons to other methods. Finally, the future directions of the application of nature-inspired paradigms to the system identification problem are discussed, followed by the chapter conclusions.

INTRODUCTION

For more than 50 years, many techniques have been developed to control a huge variety of dynamic systems, which vary from simple and well-known mechanical systems to the dynamics of the financial market. To develop those control techniques,

DOI: 10.4018/978-1-5225-5020-4.ch001

it is fundamental to know the mathematical relations between the system inputs and outputs. This necessity naturally led to the development of techniques to find the mathematical realizations of the systems to be controlled. These realizations are mathematical models that, for a given domain, behave as close as possible to the system to be modeled. The determination of the realizations of a given dynamical system is defined as system identification.

Given the huge variety of the existent systems, there are many models that can be used to generate a system realization and, for this reason, there are also many techniques that can be applied to reach this objective. Generally, the starting point is the information available about the system to be studied. Depending on the available information, one of those three techniques may be applied: the white, grey or black box modelling. Those techniques might be applied to any kind of system, including linear, non-linear, time variant, time invariant, monovariable and multivariable ones.

If the laws that govern the system behavior are reasonably known and if there is an estimate of the parameters involved in the problem, the system equations can be written from the known dynamics using the estimated parameters and a mathematical realization is then determined. This technique is known as white-box identification, since all the relevant details about the system are available. The models obtained with this technique are reasonably accurate for simple and well-studied systems operating on a known region of the domain.

For more complex physical systems, sometimes the structure of the equations is known but the parameters are not, either because they are complicated to measure or because their values vary depending on the ambient conditions. To obtain realizations for those systems, it is possible to write the equations that relate their outputs to their inputs as functions of the unknown parameters, to collect input and output data from the system operation and to estimate the parameters as the set that minimizes the error between the real system outputs and the model outputs. It is also possible to collect the output signal statistical characteristics and to determine the set of parameters for which the model produces the outputs with the maximum likelihood to the real system outputs. Those methods are known respectively as error minimization and maximum likelihood. In this case, where the model structure is known but the parameters are not, the system identification using any of the methods cited is known as grey-box.

If both the system structure and the parameters are unknown, there is necessary to apply techniques capable to determine the model structure and the parameters. There is also important to establish an information criterion to reach a compromise between the model accuracy and the model complexity, in order to avoid too complex models that do not result in an accuracy much better than simpler ones. For linear systems, the subspace methods allow the determination of generic state space models without the necessity of any initial guess about the system order. For non-linear systems, linear combinations of the results of non-linear functions applied to the inputs can be used to model the unknown dynamics. These nonlinear functions must be bases of the functions space, such as polynomials, sigmoid funcions, radial basis functions, etc. That functions can also be applied recursively, as observed on neural networks. Once a technique is defined, the identification procedure consists on defining the set of parameters and model structures that minimize the information criterion. In this case, the identification method is known as black-box, since no information about the system is available a priori.

For the grey-box and the black-box approaches, the system identification is an optimization problem, where the objective is to find the solutions that minimize the output error, or maximize the likelihood between the systems and the model outputs, or minimize the information criterion. From this point of view, natural inspired paradigms might be used to solve this kind of problem, since many of those paradigms were developed to determine the solutions of optimization problems, such as the evolutionary algorithms.

For the time variant system identification, the application of evolutionary algorithms is even more attractive, since in this case the system parameters vary along the time, and the evolutionary approach allows the population of possible solutions to continuously evolve to the optimal set of parameters at each time instant.

In this chapter, the applications of natural paradigms on system identification are discussed. For this, a review of the recent applications of those paradigms to solve this kind of problem is presented and then an immuno-inspired algorithm implemented by the authors to identify linear multivariable time variant systems is detailed.

Background

The application of natural paradigms to solve the optimization problem related to the system identification has been observed since the beginning of the 21st century, following the development of natural inspired algorithms and the enhance of the computational capacity verified in the last decade of the 20th century.

An approach from the first decade of the 21st century is the one described in (Rodriguez-Vazquez, Fonseca, & Fleming, 2004). In this chapter, the authors applied the multiobjective genetic programming to identify a nonlinear time invariant simple input-simple output (SISO) system, which was a gas turbine. The genetic programming approach allowed the determination of a nonlinear auto regressive model with exogenous inputs (NARX) without previous assumptions about the system structure or system parameters, configuring a black-box system identification. The basis function used was polynomial and the individual's fitness was calculated based on many criteria, involving performance indexes and model complexity, following the idea of the information criterion used in the common black-box system identification. To deal with this criteria diversity, a Pareto-optimality approach was applied. The results showed a good agreement between the model and the system output data.

On the following year, an article was published showing the application of the evolutionary approach to identify the structure and parameters of a time invariant mechatronic linear system (Iwasaki, Miwa, & Matsui, 2005). In that article, the authors used a classical genetic algorithm to identify the two-mass resonant system transfer function parameters. The system studied was linear and time invariant. Both the system and the system structure were determined by the proposed algorithm, which optimizes a fitness function that incorporates an information criterion. The results were compared to the results obtained with a white-box modelling procedure, and the conclusion was that the results obtained with the evolutionary black-box approach were closer to the actual system response due to the modelling of unpredicted phenomena.

Natural approaches have also been used to identify time variant linear and non-linear systems. In the reference (Wakizono, Hatanaka, & Uosaki, 2006), an immune mechanism based on the clonal selection algorithm proposed in (de Castro & Von Zuben, 2002) was proposed to switching linear system and nonlinear system identification. The models used in the reference were based on transfer functions and the choice of the immune mechanism was due to the capacity of this algorithm to track previous optimal solutions from the set of memory cells. The results presented in the reference showed that the approach was effective to model the systems studied.

In (Zakaria, Jamaluddin, Ahmad, & Loghmanian, 2010) the authors applied a multiobjective evolutionary algorithm to determine the parameters of three time invariant nonlinear multivariable systems, where two of them were benchmarks with a known model and one of them an actual system. The two objectives of the proposed algorithm were the minimization of the model complexity and the minimization of the mean square error between the benchmark or the real systems outputs and the model's outputs, following the common black-box approach. The models used were NARX (nonlinear auto regressive with exogenous inputs) and the algorithm chosen to solve the optimization problem was an elitist non-dominated sorting genetic algorithm, that is a genetic algorithm with the capacity of keeping the better solutions found in the population along the generations. The results obtained for the two benchmarks showed a close agreement between the known parameters and the estimated ones, and the outputs obtained with the model created to simulate the real system were close to the real system outputs, with residuals with an order of magnitude two times smaller than the output data.

The combination of natural techniques with other computational intelligence algorithms has also been used to solve the system identification problem. In (Li & Li, 2012), an evolutionary algorithm combining quantum computation and a particle swarm algorithm was proposed and used to identify the parameters from a second order time invariant linear SISO system. The parameters were identified by solving an optimization problem stated as the minimization of the mean square error between the system and the model outputs. The results were compared to the ones obtained with a conventional genetic algorithm and a pure quantum inspired genetic evolutionary algorithm, showing comparable performances, even when the system output data was corrupted by noise.

The time series realization, that is the stochastic equivalent to the system identification problem, was addressed by the authors in the reference (Giesbrecht & Bottura, 2011). In this reference, the multivariable time series realization was stated as an optimization problem and solved with an immuno-inspired method. In a recent paper (Giesbrecht & Bottura, 2016) the authors stated the time series problem in an alternative way, and also applied a natural inspired method to find realizations of a given time series. In both papers, the results obtained with the heuristic method were more accurate than other more usual methods due to the stochastic nature of the problem.

The time series forecasting, that is related to the time series realization, was also studied based on a natural inspired paradigm. In (Koshiyama, Escovedo, Dias, Vellasco, & Pacheco, 2012) a genetic programming approach was applied to search for a nonlinear combination of forecasts generated by different time series models in order to obtain the optimal approximation for an observed time series. The results were compared to an optimal linear combination and the conclusion was that the nonlinear combinations obtained with the proposed method performed better than the optimal linear combination.

The particle swarm optimization (PSO), that is another natural inspired paradigm based on the movement of particles on the space, was also used to solve the system identification problem. In (Tang, Xie, & Xue, 2015) a new algorithm based on the particle swarm optimization and named comprehensive learning particle swarm optimization (CLPSO) is introduced and applied to identify the parameters of structural systems. The results were compared to the standard PSO showing a better performance of the proposed method.

The majority of the results presented so far concern the application of natural paradigms, mainly evolutionary techniques, to solve the SISO system identification problem. Even on the works where the single input multiple output (SIMO) or the multiple input multiple output (MIMO) systems were considered, the transfer functions or the difference equations that model the system were split for each output and optimized one by one. It is possible to identify a single state space model to linear MIMO systems, but the main difficulty related to this approach is the curse of dimensionality, since the search space increases as the system order does.

In (Giesbrecht & Bottura, 2015), the authors proposed an algorithm following an immuno-inspired paradigm to identify discrete state space models for time variant MIMO systems with unknown structure. To avoid the curse of dimensionality, the algorithm population was initialized using a subspace identification method. In this manner, the candidate solutions start in a solutions space region to the desired solutions, allowing the convergence in a reasonable amount of time. This algorithm also takes the advantage of the capacity of the immuno-inspired algorithms to track time variant solutions. In this manner, as the system parameters vary along the time, the individuals in the population also evolve to track the set of parameters that minimize the output error at that instant of time.

In this chapter, the algorithm proposed in (Giesbrecht & Bottura, 2015) is detailed. To do so, some important concepts related to the subspace methods for MIMO system identification, to time variant system identification and to the immuno-inspired algorithms are presented. In sequel, the proposed algorithm is detailed, what is followed by the application of it to identify a benchmark system. Then the future research directions and the conclusions are presented.

MAIN FOCUS OF THE CHAPTER

State Space System Identification

State space discrete system identification is the name given to the techniques created to determine a state space model that describes a discrete time invariant causal dynamic system. Many state space system identification techniques have been developed to identify time invariant multivariable dynamic systems, such as the ones presented on the references (Verhaegen & Verdult, 2007), (Young, 2011), (Barreto, 2002).

Basically, these techniques take into account all available system input and output samples, estimate the Markov parameters and from these parameters some algebraic manipulations are made to find the matrices of a linear time invariant model that has outputs similar to the system outputs when excited by the same input. Since these techniques are based on the whole set of samples available, only linear time invariant systems can be modeled correctly. The main advantage of the state space approach is that a multivariable input multivariable output (MIMO) dynamic system can be modeled with no prior knowledge about the system order.

Depending on the approach, a special input may or may not be needed to identify the system. In the following sections two approaches are discussed. The first is the discrete impulse response method. In this approach, a discrete impulse is applied as input to the system and from the outputs the state space model matrices can be found. The second approach discussed in this section is the Multivariable Output-Error

State Space (MOESP) method, proposed by Verhaegen and Dewilde (Verhaegen & Dewilde, 1992). In this approach, the system input can be any signal and using this signal and the system output is possible to identify the system.

Multivariable Discrete Impulse Response

A fundamental concept in discrete time MIMO state space system identification is the multivariable discrete impulse response. From this concept, the definition of the Markov Parameters and the concepts of reachability and observability arise directly. These concepts are fundamental to understand the algorithm developed in this paper and also to compare the behavior of different MIMO system state space identification algorithms. For this reason, in this section the multivariable discrete impulse response is defined in a formal way.

Let $y(k) \in \Re^2$ be the l-dimensional output at instant k when the time invariant discrete causal MIMO system is excited by a m-dimensional input $u(k) \in \Re^m$. Since the system is supposed to be causal, the outputs at instant k depend only on the inputs at instants between 0 and k. The relation between the outputs and inputs can then be represented by the equation below:

$$y(k) = \sum_{i=0}^{k} G(i)u(k - i) \tag{1}$$

where $G(i)\in\Re^{1Xm}$, $0\leq i\leq k$ are the impulse response matrices that define the system.

To find the set of matrices $G(i)$ that describe a time invariant discrete causal MIMO system, a set of multivariable discrete impulses can be applied as inputs and the outputs will be the columns of matrices $G(i)$ as is shown below.

By definition, let $u_j(k)$ be the j-th discrete impulse element defined in the following manner:

$$u_j(k) = \begin{cases} [\delta(1, j) \quad \delta(2, j) \quad \dots \quad \delta(m, j)]^T & k = 0 \\ \mathbf{0} \in \Re^m & k \neq 0 \end{cases} \tag{2}$$

where *s(i,j)* is the following function:

$$\delta(i, j) = \begin{cases} 1 & if \quad i = j \\ 0 & if \quad i \neq j \end{cases} \tag{3}$$

The definition above means that the discrete impulse elements are the following:

$$u_1(k) = \begin{cases} [1 \quad 0 \quad \dots \quad 0]^T & k = 0 \\ \mathbf{0} \in \Re^m & k \neq 0 \end{cases} \tag{4}$$

$$u_2(k) = \begin{cases} [0 \quad 1 \quad \dots \quad 0]^T & k = 0 \\ \mathbf{0} \in \Re^m & k \neq 0 \end{cases} \tag{5}$$

$$u_m(k) = \begin{cases} [0 \quad 0 \quad \dots \quad 1]^T & k = 0 \\ \mathbf{0} \in \Re^m & k \neq 0 \end{cases} \tag{6}$$

Let $u_1(k)$ be applied as input to a time invariant discrete causal MIMO system represented by equation 1. Then the outputs $y(k)$ will be, for $k = 0$

$$y(0) = \sum_{i=0}^{k} G(i)u_1(0 - i) = G(0)u_1(0) \tag{7}$$

that is:

$$y(0) = \begin{bmatrix} G_{11}(0) & \dots & G_{1m}(0) \\ \vdots & \ddots & \vdots \\ G_{l1}(0) & \dots & G_{lm}(0) \end{bmatrix} \begin{bmatrix} 1 \\ \vdots \\ 0 \end{bmatrix} = \begin{bmatrix} G_{11}(0) \\ \vdots \\ G_{l1}(0) \end{bmatrix} \tag{8}$$

for $k = 1$

$$y(1) = \sum_{i=0}^{\infty} G(i)u_1(1 - i) = G(1)u_1(0) \tag{9}$$

that is:

$$y(1) = \begin{bmatrix} G_{11}(1) & \cdots & G_{1m}(1) \\ \vdots & \ddots & \vdots \\ G_{l1}(1) & \cdots & G_{lm}(1) \end{bmatrix} \begin{bmatrix} 1 \\ \vdots \\ 0 \end{bmatrix} = \begin{bmatrix} G_{11}(1) \\ \vdots \\ G_{l1}(1) \end{bmatrix} \tag{10}$$

Similarly, it can be proved that if the j-th discrete impulse element is applied to the system the output at instant k will be:

$$y(k) = \begin{bmatrix} G_{1j}(l) \\ \vdots \\ G_{lj}(k) \end{bmatrix} \tag{11}$$

Consequently, if all m discrete impulse elements are applied to the system, all m columns of all matrices $G(i)$ can be determined. Since the matrices $G(i)$ are obtained as the system response to a multivariable discrete impulse, this set of matrices is defined as system impulse response.

State Space Models and Markov Parameters

In this section two key concepts for State Space System Identification are discussed and related to the system impulse response matrices defined in the previous section. These concepts, which are the State Space Models and the Markov Parameters, are fundamental to understand the algorithm developed in this paper and are the basis criteria to find out if a time variant system identification method succeeds.

The MIMO systems can be represented by its State Space Models, in which the past is summarized in a variable defined as state and just four matrices and the initial state are necessary to find the system output at any instant. The state space model is defined in the following manner:

$$\begin{cases} x(k+1) = Ax(k) + Bu(k) \\ \quad y(k) = Cx(k) + Du(k) \end{cases} \tag{12}$$

where $x(k) \in \Re^n$ is defined as the system state at instant k, $A \in \Re^{nXn}$ is the state transition matrix, $B \in \Re^{nXm}$ is a matrix that relates the input $u(k) \in \Re^m$ to the state, $C \in \Re^{lXn}$ is the matrix that relates the output $y(k) \in \Re^l$ to the state and $D \in \Re^{lXm}$ is the matrix that relates the outputs to the inputs.

9

It is possible to relate the impulse response matrices $G(i)$ to the state space model matrices as will be discussed in sequel. This is achieved by exciting each one of the m system inputs with one of the m discrete impulse elements and calculating the outputs as state space matrices functions.

If the system described in equation 12 is submitted to the input $u_1(k)$ defined in equation 4 and supposing that the initial state is $x(0) = \mathbf{0} \in \Re^n$, the state and outputs will be, for $k = 0$:

$$x(1) = \begin{bmatrix} x_1(1) \\ x_2(1) \\ \vdots \\ x_n(1) \end{bmatrix} = Ax(0) + Bu_1(0) = \begin{bmatrix} b_{11} \\ b_{21} \\ \vdots \\ b_{n1} \end{bmatrix} \qquad (13)$$

$$y(0) = \begin{bmatrix} y_1(0) \\ y_2(0) \\ \vdots \\ y_l(0) \end{bmatrix} = Cx(0) + Du_1(0) = \begin{bmatrix} d_{11} \\ d_{21} \\ \vdots \\ d_{l1} \end{bmatrix} \qquad (14)$$

for $k = 1$:

$$x(2) = \begin{bmatrix} x_1(2) \\ x_2(2) \\ \vdots \\ x_n(2) \end{bmatrix} = Ax(1) + Bu_1(1) = A \begin{bmatrix} b_{11} \\ b_{21} \\ \vdots \\ b_{n1} \end{bmatrix} \qquad (15)$$

$$y(1) = \begin{bmatrix} y_1(1) \\ y_2(1) \\ \vdots \\ y_l(1) \end{bmatrix} = Cx(1) + Du_1(1) = C \begin{bmatrix} b_{11} \\ b_{21} \\ \vdots \\ b_{n1} \end{bmatrix} \qquad (16)$$

for $k = 2$:

$$x(3) = \begin{bmatrix} x_1(3) \\ x_2(3) \\ \vdots \\ x_n(3) \end{bmatrix} = Ax(2) + Bu_1(2) = A^2 \begin{bmatrix} b_{11} \\ b_{21} \\ \cdots \\ b_{n1} \end{bmatrix} \tag{17}$$

$$y(2) = \begin{bmatrix} y_1(2) \\ y_2(2) \\ \vdots \\ y_l(2) \end{bmatrix} = Cx(2) + Du_1(2) = CA \begin{bmatrix} b_{11} \\ b_{21} \\ \vdots \\ b_{n1} \end{bmatrix} \tag{18}$$

Consequently, for any k the system response to the first discrete impulse element $u_1(k)$ is given by the following relation:

$$\begin{bmatrix} g_{11}(k) \\ g_{12}(k) \\ \vdots \\ g_{l1}(k) \end{bmatrix} = \begin{bmatrix} y_1(k) \\ y_2(k) \\ \vdots \\ y_l(k) \end{bmatrix} = \begin{cases} \begin{bmatrix} d_{11} \\ d_{21} \\ \vdots \\ d_{l1} \end{bmatrix} & k = 0 \\[4mm] CA^{k-1} \begin{bmatrix} b_{11} \\ b_{21} \\ \vdots \\ b_{n1} \end{bmatrix} & k \neq 0 \end{cases} \tag{19}$$

If the system is subjected to the second element of discrete impulse with the null initial state, then for $k = 0$ the following states and outputs will be obtained:

$$x(1) = \begin{bmatrix} x_1(1) \\ x_2(1) \\ \vdots \\ x_n(1) \end{bmatrix} = Ax(0) + Bu_2(0) = \begin{bmatrix} b_{12} \\ b_{22} \\ \vdots \\ b_{n2} \end{bmatrix} \tag{20}$$

$$y(0) = \begin{bmatrix} y_1(0) \\ y_2(0) \\ \vdots \\ y_l(0) \end{bmatrix} = Cx(0) + Du_2(0) = \begin{bmatrix} d_{12} \\ d_{22} \\ \vdots \\ d_{l2} \end{bmatrix} \tag{21}$$

for $k = 1$:

$$x(2) = \begin{bmatrix} x_1(2) \\ x_2(2) \\ \vdots \\ x_n(2) \end{bmatrix} = Ax(1) + Bu_2(1) = A \begin{bmatrix} b_{12} \\ b_{22} \\ \vdots \\ b_{n2} \end{bmatrix} \tag{22}$$

$$y(1) = \begin{bmatrix} y_1(1) \\ y_2(1) \\ \vdots \\ y_l(1) \end{bmatrix} = Cx(1) + Du_2(1) = C \begin{bmatrix} b_{12} \\ b_{22} \\ \vdots \\ b_{n2} \end{bmatrix} \tag{23}$$

for $k = 2$:

$$x(3) = \begin{bmatrix} x_1(3) \\ x_2(3) \\ \vdots \\ x_n(3) \end{bmatrix} = Ax(2) + Bu_2(2) = A^2 \begin{bmatrix} b_{12} \\ b_{22} \\ \vdots \\ b_{n2} \end{bmatrix} \tag{24}$$

$$y(2) = \begin{bmatrix} y_1(2) \\ y_2(2) \\ \vdots \\ y_l(2) \end{bmatrix} = Cx(2) + Du_2(2) = CA \begin{bmatrix} b_{12} \\ b_{22} \\ \vdots \\ b_{n2} \end{bmatrix} \tag{25}$$

Consequently, for any k the second impulse response is the following:

$$
\begin{bmatrix} g_{12}(k) \\ g_{22}(k) \\ \dots \\ g_{l2}(k) \end{bmatrix} = \begin{bmatrix} y_1(k) \\ y_2(k) \\ \dots \\ y_l(k) \end{bmatrix} = \begin{cases} \begin{bmatrix} d_{12} \\ d_{22} \\ \dots \\ d_{l2} \end{bmatrix} & k = 0 \\ CA^{k-1} \begin{bmatrix} b_{12} \\ b_{22} \\ \dots \\ b_{n2} \end{bmatrix} & k \neq 0 \end{cases}
\tag{26}
$$

From the development above it can be noticed that, for each discrete impulse element applied to the system, a system impulse response matrix column is found, and this impulse response matrix is related to B, C and D, in the following manner:

$$
G(i) = \begin{cases} D & k = 0 \\ CA^{i-1}B & k \neq 0 \end{cases}
\tag{27}
$$

The impulse response matrices are also defined as Markov parameters. Since it is possible that more than one quadruple {*A, B, C, D*} satisfy the equation 27, the state space model that represents a system is not unique, but the impulse response, or the Markov parameters, are unique. Once the impulse response matrices are determined, the state space system matrices can be found from the relation shown in equation 27 and some algebraic relations, as can be found in (Ho & Kalman, 1966) for the continuous system identification and in (Aoki, 1987) for discrete time series realization, that is a problem similar to the state space discrete system identification.

Observability and Reachability

From the concepts and definitions discussed above, two other useful definitions can be derived. These definitions are the observability and reachability properties of a system, and are described below.

Let a system with initial state equal to $x(0) = \mathbf{0} \in \Re^n$ be submitted to an arbitrary input until the time i and from this instant to the future the input is $\mathbf{0} \in \Re^n$. Since $u(i) = \mathbf{0} \in \Re^m, i \geq k+1$, the outputs at instants $i+1$ depend only on the state at instant $i+1$ and this relation, derived from the equation 12, is the following:

$$\begin{bmatrix} y(i+1) \\ y(i+2) \\ y(i+3) \\ \vdots \end{bmatrix} = \begin{bmatrix} C \\ CA \\ CA^2 \\ \vdots \end{bmatrix} x(i+1) \tag{28}$$

Defining the matrix at left of equation 28 as $y^+(k+1)$ and the matrix at right as O, the equation 28 can be rewritten as:

$$y^+(i+1) = \mathcal{O}x(i+1) \tag{29}$$

The matrix O contains the relation between an output set in the future and the state at instant $i+1$. For this reason, the matrix O is defined as observability matrix. In other words, from this matrix is possible to observe the state at instant $i+1$ from any future output with the following relation:

$$x(i+1) = \mathcal{O}^\dagger y^+(i+1) \tag{30}$$

where $*^\dagger$ is the pseudoinverse of $*$.

As can be seen from the linear system shown in equation 30, if the matrix O rank is equal or greater than the system order n, any state can be determined from any set of outputs and the system is defined as observable.

Similarly, the state at instant $i+1$ depends only on the inputs until the instant i and the relation between state and inputs is the following:

$$x(i+1) = \begin{bmatrix} B & AB & A^2B & \cdots \end{bmatrix} \begin{bmatrix} u(i) \\ u(i-1) \\ u(i-2) \\ \vdots \end{bmatrix} \tag{31}$$

or, similarly as the definitions made for the observability matrix,

$$x(i+1) = \mathcal{C}u^-(i) \tag{32}$$

where $\mathcal{C}$ is a matrix that defines how the state $x(i+1)$ was reached by the system with the inputs $u^-(i)$. For this reason, the matrix $\mathcal{C}$ is defined as reachability matrix. To reach a determined state, an input set can be defined by the following relation:

$$u^-(i) = \mathcal{C}^\dagger x(i+1) \tag{33}$$

so, if the reachability matrix has rank equal or greater than n it is possible to define an input set that reaches any state, and the system is defined as reachable.

In this work, the reachability and the observability properties were used as constraints as discussed in the section named time variant multivariable system identification as an optimization problem.

MOESP Method

The second method discussed in this section is the Multivariable Output-Error State Space (MOESP), proposed by Verhaegen and Dewilde at (Verhaegen & Dewilde, 1992). This method is based on a LQ decomposition of a matrix containing output and input data. Let the system inputs and outputs from t to an arbitrary instant *k-1* be concatenated in two matrices as defined below:

$$y_{t|k-1} = \begin{bmatrix} y(t) \\ y(t+1) \\ \vdots \\ y(t+k-1) \end{bmatrix} \tag{34}$$

$$u_{t|k-1} = \begin{bmatrix} u(t) \\ u(t+1) \\ \vdots \\ u(t+k-1) \end{bmatrix} \tag{35}$$

then it is possible to show that:

$$y_{t|k-1} = \mathcal{O}_k x(t) + \Psi_k u_{t|k-1} \tag{36}$$

where

$$\mathcal{O}_k = \begin{bmatrix} C \\ CA \\ \vdots \\ CA^{k-1} \end{bmatrix} \tag{37}$$

$$\Psi_k = \begin{bmatrix} D & 0 & 0 & 0 \\ CB & D & 0 & 0 \\ \vdots & \vdots & \ddots & \vdots \\ CA^{k-2}B & \dots & CB & D \end{bmatrix} \tag{38}$$

If the matrices $u_{t|k-1}$, $y_{t|k-1}$ and $x(t)$ for $t = 0 \dots N-1$, where N is the total number of inputs and outputs available, are concatenated side by side, the following matrices can be defined:

$$U_{0|k-1} = \begin{bmatrix} u_{0|k-1} & u_{1|k} & \dots & u_{N-1|k+N-2} \end{bmatrix} \tag{39}$$

$$Y_{0|k-1} = \begin{bmatrix} y_{0|k-1} & y_{1|k} & \dots & y_{N-1|k+N-2} \end{bmatrix} \tag{40}$$

$$X_{N-1} = \begin{bmatrix} x(0) & x(1) & \dots & x(N-1) \end{bmatrix} \tag{41}$$

and then the following extended state space model can be written:

$$Y_{0|k-1} = \mathcal{O}_k X_{N-1} + \Psi_k U_{0|k-1} \tag{42}$$

Concatenating the matrices $U_{0|k-1}$, $Y_{0|k-1}$ and proceeding a LQ decomposition, the following relation can be found:

$$\begin{bmatrix} U_{0|k-1} \\ Y_{0|k-1} \end{bmatrix} = LQ = \begin{bmatrix} L_{11} & 0 \\ L_{21} & L_{22} \end{bmatrix} \begin{bmatrix} Q_1^T \\ Q_2^T \end{bmatrix} \tag{43}$$

where $L_{11} \in \Re^{kmXkm}$ and $L_{22} \in \Re^{klXkl}$ are lower triangular matrices, $Q_1^T \in \Re^{kmXN}$ and $Q_2^T \in \Re^{klXN}$ are orthonormal and $L_{21} \in \Re^{klXkm}$.

From this decomposition, the equation 42 can be rewritten as shown below:

$$L_{21}Q_1^T + L_{22}Q_2^T = \mathcal{O}_k X_{N-1} + \Psi_k L_{11}Q_1^T \tag{44}$$

Post-multiplying both sides of equation 44 by Q_2 results in:

$$L_{22} = \mathcal{O}_k X_{N-1} Q_2 \tag{45}$$

a singular value decomposition (SVD) is then applied to L_{22}, resulting in the following:

$$L_{22} = \begin{bmatrix} U_1 & U_2 \end{bmatrix} \begin{bmatrix} \Sigma_1 & 0 \\ 0 & 0 \end{bmatrix} \begin{bmatrix} V_1 \\ V_2 \end{bmatrix} = \mathcal{O}_k X_{N-1} Q_2 \tag{46}$$

and then:

$$\mathcal{O}_k = U_1 \Sigma_1^{\frac{1}{2}} \quad X_{N-1} Q_2 = \Sigma_1^{\frac{1}{2}} V_1 \tag{47}$$

Once the matrix $\mathcal{O}_k$ is found, is easy to find the matrices A and C of the state space system. Let $\mathcal{O}_{k\uparrow}$ be the following matrix:

$$\mathcal{O}_{k\uparrow} = \begin{bmatrix} CA \\ CA^2 \\ \vdots \end{bmatrix} = \begin{bmatrix} C \\ CA \\ \vdots \end{bmatrix} A = \mathcal{O}_k A \tag{48}$$

then:

$$A = \mathcal{O}_k^\dagger \mathcal{O}_{k\uparrow} \tag{49}$$

and C is the first $l \, X \, n$ block of O.

The matrices B and D can be found by observing the following relations, that come from the orthogonality between U_1 and U_2 guaranteed by the SVD:

17

$$U_2^T L_{22} = 0 \quad U_2^T \mathcal{O}_k = 0 \tag{50}$$

Then, multiplying both sides of equation 44 by U_2^T the following relation is found:

$$U_2^T (L_{21} Q_1^T + L_{22} Q_2^T) = U_2^T (\mathcal{O}_k X_{N-1} + \Psi_k L_{11} Q_1^T) \Rightarrow$$

$$\Rightarrow U_2^T L_{21} Q_1^T = U_2^T \Psi_k L_{11} Q_1^T \Rightarrow$$

$$\Rightarrow U_2^T L_{21} = U_2^T \Psi_k L_{11} \tag{51}$$

$$\Rightarrow U_2^T L_{21} L_{11}^{-1} = U_2^T \Psi_k$$

Splitting U_2^T in blocks with l columns defined as L_i and splitting the matrix $U_2^T L_{21} L_{11}^{-1}$ in blocks with m columns defined as M_i, the following relation is valid:

$$\begin{bmatrix} M_1 & \cdots & M_k \end{bmatrix} = \begin{bmatrix} L_1 & \cdots & L_k \end{bmatrix} \Psi \tag{52}$$

then, opening the matrix Ψ the following linear system can be written:

$$L_1 D + \ldots + L_{k-1} CA^{k-3} B + L_k CA^{k-2} B = M_1$$

$$L_2 D + \ldots + L_{k-1} CA^{k-4} B + L_k CA^{k-3} B = M_2$$

$$\vdots \tag{53}$$

$$L_{k-1} D + L_k CB = M_{k-1}$$

$$L_k D = M_k$$

and from this system the matrices B and D can be found.

As can be noticed from the discussion above, the MOESP method can be used just for time invariant systems and a large amount of data is needed to estimate the quadruple $\{A, B, C, D\}$ that constitutes a state space model for the system.

Although MOESP is not suitable to solve the time variant system identification problem, this method is used in the algorithm proposed in this work to create an initial estimate of the time variant system, as will be seen in one of the next sections of this paper.

The results of time variant system identification if only the MOESP method is used are not exact, as can be seen in the section in which an example of application is shown, but the MOESP initialization solves the problem related to the search space topology as will be seen in one of the following sections.

MOESP-VAR Algorithm

To solve the time variant system identification problem, a MOESP based algorithm was created (Tamariz, 2005) (Tamariz, Bottura, & Barreto, 2005). This algorithm works as follows: The first step is the definition of time windows. Each window contains a subset of the system input and output data. The windows lengths are defined in such a way that the system does no vary significantly during the time interval defined for each window. Then, the MOESP algorithm is applied to the output and input data contained in each window and a quadruple $\{A, B, C, D\}$ is estimated. This quadruple represents the system during the interval defined by each window.

This algorithm works well if a large amount of data is available for each window. This means that the system variations cannot be too fast in order to guarantee that a large amount of input and output data can be collected for each window, without excessive system variations during that time interval. This happens because the decompositions defined in equations 43 and 46 need large matrices to be successful, and these large matrices can be reached only if large $U_{0|k-1}$ and $Y_{0|k-1}$ matrices are available, and these matrices are large only if a large amount of input and output samples is available.

The windows size for the method discussed in this chapter can be smaller than the size required by MOESP-VAR algorithm since the method here proposed is not based on matrices decompositions as shown in the section that discusses the proposed algorithm. In a later section, the results for a fast time variant problem are shown using both algorithms and the difference between them can be clearly observed.

Immune Inspired Algorithms for Optimization

As will be discussed in a future section, in this paper the time variant system identification problem is seen as an optimization problem. To solve this optimization problem an immuno inspired algorithm is used. In this section this class of algorithms and the advantages of using it are discussed.

Immuno-inspired algorithms are computational tools inspired on biological immune system principles. Useful information about this kind of algorithms can be found at (de Castro & Von Zuben, 2000; de Castro & Timmis, 2002; de Castro & Von Zuben, 2002; de França, Coelho, Castro, & Von Zuben, 2010).

Basically, immune system works as follows: when an animal is exposed to an antigen (Ag), some B cells of its bone marrow secrete antibodies (Ab), that are molecules which goal is to recognize and bind themselves to Ags. The B cells that produced Abs with higher affinity to the Ags are encouraged to mature into non-dividing Ab secreting cells called plasma cells. Some of them are selected to become memory cells which will be used by the immune system to deal with the similar Ags in the future, and the other ones will generate clones. These clones are subjected to random mutations (receptor editing) and are not exactly equal to the original cells. This mechanism allows B cells to produce Abs with higher affinity to some Ag. On the other hand, this process also creates clones producing lower affinity Abs. The higher affinity clones are encouraged to proliferate and the lower affinity ones are eliminated by the immune system. These mechanisms are controlled by T cells. In addition to it, a set of B cells with random receptors is created at bone marrow to maintain the population diversity.

An interesting immune response aspect is that the process indicated above will happen only with B cells that produced higher affinity Abs. This aspect is known as Clonal Selection Principle. Another interesting characteristic is that immune system cells do not only recognize Abs, but also recognize other cells (idiotypic network theory). Then, the immune response is regulated by T cells that detect and encourage multiplication of higher affinity B cells and suppression of B cells that are at a shape space region near to another cell with better fitness.

The ideas taken from the immune system can be used in an optimization procedure as shown in (de Castro & Von Zuben, 2002). In this case, Abs are candidate solutions and the concept of binding an Ag is replaced by the concept of having a better fitness. The method works as follows: first of all, a set of optimization problem candidate solutions (Abs) is generated. Candidate solutions are applied to the objective function and the result is called fitness. The fitness measures how appropriate a candidate solution is for the problem. All of the solutions are cloned with slight mutations producing new antibodies (receptor editing). The clones number for each solution is proportional to the fitness of it (when considering the maximization problem), following the clonal selection principle. The new population then is submitted to threshold suppression, that is, the Abs that are near to Abs of best fitness are eliminated from the population. Then, other new feasible solutions are generated to avoid population stagnation around a local optimum. This procedure is repeated until reasonable solutions are found. This algorithm is known as Opt-AiNet (Optimization Artificial Immune Net). In Opt-AiNet algorithm there is no distinction between memory and plasma cells. The whole set of cells is submitted to steps cited above on every iteration.

The use of Opt-AINet algorithm brings many advantages to optimization problems solution. The first one is that the algorithm does not stagnate around a local optimum since new Abs are introduced on each iteration. The second advantage is that the population size is self-regulated by the suppression mechanism and, if the suppression threshold is well established, each local optimum is found. The final set of solutions tends to have the same size of the problem local optima set. This happens because if an Ab is at a local optimum region, it tends to be nearer to this point on each iteration by the receptor editing mechanism. All other solutions that are not the one nearer the optimum are suppressed. If an antibody generates descendants in a region that tends to another optimum, these new ones will tend to find these other points and will not be suppressed (once algorithm parameters are well chosen).

There are other immuno-inspired algorithms, for instance Opt-IA, proposed at (Cutello & Nicosia, 2002), and Opt-Immalg, proposed at (Cutello, Narizi, Nicosia, & Pavone, 2006). These algorithms do not use the threshold suppression and population size is not self-regulated. At (Cutello, Narizi, Nicosia, & Pavone, 2005) a comparison is made between Opt-Immalg and Opt-AINet but the second algorithm was implemented without the threshold suppression, leading to an incomplete conclusion. Since algorithm capacity to self-regulate the population size is important to solve the problem here presented, an algorithm based on the Opt-AINet was used.

Opt-AINet algorithm can be used to solve time variant discrete multivariable system state space identification by transforming the problem into an optimization problem, as it will be seen in the next section. Since this optimization problem is constrained, some modifications have to be done to the algorithm, as detailed in the following sections.

SOLUTIONS AND RECOMMENDATIONS

Time Variant Multivariable System Identification as an Optimization Problem

The time variant system identification can be defined as an optimization problem if a State Space Models Space is defined. This space contains all possible matrices quadruples $\{A, B, C, D\}$ with the desired dimensions, supposed known a priori. Each state space model is seen as a point in this space and the idea is to find the point that minimizes the error between the system and the model outputs to the same input signal. This point at the state space models space is the one that represents the system for that set of inputs and outputs.

Supposing that the system to be modeled is time variant, if it suffers a variation along the time another point in the state space models space will be model that represents the system, but since the variations of the system are supposed to be slight, this new optimum point is in a region of the State Space Models Space around the former model. Therefore, a heuristic algorithm can find the new model without too much effort.

In other words, in this work the time variant multivariable system identification is treated as an optimization problem in the following way: at each time instant k a set of $N_w + 1$ inputs and outputs is taken. This set, defined as time window, contains the inputs between the time instant $k - (N_w / 2)$ and $k + N_w / 2$ and the outputs between $k - (N_w / 2) + 1$ and $k + N_w / 2 + 1$. The optimization problem is to find the matrix quadruple $\{ A_{est}, B_{est}, C_{est}, D_{est} \}$ that describes a state space model (see equation 12) that when excited by inputs contained in the time window, produces the better approximation to the outputs contained in the same time window. Once this quadruple is found, the next time window is taken and the optimization algorithm runs again. This procedure is repeated until the time windows cover all data available.

This procedure allows determining a different model for each time window and therefore can be used to model time variant systems.

The optimization problem details and the definitions of the search space, candidate solutions, objective function, constraints and search space topology are discussed in sequel.

Optimization Search Space

The search space in the optimization problem related to the multivariable time variant system identification is the union of the four spaces where the matrices A, B, C, and D lie.

It is, $\Re^{nXn} \cup \Re^{nXm} \cup \Re^{lXn} \cup \Re^{lXm}$. This search space is huge and also has a not very well-behaved topology as will be shown by an example in the end of this section.

Candidate Solutions

The candidate solutions to this optimization problem are quadruples $\{ A_{est}, B_{est}, C_{est}, D_{est} \}$, which are points in the search space defined above. These quadruples define models following the structure shown in equation 12. Each one of these models, when submitted to the input $u(k)$, produce estimated outputs $y_{est}(k)$. These outputs can be compared to the system outputs allowing the creation of an objective function described below. In immuno-inspired algorithms context, the quadruples $\{ A_{est}, B_{est}, C_{est}, D_{est} \}$ are also defined as antibodies.

Objective Function

For an arbitrary time window, let mod_e be a vector containing in each position the absolute value of the l-dimensional difference between the system output, and the output estimated with a candidate solution $\{ A_{est}, B_{est}, C_{est}, D_{est} \}$, for each sample in the window, it is:

$$mod_e = \begin{bmatrix} | y(k - (N_w / 2) + 1) - y_{est}(k - (N_w / 2) + 1) | \\ | y(k - (N_w / 2) + 2) - y_{est}(k - (N_w / 2) + 1) | \\ \vdots \\ | y(k + (N_w / 2) + 1) - y_{est}(k + (N_w / 2) + 1) | \end{bmatrix} \tag{54}$$

The objective function to be maximized is the following:

$$F(mod_e) = \frac{N_w + 1}{\sum\limits_{i=1}^{N_w + 1} mod_e(i)} \tag{55}$$

The variable $N_w + 1$ is at the numerator to allow the comparison between objective function values for cases with different time windows lengths. The error sum is at denominator and consequently the objective function will be greater if the error is smaller. In the immuno-inspired optimization algorithms context, the function F calculated for a candidate solution, or antibody $\{ A_{est}, B_{est}, C_{est}, D_{est} \}$, is defined as the fitness of this candidate solution.

Constraints

The candidate solutions $\{ A_{est}, B_{est}, C_{est}, D_{est} \}$ must satisfy the following constraints: The matrix A_{est} must imply on a stable model, which in discrete case means that its eigenvalues must be inside the unit circle. The matrices B_{est} and C_{est} must produce model's outputs reasonably close to the system outputs, in other words, they must imply on outputs that do not make the error go to infinity.

The observability and reachability are also constraints to the optimization problem. To check if a candidate solution defined by a quadruple { A_{est}, B_{est}, C_{est}, D_{est} } implies on an observable model, matrices A_{est} and C_{est} are taken to evaluate the observability matrix rank. If the observability matrix rank is greater than model order, the model is observable. To check the reachability property, the matrices A_{est} and B_{est} are taken and the reachability matrix rank is evaluated. If the rank is greater than model order, the model is reachable, as discussed before.

Search Space Topology

To illustrate the search space in the optimization problem proposed in this paper, the following simpler but similar example is proposed. Let:

$$C = [1.231862 \quad -0.719364]$$

be a 1x2 matrix and x_0 the following 2x1 vector:

$$x_0 = \begin{bmatrix} 0.3601 \\ 0.2725 \end{bmatrix}$$

and

$$y_0 = Cx_0 = 0.2476$$

For i and j varying in a range between -2 and 2 in steps of 0.01, a set of $C_{est}(i, j)$ matrices was defined in the following way:

$$C_{est}(i, j) = [i \quad j]$$

with these matrices, the numbers $y_{0est}(i, j) = C_{est}(i, j)x_0$ were calculated. For each $C_{est}(i, j)$ the fitness was calculated according to the following equation:

$$F_s(C_{est}(i, j)) = \frac{1}{|y_0 - y_{0est}(i, j)|}$$

that is equivalent to the equation 55. The results of F_s for each $C_{est}(i, j)$ are plotted in Figure 1.

From the figure is easy to see that the surface of the problem is not well behaved since it has high peaks and the derivatives are also very high. Consequently, if a heuristic algorithm is used to solve the optimization problem of finding the $C_{est}(i, j)$ that best represents C, at least one of the random candidate solution must fall in a very restricted region of the space. Since this has a low probability to happen, this is a hard optimization problem to be solved by heuristic algorithms.

The problem studied in this paper is even harder than the example proposed in this section since it has four matrices with dimensions higher than the one shown. As shown in the next section, an initialization step was implemented to deal with this problem. This step puts the candidate solutions in a region near the optimal solutions to be found.

Proposed Algorithm

As shown in the last section, the optimization problem related to the time variant system identification is constrained and has a search space that is not favorable to heuristic algorithms since the peaks are high and with high derivatives. On the other

Figure 1. Results of calculating the fitness F_s to each $C_{est}(i,j)$

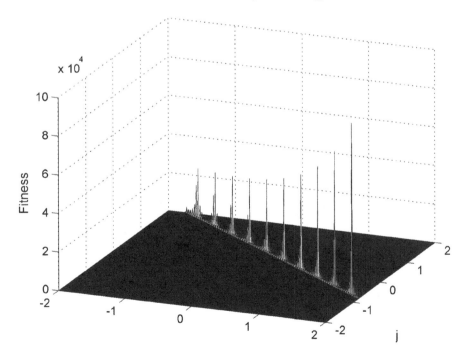

hand, considering that the system variations are continuous in time, once a solution is found, it is easy to follow slight variations of it by making small disturbances to the solution found in the previous time. More than that, if an immuno-inspired algorithm is used, it is guaranteed that, if the suppression threshold is well chosen, a solution that solves the problem in the past is kept in the population and consequently, if the system comes back to a previous situation, the solution is easier to be found.

The analogy between the optimization problem treated in this chapter and the immune system is the following: the antibodies are the quadruples { $A_{est}, B_{est}, C_{est}, D_{est}$ } and antigens are the time variant system matrices at each instant k represented by the quadruple {A, B, C, D}. If the system varies in time, or in other words, if the antigen suffers mutations, the quadruple { $A_{est}, B_{est}, C_{est}, D_{est}$ } will be mutated until it fits to the new system, or in other words, the B cells that secrete the antibodies will suffer mutation to fit the mutated antigen. If the system changes again, the estimated quadruple will be changed again to increase the fitness, but the previous solution will be kept in the organism. If the system comes back to a situation where it was before, the organism has already learned how to deal with that and the correct antibody will be used.

The main advantage of the immuno-inspired algorithms to other heuristic algorithms in this case is that previous solutions are kept in the population, without overpopulating the organism, what would imply on a huge computational effort.

The data used by the algorithm proposed in this paper is a set of inputs and outputs obtained from an actual or a benchmark time variant system. The outcomes are the models that describe the system at each instant of time. The algorithm steps are described below:

Algorithm Initialization

Before the main loop starts, an initialization is run to define the initial set of candidate solutions of the algorithm. The steps in this initialization are described below:

Step 1: An initialization window is defined containing N_{ini} samples of the inputs and outputs of the dynamic system to be modeled for time instants $0 \le k \le N_{ini} - 1$. This number of samples is considerably smaller than the total volume of data available but must be big enough to the MOESP algorithm work. In this definition $u_{ini} = input(:,1:N_{ini} - 1)$ and $y_{ini} = output(:,1:N_{ini} - 1)$ are the set of the first N_{ini} samples of inputs and outputs of the system.

Step 2: The MOESP algorithm described in the beginning of this paper is applied to the inputs u_ini and outputs y_ini contained in the initialization window to find a state space model that defines an initial quadruple { A_{ini}, B_{ini}, C_{ini}, D_{ini} } of matrices, as shown in the command below:

$$\{A_{ini}, B_{ini}, C_{ini}, D_{ini}\} = MOESP(u_{ini}, y_{ini})$$

Step 3: The initial quadruple { A_{ini}, B_{ini}, C_{ini}, D_{ini} } is cloned creating $N_{clonesini}$ clones, which are copies of this initial quadruple. Each one of the clones is then disturbed, it means, each matrix inside each clone is added to a disturbance, which is a random matrix of the same dimensions. This procedure defines the initial population. The disturbance of the clones is made such a way that is guaranteed that the solutions satisfy the constraints defined for the problem, as will be seen later in this section.

To create the disturbance for each clone, a positive real variable defined as Disturbance Order of Magnitude (DOM) and a pseudorandom matrices generator are used. This generator is a routine that generates matrices with a predetermined dimension filled with pseudorandom numbers taken from an uniform distribution between 0 and 1. Subtracting a matrix with all elements equal to 0.5 from the pseudorandom matrix and multiplying the result by the positive real number DOM, a disturbance random matrix with elements from a uniform distribution between –DOM/2 and DOM/2 is obtained.

Let rand(i,j) be the command to generate a matrix with i rows and j columns filled with pseudorandom numbers taken from an uniform distribution between 0 and 1 and ones(i,j) the command to generate a matrix with i rows and j columns filled with ones. Then a disturbance to the matrix A_{ini} of each clone is obtained with the following command:

Disturbance_A=DOM(rand(n,n)-0.5*ones(n,n))*

This disturbance is then added to A_{ini} defining a possible first matrix of each disturbed clone, defined as A_{qq}.

A_qq=A_ini+ Disturbance_A

The matrices must satisfy the constraints discussed before. For the matrix A this means that every eigenvalue of it must be inside the unit circle. To guarantee this, the eigenvalues of A_{qq} are calculated and if they are all inside the unit circle the matrix is considered part of a feasible solution and becomes one of the matrices of the quadruple that defines the candidate solution, receiving the name A_{est}. If not, a new disturbance is generated following the same rule and added again to A_{ini}. This is done until a feasible matrix A appears. The pseudo code is the following:

While all eingenvalues of A_{qq} are not inside the unit circle

Disturbance_A=DOM*(rand(n,n)-0.5*ones(n,n))

A_qq=A_ini+ Disturbance_A

Check the eigenvalues of A_qq

End

A_est=A_qq

Once the A_est matrix of each clone is defined, a similar procedure is applied to disturb the B_est and the C_est matrices of each clone, using basically the same functions adapted to the dimension of each matrix and to the constraints related to B_est and C_est:

While (A_{est} , B_{qq}) is not a reachable pair and B_{qq} does not satisfy its constraints

Disturbance$_B$ =DOM*(rand(n,m)-0.5*ones(n,m))

$B_{qq} = B_{ini} + Disturbance_B$

Check if the pair (A_{est} , B_{qq}) is reachable

End

$B_{est} = B_{qq}$

While (A_{est} , C_{qq}) is not an observable pair and C_{qq} does not satisfy its constraints

Disturbance$_C$ =DOM*(rand(l,n)-0.5*ones(l,n))

$$C_{qq} = C_{ini} + Disturbance_C$$

Check if the pair (A_{est} , C_{qq}) is observable

End

$$C_{est} = C_{qq}$$

For the matrix D_{est} there is no constraint, so this is created simply adding the disturbance to the matrix D_{ini}, found with the MOESP algorithm.

$$Disturbance_D = DOM*(rand(l,m)-0.5*ones(l,m))$$

$$D_{qq} = D_{ini} + Disturbance_D$$

Each one of the clones is disturbed with the procedure described above, creating the initial population of the problem.

Algorithm Iterations

Once the initial population is defined, the algorithm starts its main loop that contains the steps described below:

Step 4: For each instant $k > N_{ini}$, a set of samples containing the system inputs between the time instants $k - (N_w / 2)$ and $k + N_w / 2$, and the system outputs between $k - (N_w / 2) + 1$ and $k + N_w / 2 + 1$ is taken, where N_w is the window length. This set of data is defined as time window and represents the input and output data of the system around the time instant k.

Step 5: The fitness of the antibodies in the population is evaluated. To calculate the fitness of each antibody, the inputs of the system taken from the set of the samples of the time window are given as inputs to each model defined by each quadruple that represents each antibody in the population. Then the distance between the outputs of the model and the outputs of the system for each time instant inside the time window is calculated as the Euclidian distance between the two vectors, and fitness is calculated as described in equation 55. As seen before, if the antibody is a quadruple of matrices that represents a model that is a good approximation for the system, the outputs of this model will be similar to the outputs of the system and the fitness of this antibody will be high. If the antibody is a quadruple of matrices that do not represent the system, its outputs will be far from the system outputs and its fitness will be low.

Step 6: Each antibody at the population is cloned and the number of clones created for each antibody is proportional to the antibody fitness. Each clone is disturbed following the same procedure detailed in step 3 of the algorithm initialization, that means that the disturbances, that are matrices with elements created randomly with an uniform distribution between 0 an 1, subtracted by 0.5 and multiplied by DOM, are added to each one of the four matrices of the clone until feasible matrices are obtained. As the number of iterations gets bigger, the variable DOM decays. It means that in each iteration this variable is multiplied by a number between 0 and 1 in such a way that the disturbances become smaller as the candidate solutions converge to the optimum.

Step 7: The distances between the antibodies in the population are calculated. In this paper the distance between to quadruples of matrices is defined as the sum of the distances between the correspondent matrices in each quadruple. For example, let {A1, B1, C1, D1} and {A2, B2, C2, D2} be two quadruples of matrices that define two different antibodies and let dist() be an operator that defines distances. Then:

dist({A1, B1, C1, D1}, {A2, B2, C2, D2}) = dist(A1,A2)+dist(B1,B2)+dist(C1,C2)+dist(D1,D2)

In this paper the distance between two matrices is defined based on the Euclidean distance between two vectors, which is the square root of the sum of the differences between each term squared. So, in this paper the distance between two matrices is defined as the square root of the sum of the differences between each term of the matrices squared.

For example, let A1(i,j) be the term in the line i and column j f the matrix A1, and the same for the others matrices. The distance between the two antibodies {A1, B1, C1, D1} and {A2, B2, C2, D2} is defined in this paper as:

$$
\begin{aligned}
dist \quad &= \quad \sqrt{(A1(1,1) - A2(1,1))^2 + (A1(1,2) - A2(1,2))^2 + \ldots + (A1(2,1) - A2(2,1))^2 + \ldots + (A1(n,n) - A2(n,n))^2} \; + \\
&= \quad + \sqrt{(B1(1,1) - B2(1,1))^2 + (B1(1,2) - B2(1,2))^2 + \ldots + (B1(2,1) - B2(2,1))^2 + \ldots + (B1(n,m) - B2(n,m))^2} \; + \\
&= \quad + \sqrt{(C1(1,1) - C2(1,1))^2 + (C1(1,2) - C2(1,2))^2 + \ldots + (C1(2,1) - C2(2,1))^2 + \ldots + (C1(l,n) - C2(l,n))^2} \; + \\
&= \quad + \sqrt{(D1(1,1) - D2(1,1))^2 + (D1(1,2) - D2(1,2))^2 + \ldots + (D1(2,1) - D2(2,1))^2 + \ldots + (D1(l,m) - D2(l,m))^2} \; +
\end{aligned}
$$

Step 8: The antibodies that are around another one with better fitness, that is, he ones that have a distance to an antibody with better fitness smaller than a suppression threshold, are eliminated from the population.

Step 9: The fitness of each antibody is calculated as discussed in step 5. If the better fitness is greater than a value defined as F_{req} (required fitness), then k is incremented and the algorithm goes to step 4 defining a new time window. Otherwise random antibodies are created respecting the constraints of the problem in a procedure similar to the discussed in the step 3 and are added to the population. With this new population the algorithm goes to step 6 and the current time window solutions are refined. If the end of inputs and outputs data is reached, the algorithm is finalized.

The pseudocode that describes the main loop is shown in Box 1.

Box 1.

---

k=N_ini+1

While k+(Nw/2)+1 is smaller or equal to the number of input and output samples available

u_window=input(:,k-(Nw/2):k+(Nw/2));

y_window=output(:,k-(Nw/2+1):k+(Nw/2)+1)

Evaluate the fitness of the antibodies for u_window and y_window;

while the maximum fitness in the population is below the required fitness

For each antibody in the population

        Create a number of clones proportional to its fitness

        Disturb each clone considering the constraints

End

Varibable DOM Decays

Calculate the distance between all antibodies

For each pair of antibodies in the population

    If the distance is below the suppression threshold

        Eliminate the antibody with the smaller fitness

    End

  End

Evaluate the fitness of the antibodies for u_window and y_window;

End

Takes the next time step (k=k+1)

End

An important aspect of the algorithm is that it is implemented in such a manner that if the system does not vary between $k - (N_w / 2)$ and $k + (N_w / 2) + 1$, the same quadruple that had good fitness for the time window between $k - (N_w / 2)$ and $k + (N_w / 2)$ will have a good fitness for the time window between $k - (N_w / 2) + 1$ and $k + (N_w / 2) + 1$, and almost surely no iteration will be needed in this new time window, since the maximum fitness of the population will be bigger than the minimum fitness required.

If the system suffers a small variation between two subsequent time windows, just slight variations of the quadruple will be needed to find a quadruple that, when applied to the inputs, results in an output with a desired fitness.

In the following section, an example of application is shown. In this example, the system does not vary during the first instants of time and then, in the middle of the experiment starts varying. The behavior described in the two paragraphs above is clearly observed when the number of iterations is compared to the derivative of the system variation, as will be shown.

Example of Application

To test the algorithm proposed in this paper, a tridimensional white noise with N=1000 samples was given as input to a linear time variant benchmark system with the structure shown in equation 12, with the following time variant matrices:

$$A(k) = \begin{bmatrix} 0.2128 & f(k) & 0.1979 & -0.0836 \\ 0.1808 & 0.4420 & -0.3279 & 0.2344 \\ -0.5182 & 0.1728 & -0.5488 & -0.3083 \\ 0.2252 & -0.0541 & -0.4679 & 0.8290 \end{bmatrix} \tag{56}$$

where:

$$f(k) = \begin{cases} 0.1360 & k < 200 \\ 0.1360 - \sin(\dfrac{k - 200}{200}) & 200 \leq k \leq 828 \\ 0.1360 & k > 828 \end{cases} \tag{57}$$

$$B(k) = \begin{bmatrix} -0.0101 & 0.0317 & -0.9347 \\ -0.0600 & 0.5621 & 0.1657 \\ -0.3310 & -0.3712 & -0.5846 \\ -0.2655 & 0.4255 & 0.2204 \end{bmatrix} \tag{58}$$

$$C(k) = \begin{bmatrix} 0.6557 & -0.2502 & -0.5188 & -0.1229 \\ 0.6532 & -0.1583 & -0.055 & -0.2497 \end{bmatrix} \tag{59}$$

$$D(k) = \begin{bmatrix} -0.4326 & 0.1253 & -1.1465 \\ -1.6656 & 0.2877 & 1.1909 \end{bmatrix} \tag{60}$$

These matrices are similar to the benchmark that can be found in the third chapter of the reference (Tamariz, 2005). The only difference is the variation proposed in the term (1,2) of the matrix A.

The variation of each element of the matrix $A(k)$ along k is shown in Figure 2. Although only one element of only one matrix of the benchmark system changes along k, the system Markov parameters are deeply affected, as can be seen in Figures 3, 4, 5 and 6, where the variation of the first four Markov parameters $C(k)B(k)$, $C(k)A(k)B(k)$, $C(k)A^2(k)B(k)$ and $C(k)A^3(k)B(k)$ are shown.

The benchmark system outputs were collected and the algorithm proposed in this paper was applied to the benchmark system inputs and outputs with $N_{ini} = 40$ and $N_w = 19.$. The algorithm result was a time variant system with the following structure:

$$\begin{cases} x_{est}(k+1) = A_{est}(k)x(k) + B_{est}(k)u(k) \\ y(k) = C_{est}(k)x(k) + D_{est}(k)u(k) \end{cases} \tag{61}$$

where each matrix variation along k is shown in Figures 7, 8, 9 and 10. As can be seen from the figures, the matrices found with the algorithm proposed in this paper are different from the matrices defined for the benchmark system. More than that, the matrices B_{est}, C_{est}, and $D_{est}(k)$ shown in Figures 8, 9 and 10 are time variant, differently from the benchmark matrices $B(k)$, $C(k)$ and $D(k)$ defined respectively in equations 58, 59 and 60, that do not vary along time.

Figure 2. Variation of each A(k) element along k for the benchmark system

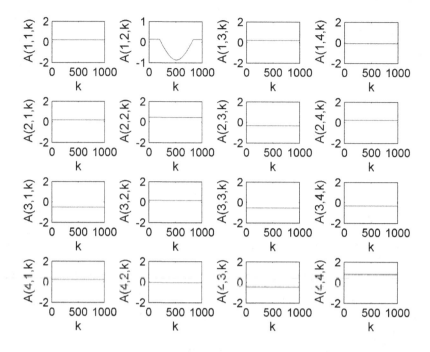

Figure 3. Benchmark system C(k)B(k) Markov parameter variation along k

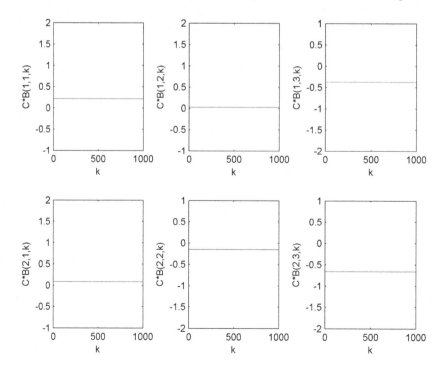

Figure 4. Benchmark system C(k)A(k)B(k) Markov parameter variation along k

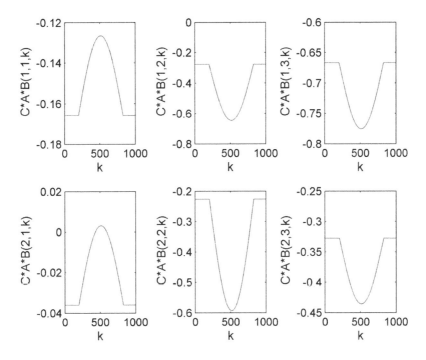

Figure 5. Benchmark system C(k)A²(k)B(k) Markov parameter variation along k

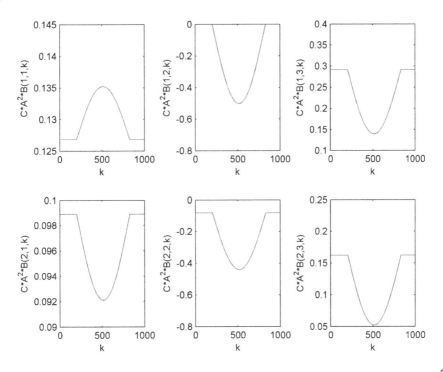

Figure 6. Benchmark system $C(k)A^3(k)B(k))$ Markov parameter variation along k

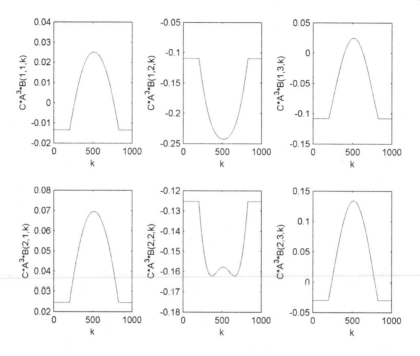

Figure 7. Variation of each estimated Aest(k) element along k. Each plot represents one element

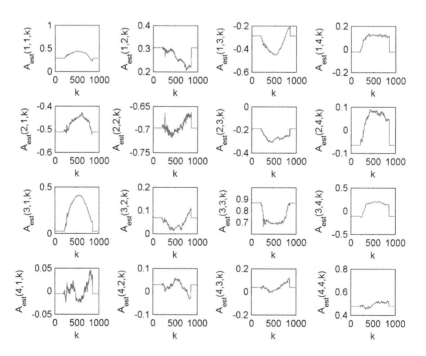

Figure 8. Variation of each estimated Best(k) element along k. Each plot represents one element

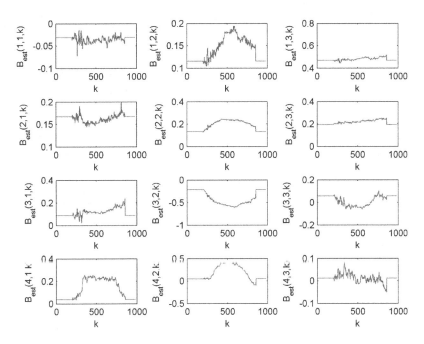

Figure 9. Variation of each estimated Cest(k) element along k. Each plot represents one element

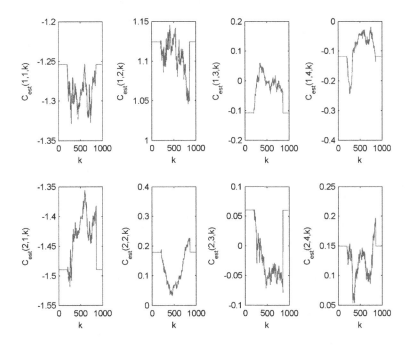

Figure 10. Variation of each estimated Dest(k) element along k. Each plot represents one element

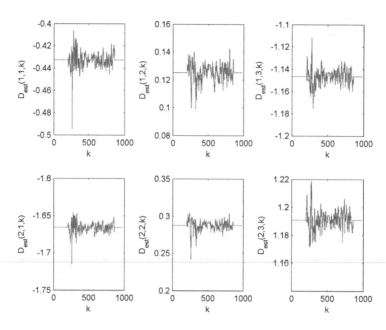

Figure 11. Markov parameters for the benchmark and the estimated system. In blue continuous line is plotted the C(k)B(k) Markov parameter for the benchmark System and in red crosses is plotted the Cest(k)Best(k) Markov parameter for the estimated system

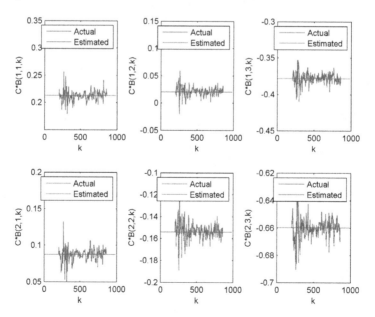

Although the estimated matrices found with the algorithm presented in this paper are different from the ones defined in the benchmark system, the time variant Markov parameters calculated with the estimated matrices are similar to the benchmark system Markov parameters, as can be seen in Figures 11, 12, 13 and 14, where the first four Markov parameters obtained with the estimated matrices are plotted together with the benchmark system Markov parameters. This shows that, even with different matrices, the estimated system impulse response is near the benchmark system impulse response, which means that the estimated system is a good approximation for the benchmark system.

The same input used to generate the benchmark system outputs was applied to the time variant system obtained with the algorithm proposed in this paper. For comparison, this input was also applied to the quadruple { A_{ini}, B_{ini}, C_{ini}, D_{ini} }

Figure 12. Markov parameters for the benchmark and the estimated system. In blue continuous line is plotted the C(k)A(k)B(k) Markov parameter for the benchmark System and in red crosses is plotted the Cest(k) Aest(k)Best(k) Markov parameter for the estimated system

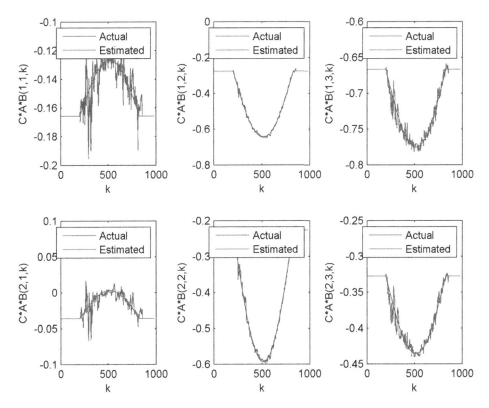

Figure 13. Markov parameters for the benchmark and the estimated system. In blue continuous line is plotted the C(k)A²(k)B(k) Markov parameter for the benchmark System and in red crosses is plotted the Cest(k) Aest² (k)Best(k) Markov parameter for the estimated system

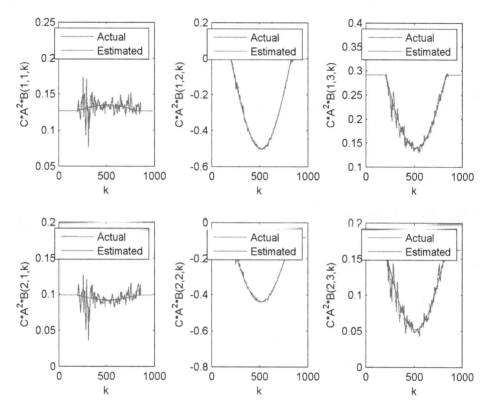

obtained during the MOESP initialization and for time variant matrices found with the MOESP-VAR algorithm using a window with the same length as the one used for the immuno-inspired algorithm, which is 19.

The outputs from the benchmark system, from the time variant system obtained by the algorithm proposed in this paper, from the system defined by the quadruple $\{ A_{ini}, B_{ini}, C_{ini}, D_{ini} \}$ and from the system found with MOESP-VAR algorithm are shown in Figures 15 and 16.

At the Figure 15 the time interval is in a region where the system does not vary. From this figure is easy to see that the outputs from the system obtained by the method proposed in this paper and the outputs from the system defined by the initialization quadruple are near the benchmark system outputs. It is as expected since in this interval the time variant benchmark system has the same matrices that

Figure 14. Markov parameters for the benchmark and the estimated system. In blue continuous line is plotted the C(k)A³(k)B(k) Markov parameter for the benchmark System and in red crosses is plotted the Cest(k) Aest³ (k)Best(k) Markov parameter for the estimated system

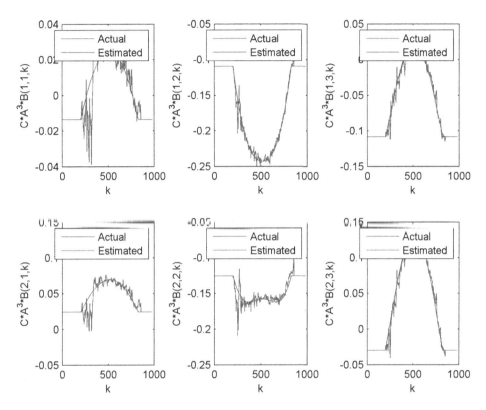

are used in the MOESP initialization step. On the other hand, the outputs obtained with MOESP-VAR algorithm in some cases are far from the actual outputs. This happens because the window size is too small to get good estimates from the sample matrices decomposition.

At the Figure 16 are shown the outputs in an interval where the benchmark system is under the greatest variation in the experiment (near k = 200). From this figure is easy to see that the outputs obtained with the system found in the MOESP initialization are still accurate, since the model is still near the original benchmark system for which the MOESP initialization was applied. The outputs obtained with the algorithm proposed in this paper are also accurate. The outputs obtained with the system found in MOESP-VAR algorithm are not accurate since at this point the system suffers a big variation and the input and output samples do not satisfy the hypothesis that the system do not change along time.

Figure 15. Outputs in the interval 100<k<110. In green continuous line are shown the benchmark system outputs. In black crosses are shown the outputs from the system obtained in MOESP initialization, in red x are shown the outputs obtained with MOESP-VAR and in blue stars are shown the outputs from the system obtained with the algorithm proposed in this paper

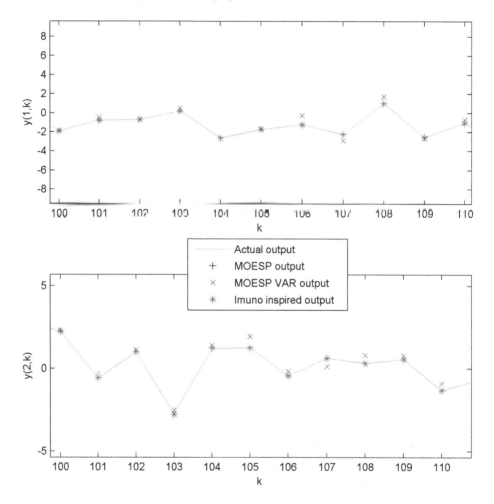

At the Figure 17 is shown a time interval where the system is farther from the system for which the initialization was made (around k=515). As expected, the outputs obtained with the model found at MOESP initialization are far from the actual outputs since at that interval the system is different from the one for which the initialization was made. The outputs obtained with the system found with MOESP-VAR algorithm are near the actual outputs since the system is not under

Figure 16. Outputs in the interval 200<k<210. In green continuous line are shown the benchmark system outputs. In black crosses are shown the outputs from the system obtained in MOESP initialization, in red x are shown the outputs obtained with MOESP-VAR and in blue stars are shown the outputs from the system obtained with the algorithm proposed in this paper

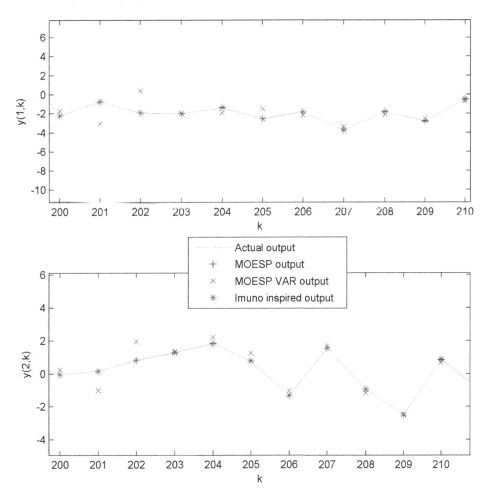

a big variation during this interval. The results obtained with the system estimated by the algorithm proposed in this paper are near to the actual outputs.

To give a general idea about the errors found with the three methods compared in this paper, the absolute values of them are plotted in the Figure 18. From the figure it is easy to see that the Immuno-Var method proposed in this paper has a very small error in the major part of the iterations. The error of the proposed method is

Figure 17. Outputs in the interval 520<k<520. In green continuous line are shown the benchmark system outputs. In black crosses are shown the outputs from the system obtained in MOESP initialization, in red x are shown the outputs obtained with MOESP-VAR and in blue stars are shown the outputs from the system obtained with the algorithm proposed in this paper

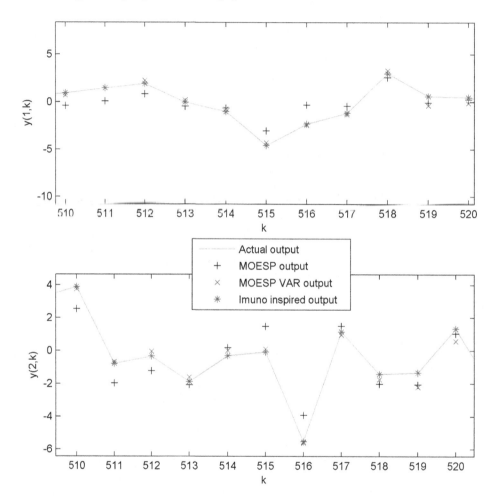

significant only in the beginning and the end of the iterations, where the window is not well defined. From the figure is possible to see that the error in MOESP is considerably big in the region around 200<k<800. In this region, the system is far from his initial condition and the MOESP method is not capable to model it. The error of the MOESP-VAR is always considerably big because the size of the window does not allow the correct calculation of the Markov Parameters correctly because the changes in the benchmark system are considerably high.

To compare analytically the results obtained with the three algorithms, the fitness defined at equation 55 was calculated for the whole set of outputs for the three methods. The results are shown in Table 1.

From the table is possible to see that the algorithm proposed in this paper has a fitness bigger than the MOESP and MOESP-VAR fitness, what is expected from the results found in Figure 18. This means that the error between the outputs obtained with the system estimated by the algorithm proposed in this paper and the actual output is smaller than the errors from the other two algorithms. An interesting result is that the fitness for MOESP is greater than the fitness obtained for MOESP-VAR. This happens because the window size is too small to allow system estimations by MOESP-VAR. In order to check this result, another run was made with MOESP-VAR with a window size equal to 41 and the fitness obtained was 3.2264, which is greater than the MOESP one but still far from the result obtained with the algorithm proposed in this paper.

Figure 18. Absolute values of the errors obtained with the three methods compared in this chapter

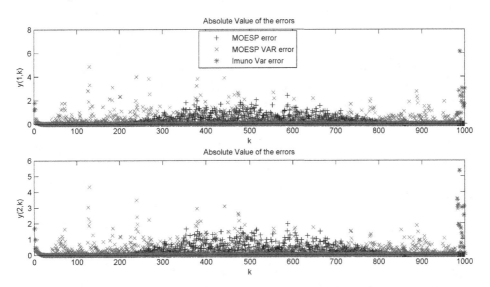

Table 1. Fitness calculated for the outputs obtained with the systems found with MOESP, MOESP-VAR and the algorithm proposed in this paper Immuno VAR)

MOESP	MOESP-VAR	Immuno-VAR
2.7129	1.5562	12.7997

With the proposed algorithm behavior is also possible to determine if a system is time variant or not. This is possible by observing the number of iterations needed to reach the desired fitness for each window. If the number of iterations is small, the system does not vary in time. Otherwise, the system suffers a variation.

In Figure 18 is shown the number of iterations needed to the algorithm find the desired fitness for each window. From this figure, it is clear that the system variation starts when k > 200, as it really happens. More than that, comparing this figure with Figures 3, 4, 5 and 6 that show the benchmark system Markov parameters variations along k, it is possible to see that the number of iterations is proportional to the system variations, or in other words, is proportional to the Markov parameters derivatives.

FUTURE RESEARCH DIRECTIONS

This chapter has shown some natural inspired approaches to solve the system identification problems and detailed an immuno-inspired method to identify time variant MIMO linear systems. The application of natural inspired approaches to the system identification problems has proved to be an interesting alternative for both linear and nonlinear system identification problems. The main issue related to these techniques is that the computations involved are massive, and grow exponentially with the system complexity. For this reason, nowadays the computational costs of the online recursive identification using natural paradigms is practically prohibitive for real systems that present nonlinearities and high order phenomena. An interesting future research would be the application of natural inspired approaches that can be parallelized, such as the co-evolutionary techniques. In this way, the burden of the massive calculations can be divided by many processors, allowing a faster response.

CONCLUSION

From the results shown in this chapter, the conclusion is that the immuno-inspired algorithm here proposed is able to follow the variations of a time variant MIMO system. If only the MOESP algorithm is used to identify the time variant system as a time invariant system, the estimated outputs are different from the benchmark system outputs. The immuno-inspired algorithm proposed in this paper can also follow system variations faster than the ones that can be followed by MOESP-VAR algorithm. The proposed algorithm is also able to follow the Markov parameters variations along time, showing that the immuno-inspired tool is useful to follow fast variations in time variant systems.

Figure 19. Number of iterations taken to reach the minimum fitness

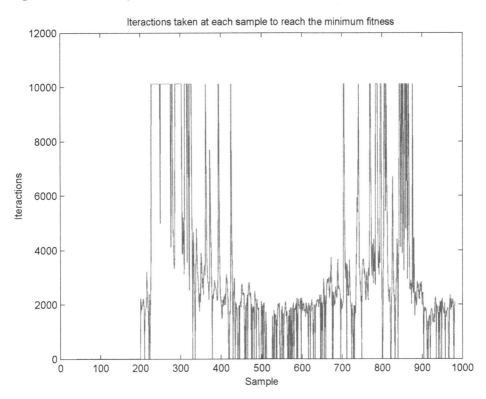

The approach used in this paper to identify a dynamic system, that was interpreting a state space model as a point in a space and searching this space to find the point that optimizes the error between the model output and the actual output, was crucial to establish the technique to solve the problem. The method here proposed can be used to identify real time varying systems, and since it is recursive, a real time varying system can be identified online.

From the method described in this chapter and the recent researches on the application of natural inspired paradigms to solve the system identification problem, it is possible to notice that the most important challenge to be addressed is the high computational cost of those algorithms. For this reason, future researches on faster algorithms and parallel approaches are expected.

ACKNOWLEDGMENT

This research received no specific grant from any funding agency in the public, commercial, or not-for-profit sectors.

REFERENCES

Aoki, M. (1987). *State Space Modeling of Time Series*. Springer-Verlag. doi:10.1007/978-3-642-96985-0

Barreto, G. (2002). *Modelagem computacional distribuída e paralela de sistemas e de séries temporais multivariáveis no espaço de estado* (PhD thesis). Universidade Estadual de Campinas.

Cutello, V., Narizi, G., Nicosia, G., & Pavone, M. (2005). Clonal selection algorithms: A comparative case study usign effective mutation potentials. In *4th Intl. Conference on Artificial Immune Systems*, (pp. 13-28). Academic Press. doi:10.1007/11536444_2

Cutello, V., Narizi, G., Nicosia, G., & Pavone, M. (2006). Real coded clonal selection algorithm for global numerical optimization using a new inversely proportional hypermutation operator. In *21st Annual ACM Symposium on Applied Computing*, (pp. 950–954). Academic Press.

Cutello, V., & Nicosia, G. (2002). An immunological approach to combinatorial optimization problems. In Advances in Artificial Intelligence IBERAMIA, (pp. 361-370). Academic Press.

de Castro, L. N., & Timmis, J. (2002). *Artificial Immune Systems - A new computational intelligence approach*. Springer Verlag.

de Castro, L. N., & Von Zuben, F. J. (2000). The clonal selection algorithm with engineering applications. In *Workshop proceedings of the GECCO 2000*, (pp. 36-37). Academic Press.

de Castro, L. N., & Von Zuben, F. J. (2002). Learning and optimization using the clonal selection principle. *IEEE Transactions on Evolutionary Computation*, 6(3), 239–251. doi:10.1109/TEVC.2002.1011539

de França, F. O., Coelho, G. P., Castro, P. A., & Von Zuben, F. J. (2010). Conceptual and Practical Aspects of the aiNet Family of Algorithms. *International Journal of Natural Computing Research*, 35.

Giesbrecht, M., & Bottura, C. P. (2011). Immuno inspired approaches to model discrete time series at state space. In *Proceedings of the Fourth International Workshop on Advanced Computational Intelligence* (pp. 750-756). Wuhan: IEEE. doi:10.1109/IWACI.2011.6160107

Giesbrecht, M., & Bottura, C. P. (2015). Recursive Immuno-Inspired Algorithm for Time Variant Discrete Multivariable Dynamic System State Space Identification. *International Journal of Natural Computing Research*, 32.

Giesbrecht, M., & Bottura, C. P. (2016). An immuno inspired proposal to solve the time series realization problem. In *2016 IEEE Congress on Evolutionary Computation (CEC)* (pp. 1786-1792). Vancouver: IEEE.

Ho, B. L., & Kalman, R. E. (1966). Effective construction of linear state variable models from input-output functions. *Regelungstechnik -zeitschrift für steuern, regeln und automatisieren*, 545–548.

Iwasaki, M., Miwa, M., & Matsui, N. (2005). GA-based evolutionary identification algorithm for unknown structured mechatronic systems. *IEEE Transactions on Industrial Electronics*, *52*(1), 300–305. doi:10.1109/TIE.2004.841075

Koshiyama, A. S., Escovedo, T., Dias, M. D., Vellasco, M. M., & Pacheco, M. A. (2012). Combining Forecasts: A Genetic Programming Approach. *International Journal of Natural Computing Research*, 18.

Li, H., & Li, S. (2012). Quantum particle swarm evolutionary algorithm with application to system identification. In *Proceedings of 2012 International Conference on Measurement, Information and Control* (pp. 1032-1036). Harbin: IEEE. doi:10.1109/MIC.2012.6273477

Rodriguez-Vazquez, K., Fonseca, C., & Fleming, P. (2004). Identifying the structure of nonlinear dynamic systems using multiobjective genetic programming. *IEEE Transactions on Systems, Man, and Cybernetics. Part A, Systems and Humans*, *34*(4), 531–545. doi:10.1109/TSMCA.2004.826299

Tamariz, A. D. (2005). *Modelagem computacional de dados e controle inteligente no espaço de estado* (PhD thesis). Universidade Estadual de Campinas.

Tamariz, A. D., Bottura, C. P., & Barreto, G. (2005). Iterative MOESP type algorithm for discrete time variant system identification. *Proceedings of the 13th Mediterranean Conference on Control and Automation (MED 2005)*. doi:10.1109/.2005.1467048

Tang, H., Xie, L., & Xue, S. (2015). Usage of Comprehensive Learning Particle Swarm Optimization for Parameter Identification of Structural System. *International Journal of Natural Computing Research*, 15.

Verhaegen, M., & Dewilde, P. (1992). Subspace model identification - part I: The output-error state-space model identification class of algorithms. *International Journal of Control*, *56*(5), 1187–1210. doi:10.1080/00207179208934363

Verhaegen, M., & Verdult, V. (2007). *Filtering and System Identification – A Least Squares Approach.* Cambridge University Press. doi:10.1017/CBO9780511618888

Wakizono, M., Hatanaka, T., & Uosaki, K. (2006). Time Varying System Identification with Immune Based Evolutionary Computation. In *2006 SICE-ICASE International Joint Conference* (pp. 5608-5613). Busan: IEEE. doi:10.1109/SICE.2006.315098

Young, P. C. (2011). *Recursive Estimation and Time Series Analysis* (2nd ed.). Springer-Verlag. doi:10.1007/978-3-642-21981-8

Zakaria, M. Z., Jamaluddin, H., Ahmad, R., & Loghmanian, S. M. (2010). Multiobjective Evolutionary Algorithm Approach in Modeling Discrete-Time Multivariable Dynamics Systems. In *Second International Conference on Computational Intelligence, Modelling and Simulation* (pp. 65-70). Bali: Academic Press. doi:10.1109/CIMSiM.2010.55

Chapter 2
Comprehensive Learning Particle Swarm Optimization for Structural System Identification

Hesheng Tang
Tongji University, China

Xueyuan Guo
Tongji University, China

Lijun Xie
Tongji University, China

Songtao Xue
Tohoku Institute of Technology, Japan

ABSTRACT

This chapter introduces a novel swarm-intelligence-based algorithm named the comprehensive learning particle swarm optimization (CLPSO) to identify parameters of structural systems, which is formulated as a high-dimensional multi-modal numerical optimization problem. With the new strategy in this variant of particle swarm optimization (PSO), historical best information for all other particles is used to update a particle's velocity. This means that the particles have more exemplars to learn from and a larger potential space to fly, avoiding premature convergence. Simulation results for identifying the parameters of a five degree-of-freedom (DOF) structural system under conditions including limited output data, noise polluted signals, and no prior knowledge of mass, damping, or stiffness are presented to demonstrate improved estimation of these parameters by CLPSO when compared with those obtained from PSO. In addition, the efficiency and applicability of the proposed method are experimentally examined by a 12-story shear building shaking table model.

DOI: 10.4018/978-1-5225-5020-4.ch002

INTRODUCTION

Nowadays, system identification with good accuracy and general practicality is quite a significant tool for assessing the performance of structures in civil engineering. The goal of system identification is to estimate the "best" set of parameter values, which minimizes the error between the actual physically measured response of a system and the simulated response. This parameter estimation problem can be formulated as a non-convex, nonlinear optimization problem, and can therefore be solved using global optimization techniques.

Recently, some researchers tried to use some sort of heuristic intelligent optimization algorithms to tackle system identification problems with limited and noise contaminated measurements. Simulated annealing (SA) have been implemented for model updating techniques that optimize a finite element model to accurately describe the dynamic behaviour of structures (Levin & Lieven, 1998). Genetic algorithm (GA) have been successfully applied to the identification of the elastic constants of composite materials (Cunha et al., 1999) and the main properties of a base-isolated concrete bridge under static and dynamic loading conditions (Chisari et al., 2015). Evolution strategy (ES) algorithms have been presented for the identification of multiple degree-of-freedom (DOF) systems (Franco et al., 2004). Tang et al.(2008) have applied a differential evolution (DE) strategy to parameters estimation of structural systems. Particularly, in the field of structural damage detection, GA has been used to identify damage severity of trusses (Chou & Ghaboussi, 2001), to detect crack in structural elements (Buezas et al., 2011) and to solve the global system identification problem in shear-type building structures. These references (Koh et al., 2003; Perry et al., 2006) have presented a modified GA based on migration and artificial selection strategies to improve the computational performance in terms of identification accuracy and computational speed. An approach based on GA combined with artificial neural networks has been employed for damage detection on a three-story steel frame (Betti et al., 2015). Although many GA versions have been developed, they are still time consuming. SA has proven to be thorough and reliable, but is generally too slow and inefficient to be of practical use with larger modelling problems (Mayer, 2002).

In the past decades, swarm intelligence algorithms have received a lot of attention in optimization problems (Piotrowski et al., 2017). As a novel evolutionary computation technique, particle swarm optimization (PSO) (Kennedy & Eberhart, 1995) has attracted much attention and has wide applications, owing to its simple concept, easy implementation and quick convergence (Poli et al., 2007; Banks et al., 2008; Der Valle et al., 2008). PSO works to iteratively improve a swarm of candidate solutions, which are called particles, in the case of an objective function. PSO has been successfully applied in many fields, such as function optimization, fuzzy system control, layout optimization, feature selection, simulation and identification, automatic target detection, optimal design, parameters estimation and damage identification (Hassan et al., 2011; He & Wang, 2007; Gholizadeh, 2013; Xue et al., 2013; Kennedy et al., 2001; Liang et al., 2006; Perera et al., 2010; Shi, 2001; Xue et al., 2009; Tang et al., 2013).

The particle swarm optimizer shares the ability of the genetic algorithm to handle arbitrary nonlinear cost functions, but with a much simpler implementation. Boeringer & Werner (2003) have investigated the performance of GA and PSO for a phased array synthesis problem. The results show that some optimization scenarios are better suited to one method versus the other, which implies that the two methods traverse the problem hyperspace differently. In another publication (Mouser & Dunn, 2005), the authors compared the performance of GA and PSO for optimizing a structural dynamics model. The results show that the PSO significantly outperformed the GA. Also, the PSO is much easier to configure than the GA and is more likely to produce an acceptable model.

Although it has been shown that the PSO performs well on many optimization problems, it may easily get trapped in a local optimum when solving complex multimodal problems (Clerc & Kennedy, 2002; Van den Bergh & Engelbrecht, 2006). Some researchers have theoretically investigated the significance of velocity updates rules in PSO, and the results have shown that the absence of adequate diversity leads to premature convergence (Wilke et al., 2010; Huang et al., 2012; Civicioglu & Besdok, 2013; Bonyadi et al., 2014). In order to enable the diversity of the swarm to be preserved to discourage premature convergence, three new learning strategies to make the particles have different learning exemplars for different dimensions have recently been employed, including elite learning strategy, multi-exemplars learning strategy and comprehensive learning strategy. The comprehensive learning PSO (CLPSO) has been proposed (Liang et al., 2004; Liang et al., 2006), since it showed the great improvement of the performance on complex multimodal problems. Huang et al. (2006) presented a CLPSO based method to handle multiple objective optimization problems, as well as a variant of CLPSO proposed by Ali & Khan (2013). In a recent article (Majhi & Panda, 2009) the CLSPO based algorithm has been applied to identify the feed-forward and feedback coefficients of IIR systems. In another paper (Gao & Hailu, 2010), the CLPSO has been employed to solve multimodal optimization problems with problem-specific constraints and mixed variables, showing the advantages in terms of solution accuracy and computational cost. It is reported that the CLPSO algorithm outperforms the existing standard recursive LMS (RLMS), GA and PSO based methods in terms of minimum mean square error (MSE) after convergence, execution time and product of population size and number of input samples used in training. Further, this method exhibits significant improvement in convergence behaviour under multimodal situation compared to those obtained by GA and PSO methods.

In the realm of structural engineering, identification of structural systems with unknown mass, stiffness and damping properties – is a challenging problem rarely considered due to the difficulty encountered in many identification methods. Thus, the main motive of this paper is to propose a new algorithm using a powerful PSO technique for identification of a structural system with unknown mass, stiffness, damping properties, limited and noise contaminated measurements which does not converge to local minima and thus expected to provide accurate estimates of the parameters.

In this chapter the identification of structural system is carried out using the CLPSO algorithm. Since the proposed technique is capable of converging to the global solution for multimodal optimization problems, it is a good candidate for identification of structural systems. Simulation results for identifying the parameters of a 5-DOF structure are presented to demonstrate the effectiveness of the proposed method. Moreover, an experimental investigation of the shaking table test data of a 12-storey RC-frame structure model (Lu et al., 2003) of the feasibility of using the CLPSO for identifying structural parameters is presented in this chapter. The identified results are compared with results calculated directly from the experiments to verify the proposed approach.

BACKGROUND

PSO Algorithm

Particle swarm algorithms have recently emerged as a powerful tool for solving many difficult optimization problems (Kennedy & Eberhart, 1995; Kennedy et al., 2001; Shi, 2001). The development of PSO algorithms has drawn the inspiration from the social behaviour of groups of individuals as observed in nature, like insects or birds. These animals are able to explore the space in search of a common goal (e.g. food) by moving in a coordinated and competitive manner. From an optimization viewpoint, a swarm represents a set of potential solutions to an optimization problem, and this set moves through the solution space in search of a better location by following a pre-specified motion model. The PSO algorithms are easy to implement in terms of requirements of only primitive mathematical operators, and are not computationally expensive as regards both memory requirements and speed. Besides, the PSO algorithms have widely applied to continuous optimization rather than ant colony optimization algorithms, another class of swarm intelligence algorithms, which are suitable for solving dispersed optimizes question problems (Dorigo et al., 2005; Castro, 2007).

In PSO, candidate solutions of a population, called particles, coexist and evolve simultaneously based on the knowledge shared with neighbouring particles. While flying through the problem search space, each particle generates a solution using directed velocity vector. Each particle modifies its velocity to find a better solution (position) by applying its own flying experience (i.e., memory of having found the best position in earlier flights) and the experience of neighbouring particles (i.e., the best solution found by the population). Recent work indicates that use of a constriction factor in the first version of PSO may be necessary to insure convergence of the particle swarm algorithm (Clerc, 1999). In this variant PSO, the dth dimension of the ith particle updates its positions θ_i^d and velocities v_i^d as shown below:

$$v_i^d \leftarrow w * v_i^d + c1 * r1 * (pbest_i^d - \theta_i^d) + c2 * r2 * (gbest^d - \theta_i^d) \tag{1}$$

$$\theta_i^d \leftarrow \theta_i^d + \kappa v_i^d, \ \kappa = \frac{2}{\left|2 - \phi - \sqrt{\phi^2 - 4\phi}\right|}, \phi = c1 + c2 > 4 \tag{2}$$

where $\boldsymbol{\theta}_i = (\theta_i^1, \theta_i^2, \cdots, \theta_i^D)$ is the position of the ith particle, D is the number of the parameters to be optimized, $\mathbf{v}_i = (v_i^1, v_i^2, \cdots, v_i^D)$ represents the velocity of particle i, $\mathbf{pbest}_i = (pbest_i^1, pbest_i^2, \cdots, pbest_i^D)$ is the best previous position yielding the best fitness value for the ith particle, and $\mathbf{gbest} = (gbest^1, gbest^2, \cdots, gbest^D)$ is the best position discovered by the whole population. Acceleration constants, $c1$ and $c2$ indicate the weighting of stochastic acceleration terms that pull each particle toward *pbest* and *gbest* positions, respectively. Proper fine-tuning of the parameters may result in faster convergence of the algorithm, and alleviation of the local minima. It might be even better to choose a larger cognitive parameter, $c1$ than a social parameter, $c2$ but with $c1+c2 >4$ (Clerc, 1999). $r1$ and $r2$ are two independently uniformly distributed random numbers in the range [0, 1]. w is the particle inertia weight. The inertia weight is used to balance the global and local search abilities. The authors' approach incorporates a linearly time-decreasing inertia weight over the course of the search (Shi & Eberhart, 1998). On the other hand, the population size S is chosen in the range 20 ~ 40 for most case studies, considering the trade-off between the computational efficiency and the precision of the global identification.

The Implementation Scheme of the PSO Algorithm

Step 1: Input the number of dimensions D, the population size S. Initialize the process including the initial D dimensional position vector and the initial D dimensional velocity vector for each particle.

Step 2: Compute the new position of each particle according to its current position and velocity.

Step 3: Compute the best previous position *pbest* of each particle and the best position discovered by the whole population *gbest* according to the fitness (objective)-based rule.

Step 4: Update all particles' velocities according to Eq. (1).

Step 5: Update all particles' positions according to Eq. (2).

Step 6: Check the terminal criteria. If the criteria are satisfied, stop. Otherwise, back to step 3.

CLPSO Algorithm

This chapter employs a comprehensive learning strategy described by Liang et al. (2004). In this learning strategy, all particles' *pbests* in the population can potentially be used as exemplars to guide a particle's flying direction, while the original PSO only uses particle's own *pbest* and *gbest* as the exemplars. In addition, instead of learning from the same exemplar particle for all dimensions in the original PSO, in the new strategy each dimension of a particle may learn from the corresponding dimension of a different particle's *pbest,* avoiding getting trapped in into local optimum. To ensure that a particle learns from good exemplars and to minimize the time wasted on poor directions, this strategy does not allow the particle to learn from exemplars across all generations. Only if the particle ceases improving for a certain number of generations, called the refreshing gap m, is the particle permitted to learn. In this new learning strategy, the following velocity updating equation is used:

$$v_i^d \leftarrow w * v_i^d + c * r * (pbest_{I_i^d}^d - \theta_i^d) \tag{3}$$

where I_i^d defines which particles' *pbests* the particle i should follow. $pbest_{I_i^d}^d$ can be the corresponding dimension of any particle's that includes its own *pbest*, and the decision depends on probability Pc, i.e., the learning probability, which can have different values for different particles. The comprehensive learning strategy for updating *pbest* after a particle ceases improving for the refreshing gap m is demonstrated in Table 1.

Table 1. Pseudo-code for selection of exemplar dimensions for particle i and updating pbest$_i$

For each dimensional variable d in total length of dimension D of particle i
    Generate a random number rc from a uniform distribution between 0 and 1
    If $rc < Pc_i$
$I_1 = $ ceil($NP \times$ rand(1,D)) /ceiling operation, NP is the population size/
    $I_2 = $ ceil($NP \times$ rand(1,D)) /ceiling operation/
    If particle I_1 is better than particle I_2 /tournament selection in terms of the fitness (objective) values /

$$pbest_i^d = pbest_{I_1}^d$$

    else

$$pbest_i^d = pbest_{I_2}^d$$

    End If
    End If
EndFor

Note: ceiling operation: ceil(A) rounds the elements of A to the nearest integers greater than or equal to A.

In the learning strategy, each particle learns potentially from all particles' *pbests* in the swarm. During the search process, each dimension of a particle has an equal chance to learn from other particles. For each particle, some dimensions of other particles' *pbests* are randomly chosen according to a probability *Pc*, called learning probability. *Pc* determines how many dimensions are chosen to learn from other particles' *pbests*. Each particle has its own *Pc$_i$*, which could be different from that of other particles. For each dimension of particle *i*, a random number is generated. If this random number is larger than *Pc$_i$*, the corresponding dimension will learn from its own *pbest*; otherwise, it will learn from another particle's *pbest*. A tournament selection procedure is employed when the particle's dimension learns from another particle's *pbest*. In this selection strategy, two particles are randomly chosen out of the population, which excludes the particle being updated. Then these two particles' *pbests* are compared in terms of the fitness (objective) values and the better one will be selected. The winner's *pbest* is used as the exemplar to learn from for that dimension. If all exemplars of a particle are its own *pbest*, then one dimension is randomly selected to learn from another particle's *pbest*'s corresponding dimension. These operations increase the diversity of swarms which results in enhanced performance when solving complex multimodal problems. The refresher gap parameter *m* also influences the results as it affects the convergence velocity. An extended study of the parameter setting is given by Clerc & Kennedy (2002) and Liang et al. (2006). In the authors' experiments, better results were obtained when the refreshing gap was set to 0.6-0.8 times the dimension. The proposed algorithm is given in Table 2. For a detailed explanation of CLPSO algorithm, reader is referred to Liang et al. (2006).

Table 2. Pseudo-code for the CLPSO algorithm

Initialize a population of particles with random positions and velocities.
  For k=1 to Max_gen / Max_gen is maximum evolution generation /
    Update *gbest* according to the fitness (objective)-based rule
    For i=1 to *NP* /*NP* is the population size /
      Update *pbest*$_i$ after a particle ceases improving for the refreshing gap m according to comprehensive learning strategy. / see Table 1. /
        For d=1 to D / D denotes dimension of the particle /

Update the velocity v_i^d in terms of Eq. (3)
Restrict velocity if it exceeds the range specified:

$$v_i^d = \min(v_{max}^d, \max(-v_{max}^d, v_i^d))$$

Update the positions θ_i^d in terms of Eq. (2)
        End For d
      End For i
      Update *pbest*$_i$ according to the fitness (objective)-based rule
      Stop if a stop criterion is satisfied
    End For k

CLPSO BASED IDENTIFICATION OF STRUCTURAL SYSTEMS

The identification problem can be considered as a non-convex nonlinear optimization problem in which the error between the actual physical measured response of a structure and the simulated response of a numerical model is minimized. To show this in more detail, the authors consider a general physical system:

$$\mathbf{y}(k) = f(\mathbf{u}(k), \boldsymbol{\theta}) \tag{4}$$

where $\mathbf{y} \in R^q$ denotes the system output, $u \in R^p$ denotes system input, $\boldsymbol{\theta} = (\theta_1, \theta_2, \cdots, \theta_D)$ are the D parameters to be estimated and $k = 0,1,\ldots,T$ denote the kth discrete time step.

For successful identification, the candidate system, $\hat{\mathbf{y}}(k) = f(\mathbf{u}(k), \hat{\boldsymbol{\theta}})$, must be able to accurately reproduce the output of the physical system for any given input. Therefore, the authors' interest lies in minimizing the predefined error norm of the outputs, e.g., the mean square error (MSE) function:

$$F(\boldsymbol{\theta}) = \frac{1}{T} \sum_{k=1}^{T} \left\| \mathbf{y}(k) - \hat{\mathbf{y}}(k) \right\|^2 \tag{5}$$

where $\hat{\mathbf{y}}(k) = f(\mathbf{u}(k), \hat{\boldsymbol{\theta}})$ is the output of the model with estimated parameters and $\|\cdot\|$ represents the Euclidean norm of vectors. Formally, the optimization problem requires finding a vector $\boldsymbol{\theta} \in R^D$ so that a certain quality criterion is satisfied, i.e., the error norm $F(\bullet)$ is minimized. The function $F(\bullet)$ is commonly known as a fitness function or an objective function. In PSO, a fitness function is typically used, which reflects the accuracy of a solution. Thus, the problem of identification thus is treated as a linearly constrained multi-dimensional nonlinear optimization problem:

$$\min F(\boldsymbol{\theta}), \boldsymbol{\theta} = (\theta_1, \theta_2, \cdots, \theta_D)$$

$$s.t. \quad \boldsymbol{\theta} \in R^n \Big| \theta_{\min,i} \leq \theta_i \leq \theta_{\max,i} \qquad \forall i = 1, 2, \cdots, D \qquad (6)$$

where $\theta_{\max}$ and $\theta_{\min}$ denote the upper and the lower bounds of n parameters, respectively.

For an n-DOF structural system, its dynamic equation of motion can be expressed as

$$\mathbf{M\ddot{x}}(t) + \mathbf{C\dot{x}}(t) + \mathbf{Kx}(t) = \mathbf{u}(t) \qquad (7)$$

where *M*, *C* and *K* are the mass, damping and stiffness matrices, respectively, $\ddot{\mathbf{x}}(t), \dot{\mathbf{x}}(t), x$ are the acceleration, velocity and displacement vector and *u* is the input force vector.

Therefore, the system is completely described by the following set of parameters:

$$\boldsymbol{\theta} = (m_1, \cdots, m_n, k_1, \cdots, k_n, c_1, \cdots, c_n) \qquad (8)$$

where m_i, c_i and k_i are mass, damping and stiffness of the *i*th DOF, respectively.

The identification of structural system is a batch type optimization problem. In each iteration step in the process of optimization, the parameters $\boldsymbol{\theta}$ will be updated. Thus, the dynamic equation needs to be solved iteratively in order to obtain the new model output $\hat{\mathbf{y}}(k)$ for each updating step. The model output $\hat{\mathbf{y}}(k)$ consists of a combination of the full or partial set of the acceleration, velocity or displacement.

Like the other stochastic search optimization algorithms, the search for an optimum in the feasible search space could be conducted in theory. However, in structural system identification using dynamic analysis, not all sets of parameters in the specified search space might provide physically plausible solutions to the problem (Franco et al., 2004). Restricting the search space to the feasible region might be difficult because the constraints are not simple. In this study, a preserving feasibility strategy is employed to deal with the constraints. When updating the memories (*pbest* and *gbest*), all the particles only keep feasible solutions in their memory. During the initialization process, all particles are started with feasible solutions. To find the optimum in the feasible space, each particle searches the whole space but only tracks feasible solutions, i.e., to calculate the fitness value of a particle and update its *pbest* and *gbest* only if the particle is in the range.

SOLUTIONS AND RECOMMENDATIONS

Simulation Results and Comparisons

To assess the effectiveness of the parameter estimation technique with the CLPSO presented above, numerical simulations of a five-storey shear-type structure system (Figure 1) with properties as mentioned in Table 3 are performed, and the mass, stiffness and damping of the structure are to be identified. The authors consider the structure subjected to the Niigata earthquake excitation (Japan, 2000). It is assumed that the structure is excited by known forces and that the response of the structure, in terms of accelerations, is recorded at some given points.

In this simulation study, partial measurements are available, i.e., $\mathbf{y}(t) = (\ddot{x}_2, \ddot{x}_4, \ddot{x}_5)$. The parameters of CLPSO algorithm are set as follows: swarm size NP = 20, maximum evolution generation Max_gen = 500 (stopping condition), and c1 = 2.8, c2 = 1.3, c=1.494, m=0.8D. There was no strict theoretical rule to define the *Pc* value until now. Recent studies (Liang et al., 2004; Liang et al., 2006) reported that different values of *Pc* yielded a solution which is different from that obtained by taking the same *Pc* for all particles. If different values of *Pc* for different particles

Table 3. Structural properties

Stiffness(kN/m)	Value
k_1	2.485e5
k_2	1.921e5
k_3-k_5	1.522e5
Mass(kg)	**Value**
m_1	2.762e3
m_2	2.760e3
m_3-m_5	2.300e3
Damping(kN·s/m)	**Value**
c_1	3.129e3
c_2	2.536e3
c_3-c_5	2.030e3

Figure 1. N-DOF structure

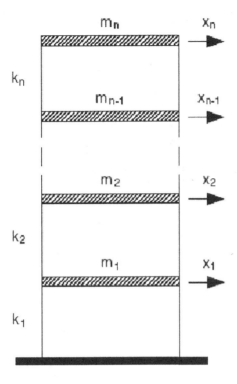

are taken, then the particles have different levels of exploration and exploitation ability in the population. The authors empirically developed the following expression to set a Pc_i value for each particle:

$$Pc_i = 0.05 + 0.45 \frac{\exp\left(\dfrac{5(i-1)}{NP-1}\right) - 1}{\exp(5) - 1} \tag{9}$$

where NP is the population size and i is the particle's ID.

The statistical simulation results (20 independent runs) of the PSO method are shown in Table 4, along with the results obtained with the CLPSO for the sake of comparison, where "best", "mean" and "variance" denote the best result, mean result and the variance of a certain number of runs respectively. The results obtained with the proposed particle swarm methodology are obtained using the same search space. The search space is defined as follows: The upper bounds of the parameters are set to two times their actual values and the lower bounds are set to half of their actual values.

Table 4. Statistical simulation results of PSO and CLPSO without noise corruption

Paras.	True value	Estimation by PSO			Estimation by CLPSO		
		Best	Mean	Variance	Best	Mean	Variance
k_1	2.485e5	2.3783e5	2.3164e5	8.7543e3	2.5095e5	2.5283e5	2.6525e2
k_2	1.921e5	1.8681e5	2.0635e5	2.7645e3	1.9230e5	1.9246e5	2.3222e2
k_3	1.522e5	1.5359e5	1.5392e5	4.6179e2	1.5202e5	1.5143e5	3.2660e2
k_4	1.522e5	1.5535e5	1.5736e5	2.8441e3	1.5147e5	1.5078e5	9.6341e1
k_5	1.522e5	1.5165e5	1.5092e5	1.0361e3	1.5266e5	1.5317e5	7.1563e2
m_1	2.762e3	2.7146e3	2.6949e3	2.7915e1	2.7771e3	2.7851e3	1.1252e1
m_2	2.760e3	2.7548e3	2.7256e3	4.1299e1	2.7628e3	2.7645e3	2.3662e1
m_3	2.300e3	2.2588e3	2.2435e3	2.1670e1	2.3045e3	2.3091e3	6.4656e0
m_4	2.300e3	2.3088e3	2.3328e3	3.3953e1	2.3015e3	2.3023e3	1.0399e1
m_5	2.300e3	2.2878e3	2.3203e3	4.5995e1	2.3029e3	2.3042e3	1.9342e1
c_1	3.129e3	2.8714e3	2.9396e3	9.6538e1	3.1374e3	3.1486e3	9.9503e0
c_2	2.536e3	2.6794e3	2.8802e3	2.8387e1	2.5383e3	2.5403e3	2.8502e0
c_3	2.030e3	2.0381e3	2.0393e3	1.7399e1	2.0291e3	2.0238e3	7.5061e0
c_4	2.030e3	2.0539e3	2.0699e3	2.2521e1	2.0227e3	2.0157e3	9.9593e0
c_5	2.030e3	2.0287e3	2.0432e3	2.0544e1	2.0356e3	2.0381e3	7.8564e0

As shown in Table 4, once again it is clear that the best, average, and the variance results obtained by the CLPSO are better than those obtained by the PSO. In addition, the average result obtained by the CLPSO is even better than the best result obtained by the PSO. Also, the values of estimated parameters obtained by the CLPSO are still very close to the true values of original parameters. Therefore, it is concluded that CLPSO is more effective and robust than the PSO in this example. The CLPSO seems to be more effective in escaping local optima and in searching for the global optimum on this identification problem.

In addition, the authors present typical simulation results (including the convergent processes of objective value and all parameters) for the examples in Figures 2-3. From these figures, the authors observe that the PSO seemed to have more difficulty in locating the solution than the CLPSO. Since the CLPSO has a large potential search space, it did not converge as fast as the original PSO. CLPSO achieved better results than the original PSO. The CLPSO might be able to locate the global optimum region in the identification problem easier than the PSO.

It can be seen in Figure 3 that the fitness value obtained in CLPSO is very low, and therefore, is close to the global minimum; whereas, in the PSO, a marginally higher cost is obtained, which is further away from the global minimum. These

Figure 2. One typical simulation result of PSO and CLPSO without noise corruption

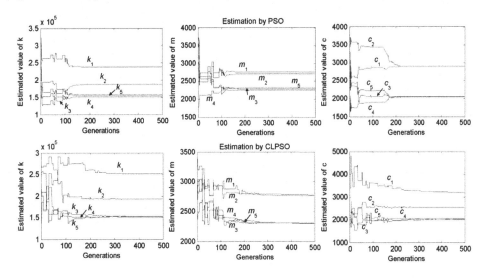

Figure 3. One typical convergence characteristics of estimation

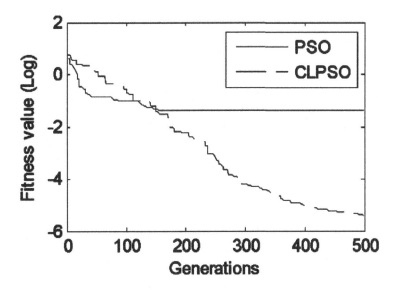

results imply that the CLPSO is more effective in solving problems with less linkage. This property is due to the PSO's dimension-wise updating rule, as well as CLPSO's learning of different dimensions from different exemplars. With the new updating rule, different dimensions may learn from different exemplars, because of which, the CLPSO explores a larger search space than the standard PSO. The larger search space is not achieved randomly. Instead, it is based on the historical search experience. Because of this, the CLPSO performs better than original the PSO for the identification problems in this chapter.

The numerical simulations conducted on the noise corruption scenario are repeated (20 independent runs) on the identification problems. In the cases considering noise, the measurements are polluted with Gaussian, zero mean and white-noise sequences, the root mean- square (RMS) value of which is adjusted to be a certain percentage of the unpolluted time histories. The identification results for measurements corrupted with 3%, and 7% RMS noise are summarized in Table 5.

In general, for all cases studied, the authors can see that the errors are ranging from 0.4 to 4.1% for the CLPSO in the mass and stiffness parameters and much higher in the damping parameters, ranging from 1.0 to 6.4%, and from 1.2% to 10.7% for the PSO. The largest relative errors are usually observed in the damping coefficients. The results show that the CLPSO and the PSO seem to perform well in other less polluted cases, yielding very accurate results for the noise-free case but accruing more error as the noise level increases.

Table 5. Statistical simulation results of CLPSO and PSO with noise corruption

Paras.	True value	Estimation by PSO		Estimation by CLPSO	
		3%	*7%*	*3%*	*7%*
m_1	2.762e3	2.828e3(2.4)	2.855e3(3.4)	2.795e3(1.1)	2.828e3(2.4)
m_2	2.760e3	2.863e3(3.7)	2.907e3(5.3)	2.784e3(0.8)	2.650e3(3.5)
m_3	2.300e3	2.219e3(3.5)	2.192e3(4.7)	2.314e3(0.6)	2.337e3(1.6)
m_4	2.300e3	2.438e3(4.6)	2.459e3(6.9)	2.262e3(1.7)	2.385e3(3.7)
m_5	2.300e3	2.374e3(3.2)	2.183e3(5.1)	2.344e3(1.9)	2.245e3(2.4)
k_1	2.485e5	2.328e5(6.3)	2.297e5(7.6)	2.518e5(1.3)	2.565e5(3.2)
k_2	1.921e5	2.018e5(5.0)	2.044e5(6.4)	1.889e5(1.7)	1.865e5(2.9)
k_3	1.522e5	1.591e5(4.5)	1.630e5(7.1)	1.536e5(0.9)	1.578e5(3.7)
k_4	1.522e5	1.581e5(3.9)	1.431e5(6.2)	1.550e5(1.8)	1.562e5(2.6)
k_5	1.522e5	1.446e5(4.6)	1.627e5(6.9)	1.500e5(1.5)	1.460e5(4.1)
c_1	3.129e3	3.339e3(6.7)	2.822e3(9.8)	3.214e3(2.7)	3.162e3(3.9)
c_2	2.536e3	2.406e3(5.1)	2.772e3(9.3)	2.612e3(3.0)	2.655e3(4.7)
c_3	2.030e3	2.125e3(4.7)	2.25e3(10.7)	1.965e3(3.7)	1.935e3(5.8)
c_4	2.030e3	1.911e3(5.9)	2.192e3(8.4)	2.069e3(1.9)	2.160e3(6.4)
c_5	2.030e3	2.144e3(5.6)	1.843e3(9.2)	2.082e3(2.6)	2.122e3(4.6)

Note: Relative errors of identification are in parentheses expressed in %.

Experiment Arrangement

A benchmark test of a 12-storey reinforced concrete frame model with a scale of 1:10 was used for analysis in this chapter. The test frame floor height was 0.3m, total height was 3.6m, and floor plan was 0.6m×0.6m. The model fixed on the shaking table is shown in Figure 4. Unidirectional (horizontal x-direction) excitations were applied, including El Centro earthquake record (1940, N-S component) and the Kobe earthquake records. All of the acceleration peak values were adjusted to 0.09g and the time interval was adjusted to 0.00392s in according with the similitude relation. The structure was constructed using micro-concrete and fine steel bars.

Figure 4. Photograph of shaking table test model

Accelerometers (only even floors were fitted with instruments) and strain gauges were used to measure the dynamics response. The sensor locations and orientations of the test system and the dimensions of the structure model are shown in Figure 5.

From the material properties of the shear building, the theoretical value of mass and stiffness of each floor can be calculated. With an additional mass placed on each floor of the building model accord with the similitude relation, the additional mass of the roof is 19.7kg, and the other floors have the same additional mass of 19.4 kg.

Experimental Results and Discussions

In this experiment, the parameters are set as follows: swarm size $NP = 30$, maximum evolution generation Max_gen = 500 (stopping condition), and $c1 = 2.4$, $c2 = 1.7$, $c=1.494$, $m=0.8D$. The search space is defined as follows: The upper bounds of the stiffness parameters are set as 1.8θ and the lower bounds are set as 0.7θ. Table 6 presents the "means" and "variances" of the 20 runs of the two algorithms on the shaking table system respectively. In addition, we present typical estimation results, including the convergent processes of objective value and all parameters for the two methods, in Figures 6 and 7.

Figure 5. Sensor locations and orientations of test system and the dimensions of the model

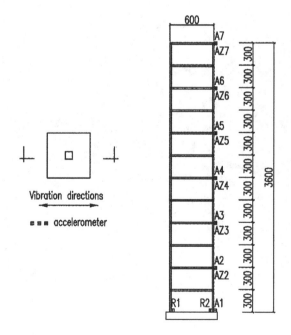

Table 6. Statistical simulation results of shaking table data

Paras.	Theoretical value	Estimation by PSO		Estimation by CLPSO	
		Mean	Variance	Mean	Variance
m_{12}	45.06	47.1896	4.3888	46.8435	2.9857
m_1-m_{11}	49.48	54.0167	5.8722	52.1458	4.3240
k_1	5.529e3	5.6779e3	7.3743e2	5.8461e3	3.8143e2
k_2-k_{12}	2.723e3	2.3110e3	2.1347e2	2.4209e3	1.3974e2
c_1	1.457e2	1.6850e2	14.4634	1.5774e2	8.5420
c_2-c_{12}	0.741e2	0.6506e2	12.6821	0.6715e2	9.2789

Figure 6. One typical simulation result of shaking table test model

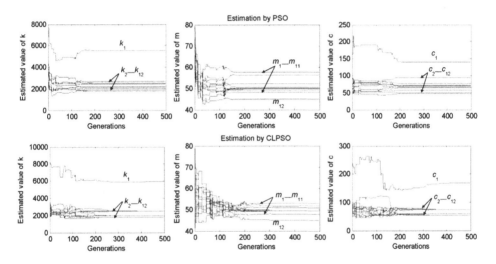

Results summarized in the Table 6 indicate the estimated results of the two methods a little far from the theoretical values. In reality measurements always have noise, so it is anticipated that the results obtained by using the CLPSO approach and the theoretical values should be different from the real values. However, the fitness values illustrated in Figure 7 are very small. The result indicates that the estimated parameters fit the real model system very well. Although the damping identification results have relatively large variances, considering the complex nature of the damping mechanism, the identification results are also acceptable.

In order to test statistical difference of the numerical simulation results of the CLPSO, two sets of results (each 20 independent runs) with mean, μ_1, μ_2 and variance, S_1, S_2 are presented, and the standard t-test is used. If μ_1 and μ_2 are defined as the

Figure 7. One typical estimation convergence characteristics of shaking table test model

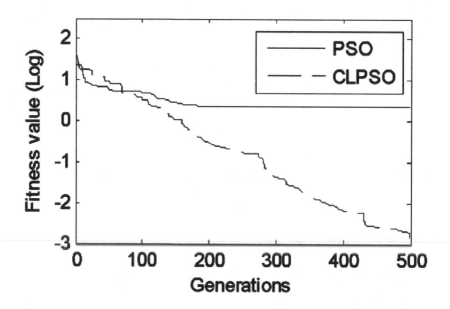

mean values of the parameters obtained from the two different sets, then a hypothesis test may be set up as follows to determine if their differences are significant:

H_0: The differences between μ_1 and μ_2 are not statistically significant,
H_1: The differences between μ_1 and μ_2 are statistically significant,

where H_0 and H_1 are the null and alternate hypothesis, respectively. The significance level of the test is set at 0.05.

Table 7 shows the decision results for the numerical simulation study. It is observed that the computed t-score are all less than the value of 2.024 ($t_{0.95,38}$), the null hypothesis H_0 is accepted and the alternate hypothesis H_1 is rejected, which indicates the differences between the mean values of two sets not statistical significance using Student's t-test. Also note that the null hypothesis H_0 is accepted for PSO in this example.

Therefore, these results indicate that the proposed technique is a feasible method for approximating structural characteristics using the partial recorded data without prior knowledge of mass. In general, comparing the results and the convergence graphs, the CLPSO surpasses the standard PSO algorithm. It is also note that the

Table 7. Hypothesis test results of CLPSO

Paras.	μ_1	S_1	μ_2	S_2	Decision	t-score
m_{12}	46.8435	2.9857	46.0316	2.8769	H_0	1.4996
m_1-m_{11}	52.1458	4.324	53.212	3.9751	H_0	1.5281
k_1	5846.1	381.43	5839.32	378.01	H_0	1.1003
k_2-k_{12}	2420.9	139.74	2427.03	137.02	H_0	1.6479
c_1	157.74	8.542	156.21	8.4431	H_0	1.6602
c_2-c_{12}	67.15	9.279	68.60	8.9794	H_0	1.5176

unknown mass systems presents a far greater challenge when compared with systems in which the mass is known. Thus, a smaller search space for mass in practical applications may be adopted, resulting in better and faster identification.

FUTURE RESEARCH DIRECTIONS

Though the CLPSO has gained increasing popularity in many optimization problems in the last decades, it still has rarely been applied in structural parameters and damage identification. The CLPSO will be widely applied in health monitoring, non-destructive evaluation, and active control. An issue for future research is to use the CLPSO to solve the parameters identification in time varying systems. Besides, the developed CLPSO has the advantage of diversity avoiding premature convergence with great global searching characteristic. This means that the convergence process will slow down greatly when the CLPSO is used in high degree of freedom structures. Thus, further research will exploit the integration of other heuristic algorithms, in order to accelerate convergence process and improve the global searching ability simultaneously

CONCLUSION

This chapter has suitably employed the recently developed CLPSO to identify the parameters of structural systems. The performance of the proposed method has been illustrated by numerical simulation as well as model shaking table tests of a RC-frame structure. A hypothesis test involving the t-test is used to prove that the differences of the estimation results are not statistically significant. Simulation study reveals that the CLPSO surpasses the existing standard PSO algorithm on unknown mass case, and especially significantly improves the results on partial output scenario. Further, this method has no special requirements regarding the number and location of output measurements from the shaking table test. Even when all properties of the structure are unknown, the proposed method can still converge to give promising results.

ACKNOWLEDGMENT

This study was partially supported by the National Natural Science Foundation of China (Grant No. 51178337 and 50708076), Basic Research of the State Key Laboratory for Disaster Reduction in Civil Engineering of Tongji University (Grant No. SLDRCE11-B-01) and the Kwang-Hua Fund for College of Civil Engineering, Tongji University. The authors thank Prof. Suganthan of Nanyang Technological University for providing original codes to improve this chapter.

REFERENCES

Ali, H., & Khan, F. A. (2013). Attributed multi-objective comprehensive learning particle swarm optimization for optimal security of networks. *Applied Soft Computing*, *13*(9), 3903–3921. doi:10.1016/j.asoc.2013.04.015

Banks, A., Vincent, J., & Anyakoha, C. (2008). A review of particle swarm optimization. Part II: Hybridisation, combinatorial, multicriteria and constrained optimization, and indicative applications. *Natural Computing*, *7*(1), 109–124. doi:10.1007/s11047-007-9050-z

Betti, M., Facchini, L., & Biagini, P. (2015). Damage detection on a three-storey steel frame using artificial neural networks and genetic algorithms. *Meccanica*, *50*(3), 875–886. doi:10.1007/s11012-014-0085-9

Boeringer, D. W., & Werner, D. H. (2003). A comparison of particle swarm optimization and genetic algorithms for a phased array synthesis problem. *IEEE International Symposium on Antennas and Propagation*, 181-184. doi:10.1109/APS.2003.1217430

Bonyadi, M. R., Michalewicz, Z., & Li, X. (2014). An analysis of the velocity updating rule of the particle swarm optimization algorithm. *Journal of Heuristics*, *20*(4), 417–452. doi:10.1007/s10732-014-9245-2

Buezas, F. S., Rosales, M. B., & Filipich, C. P. (2011). Damage detection with genetic algorithms taking into account a crack contact model. *Engineering Fracture Mechanics, 78*(4), 695–712. doi:10.1016/j.engfracmech.2010.11.008

Castro, L. N. D. (2007). Fundamentals of natural computing: An overview. *Physics of Life Reviews, 4*(1), 1–36. doi:10.1016/j.plrev.2006.10.002

Chisari, C., Bedon, C., & Amadio, C. (2015). Dynamic and static identification of base-isolated bridges using genetic algorithms. *Engineering Structures, 102*(11), 80–92. doi:10.1016/j.engstruct.2015.07.043

Chou, J., & Ghaboussi, J. (2001). Genetic algorithm in structural damage detection. *Computers & Structures, 79*(14), 1335–1353. doi:10.1016/S0045-7949(01)00027-X

Civicioglu, P., & Besdok, E. (2013). A conceptual comparison of the cuckoo-search, particle swarm optimization, differential evolution and artificial bee colony algorithms. *Artificial Intelligence Review, 39*(4), 315–346. doi:10.1007/s10462-011-9276-0

Clerc, M. (1999). The swarm and the queen: towards a deterministic and adaptive particle swarm optimization. *Evolutionary Computation, 1999. CEC 99. Proceedings of the 1999 Congress on.* doi:10.1109/CEC.1999.785513

Clerc, M., & Kennedy, J. (2002). The particle swarm - explosion, stability, and convergence in a multidimensional complex space. *Trans. Evol. Comp, 6*(1), 58–73. doi:10.1109/4235.985692

Cunha, J., Cogan, S., & Berthod, C. (1999). Application of genetic algorithms for the identification of elastic constants of composite materials from dynamic tests. *International Journal for Numerical Methods in Engineering, 45*(7), 891–900. doi:10.1002/(SICI)1097-0207(19990710)45:7<891::AID-NME610>3.0.CO;2-1

Der Valle, Y., Venayagamoorthy, G. K., Mohagheghi, S., Hernandez, J. C., & Harley, R. G. (2008). Particle swarm optimization: Basic concepts, variants and applications in power systems. *IEEE Transactions on Evolutionary Computation, 12*(2), 171–195. doi:10.1109/TEVC.2007.896686

Dorigo, M., & Blum, C. (2005). Ant colony optimization theory: A survey. *Theoretical Computer Science, 344*(2–3), 243–278. doi:10.1016/j.tcs.2005.05.020

Franco, G., Betti, R., & Lus, H. (2004). Identification of structural systems using an evolutionary strategy. *Journal of Engineering Mechanics, 130*(10), 1125–1139. doi:10.1061/(ASCE)0733-9399(2004)130:10(1125)

Gao, L., & Hailu, A. (2010). Comprehensive learning particle swarm optimizer for constrained mixed-variable optimization problems. *International Journal of Computational Intelligence Systems, 3*(6), 832–842. doi:10.1080/18756891.2010.9727745

Gholizadeh, S. (2013). Layout optimization of truss structures by hybridizing cellular automata and particle swarm optimization. *Computers & Structures, 125*(1), 86–99. doi:10.1016/j.compstruc.2013.04.024

Hassan, F. R., Koh, S. P., Tiong, S. K., Chong, K. H., & Abdalla, A. N. (2011). Investigation of induction motor parameter identification using particle swarm optimization-based RBF neural network (PSO-RBFNN). *International Journal of Physical Sciences, 6*(9), 4564–4570.

He, Q., & Wang, L. (2007). An effective co-evolutionary particle swarm optimization for constrained engineering design problems. *Engineering Applications of Artificial Intelligence, 20*(1), 89–99. doi:10.1016/j.engappai.2006.03.003

Huang, H., Qin, H., Hao, Z., & Lim, A. (2012). Example-based learning particle swarm optimization for continuous optimization. *Information Sciences, 182*(1), 125–138. doi:10.1016/j.ins.2010.10.018

Huang, V. L., Suganthan, P. N., & Liang, J. J. (2006). Comprehensive learning particle swarm optimizer for solving multiobjective optimization problems. *International Journal of Intelligent Systems, 21*(2), 209–226. doi:10.1002/int.20128

Kennedy, J., & Eberhart, R. (1995). Particle swarm optimization. *Proceedings of IEEE international conference on neural networks.* doi:10.1109/ICNN.1995.488968

Kennedy, J., Eberhart, R. C., & Shi, Y. (2001). *Swarm Intelligence.* San Francisco, CA: Morgan Kaufmann.

Koh, C. G., Chen, Y. F., & Liaw, C. Y. (2003). A hybrid computational strategy for identification of structural parameters. *Computers & Structures, 81*(2), 107–117. doi:10.1016/S0045-7949(02)00344-9

Levin, R. I., & Lieven, N. A. J. (1998). Dynamic finite element model updating using simulated annealing and genetic algorithms. *Mechanical Systems and Signal Processing, 12*(1), 91–120. doi:10.1006/mssp.1996.0136

Liang, J. J., Qin, A. K., Suganthan, P., & Baskar, S. (2004). Evaluation of Comprehensive Learning Particle Swarm Optimizer. In N. Pal, N. Kasabov, R. Mudi, S. Pal, & S. Parui (Eds.), *Neural Information Processing* (Vol. 3316, pp. 230–235). Springer Berlin Heidelberg. doi:10.1007/978-3-540-30499-9_34

Liang, J. J., Qin, A. K., Suganthan, P. N., & Baskar, S. (2006). Comprehensive learning particle swarm optimizer for global optimization of multimodal functions. *Evolutionary Computation. IEEE Transactions on*, *10*(3), 281–295.

Lu, X. L., Li, P. Z., & Chen, Y. Q. (2003). *Benchmark Test of a 12-Story Reinforced Concrete Frame Model on Shaking Table*. Study Report of State Key Laboratory for Disaster Reduction in Civil Engineering, Tongji University (A20030609-405).

Majhi, B., & Panda, G. (2009). Identification of IIR systems using comprehensive learning particle swarm optimisation. *International Journal of Power and Energy Conversion*, *1*(1), 105–124. doi:10.1504/IJPEC.2009.023478

Mayer, D. G. (2002). *Evolutionary algorithms and agricultural systems*. Springer. doi:10.1007/978-1-4615-1717-7

Mouser, C. R., & Dunn, S. A. (2005). Comparing genetic algorithms and particle swarm optimisation for an inverse problem exercise. *The ANZIAM Journal*, *46*, C89–C101. doi:10.21914/anziamj.v46i0.949

Perera, R., Fang, S. E., & Ruiz, A. (2010). Application of particle swarm optimization and genetic algorithms to multiobjective damage identification inverse problems with modelling errors. *Meccanica*, *45*(5), 723–734. doi:10.1007/s11012-009-9264-5

Perry, M. J., Koh, C. G., & Choo, Y. S. (2006). Modified genetic algorithm strategy for structural identification. *Computers & Structures*, *84*(8), 529–540. doi:10.1016/j.compstruc.2005.11.008

Piotrowski, A. P., Napiorkowski, M. J., Napiorkowski, J. J., & Rowinski, P. M. (2017). Swarm intelligence and evolutionary algorithms: Performance versus speed. *Information Sciences*, *384*, 34–85. doi:10.1016/j.ins.2016.12.028

Poli, R., Kennedy, J., & Blackwell, T. (2007). Particle swarm optimization: An overview. *Swarm Intelligence*, *1*(1), 33–57. doi:10.1007/s11721-007-0002-0

Shi, Y. (2001). Particle swarm optimization: developments, applications and resources. *Proceedings of the Congress on Evolutionary Computation*, 81-86.

Shi, Y., & Eberhart, R. (1998). A modified particle swarm optimizer. *Proceedings of IEEE International Conference on Evolutionary Computation*, 69-73.

Tang, H., Xue, S., & Fan, C. (2008). Differential evolution strategy for structural system identification. *Computers & Structures*, *86*(21), 2004–2012. doi:10.1016/j.compstruc.2008.05.001

Tang, H., Zhang, W., Xie, L., & Xue, S. (2013). Multi-stage approach for structural damage identification using particle swarm optimization. *Bulletin of Mathematical Biology*, *11*(1), 2289–2303.

Van den Bergh, F., & Engelbrecht, A. P. (2006). A study of particle swarm optimization particle trajectories. *Information Sciences*, *176*(8), 937–971. doi:10.1016/j.ins.2005.02.003

Wilke, D. N., Kok, S., & Groenwold, A. A. (2010). Comparison of linear and classical velocity update rules in particle swarm optimization: Notes on diversity. *International Journal for Numerical Methods in Engineering*, *70*(8), 985–1008. doi:10.1002/nme.1914

Xue, B., Zhang, M., & Browne, W. N. (2013). Particle swarm optimization for feature selection in classification: A multi-objective approach. *IEEE Transactions on Cybernetics*, *43*(6), 1656–1671. doi:10.1109/TSMCB.2012.2227469 PMID:24273143

Xue, S., Tang, H., & Zhou, J. (2009). Identification of Structural Systems Using Particle Swarm Optimization. *Journal of Asian Architecture and Building Engineering*, *8*(2), 517–524. doi:10.3130/jaabe.8.517

KEY TERMS AND DEFINITIONS

Evolutionary Computation: Evolutionary computation is a class of algorithms for global optimization with a metaheuristic or stochastic optimization character inspired by biological evolution, and the subfield of artificial intelligence and soft computing studying these algorithms.

Genetic Algorithm: A metaheuristic inspired by the process of natural operators such as mutation, crossover, and selection is employed to generate high-quality solutions to optimization and search problems. The evolution, an iterative process, makes a population of candidate solutions be evolved toward better solutions with the population in each iteration called a generation.

Global Optimization: In many nonlinear optimization problems, a branch of applied mathematics and numerical analysis is applied to find the global minimum (or maximum) of a function or a set of functions with a large number of local minima and maxima, according to a set of bound and more general constraints.

Heuristic Algorithm: A technique using rules based on precious experience in a reasonable time frame in order to solve a problem more quickly compared with classic methods, or find an approximate solution when classic methods are unable to find exact solution.

Particle Swarm: A population (called a swarm) of candidate solutions (called particles) are moved around by a computational method in the search-space according to simple mathematical formulae over the particle's position and velocity. The particle swarm is expected to be moved toward the best solutions.

Premature Convergence: In case of genetic variation, a population for an optimization problem converges too early leading to it being suboptimal. This means that through the aid of genetic operators, offspring solutions generated by the parental solutions are not able to outperform their parents.

Simulated Annealing: When the search space is discrete, it is a probabilistic metaheuristic often used to approximate the global optimum of a given function, reducing a minimization of a function of large number of variables to the statistical mechanics of equilibration of the mathematically equivalent artificial multi-objective system.

Stochastic Optimization: It is an optimization process that generates and uses random variables involving random objective functions or random constraints, which also includes methods with random iterates.

System Identification: A significant tool using statistical methods to build mathematical models of dynamical systems with the best set of parameter values, which minimizes the error between the actual physically measured response of a system and the simulated response.

Chapter 3

Finding Optimal Input Values for Desired Target Output by Using Particle Swarm Optimization Algorithm Within Probabilistic Models

Goran Klepac
Raiffeisenbank Austria, Croatia

ABSTRACT

Developed predictive models, especially models based on probabilistic concept, regarding numerous potential combinatory states can be very complex. That complexity can cause uncertainty about which factors should have which values to achieve optimal value of output. An example of that problem is developed with a Bayesian network with numerous potential states and their interaction when we would like to find optimal value of nodes for achieving maximum probability on specific output node. This chapter shows a novel concept based on usage of the particle swarm optimization algorithm for finding optimal values within developed probabilistic models.

INTRODUCTION

Predictive model development is demanding process. It demands precise and objective determination of sample construction, target variable construction, attribute relevance analysis, model testing and many other activities which will guarantee that developed model is robust, stable, reliable and predictive.

DOI: 10.4018/978-1-5225-5020-4.ch003

If we are talking about predictive models with binominal output and predictive models based on logistic regression, neural networks or similar techniques, than determination of initial states of variable values for achieving specific output are relatively simple. It can be manual process, but achievable from perspective of human effort.

Reason why someone would like to find out which values of input variables will cause best fit for specific output is that we would like to find out typical case, or profile. That means if we would like to find out typical profile of churner based on developed binominal predictive model we should find combination of input values which will result with maximum output value in zone of wanted output.

Things became more complicated when we have multinomial output from predictive models.

Main advantage of binominal output usage is ability to understand relations between target variable and potential predictors and business logic check.

From technical point of view, data mining techniques like neural networks, and logistic regression by the nature of their algorithms, prefers to operate with values between 0 and 1. Dummy variables could be interpreted as membership declaration with 0 and 1 values. If some value belongs into specific class represented as dummy variable, it is true and dummy variable has value "1" otherwise "0".

Robust and stable predictive models have few attributes incorporated into model. It could be 6-10 of most predictive attributes. As it is evident initial data sample could contain more than hundreds of potential predictors. Some of them are original variables from databases as socio demographic values assigned to each customer, and other has behavioural characteristics defined by experts and extracted from existing transactional data.

Attribute relevance analyse has two important functions:

- Recognition of most important variables which has greatest impact on target variable
- Understanding relations and logic between most important predictor and target variable, and understanding relations and logic between most important predictors from target variable perspective

Contrary to assurance that powerful hardware and sophisticated software can substitute need for attribute relevance analyse, attribute relevance analyse is important part of each kind of analysis which operates with target variable. Recognition of most important variables, which has greatest impact on target variable, reduces redundancy and uncertainty at model development process stage. It provides robustness of the model and model reliability. Attribute relevance analyze besides importance measuring, evaluates attribute characteristics. Attribute characteristics evaluation includes measuring attribute values impact on target variables. It helps on understanding relations and logic between most important predictor and target variable, and understanding relations and logic between most important predictors from target variable perspective. After attribute relevance analysis stage, analyst has initial picture about churner profile and behaviour. This stage often opens many additional questions related to revealed relations and sometimes induces construction of new behavioural (derived) variables, which also should pass attribute relevance analysis process.

From perspective of predictive modelling there are two basic data sample types for predictive churn model development:

- Data sample with binomial target variable
- Data sample with multinomial target variable

Data sample with multinomial target variable contains target variable with more than two finite states.

Biggest challenge is to find out combination of input values which will result with maximum output value in zone of wanted output in situation when we have multinomial output (multinomial target variable) from predictive models and predictive models based on structures like Bayesian networks.

Reason for that is in their complexity based on links between chance nodes. It means that predictive models based on Bayesian networks demands different approach in situation when we would like to use it for finding of optimal combination of input values which will produce desired output.

In those cases it is almost impossible to find out optimal combination of variable values for achieving desired output. For that purpose appropriate approach can be usage of evolutionary computing for finding optimal values of input variables with respect of desired output and interaction within Bayesian network.

Evolutionary algorithms like particle swarm optimization algorithm will not always propose best solution, but solution which is plausible and acceptable.

Other problem is related to fact that evidence means certain event, which implies potential usage of binary states as outputs from chance nodes within Bayesian network. It leads us to on binary PSO usage and adoption, except in situation when we do not have intention to set all chance nodes as a certain events. It depend on potential solution, but for sure it demands additional research and conclusions for finding optimal approach for usage Bayesian networks with PSO algorithm for finding optimal solution.

As an illustration proposed methodology will be applied as a tool for profiling on developed Bayesian network which makes prediction about shopping preferences.

Model which regarding input variables as predictors evaluate shopping preferences, will be used for finding optimal values of predictor for buying specific product.

Most important feature of presented methodology is ability to recognize important areas and customer characteristics where changes became significant in comparison with previous period. Particle swarm optimization algorithm as a profiling tool usage, in combination with predictive models has additional advantage. This could be the base for strategic business decisions, regarding observed market trends.

Predictive models complexity rises with number of input variables, as well as number of states in output variable. Greater impact on complexity has increasing number of states in output variable.

In other words, it is great challenge to recognize typical profile of customer which prefers buying, or usage product of service e.g. "A" in situation where we use predictive models which has function to predict probability of buying, or usage for n product where n >2.

Complexity from other side rises with higher number of predictors, because they cause numerous potential combinations regarding state from output variable.

Main advantage of proposed solution is automatic determination of profiles in situation, where we have combinatory explosion caused by numerous nodes and their states within Bayesian network model.

Variables which are part of predictive models should contain strong business logic approved and checked with people from business practice. Approved and checked business logic assures also trust into developed model, because a business user also on quantitative models looks as on black boxes, especially when it is complex. Understanding inputs and logic of those inputs, which is in line with their perception of their problem area, could result on better cooperation and better results in decision making. Particle swarm optimization algorithm operates on trusted variables for seeking additional information on profiles.

Profiling could be wrongly identified as segmentation modeling. Those two types of models have common points but it is different type of models. Profiling models gives holistic picture of typical churner/buyer/ users as member of some population or as a member of the segment recognized thought segmentation process. Profiling models does not lay on social demographic data only, they also could be constructed by using behavioral and temporal characteristics. Profiling models could provide information how different is for example members of each segments recognized thought segmentation process. It could be trigger for decision about churn mitigation policy, or further analysis processes. Profiling analysis could include variety of data mining techniques.

Integral part of the chapter is case study in domain of insurance.

The case study will present the usage of the particle swarm optimization algorithm as a tool for finding the riskiest profiles based on previously developed Bayesian network. As explained in introduction, particle swarm optimization algorithm will be used as a tool which should find optimal values of input variables (within developed predictive models) as referent values for maximization of probability value of some risky event. It means that particle swarm optimization algorithm will be used as a tool which should find optimal values of input variables within developed predictive models as referent values for maximization value of probability that customer will select/buy some product or service. Using given results, insurance company can make profiles of the riskiest insurance users, even in the situation affected by combinatory explosion, caused by numerous nodes and their states within Bayesian network model. This approach will help company to better understand a cause of riskiness of events in an environment where numerous factors and influence overlaps exist.

Proposed methodology is applicable not only on Bayesian networks, it can be applied on each complex probabilistic model. Additional advantage of proposed solution is that it is not focused only on previously determined aim variable. On such complex structures like Bayesian networks each node can act target variable and proposed methodology can be adopted for finding optimal values within existing nodes with respect to desired output of selected target node value.

Such methodology is fruitful ground for profile transition evaluation and monitoring. In case of temporal component introduction within model, it is possible to monitoring profile changes with respect of selected target variable.

It means that profile transition in case of complex analytical environment can be analysed and compared, which is valuable piece of information for business decision purposes.

Background

There are numerous case studies dedicated to predictive modeling in business and usage of data mining techniques for building predictive models for purposes like churn detection (Abbasimehr, 2011), next best offer, fraud detection (Larose, 2005; Klepac, 2010; Klepac, 2014; Klepac, 2015). In the case of predictive modeling, particle swarm optimization (PSO) algorithm is mostly used as an algorithm for learning optimization in neural networks (Clerck, 2013; Kurbatsky, 2014; Russel, 2001). Particle swarm optimization algorithm is used in many areas, mostly for solving problems in the domain of optimization (Adhikari, 2013; Anagnostopoulos, 2012; Babahajyani 2014; El-Shorbagy, 2013; Gonsalves, 2015).

In literature, particle swarm optimization algorithm is not recognized as a methodology that can directly contribute to risk or customer profiling. It is mostly used as a tool for neural networks optimization, which could be used as a tool for profiling or for clustering purposes (Devi, 2014; Konstantinos, 2010; Xing, 2014).

Particle swarm optimization algorithm has a great potential in solving problems which are not primarily focused on optimization (Singh, 2010; Tosun, 2014; Yosuf, 2010; Acharjya 2015).

Problems in the domain of business could be used by the adoption and inventive usage of PSO algorithm (Olson, 2011; Rajesh 2013; Xing, 2014a). Beside optimization for neural networks in business domain, PSOs are also used as a learning optimization tool in engineering, environmental science, or social sciences (Clerk, 2013; Olson, 2011, Russel, 2001; Yin, 2014).

Neural networks and particle swarm optimization algorithm could be also used in the area of time series forecasting (Adhikari, 2013; Alam, 2014). This approach is the same as in the situation where particle swarm optimization algorithm has been used as a tool for learning optimization for neural networks on non-temporal data. Main differences are related to the nature of temporal data and their characteristics, which requires for a different approach in building predictive models by using neural networks.

Different types of neural network algorithms (Alexander, 1995; Zhang, 2000; Zuo, 2012) demand different approach in usage of soft computing techniques (Devi, 2014), along with neural networks. It means that, for example, in the situation where particle swarm optimization algorithm has been used as a as tool for learning optimization for neural networks, considering fact that we try to optimize learning for error back propagation model or for self organizing maps, it demands different approach in particle swarm optimization algorithm usage (Janecek, 2015). Evolutionary algorithms, as well as particle swarm optimization algorithm, can be applied in various business areas (Arora, 2013; Nguyen, 2010; Taleizadeh, 2013). One of the areas is customer relationship management systems. Usage of data mining techniques in customer relationship management systems, are mostly concentrated on finding a typical profile of the churner, buyer or subscriber (Giudici, 2003; Giudici, 2009). Neural networks play significant role in predictive modeling as well as in profiling. Considering the anatomy of a neural network and the final output of modeling with neural networks, it is obvious that profiling in the case of multinomial output from the model is not an easy task (Larose, 2005). Profiling, on the other hand, can be interpreted as a diversification task. In case that predictive model exists, it can be used as a base for diversification. Particle swarm optimization algorithm has a potential for diversification tasks (Cheng, 2013; Kress, 2010; Konstantinos, 2010; Klepac, 2015a; Klepac, 2016). This idea leads us to the concept presented in this chapter, in which the particle swarm optimization algorithm became a tool for diversification (profiling) based on the predictive model constructed using a neural network.

Evolutionary approach, which is one of the particle swarm optimization algorithm characteristics, provides opportunity for finding optimal solution to aimed profiles. This approach saves time and human work on manual profiling and speeds up the profiling process. On the other hand, it could give a perspective for changes in customers' profile characteristics through time in case when it is used in appropriate way as a part of a more complex system for profile analysis. Beside neural networks which have been used in combination with PSO algorithm, we propose usage of Bayesian networks (Jensen, 2001) in combination with PSO algorithm. Bayesian networks are much more complex structures looking from perspective of PSO algorithm usage than neural networks. In general, by using the proposed approach, each node in a Bayesian network could be observed as a target variable (Jensen, 2001; Okun, 2014; Kaur 2015).

IMPORTANCE OF RISK PROFILING

Customer profiling, is one of the most important techniques in customer relationship management (Kim et al, 2009). Campaign planning, new product development, cross selling activities, up-sell activities and many other activities related to customer portfolio management are closely related with customer profiles. It is the same situation in which we would like to measure risk of insurance company clients. It is unrealistic to expect that whole customer portfolio has similar or even the same profile characteristics regarding the risk. Risk characteristics are very dependable on behavioral characteristics and its relation to probability of making some unexpected event which will cause additional cost to insurance company. For insurance companies which have a small number of products and services in their portfolio, risk profiling is an easier task in comparison to insurance companies with a large number of products and services (Agosta, 2000).

Even in situation where a company has a limited set of products and services, risk profiling is not a trivial task. Profiling is not (should not be) concentrated solely on socio-demographic characteristics. Risk profiling should also take into consideration customer behavioral characteristics. Customer behavioral characteristics are not obvious and recognizable as socio-demographic variables (Aleksander, 1995). Although socio-demographic characteristics could be represented with a set of standard variables such as age, gender, region, etc., and company can use those profiles within those variables (which is not recommended), risk profiling is still not an easy task. It should be done considering target variable which represents usage of some products or a group of products. Considering customer behavioral characteristic as a part of profiling, it makes profiling more complicated. First problem in situation when companies decide to include behavioral characteristics as a profiling element is related to relevant behavioral characteristics recognition, which is significant for profiling (Almeida & Sanots, 2014; Baksi, 2014). Behavioral characteristics are more powerful determinants for profiling than socio-demographic characteristics. Problem with this approach is the fact that it is not easy to recognize key behavioral characteristics which will show "typical" risk profile.

PARTICLE SWARM OPTIMIZATION ALGORITHM AND PROFILING FROM PREDICTIVE MODELS

Relationship Between Predictive Modeling and Profiling

Final result of predictive modeling should not be a predictive model, at least not as the only goal in the process. Predictive modeling should also be concentrated on understanding reasons and causes of events, which is a scope of predictive modeling process. In case of predictive modeling for recommendation systems (e.g. next best offer) for buying preferences it is important to understand profiles and characteristics, including those which of them has the highest odds for selection of specific items. In general, a predictive model contains a determined number of variables, and profiles are determined with their values. It means that a referent profile, in light of a predictive model, is determined by a finite number of variables which contain specific values or scales within variables.

Understanding of those relations and values leads us to deeper understanding of client preferences which could be a strong base for further hypothesis generation concentrated on deeper understanding and further analytics of customer behavior and preferences (Alippi, 2003). Predictive model development at its final stage provides a tool for probability calculation, but the development phase should reveal main characteristic of portfolio structure and basic information about important variables that have greatest influence on customer decisions. Data cleaning, data preprocessing, factor analysis and attribute relevance analysis make a significant contribution to this goal.

Predictive model complexity increases with the number of input variables as well as the number of available states in output variable. Greatest impact on complexity has the increasing number of states in output variable and researcher should pay attention to this fact (Bang et al., 2009; Barry & Linhoff, 1997). On the other hand, complexity will be increased by raising the number of predictors, because they cause numerous potential combinations regarding output variable state. During the developing phase, in case of models with output variables with two possible states, it is easier to determine profiles for two different states. First reason lies in the fact that measures for attribute relevance analysis like Information Value and Weight of evidence provide a clear picture of zones which have higher impact on observed binary states. When the number of states in output variable from predictive model is greater than 2, model complexity is rising and, in the stage of model development the common task for understanding profiles is the recognition of those attributes which have the greatest impact on aim variables with multiple states. It could be helpful for the general scope to look at their impact on preferences, but it is not sufficient for the typical profile recognition for a specific product or service. Often in that case, users try to manually find typical profile by varying values of predictors for each state in output variable within the model. It is time a consuming and imprecise process, and in case of numerous states in output variable, few of the output states are usually covered in this way. It is rather complex considering all difficulties connected with profiling from predictive models, especially in situation where number of states in output variable from predictive model is greater than 2 (Barry & Linhoff, 2000).

Attribute Relevance Analysis and Profiling

Robust and stable predictive models have several attributes incorporated into the model. It could be 6-12 of most predictive attributes (Dressner, 2008). Initial data sample could contain more than hundreds of potential predictors. Some of them could be socio-demographic values assigned to each customer and others could be behavioral characteristics defined by experts and extracted from existing transactional data as derived variables.

Attribute relevance analysis has two important functions or characteristics:

- Recognition of most important variables which have the greatest impact on target variable,
- Understanding relations and logic between the most important predictor and target variable and understanding relations and logic between the most important predictors from the target variable perspective.

Both functions and characteristics are aligned with customer profile recognition, especially in the situation when we are developing predictive model for probability calculation of product or services buying behavior. Apart from measuring the importance, attribute relevance analysis also evaluates attribute characteristics. Attribute characteristics evaluation include measuring attribute values impact on target variables. It helps understanding relations and logic between the most important predictor and target variable, and understanding relations and logic between most important predictors from the target variable perspective.

After attribute relevance analysis phase, analyst has initial picture about profiles, which includes behavioral characteristics as well.

From the perspective of predictive modeling there are two basic types of predictive models important from the profiling point:

- Predictive models with binomial target variable,
- Predictive models with multinomial target variable.

In case of predictive models with binomial target variable, common approach for attribute relevance analysis is the usage of Weight of Evidence and Information Value calculation by using following formulas:

$$WoE = \ln\left(\frac{Dnb}{Db}\right) WoE = \ln\left(\frac{Dnb}{Db}\right)$$

$$IV = \sum_{i=1}^{n}\left(Dnb_i - Db_i\right) \sum_{i=1}^{n}\left(Dnb_i - Db_i\right) * \ln\left(\frac{Dnb_i}{Db_i}\right) \ln\left(\frac{Dnb_i}{Db_i}\right)$$

Weight of evidence is calculated as a natural logarithm of ratio between distributions of e.g. non-buyers (D_{nb}) and e.g. buyers (D_b) in distribution spans. Information value is calculated as a sum of differences between the distribution of non-buyers and buyers in distribution spans and product of corresponding weight of evidence.

In situation with multinomial target variable it is much more complicated and almost impossible even manually to make typical profiles like: "buyer of product A", "buyer of product B", … "buyer of product N". In case of predictive models with multinomial target variable, common approach for attribute relevance analysis is the usage of e.g. information gain calculation.

Information gain can be calculated by the following formula (Han, 2006):

$$Info\left(D\right) = -\sum_{i=1}^{n} p_i \log_2\left(p_i\right) Info\left(D\right) = -\sum_{i=1}^{n} p_i \log_2\left(p_i\right)$$

where p_i is the probability that an arbitrary tuple in D belongs to class C_i (Han, 2006). This measure is recommended for usage in situations where output variable has more than 2 states for prediction. There are many measures which can be used for this purpose. *Info gain* is presented as one possible solution for attribute relevance analysis in situations when we are operating with more than 2 states in output variable.

In that case we do not have clear cuts in impact zones, and zones are overlapping. It makes profiling more complicated and it is hard or even impossible to make profiling in the same way as in the situation with binary output. Different output classes for the same predictor in the same zones could have significant influences for several output classes. Also, those zones (bins) could be different for different output classes with different info gain values through observed zones. Information gain is a valuable measure for attribute relevance analysis and for finding appropriate predictors, which will be the base for the predictive model. In both situations goal is to maximize probability for specific product to be bought in case when we try to recognize typical profile. Manually, it is a relatively easy task in situation with binary output from predictive model. In situation when predictive model has more than 2 output states and 6-12 predictors, efficient profiling becomes a very complex task.

Assume that there is a business problem in which a company develops a predictive model with more than 2 output states. Output states represent probability for buying a specific product or service. Predictive model contains ten to twelve variables as predictors. Predictive model contains several states of output variable with overlapping for different predictors for different output states (Elamvazuthi et al, 2012; Feng et al, 2009). This situation is the main reason (beside many output states in aim variable) for difficulties in profiling based on predictive models and difficulties in finding clear cut in predictors regarding profiling, as well as finding a clear distinction between profiles which are related to specific value of output state (Garrido et al, 2008).

Using Particle Swarm Optimization Algorithm as an Automatic Profiling Tool From Bayesian Networks

Profiling by using particle swarm optimization algorithm could be done for each predictive model based on different methods (neural networks, support vector machines, Bayesian networks). Bayesian network model for finding risk profiles should be constructed in way that target variable contains probabilities for j number of products (Janecek & Tan, 2011; Kawamura & Suzuki, 2011; Yavuz, 2006). Parental nodes contain behavioral characteristics recognized as crucial for risk evaluation in process of attribute relevance analysis.

Attribute Relevance Analysis Process

Formally, we can express it as:

$Pr[P_j] = Pr[\text{node parents}]$

Or more precisely as:

$$Pr\left[P_j\right] = \prod_{i=1}^{n} Pr\left[P_j \mid Y_i, \dots, Y_n\right] \, Pr\left[P_j\right] = \prod_{i=1}^{n} Pr\left[P_j \mid Y_i, \dots, Y_n\right]$$

where:

Pr[P$_j$] – represents risk probability for j insurance product or service.

Y$_i$ – represents behavioral characteristics within Bayesian network expressed as a state value of Bayesian network node.

For discovering risk profile which has the highest risk for product j, it is necessary to find such combination of Y$_1$ to Y$_n$ values which gives maximum value of P$_j$. From the perspective of Bayesian networks, task is to find combination of evidences in nodes which will maximize value of P$_j$.

Manual approach, which includes trial and error iterations, could easily be interpreted as manual evolutional process, similar to algorithms based on evolutional principles. This process is time consuming, to costly, imprecise and with an uncertain outcome.

Bayesian networks are not classical probabilistic models mostly because of the fact that relations between nodes could be created automatically, or based on expert knowledge. The experience shows that combination of both approaches provides best results. However, if we consider the nature of Bayesian networks (where almost each node can be observed as a potential target variable of its parental nodes), we recommend information gain calculation for each node which can be recognized as a "child" node. This approach will contribute in higher stability and reliability of the model.

For discovering client profile which has the highest risk on product usage j, it is necessary to find such a combination of Y$_1$ to Y$_n$ values which gives maximum value of P$_j$. Maximum value of P$_j$ for j-th product, in model should not always be 1.

Manual approach, which includes trial and error iterations, could easily be interpreted as manual evolutional process similar to algorithms based on evolutional principles. This process is, as explained, time consuming, too costly, and imprecise and with uncertain outcome. In situation when we have numerous products which is included in model (huge number of j) it is almost impossible to finish this task manually with satisfactory results. On the other hand, it is a complex task to consider all problems regarding overlapping values from information gain calculation with respect to aim variable. For the optimal solution we propose usage of particle swarm optimization algorithm.

Results of this approach improve and speed up profiling in situation when we would like to determine profiles from complex predictive models with many predictors and many outputs from the aim variable. This leads to the fact that same methodology could be used periodically for monitoring changes in customer risk. From the perspective of decision support system, it is valuable information.

Particle swarm optimization for this purpose could be used as:

$$v = v_c + c_1 r_1 (pbest - Y_i) + c_2 r_2 (gbest - Y_i)$$

$$Y_i = Y_i + v$$

where:

Y_i'- is i-th particle in swarm. It is input value from a Bayesian network initially generated randomly or by random selection from empirical data. We generate swarm of size N randomly using uniform distribution. Values of particle are in range (0, 1), which represents normalized value in the Bayesian network.

Gbest: Best solution of swarm
pbest: Best solution for particular particle
c_1, c_2: Acceleration factors range (0,4)
r_1, r_2: Random value range (0,1), factor which stops quick converging
v: is Velocity
v_c: Current velocity

Number of particles is determined by the number of input variables in the predictive model. Basic algorithm for each j-th product where criteria is maximization of P_j using a predictive model (Bayesian network in presented case), using Y_1 to Y_n as particles and swarm of size N is:

1. *For each j-th product*
2. *Initialize swarm of size N and randomly assign initial values of particles from Y1' to Yn' in range (0,1)*
3. *Evaluate fitness (for each particle)*
4. *Calculate pbest, gbest and v*
5. *Calculate new position for each particle*
6. *Go to 3 until reaching stopping criteria (stopping criteria could be convergence, predefined number of iteration or decreasing fitness trend)*

As a final result, after stopping condition is satisfied, profiles (values of Y_1 to Y_n) should be appointed for each product (j-th product). Values of Y_1' to Y_n' for j-th product show typical risky profile in relation to j-th product with maximized P_j value which represents probability of bad event for j-th product or service.

Particle swarm optimization algorithm presented in this way becomes a powerful tool for automatic risk profile detection based on the created predictive model. Evolutionary approach integrated within the particle swarm optimization algorithm speeds up the process of finding profiles which fit best a specific state in the output variable. This approach gives opportunity to companies for making periodic, frequent profiling in service of profile monitoring.

Beside recognized profiles using PSO algorithm, in situation when output variable has many states, interesting information could be found about similarity between generated profiles based on input values for each correspondent output value which represents willingness for buying a specific product or service.

It could be extracted by using Euclidian distances by formula:

$$D\left(o,i\right) = \sqrt{\left(Y_{o,1} - Y_{i,1}\right)^2 + \left(Y_{o,2} - Y_{i,2}\right)^2 + ... + \left(Y_{o,n} - Y_{i,n}\right)^2}$$

$$D\left(o,i\right) = \sqrt{\left(Y_{o,1} - Y_{i,1}\right)^2 + \left(Y_{o,2} - Y_{i,2}\right)^2 + ... + \left(Y_{o,n} - Y_{i,n}\right)^2}$$

Where:

D(o,i): Distance between the observed profile and the tested profile (observed profile $(Y_{o,n})$ is the profile for which we would like to find the most similar one, and tested profiles $(Y_{i,n})$ are the remaining profiles) .

$Y_{o,n}$: The input values from observed profile calculated with PSO algorithm, for which we are searching nearest profile in the list of candidates for comparison, determined with PSO algorithm.

$Y_{i,n}$: The input values from predictive models calculated with PSO algorithm which make the list of candidates for comparison as the nearest profile, calculated with PSO algorithm.

Proposed methodology could be the base for new clustering approach. These clustering methods focus on similarity of product or service usage.

Results Based on Empirical Data

Described methodology has been applied on empirical data of one insurance company from Croatia. In their portfolio there are more than eighty insurance products and services. Company strategy was to make predictive models on a product group level. Product groups have been made on products which were recognized as strategic products for this company. Nine groups of product were created based on business logic and similarity criteria. Single client can be present in multiple groups in data sample if it uses more than one insurance product. Based on that, learning sample has been divided on development sample and test sample on 80:20 ratios. Bayesian network model has been developed and it was the base for particle swarm optimization algorithm appliance. Developed model of Bayesian network had ninteen nodes (one output node) and that fact determines the number of particles in the individual case. Initial swarm was constructed with seven members for each of fourteen groups.

Stopping criteria for PSO algorithm was achieving fitness of any particle within swarm greater or equal than 0.80 (on scale from 0..1 which represents probability for buying observed product), or keeping similar (6% changes) or repeating fitness (recognized repeating patterns similar to e.g.: 0.5, 0.6,0.5, 0.6, 0.5) on swarm in last 200 epoch, with fitness within swarm less than 0.80.

In the case of meeting criteria, where any particle within swarm are greater or equal than 0.80, algorithm remembers the values and tries to achieve better results until convergence.

Final profiling results by using PSO algorithm are shown in Table 1.

Success rate for profiling was 66.66% (6 successfully recognized profiles of 9). From results, it is evident that successfully recognized profiles have lower number of epochs. One of the reasons was that successfully recognized profiles were joined with stopping criteria earlier. In the case of unsuccessful profiling, the number of epoch is higher. Reason for that is in observing 200 epochs in which fitness changes are within 5% or recognition of repeating patterns above fitness value of 0.80. Analysis makes profiles of most risky clients by product usage. In other words, analysis shows which profiles generate most costs to company regarding the usage of insurance products.

With successful profiles recognition results, similarity has been calculated. Similarity definition means that two profiles are similar if they have less than 15% of differences. Reason for that is to avoid situation where two profiles are declared as similar because other are much more different from the observed one and differences between them are e.g. 60%. From business and decision-making perspective, those profiles are not similar.

Results of similarity calculation are shown in Table 2.

Table 1. Profiling results

Group number	Best fitness (0..1)	Number of epochs in PSO	Successful profiling
1.	0.23	1131	No
2.	0.65	1337	No
3.	0.88	573	Yes
4.	0.97	588	Yes
5.	0.95	758	Yes
6.	0.81	505	Yes
7.	0.82	366	Yes
8.	0.41	2444	No
9.	0.63	3821	No

Table 2. Similar profiles

Profile based on group number	Similar to profile based on group number
3	6
4	7

Further analysis shows that similar profiles are different in average with 3-4 variables of 19. Similarity analysis shows that risky car insurers show similar behavioral characteristics. Recognized similar group numbers shows similar behavioral characteristics regarding the number of crash accidents and other characteristics in relation to observed product usage. Main differences were on socio-demographic characteristics and vehicle types. Considering that, conclusion is that risky behavior is mainly driven by mindsets, behavioral characteristics and less by socio-demographic characteristics and vehicle types.

FUTURE RESEARCH DIRECTIONS

This chapter shows usage of Bayesian networks with PSO algorithm for risk profiling. As it was shown, the same methodology could be applied on any type of trained predictive model. Subject of future research could be aimed on usage of presented methodology with predictive models based on decisions trees, logistic regression, support vector machines and other data mining techniques. Each mentioned technique has some characteristics which require an individual approach for finding technical solution for risk profiling.

Other interesting topic is clustering and usage of e.g. K-means clustering on profiles recognized by PSO algorithm usage based on predictive model (Hemalatha, 2012; Hussain & Liatsis, 2009). Clustering could recognize similar profiles and consolidate similar profiles together. In the end, it could imply revelation that customers which buy product groups A,B,C,D are similar to customers which buy product groups E,F,G,H.

Additionally, decision trees could be used for finding common denominator within clusters, as well as common differences between clusters. All those information are valuable from the perspective of business decision-making.

DISCUSSION

Predictive model developing is not only the approach for cases in which a company develops predictive models in, for example, insurance industry. Developing process should be used for understanding relations and key drivers (influencers) for appearance which we are modeling (Malhotra, 2014). It is much easier to achieve some result in situation where we have a binary output in target variable, and it becomes complicated in situations with models which have more than 2 states in aim variable.

Predictive models should not be used only as a probabilistic calculator because in that case business background remains unknown and hidden. Understanding of business background is a crucial factor for strategic management. Knowledge about typical users of insurance company product is the base for strategic business activities. Profile changes demand changes in marketing strategies and marketing planning, as well as changes in company policies. Significant profile transformation demands greater changes in marketing strategies. Portfolio management demands continuous portfolio monitoring, especially when a company operates with a large number of products on the market which are covered with some predictive models which calculate probability that some bad event will happen.

Presented model is an appropriate and efficient solution in this case, and it can also be used as an element of more complex systems. Particle swarm optimization algorithm in combination with built predictive model is a solid base for automation of risk profiling processes (Pacini et al, 2013; Qi et al, 2009; Sharkey 2006). Periodical processing on available data with particle swarm optimization algorithm in combination with built predictive model should result with derived typical risky profiles, and what is more important with migration trends (differences) of some characteristics within profiles. Those results observed over some period of time could give a much clearer picture about changes in risk profiles, and could be the trigger for market policy changes with intention of reducing costs.

As it can be seen from presented empirical results, there is no guarantee that the proposed model will be successful for generating risky profiles for all the products covered with predictive model. However, empirical results show that it is efficient for most of the modalities of output variable. It implies that the proposed methodology could be efficient for the intended purpose. Additional advantage of the proposed model is the ability to calculate similarity between profiles. It is a useful functionality in situations where companies try to find "profile clusters", and profile clustering is useful in situations where companies try to optimize market activities and save costs of marketing.

Generic profile calculation has some additional advantages in combination with functions for distance calculation. In combination, that methodology could give an answer to the question of which is the main similarity between portfolio members regarding risky behavior. Regarding the nature of the market which can change over time, same methodology can provide information about profile migration which could be presented with profile migration maps for specific products or group of products. Also, it can provide an answer to the following question: Do risky profiles for several targeted products become more diversified or more similar over time? That information is a valuable source for portfolio management.

It is not difficult to assume benefits of applying additional data mining methods like SOM and decision trees to this concept. In case where we generate profiles based on particle swarm optimization algorithm in combination with built predictive model, SOM's could be used for customer profile clustering. Clustered profiles, which contain behavioral characteristics processed with decision trees, could give an insight into key risk factors and main differences in recognized segments.

In general, it leads us to conclusion that instead of single profile monitoring a company can also monitor profile groups (Shi, 2012; Yusoff et al, 2012). Also, same as for single profiles, periodical processing on profile group level over time could give better and clearer picture about changes in risk profiles on recognized group level and could be used as a trigger for further market activities, as well as a generator of new ideas.

ROLE OF BIG DATA

Big data phenomena, which manifested on exponential growth of data size, demands new approaches on data analytics and innovative methods for data capturing, storage, sharing, and analysis. Along with technical solutions, which should challenge data complexity, data volume and variety challenges in the big data era are also addressed on capturing the full potential of big data.

Analytical projects which include data mining as a key factor of solutions, shows more and more complexity, and needs a variety of data sources for efficient hidden knowledge revealing, which can be used in decision making. Big data analytics integrates a variety of disciplines from traditional data mining techniques along with social network analysis and text mining. Scientific research are mostly concentrated (in context of big data) on data sampling (Webb, 2014), parallel processing in the big data environment, technologies for big data, problems with sampling in the big data environment, and strategic business aspects of big data analysis should not be neglected

Richness of data sources does not guarantee a successful analytical process if it is not well and objectively planned, with clear aims and understanding of business problems. Often, it is hard to make clear analytical objectives for big data environment, where data volume and complexity is bigger than in traditional local data environment. Even in such conditions, unclear vision and methodology on how to achieve analytical aim based on business needs could be crucial for project failure or success.

In the big data area, requirements for clear analytical aims are crucial for setting the right analytical strategy. More choices and sources gives an opportunity for better and precise results, but also hides the potential danger of missing the point, if these kind of projects are not adequately and not strategically planned from perspective of business decision needs. Business decision needs also require strategic analytical planning, and the big data concept enters some new standards and requirements into this process . Basic ideas from perspective of business suggest the use of the most efficient disposable data sources which are reachable thought big data concept, along with new type of methodological framework for achieving better market position, by using such infrastructure.

Traditional approach in data mining analytics, which are concentrated mostly on internal data sources, should not be neglected, as advantages are present. While, it does has some limitations, because it covers limited information, contained within predefined database structures. This kind of data source, even limited by its scope, offers opportunity for making the analytical process on more or less known data with the expected type of output due to defined analytical aims.

A big data environment leads to unknown territory, where a company is often unsure what it could dig from those data sources, which are mostly unstructured, big in volume and complex, sometimes without clear vision. Along to these problems, it offers rich sources of new data, which can be combined, with internal data sources. That synergy can result with much more appropriate models and findings, which can be used for better business decisions. All of that needs proposal of the new approach, which will give a direction how to integrate those two concepts. Approach, which integrates best practice from both concepts and introduce new one concept, should result with a more efficient tool for business decision support. Big data does not only mean volume as a criterion of complexity, it also means combinatory as a criterion of complexity, which presented case study shows.

Common methodologies used for analytical purposes lean mostly on internally disposable data sources, which examine the cause usage of methods, and are mostly focused on structured databases. Projects, which are oriented on unstructured data sources like text or web, are mostly independent conceptually, and methodologically from projects like predictive fraud detection models, predictive churn detection models or segmentation models. For methodological synergies the prerequisite is data synergism, and for achieving those aims a clear strategy and knowledge on the management level (strategic, operative and organizational parts responsible for analytic solution development) should exist.

The big data phenomena should not only be observed from the perspective of huge data amounts, or be concentrated only on methodology and infrastructure for effectively processing huge data sets. Variety of data sources, often unconnected with unique relational keys, which are expected for traditional analysis purposes, are not the case if companies would like to use the benefits from data sources, which could be classified in the "big data area".

It could produce confusion especially when companies would like to use the standard analytical approach. Regarding that, it is evident that "big data analytics" are mostly concentrated on external data sources. Typically without a clear concept on how to connect internal transactional data with external data sources mostly unstructured and unconnected. The known analytical method is mostly oriented on structured data sources, and in situations when unstructured data sources are used for text mining purposes, when other type of analytical techniques should be used. Sometimes relatively lower data sets also could be declared as complex, because of their combinatory complexity.

From the perspective of a company it is very important to combine external and internal data sources, because knowledge about some global trends or attitudes about some subject or behavior, should be analyzed from the perspective of the company's portfolio. Comparison between global and local trends could give a holistic picture sufficient for decision-making. The problem lies in the fact that there is no common methodology for how to develop an efficient model, which would consolidate both data sources for developing efficient models as a base for business decision.

Achieving analytical connectivity between different types of data sources is one of the most important topics when discussing big data analytical strategies. Different types of data (structured, unstructured) can exist within company as internal data, and it is a challenge to make connectivity between them, from an analytical point of view. Making the situation much more difficult is the attempt to make connectivity between different type of data, when they exists externally and internally.

Proposed is a methodology for achieving this aim in a situation when a company develops predictive models. One of the simplest, but effective techniques which will be presented as effective for making the connection between structured and unstructured data through analytical models, is measuring impact of some used word or phrase, for example in call center on aim, variable as "churn commitment". For purposes of significant word recognition, it is recommended for long words in text discovery.

Data mining as a discipline brings a completely new direction on business planning from the last decades. Developing churn models, fraud detection models and customer segmentation have become an important element for successful business in conditions where market competition exists. Data mining has become a tool for reducing uncertainty and tool for business planning. It also has a role as a decision support instrument. Even mentioned techniques rely on huge amounts of data, in the very beginning, sources for analysis were mostly local transactional databases and local data warehouses. When a company needs to develop strategy against running churn rate, it mostly relies upon existing local transactional data or data warehouse for the modeling purposes. Similar situations for other types of problems like fraud detection or segmentation are also common. Mentioned strategies have leaned on huge amounts of data usage for finding useful patterns, mostly on local data sources.

The big data era brings new challenges, not only relative to bigger quantities of data from external and internal data sources. But also, the big data era brings with it a whole new way of strategic, analytical thinking which connects the traditional approach by using data mining techniques within internal databases, along with data sources as forums, blogs and social networks in finding the right answers for solving business problems. All of which demands a different approach in designing analytical solutions and demands new ways for analytical models to be integrated.

ROLE OF CUSTOMER PROFILE OPTIMIZATION

Data mining solutions for profiling are always complex in way of chaining and usage of more than one data mining method. Presented project in is no exception in complexity.

Usage of numerous data mining methods is not guarantee of project success. More than that it is cooperation between analyst, business insider within company, which initiate project, and creativity of all project members.

Traditional assurance, that profiling modeling is developing predictive model, which calculates probabilities, is not correct. It is more than that. We should understand customer profiles, their behavior, interaction, power to disintegrate network if we are talking about social networks.

Unfortunately there is no cookbook for profiling, each business case is a unique story, and each step forward in analysis can change initial analysis direction.

Most important of all things is to derive useful information for decision support, because main aim of business modeling with data mining methods is knowledge recognition, understanding of customer behavior which can be applied in decision-making.

Understanding of customer behaviour is key factor of market success, especially in competitive market conditions.

Extracting information from social networks is one of the aims when a company wants to understand their customers. New era of big data and social networks contributes in complexity of data sources for analytical purposes, and offers new challenges and also additional useful information for understanding customer behavior. That leads us to taking in account social network analysis as a important factor for understanding hidden relations.

Traditional data mining approach, which is commonly used, offers well known methods typically used on internal data sources. External data sources along with traditional data mining methods offer solutions for the use of text mining methods, social network analysis and expert systems which can be centrally placed for the integration of differing aspects of analysis depending upon the strategic business or/and analytical aims. Looking in that direction, answers for churn detection and mitigation of contract breaking by clients could be extracted in combination from predictive models, developed on local data sources and text patterns from forums or blogs, as well as from social networks like Facebook, twitter or other, by using appropriate analytical techniques.

Richness of data sources does not guarantee a successful analytical process if it is not well and objectively planned, with clear aims and understanding of business problems. Often, it is hard to make clear analytical objectives for big data environment, where data volume and complexity is bigger than in traditional local data environment. Even in such conditions, unclear vision and methodology on how to achieve analytical aim based on business needs could be crucial for project failure or success.

In the big data area, requirements for clear analytical aims are crucial for setting the right analytical strategy. More choices and sources gives an opportunity for better and precise results, but also hides the potential danger of missing the point, if these kind of projects are not adequately and not strategically planned from perspective of business decision needs. Business decision needs also require strategic analytical planning, and the big data concept enters some new standards and requirements into this process. Basic ideas from perspective of business suggest the use of the most efficient disposable data sources which are reachable thought big data concept, along with new type of methodological framework for achieving better market position, by using such infrastructure.

Traditional approach in data mining analytics, which are concentrated mostly on internal data sources, should not be neglected, as advantages are present. While, it does has some limitations, because it covers limited information, contained within predefined database structures. This kind of data source, even limited by its scope, offers opportunity for making the analytical process on more or less known data with the expected type of output due to defined analytical aims.

A big data environment leads to unknown territory, where a company is often unsure what it could dig from those data sources, which are mostly unstructured, big in volume and complex, sometimes without clear vision. Along to these problems, it offers rich sources of new data, which can be combined, with internal data sources.

That synergy can result with much more appropriate models and findings, which can be used for better business decisions. All of that needs proposal of the new approach, which will give a direction how to integrate those two concepts. Approach, which integrates best practice from both concepts and introduce new one concept, which should result with a more efficient tool for business decision support.

Traditional approaches in business analytics and usage of data mining methods are mostly concentrated on solving single problems like segmentation, fraud detection and churn detection on data disposable within local databases. Those data could be huge by volume, collected through transactional databases and consolidated through data warehouses.

Even if it seems complex and sufficient, it often represents a narrow set of data for specific purposes like segmentation, fraud detection and churn detection. The reason for that lies in the fact that transactional databases are not constructed, or have been rarely constructed with the intention to fulfill analytical needs. Specifically, it is evident for some exact needs like fraud detection or churn detection. Transactional databases are constructed with a general scope, and transactional business needs. This does not mean that such databases are useless for analytical purposes; it simply means that it provides a narrow set of information with which some predictive analytical data mining model or other model or reporting for specific business needs could be constructed.

Value of the existing data, dislocated within different transactional systems could be increased by integration into a data warehouse system. It still does not mean that a company does not have limited information about some problem space. Other problems in relation with the traditional analytical approach is often avoidance of unstructured data source usage for business modeling purposes, even unstructured data exists within systems like call centers data or similar sources.

Unstructured data usage is mainly focused on pure text mining analytics in connection with specific problems based on textual data sources, or in web mining analytics. Integration of structured and unstructured data sources as well as internal or external data sources (from web, blogs, social networks) is not the case when we are speaking about traditional business analytics.

All of that leads to the question regarding potential business strategy based on analytical models.

Data mining is defined as a discipline, which reveals hidden unexpected patterns from the data. From the perspective of business planning, it should serve to as an efficient business strategy. The traditional approach reveals hidden unexpected patterns from the internal, mostly structured, relational data sets, and results from those models could be plausible and usable for decision-making. Internal data, collected within a company data warehouse has (could have) limited scope on some problems such as fraud, because it does not contain enough relevant information for efficient fraud detection modeling and analytic. The developed model (in this case fraud detection model based on an internal data warehouse) could show plausible performance, but relevant patterns could stay undetected, because other data sources like blogs, social networks and web sources are not used for analytical purposes.

Contrary to traditional analytical approach, big data strategic thinking, implies knowledge extracting from additional data sources, which does not have to be relationally connected through existing databases or data warehouses. It implies using disposable knowledge from other sources, and its integration into analytical process, having in mind achieving greater efficiency for decision support.

For example, let's assume that an insurance company would like to develop a predictive model, which will calculate churn probability on the customer level. Traditional model development would be concentrated on local databases, capturing client behavior characteristics within the local database framework. This approach is a result of an adopted way of thinking, caused by the common methodology where big data and its potential are not used for building solutions. Traditional solutions offer answers about the churner's patterns (if we are observing the previous example). Other activities where clients exchange opinions about the company and share some attitudes, which at the end leads to churn, could stay unrevealed if the company does not change strategic way of analytical thinking.

Unstructured data could exist as well in internal sources, like memo fields within call center databases, which stays out of the analytical process. Analytical thinking from the perspective of big data also includes facts, that data does not have to be connected through relational keys within databases. In the described churn example it indicates that data for predictive modeling should be consolidated from data sources such as databases, blogs, forums and other unstructured data sources.

There is no guarantee that external data or internal data will deliver additional information about problems, which would be of great value for finding business solutions. The basic idea from the perspective of a big data analytical strategy is to cover all disposable and usable data sources and techniques, which potentially could be useful for additional knowledge extraction. For such purposes, during the project planning stage, it is important to have in mind all possibilities, which big data concepts could offer.

After the business aim definition, which includes strategy based on the big data paradigm, disposable data has the potential to have a strong influence on solution design and solution building. It can consolidate traditional model development along with analytical solutions, based on the big data paradigm. It is important to stress that in such situations, knowledge extraction demands much more human expert involvement. Especially in situations where results and knowledge from different kinds of models exist, and it demands expert judgment and evaluation. During the business decision process, expert explanations and conclusions play a crucial role in the understanding and interpretation of given results. This is due to the fact that results are derived from different data sources, which provide different perspectives of the problem and desire experts for their explanation.

CONCLUSION

From the perspective of risk profiling, the usage of Bayesian networks in predictive modelling is complex. Finding optimal combination of nodes with corresponding evidences, which will maximize final output, is not a trivial task. Manual tuning is noted as an inappropriate procedure, especially in cases when Bayesian network contains many nodes and has many output states. Particle swarm optimization approach can speed up the whole process that is hard to do manually.

Presented methodology has a practical value for decision support, especially in business where information about customer risky profiles is valuable for future portfolio planning, as is shown on the example of an insurance company. Additional advantage is profile similarity calculation based on given results. Additionally, described methodology can be used frequently (e.g. on quarterly basis) for determination about changes in risk profiles, which implies changes in customer behavior or preferences over time. This information is a valuable source for changes in marketing strategy and for the situation when we use an automatic process combined with PSO algorithm, because it can be turned into a semi-automated process, which is less time/resource consuming.

It is important to keep in mind that presented methodology does not guarantee success in finding risky profiles for each defined product/group of products. As it is shown in results based on empirical data, it is not surprising that for some defined product/group of products it is not possible to find a reliable risk profile. It depends on the data itself, as well as on the type of the predictive model used. Situation in which adequate profiles are recognized with certain threshold for the most of the product/group of products is acceptable.

REFERENCES

Abbasimehr, H., Tarokh, M. J., & Setak, M. (2011). Determination of Algorithms Making Balance Between Accuracy and Comprehensibility in Churn Prediction Setting. *International Journal of Information Retrieval Research*, *1*(2), 39–54. doi:10.4018/IJIRR.2011040103

Acharjya, D. P., & Kauser, A. P. (2015). Swarm Intelligence in Solving Bio-Inspired Computing Problems: Reviews, Perspectives, and Challenges. In S. Bhattacharyya & P. Dutta (Eds.), *Handbook of Research on Swarm Intelligence in Engineering* (pp. 74–98). Hershey, PA: Engineering Science Reference; doi:10.4018/978-1-4666-8291-7.ch003

Adhikari, R., & Agrawal, R. K. (2013). Hybridization of Artificial Neural Network and Particle Swarm Optimization Methods for Time Series Forecasting. *International Journal of Applied Evolutionary Computation*, *4*(3), 75–90. doi:10.4018/jaec.2013070107

Afify, A. (2013). Intelligent Computation for Manufacturing. In Z. Li & A. Al-Ahmari (Eds.), *Formal Methods in Manufacturing Systems: Recent Advances* (pp. 211–246). Hershey, PA: Engineering Science Reference; doi:10.4018/978-1-4666-4034-4.ch009

Agosta, L. (2000). *The Essential Guide to Data Warehousing*. Upper Saddle River, NJ: Prentice Hall.

Alam, S., Dobbie, G., Koh, Y. S., & Rehman, S. U. (2014). Biologically Inspired Techniques for Data Mining: A Brief Overview of Particle Swarm Optimization for KDD. In S. Alam, G. Dobbie, Y. Koh, & S. ur Rehman (Eds.), Biologically-Inspired Techniques for Knowledge Discovery and Data Mining (pp. 1-10). Hershey, PA: Information Science Reference. doi:10.4018/978-1-4666-6078-6.ch001

Aleksander, I., & Morton, H. (1995). *An introduction to neural computing*. International Thompson Computer Press.

Alippi, C. (2003). A Perturbation Size-Independent Analysis of Robustness in Neural Networks by Randomized Algorithms. In M. Mohammadian, R. Sarker, & X. Yao (Eds.), *Computational Intelligence in Control* (pp. 22–40). Hershey, PA: Idea Group Publishing; doi:10.4018/978-1-59140-037-0.ch002

Almeida, F., & Santos, M. (2014). A Conceptual Framework for Big Data Analysis. In I. Portela & F. Almeida (Eds.), *Organizational, Legal, and Technological Dimensions of Information System Administration* (pp. 199–223). Hershey, PA: Information Science Reference; doi:10.4018/978-1-4666-4526-4.ch011

Anagnostopoulos, C., & Hadjiefthymiades, S. (2012). Swarm Intelligence in Autonomic Computing: The Particle Swarm Optimization Case. In P. Cong-Vinh (Ed.), *Formal and Practical Aspects of Autonomic Computing and Networking: Specification, Development, and Verification* (pp. 97–117). Hershey, PA: Information Science Reference; doi:10.4018/978-1-60960-845-3.ch004

Arora, V., & Ravi, V. (2013). Data Mining using Advanced Ant Colony Optimization Algorithm and Application to Bankruptcy Prediction. *International Journal of Information Systems and Social Change, 4*(3), 33–56. doi:10.4018/jissc.2013070103

Babahajyani, P., Habibi, F., & Bevrani, H. (2014). An On-Line PSO-Based Fuzzy Logic Tuning Approach: Microgrid Frequency Control Case Study. In P. Vasant (Ed.), *Handbook of Research on Novel Soft Computing Intelligent Algorithms: Theory and Practical Applications* (pp. 589–616). Hershey, PA: Information Science Reference; doi:10.4018/978-1-4666-4450-2.ch020

Bakshi, K. (2014). Technologies for Big Data. In W. Hu & N. Kaabouch (Eds.), *Big Data Management, Technologies, and Applications* (pp. 1–22). Hershey, PA: Information Science Reference; doi:10.4018/978-1-4666-4699-5.ch001

Bang, J., Dholakia, N., Hamel, L., & Shin, S. (2009). Customer Relationship Management and Knowledge Discovery in Database. In J. Erickson (Ed.), *Database Technologies: Concepts, Methodologies, Tools, and Applications* (pp. 1778–1786). Hershey, PA: Information Science Reference, doi:10.4018/978-1-60566-058-5.ch107

Berry, J. A. M. Linoff Gordon, (2000). Mastering data mining. John Wiley & Sons Inc.

Berry, J. A. M., & Linoff, G. (1997). *Data mining techniques for marketing sales and customer support*. John Wiley & Sons Inc.

Cheng, S., Shi, Y., & Qin, Q. (2013). A Study of Normalized Population Diversity in Particle Swarm Optimization. *International Journal of Swarm Intelligence Research, 4*(1), 1–34. doi:10.4018/jsir.2013010101

Clerck, M. (2013). *Particle Swarm Optimization*. London: Iste.

Devi, V. S. (2014). Learning Using Soft Computing Techniques. In B. Tripathy & D. Acharjya (Eds.), *Global Trends in Intelligent Computing Research and Development* (pp. 51–67). Hershey, PA: Information Science Reference. doi:10.4018/978-1-4666-4936-1.ch003

Dresner, H. (2008). *Performance management revolution*. John Wiley & Sons Inc.

El-Shorbagy. (2013). *Numerical Optimization & Swarm Intelligence for optimization: Trust Region Algorithm & Particle Swarm Optimization*. LAP LAMBERT Academic Publishing.

Elamvazuthi, I., Vasant, P., & Ganesan, T. (2012). Integration of Fuzzy Logic Techniques into DSS for Profitability Quantification in a Manufacturing Environment. In M. Khan & A. Ansari (Eds.), *Handbook of Research on Industrial Informatics and Manufacturing Intelligence: Innovations and Solutions* (pp. 171–192). Hershey, PA: Information Science Reference; doi:10.4018/978-1-4666-0294-6.ch007

Feng, J., Xu, L., & Ramamurthy, B. (2009). Overlay Construction in Mobile Peer-to-Peer Networks. In B. Seet (Ed.), *Mobile Peer-to-Peer Computing for Next Generation Distributed Environments: Advancing Conceptual and Algorithmic Applications* (pp. 51–67). Hershey, PA: Information Science Reference. doi:10.4018/978-1-60566-715-7.ch003

Garrido, P., & Lemahieu, W. (2008). Collective Intelligence. In G. Putnik & M. Cruz-Cunha (Eds.), *Encyclopedia of Networked and Virtual Organizations* (pp. 280–287). Hershey, PA: Information Science Reference. doi:10.4018/978-1-59904-885-7.ch037

Giudici, P. (2003). *Applied Data Mining: Statistical Methods for Business and Industry*. John Wiley &Sons Inc.

Giudici, P., & Figini, S. (2009). *Applied Data Mining for Business and Industry (Statistics in Practice)*. Wiley. doi:10.1002/9780470745830

Gonsalves, T. (2015). Hybrid Swarm Intelligence. In M. Khosrow-Pour (Ed.), *Encyclopedia of Information Science and Technology* (3rd ed.; pp. 175–186). Hershey, PA: Information Science Reference. doi:10.4018/978-1-4666-5888-2.ch018

Han, J., & Kamber, M. (2006). *Data Mining: Concepts and Techniques*. Morgan Kaufmann.

Hemalatha, M. (2012). A Predictive Modeling of Retail Satisfaction: A Data Mining Approach to Retail Service Industry. In P. Ordóñez de Pablos & M. Lytras (Eds.), *Knowledge Management and Drivers of Innovation in Services Industries* (pp. 175–189). Hershey, PA: Information Science Reference. doi:10.4018/978-1-4666-0948-8.ch014

Hussain, A., & Liatsis, P. (2009). A Novel Recurrent Polynomial Neural Network for Financial Time Series Prediction. In M. Zhang (Ed.), *Artificial Higher Order Neural Networks for Economics and Business* (pp. 190–211). Hershey, PA: Information Science Reference. doi:10.4018/978-1-59904-897-0.ch009

Janecek, A., & Tan, Y. (2011). Swarm Intelligence for Non-Negative Matrix Factorization. *International Journal of Swarm Intelligence Research*, 2(4), 12–34. doi:10.4018/jsir.2011100102

Janecek, A., & Tan, Y. (2015). Swarm Intelligence for Dimensionality Reduction: How to Improve the Non-Negative Matrix Factorization with Nature-Inspired Optimization Methods. In Y. Shi (Ed.), *Emerging Research on Swarm Intelligence and Algorithm Optimization* (pp. 285–309). Hershey, PA: Information Science Reference. doi:10.4018/978-1-4666-6328-2.ch013

Jensen, F. (2001). *Bayesian networks and decision graphs*. Springer. doi:10.1007/978-1-4757-3502-4

Kaur, H., Chauhan, R., & Wasan, S. K. (2015). A Bayesian Network Model for Probability Estimation. In M. Khosrow-Pour (Ed.), *Encyclopedia of Information Science and Technology* (3rd ed.; pp. 1551–1558). Hershey, PA: Information Science Reference. doi:10.4018/978-1-4666-5888-2.ch148

Kawamura, H., & Suzuki, K. (2011). Pheromone-style Communication for Swarm Intelligence. In S. Chen, Y. Kambayashi, & H. Sato (Eds.), *Multi-Agent Applications with Evolutionary Computation and Biologically Inspired Technologies: Intelligent Techniques for Ubiquity and Optimization* (pp. 294–307). Hershey, PA. Medical Information Science Reference. doi:10.4018/978-1-60566-898-7.ch016

Kim, M., Park, M., & Park, J. (2009). When Customer Satisfaction Isn't Good Enough: The Role of Switching Incentives and Barriers Affecting Customer Behavior in Korean Mobile Communications Services. In I. Lee (Ed.), *Handbook of Research on Telecommunications Planning and Management for Business* (pp. 351–363). Hershey, PA: Information Science Reference. doi:10.4018/978-1-60566-194-0.ch022

Klepac, G. (2010). Preparing for New Competition in the Retail Industry. In A. Syvajarvi & J. Stenvall (Eds.), *Data Mining in Public and Private Sectors: Organizational and Government Applications* (pp. 245–266). Hershey, PA: Information Science Reference. doi:10.4018/978-1-60566-906-9.ch013

Klepac, G. (2014). Data Mining Models as a Tool for Churn Reduction and Custom Product Development in Telecommunication Industries. In P. Vasant (Ed.), *Handbook of Research on Novel Soft Computing Intelligent Algorithms: Theory and Practical Applications* (pp. 511–537). Hershey, PA: Information Science Reference. doi:10.4018/978-1-4666-4450-2.ch017

Klepac, G., & Berg, K. L. (2015a). Proposal of Analytical Model for Business Problems Solving in Big Data Environment. In J. Girard, D. Klein, & K. Berg (Eds.), *Strategic Data-Based Wisdom in the Big Data Era* (pp. 209–228). Hershey, PA: Information Science Reference. doi:10.4018/978-1-4666-8122-4.ch012

Klepac, G., Kopal, R., & Mršić, L. (2015). *Developing Churn Models Using Data Mining Techniques and Social Network Analysis* (pp. 1–361). Hershey, PA: IGI Global. doi:10.4018/978-1-4666-6288-9

Klepac, G., Mrsic, L., & Kopal, R. (2016). Efficient Risk Profiling Using Bayesian Networks and Particle Swarm Optimization Algorithm. In D. Jakóbczak (Ed.), *Analyzing Risk through Probabilistic Modeling in Operations Research* (pp. 91–124). Hershey, PA: Business Science Reference. doi:10.4018/978-1-4666-9458-3.ch004

Konstantinos, E. P., & Michael, N. V. (2010). Applications in Machine Learning. In K. Parsopoulos & M. Vrahatis (Eds.), *Particle Swarm Optimization and Intelligence: Advances and Applications* (pp. 149–167). Hershey, PA: Information Science Reference. doi:10.4018/978-1-61520-666-7.ch006

Konstantinos, E. P., & Michael, N. V. (2010). Established and Recently Proposed Variants of Particle Swarm Optimization. In K. Parsopoulos & M. Vrahatis (Eds.), *Particle Swarm Optimization and Intelligence: Advances and Applications* (pp. 88–132). Hershey, PA: Information Science Reference. doi:10.4018/978-1-61520-666-7.ch004

Kress, M., Mostaghim, S., & Seese, D. (2010). Intelligent Business Process Execution using Particle Swarm Optimization. In Information Resources Management: Concepts, Methodologies, Tools and Applications (pp. 797-815). Hershey, PA: Information Science Reference. doi:10.4018/978-1-61520-965-1.ch319

Kurbatsky, V., Sidorov, D., Tomin, N., & Spiryaev, V. (2014). Optimal Training of Artificial Neural Networks to Forecast Power System State Variables. *International Journal of Energy Optimization and Engineering*, 3(1), 65–82. doi:10.4018/ijeoe.2014010104

Larose, D. T. (2005). *Discovering Knowledge in Data: An Introduction to Data Mining*. John Wiley &Sons Inc.

Lee, K., & Paik, T. (2006). A Neural Network Approach to Cost Minimizatin in a Production Scheduling Setting. In J. Rabuñal & J. Dorado (Eds.), *Artificial Neural Networks in Real-Life Applications* (pp. 297–313). Hershey, PA: Idea Group Publishing. doi:10.4018/978-1-59140-902-1.ch014

Malhotra, R. (2014). SIDE: A Decision Support System Using a Combination of Swarm Intelligence and Data Envelopment Analysis. *International Journal of Strategic Decision Sciences*, 5(1), 39–58. doi:10.4018/ijsds.2014010103

Nguyen, S., & Kachitvichyanukul, V. (2010). Movement Strategies for Multi-Objective Particle Swarm Optimization. *International Journal of Applied Metaheuristic Computing*, *1*(3), 59–79. doi:10.4018/jamc.2010070105

Okun, O. (2014). Bayesian Variable Selection. In J. Wang (Ed.), *Encyclopedia of Business Analytics and Optimization* (pp. 241–250). Hershey, PA: Business Science Reference. doi:10.4018/978-1-4666-5202-6.ch023

Olson, E. A. (2011). *Particle Swarm Optimization: Theory, Techniques and Applications (Engineering Tools, Techniques and Tables)*. Nova Science Pub Inc.

Pacini, E., Mateos, C., & Garino, C. G. (2013). Schedulers Based on Ant Colony Optimization for Parameter Sweep Experiments in Distributed Environments. In S. Bhattacharyya & P. Dutta (Eds.), *Handbook of Research on Computational Intelligence for Engineering, Science, and Business* (pp. 410–448). Hershey, PA: Information Science Reference. doi:10.4018/978-1-4666-2518-1.ch016

Qi, J., Li, Y., Li, C., & Zhang, Y. (2009). Telecommunication Customer Detainment Management. In I. Lee (Ed.), *Handbook of Research on Telecommunications Planning and Management for Business* (pp. 379–399). Hershey, PA: Information Science Reference. doi:10.4018/978-1-60566-194-0.ch024

Rajesh, R., Pugazhendhi, S., & Ganesh, K. (2013). Genetic Algorithm and Particle Swarm Optimization for Solving Balanced Allocation Problem of Third Party Logistics Providers. In J. Wang (Ed.), *Management Innovations for Intelligent Supply Chains* (pp. 184–203). Hershey, PA: Business Science Reference. doi:10.4018/978-1-4666-2461-0.ch010

Russel, C. E., Yuhui, S., & Kennedy, J. (2001). *Swarm Intelligence*. Morgan Kaufmann.

Sharkey, A. J., & Sharkey, N. (2006). The Application of Swarm Intelligence to Collective Robots. In J. Fulcher (Ed.), *Advances in Applied Artificial Intelligence* (pp. 157–185). Hershey, PA: Idea Group Publishing. doi:10.4018/978-1-59140-827-7.ch006

Shi, Y. (2012). *Innovations and Developments of Swarm Intelligence Applications*. Hershey, PA: IGI Global. doi:10.4018/978-1-4666-1592-2

Singh, S., & Singh, J. N. (2012). *Application of Particle Swarm Optimization: In the field of Image Processing*. LAP LAMBERT Academic Publishing.

Taleizadeh, A. A., & Cárdenas-Barrón, L. E. (2013). Metaheuristic Algorithms for Supply Chain Management Problems. In Supply Chain Management: Concepts, Methodologies, Tools, and Applications (pp. 1814-1837). Hershey, PA: Business Science Reference. doi:10.4018/978-1-4666-2625-6.ch106

Tosun, Ö. (2014). Artificial Bee Colony Algorithm. In J. Wang (Ed.), *Encyclopedia of Business Analytics and Optimization* (pp. 179–192). Hershey, PA: Business Science Reference. doi:10.4018/978-1-4666-5202-6.ch018

Xing, B., & Gao, W. (2014). Overview of Computational Intelligence. In *Computational Intelligence in Remanufacturing* (pp. 18–36). Hershey, PA: Information Science Reference. doi:10.4018/978-1-4666-4908-8.ch002

Xing, B., & Gao, W. (2014). Post-Disassembly Part-Machine Clustering Using Artificial Neural Networks and Ant Colony Systems. In *Computational Intelligence in Remanufacturing* (pp. 135–150). Hershey, PA: Information Science Reference. doi:10.4018/978-1-4666-4908-8.ch008

Yavuz, M. C., Sahin, F., Arnavut, Z., & Uluyol, O. (2006), Generating and Exploiting Bayesian Networks for Fault Diagnosis in Airplane Engines, *Proceedings of the IEEE International Conference on Granular Computing*, 250-255. doi:10.1109/GRC.2006.1635792

Yin, P.-Y. (2004). A Discrete Particle Swarm Algorithm for Optimal Polygonal Approximation of Digital Curves J. *Vis. Comm. Image R., 15*(2), 241–260. doi:10.1016/j.jvcir.2003.12.001

Yosuf, M. S. (2010). *Nonlinear Predictive Control Using Particle Swarm Optimization: Application to Power Systems. Hidelberg, Germany: VDM Verlag Dr.* Müller.

Yusoff, N., Sporea, I., & Grüning, A. (2012). Neural Networks in Cognitive Science: An Introduction. In P. Lio & D. Verma (Eds.), *Biologically Inspired Networking and Sensing: Algorithms and Architectures* (pp. 58–83). Hershey, PA: Medical Information Science Reference. doi:10.4018/978-1-61350-092-7.ch004

Zhang, Y. Q., Fraser, M. D., Gagliano, R. A., & Kandel, A. (2000). Granular neural networks for numerical-linguistic data fusion and knowledge discovery. *IEEE Transactions on Neural Networks, 11*(3), 658–667. doi:10.1109/72.846737 PMID:18249793

Zuo, Y., & Kita, E. (2012). Stock Price Forecast Using Bayesian Network. *Expert Systems with Applications, 39*(8), 6729–6737. doi:10.1016/j.eswa.2011.12.035

Chapter 4

Multi–Thresholded Histogram Equalization Based on Parameterless Artificial Bee Colony

Krishna Gopal Dhal
Midnapore College (Autonomous), India

Mandira Sen
Tata Consultancy Services, India

Swarnajit Ray
JBMatrix Technology Pvt. Ltd., India

Sanjoy Das
University of Kalyani, India

ABSTRACT

This chapter presents a novel variant of histogram equalization (HE) method called multi-thresholded histogram equalization (MTHE), depending on entropy-based multi-level thresholding-based segmentation. It is reported that proper segmentation of the histogram significantly assists the HE variants to maintain the original brightness of the image, which is one of the main criterion of the consumer electronics field. Multi-separation-based HE variants are also very effective for multi-modal histogram-based images. But, proper multi-seaparation of the histogram increases the computational time of the corresponding HE variants. In order to overcome that problem, one novel parameterless artifical bee colony (ABC) algorithm is employed to solve the multi-level thresholding problem. Experimental results prove that proposed parameterless ABC helps to reduce the computational time significantly and the proposed MTHE outperforms several existing HE varints in brightness preserving histopathological image enhancement domain.

DOI: 10.4018/978-1-5225-5020-4.ch004

INTRODUCTION

Contrast enhancement methods have been applied for better visual interpretation. Histogram Equalization (HE) is one of the most simple and widely used method for contrast enhancement (Gonzalez, R.C., Woods, R.E. (2002)). Basically HE computes linear cumulative histogram of the original image and dispenses intensity values over its dynamic intensity range. HE based techniques have been used in medical image processing, satellite image processing etc. The method of Traditional Histogram Equalization (Gonzalez, R.C., Woods, R.E. (2002)) is described below:

The method of Traditional Histogram Equalization (Chen, S. D., Ramli, A. R. (2004)) has the following steps:

If the original image $f(i, j)$ has total W number of pixels within the dynamic range $[X_0, X_{L-1}]$, where L is the number of discrete gray levels, then the probability density function $H1(X_k)$ of intensity level X_k of the image is given by:

$$H1(X_k) = \frac{n_k}{W} \text{ for } 0 \leq k \leq L - 1 \tag{1}$$

Where, n_k is the total number of pixels with intensity level X_k. The plot of X_k vs. n_k is the histogram of image f. the cumulative density function is defined as (Chen, S. D., Ramli, A. R. (2004)):

$$CDF(X_k) = \sum_{i=0}^{k} H1(X_i) \tag{2}$$

Traditional HE maps the corresponding image into the total dynamic range $[X_0, X_{L-1}]$ with the help of the CDF as given below:

$$f(X) = X_0 + (X_{L-1} - X_0).CDF(X) \tag{3}$$

In the HE procedure the entire gray levels are distributed uniformly, HE improves the image contrast and maximizes the image entropy and also change the mean brightness of the output image to the middle of the gray level regardless of the input image's mean (Chen, S. D., Ramli, A. R. (2004), Kim, Y.T. (1997)). The equation of mean or statistical expectation $E(.)$ of the output image G is given below:

$$E\left(G\right) = G_m = \frac{1}{2}\left(X_0 + X_{L-1}\right) \tag{4}$$

Where, G_m is the mean intensity of the output image. As a result, if the Traditioanl HE is applied over images, the brightness of the image changes drastically. To preserve the original brightness, proper histogram segmentation based HE variants are reported (Chen, S. D., Ramli, A. R. (2004), Kim, Y.T. (1997), Cheng, H.D. Shi, J. (2004), Chen, S. D., Ramli, A. R. (2003), Chen, S. D., Ramli, A. R. (2003)). Brightness Preserving Bi-Histogram Equalization (BBHE) was one of the variant of THE (Chen, S. D., Ramli, A. R. (2004), Kim, Y.T. (1997)). In BBHE, histogram of the image was separated around its mean and then the two divided parts were equalized separately (Chen, S. D., Ramli, A. R. (2004), Kim, Y.T. (1997)). BBHE method preserved the original brightness up to a certain level (Chen, S. D., Ramli, A. R. (2004)). The mean intensity value of the output image was defined as:

$$E\left(G1\right) = G1_m = \frac{1}{2}\left(X_m + G_m\right) \tag{5}$$

Where, X_m is the mean intensity value of the input image. In Dualistic Sub-Image Histogram Equalization (DSIHE) proposed by Wan (Chen, S. D., Ramli, A. R. (2004)), the procedure was same as BBHE, but the histogram was separated by median instead of mean (Chen, S. D., Ramli, A. R. (2004)). The potential of preserving the original brightness was not as good in DSIHE method as BBHE method. Chen and Ramli proposed Minimum Mean Brightness Error Bi-Histogram Equalization (MMBEBHE) method (Chen, S. D., Ramli, A. R. (2003)), in which the histogram was separated using a specified threshold which preserved the minimum mean brightness error between input and output images and then the two parts were equalized independently. This technique was better than BBHE and DSIHE, but it still suffered from deficiency of contrast and brightness (Shanmugavadivu, P., Balasubramanian, K., Muruganandam, A. (2014)). The same authors presented Recursive Mean Separate Histogram Equalization (RMSHE) method where the input image was separated recursively (Chen, S. D., Ramli, A. R. (2003)). RMSHE method was better than BBHE as RMSHE could preserve the brightness well and could give natural enhancement (Chen, S. D., Ramli, A. R. (2004)). The disadvantage of RMSHE was its large time complexity for recursion. Recursive sub-histogram equalization method (RSIHE) had been proposed by Sim et. al. which was nearly same as RMSHE but histograms were separated based on its median rather than mean (Sim, K. S., Tso, C. P., Tan, Y. Y. (2007)). The main disadvantage of both methods is to find out the optimal recursion level. Therefore it can be conclude that multi-separation helps to produce better enhanced images. To solve the above discussed problem, multipeak histogram equalization with brightness preserving (MPHEBP) had been proposed byWongsritong et.al. (Wongsritong, K., Kittayaruasiriwat, K., Cheevasuvit, F., Dejhan, K. Somboonkaew, A. (1998)). In this procedure, the histogram was first smoothed by one dimensional smoothing filter and then divided based on histogram's local maximums. So the number of sub histograms depended on the number of local maximums. Experimental results proved that MPHEBP was better than BBHE in terms of preserving the original brightness. But all the above discussed techniques do not allow some sections of the histogram to expand (Ibrahim, H., Kong, N.S.P. (2007)). To overcome this problem Dynamic histogram equalization (DHE) method was reported by Wadud et. al. (Abdullah-Al-Wadud, M., Kabir, M. H., Dewan, M. A. A. Chae, O.(2007)). It is similar to MPHEBP but the histogram was separated recursively into several parts depending on local minimums to remove any presence of any dominating gray level and then all sub-histograms were mapped into a new dynamic range. The mapping function depended on the number of pixels each sub-histogram contained i.e. the sub-histogram with large number of pixels took bigger range. The main demerit of DHE was that it did not put constrain to maintain the mean brightness of the image. Therefore, DHE is not suitable for consumer electronic purpose. That's why Brightness Preserving Dynamic Histogram Equalization (BPDHE) had been proposed by Ibrahim et. al. (Ibrahim, H. Kong, N.S.P. (2007)) which is actually the extension of both MPHEBP and DHE. In BPDHE, input histogram was smoothed by Gaussian filter followed by the segmentation based on local maximums. Segmented sub-histograms were equalized like DHE and the original brightness had been maintained by normalizing the output intensity. Experimental results proved that BPDHE was better than both MPHEBP and DHE. But, the main demerits of the methods such as BPDHE are finding of proper filter size for smoothing of histogram and computation of maximums and minimums of the different histograms as derivative based methods produces several stray signs which are problematic for finding the actual number of maximums or minimums. Zuo et. al. proposed one HE variant using Otsu method for segmentation rather than mean or median of the image found better results over BBHE, DSIHE and MMBEBHE (Zuo, C., Chen, Q. Sui, X. (2013)). Entropy and Otsu based segmentation technique had been applied for better brightness prerserving enhancement field and entropy based method outperformed Otsu based method (Dhal, K. G., Das, S. (2017), Dhal, K. G., Sen, S., Sarkar, K. Das, S. (2016), Dhal, K. G., Das, S. (2017), Dhal, K. G., Sen, M., Das, S.(2017)). Therefore, from the above discussion, it can be said that proper segmentation and multi-separation significantly helps to produce the better enhanced image. In this study, one novel HE variant called Multi-thresholded Histogram Equalization (MTHE), depending on entropy based multi-level thresholding based segmentation. But, due to multithresholding, computational time of such types of HE variants increases. In order to overcome that problem with MTHE, one novel parameterless or parameterfree Artificial Bee Colony (ABC) algorithm is employed for finding the proper thresholds points. There is no human interaction needed to update the associated control parameters of the proposed ABC algorithm. Experimental results prove that the proposed MTHE outperforms the several existing HE variants in brightness preserving image enhancement domain and proposed ABC gives a better result with compare to a classical method and traditional ABC algorithm with respect to speed, robustness, and accuracy.

PROPOSED MULTI-THRESHOLDED HISTOGRAM EQUALIZATION (MTHE)

The proposed method has been developed based on entropy based multithresholding technique as it outperforms Otsu method in brightness preserving image enhancement field (Dhal, K. G., Das, S. (2017), Dhal, K. G., Sen, S., Sarkar, K. Das, S. (2016)). The methodology is discussed below.

Multi- Level Entropy Based Segmentation

Let $P = \left(p_1, p_2, p_3, \dots\dots\dots, p_n \right) \in \Delta_n$ where

$$\Delta_n = \left\{ \left(p_1, p_2, \dots\dots\dots, p_n \right) \mid p_i \geq 0, i = 1, 2, \dots\dots, n, n \geq 2, \sum_{i=1}^{n} p_i = 1 \right\}$$

is a set of discrete finite n n-ary probability distributions. Then entropy of the total image can be defined as (Sarkar, S., Paul, S., Burman, R., Das, S., Chaudhuri, S.S. (2015)):

$$H\left(P \right) = -\sum_{i=1}^{n} p_i log_2 p_i \tag{6}$$

i denote a 8 bit gray level digital image of dimension $M \times N$. P is the normalized histogram for image with $L = 256$ gray levels. Now, if there are $n - 1$ thresholds $\left(t \right)$, partitioning the normalized histogram into n classes, then the entropy for each class may be computed as,

$$H_1\left(t\right) = -\sum_{i=0}^{t_1} \frac{p_i}{P_1} \ln \frac{p_i}{P_1},$$

$$H_2\left(t\right) = -\sum_{i=t_1+1}^{t_2} \frac{p_i}{P_2} \ln \frac{p_i}{P_2},$$

$$H_n\left(t\right) = -\sum_{i=t_{n-1}+1}^{L-1} \frac{p_i}{P_n} \ln \frac{p_i}{P_n}. \tag{7}$$

Where,

$$P_1\left(t\right) = \sum_{i=0}^{t_1} p_i, P_2\left(t\right) = \sum_{i=t_1+1}^{t_2} p_i, \ldots\ldots\ldots, P_n\left(t\right) = -\sum_{i=t_{n-1}+1}^{L-1} p_i \tag{8}$$

Where, For ease of computation two dummy thresholds $t_0 = 0, t_n = L-1$ are introduced with $t_0 < t_1 < \ldots < t_{n-1} < t_n$. Then the optimum threshold value can be found by

$$\varphi\left(t_1, t_2, \ldots\ldots, t_n\right) = Arg\, max\left(\left[H_1\left(t\right) + H_2\left(t\right) + \ldots + H_n\left(t\right)\right]\right) \tag{9}$$

This maximization problem has been solved by employing one modified ABC algorithm here.

The procedure of the propose MTHE is as follows:

Step 1: Divide the histogram into several parts by using entropy based multi-thresholding method. Suppose, the optimal threshold points are $t_1, t_2, \ldots\ldots, t_{n-1}$.

Step 2: Then equalize each part individually by the following rule:

$$f^1\left(X\right) = X_0 + \left(t_1 - X_0\right) CDF_{X_0}^{t_1}\left(X\right),$$

$$f^2\left(X\right) = \left(t_1 + 1\right) + \left(t_2 - \left(t_1 + 1\right)\right) CDF_{(t_1+1)}^{t_2}\left(X\right),$$

$$f^n\left(X\right) = \left(t_{n-1} + 1\right) + \left(X_{L-1} - \left(t_{n-1} + 1\right)\right) CDF_{(t_{n-1}+1)}^{X_{L-1}}\left(X\right). \tag{10}$$

Step 3: Then unite all parts for the output image: $f^o = f^1 \cup f^2 \cup .... \cup f^n$.

Step 4: Normalize the image brightness:

Suppose the mean brightness of the input and output images are respectively M_i and M_o. To maintain the original brightness of the image normalization has been done by the following rule:

$$g(x, y) = \frac{M_i}{M_o} \times f(x, y) \tag{11}$$

Where, $f(x, y)$ and $g(x, y)$ are the input and output images respectively. This normalization step helps greatly to maintain the original brightness of the image.

Therefore, the key step of the proposed method is finding the proper threshold points within less computational time which also increases the efficicency and reduces the computational time of the proposed MTHE. In order to find out the threshold points in less time, one novel parameterless Artificial Bee Colony (ABC) algorithm has been developed which is discussed below.

PROPOSED PARAMETERLESS ABC (PLABC) ALGORITHM:

Recently, several nature inspired metaheuristic algorithms such as Cuckoo Search (CS) (Dhal, K. G., Sen, M., Das, S.(2017), Dhal, K. G., Das, S. (2017), 20], Firefly Algorithm (FA) (Dhal, K.G, Quraishi, I. M., Das, S.(2015), Dhal, K.G, Quraishi, I. M., Das, S. (2015)), Particle swarm Optimization (PSO) (Shanmugavadivu, P., Balasubramanian, K., Muruganandam, A. (2014), Gorai, A., Ghosh, A. (2009), Quraishi, I. M., Dhal, K.G, Paul Chowdhury, J., Pattanayak, K., De, M., (2012), Dhal, K, G., Namtirtha, A., Quraishi, I. M., Das, S. (2016)), Genetic Algortihm (GA) (Quraishi, I. M., De, M., Dhal, K.G, Mondal, S., Das, G., (2013), Hashemi, S., Kiani, S., Noroozi, N., Moghaddam, M. E. (2010)), Differential Evolution (DE) (Coelho, L. D. S., Sauer, J.G., Rudek, M. (2009), Dhal, K.G, Quraishi, I. M., Das, S. (2015)), Bat Algorithm (BA) (Dhal, K.G, Quraishi, I. M., Das, S. (2015), Dhal, K.G, Quraishi, I. M., Das, S. (2015)), Artificial Bee Colony (ABC) (Dhal, K., G., Das, S (2015)) and their modified versions are widely applied in image enhancement field and prove their efficiency. In this study, one parameterless ABC algorithm is developed which is the extended version of the one modified ABC algorithm applied by Dhal. et. al. (Dhal, K., G., Das, S (2015)). The traditional ABC algorithm (Dhal, K., G., Das, S (2015)) associated with few parameters and the finding of proper combination of the parameter values is time consuming. That's why a parameter free or parameter less variant has been proposed here which does not need any control over parameters.

Chaotic Sequence

Recently, chaotic sequence has been incorporated with nature inspired algorithms to enhance their capability (Dhal, K.G, Quraishi, I. M., Das, S.(2015), Dhal, K., G., Das, S (2015), Leandro, C., S., d., Viviana, C., M. (2009), Sheikholeslami, R., Kaveh, A. (2013), Coelho, L. d. S., Mariani, V. C. (2008)). Chaotic sequences are used in metaheuristic algorithms for three purposes 1. To generate random numbers 2.To generate inertia weight 3. To perform the local search. In this study the chaotic sequence has been successfully applied to update the mutation factor and crossover rate of the DE algorithm which are responsible for controlling the trade-off between exploration and exploitation. There are several chaotic generators like logistic map, tent map, gauss map, sinusoidal iterator, lozi map, chua's oscillator etc (Caponetto, R., Fortuna, L., Fazzino, S., Xibilia, M., G. (2003)). Among those logistic equation is used in this paper as it carries greater variance and outperforms others (Dhal, K.G, Quraishi, I. M., Das, S. (2017), Dhal, K., G., Das, S (2015)). The equation of logistic map is given below:

$$L_{m+1} = aL_m \left(1 - L_m\right) \tag{12}$$

a is a control parameter and $0 < a \leq 4$, L_m is the chaotic value at mth iteration. The behavior of the system mostly depends on the variation of a. Value of a is set to 4 and L_0 does not belong to $\{0, 0.25, 0.5, 0.75, 1\}$ otherwise the logistic equation does not show chaotic behavior (Coelho, L. D. S., Sauer, J.G., Rudek, M. (2009)).

Initial Population Generation

The initial population is usually created randomly. The equation of standard method is given below:

$$x_i = low + \left(up - low\right) \times \partial \tag{13}$$

x_i is the ith individual. up $\& low$ are the upper and lower bound of the search space of objective function. ∂ is the random variable that belongs to [0,1].

If the initial population carries a great variance then it helps to restrict the premature convergence of the algorithm. Average population diversity is good when ∂ is generated using logistic equation (Dhal, K.G, Quraishi, I. M., Das, S. (2017), Dhal, K., G., Das, S (2015)). In this study, logistic equation based initial population has been used.

Depending on the chaotic sequence the pseudocode of the proposed ABC is as follows:

Step 1: An objective function has been taken as Equation (9).

Step 2: Initialize Bee colony $X = \{X_i | i = 1, 2, 3, \ldots n\}$ by using logistic map based chaotic generator. where n is the number of bees or population size, and X_i is the ith bee. Here n=100.

Step 3: Each employed bee produces a new solution X_i^{t+1} in the neighbourhood by the equation given below:

$$X_i^{t+1} = X_i^t + \left(X_i^t - X_k\right) \times sign\left(rand - 0.5\right).L_m \tag{14}$$

Where, i and k are near to each other, but i ≠ k.

Step 4: Using fitness function calculate fitness (fit_i) of each solution i.

Step 5: Use the greedy criterion to update the solution.

$$if \ (fit_i^{t+1}\left(X_i\right) > fit_i^t\left(X_i\right))$$

then replaces the previous solution by new one.

Otherwise remains same

Step 6: Find the probability p_i of each X_i as follows

$$p_i = fit_i / MAX\left(fit^t\right) \tag{15}$$

fit_i is the fitness value of ith bee at t^{th} iteration. $MAX\left(fit^t\right)$ is the maximum fitness value at t^{th} iteration. So, $0 \le p_i \le 1$.

Step 7: Depending on the value of p_i and threshold the set of X_i is divided into $P_{onlooker}$ and P_{scout} sets.

$$if\left(P_i \geq 0.7\right) then\, X_i \in P_{onlooker}$$

$$otherwise\, X_i \in P_{scout}$$

Threshold value is set from experience for multi-thresholding problem.

Step 8: Onlooker bees process the set $P_{onlooker}$ by the following equation:

$$X_i^{t+1} = X_i^t + \left(X_i^t - X_k\right) \times L_m \tag{16}$$

Where, i and k are near to each other, but $i \neq k$ and X_i, $X_k \in P_{onlooker}$

Step 9: P_{scout} set is process by the following equation:

$$X_i^{t+1} = X_i^t + \left(max - min\right) \times L_m \tag{17}$$

max and min are the parameter value of most fittest and less fittest solution respectively.

Step 10: Find the current best and visualize the result.

Stopping Conditions

Find the optimal stopping condition is a challenging matter. It has been chosen experimentally. It stopping conditions are:

1. When the fitness value of the global best solution does not change for continuous 20 iterations for a specific image.
2. But the maximum limit of iterations number is 500 to find the optimal parameters.

EXPERIMENTAL RESULTS

The experiment has been performed over 40 histopathological images with MatlabR2012b with x64-based PC, Intel(R) Core(TM) i3-CPU with 4 GB RAM. Performance of proposed method is tested with the help of two well-known image quality assessment matrices such as Absolute mean brightness error (AMBE) (Dhal, K.G, Quraishi, I. M., Das, S. (2017)), Quality Index based on Local Variance (QILV)

(Dhal, K. G., Das, S. (2017), Dhal, K. G., Sen, M., Das, S.(2017), Dhal, K. G., Das, S. (2017)). The performance of the PLABC and traditional ABC are evaluated in terms of Mean Computational time (MCT), Mean Fitness value (Fit_m) and Standard Deviation (Fit_{std}) over 40 images which are given in Table 1. PLABC proves that it has a better convergence rate with the better ability of finding global optima within less computational time compares to traditional ABC.

Figure 1 represents the histopathological images and their histograms indicating the threshold points which are found by employing MTHE with 3-level Entropy based thresholding. Figure 3 and 4 represent the enhanced images finding by employing different methods such as HE (R.C.Gonzalez, R.E.Woods (2002)), BBHE (Kim, Y.T. (1997)), DSIHE (Chen, S. D., Ramli, A. R. (2004)), MMBEBHE (Chen, S. D., Ramli, A. R. (2003)), RMSHE with recursion level 3 (Chen, S. D., Ramli, A. R. (2003)), RLBHE (Zuo, C., Chen, Q. Sui, X. (2013)) and proposed MTHE with 3-level thresholding. Visual analysis of Figure 3 and 4 reveal that proper enhancement occurs when MTHE applied over histopathological images. In the most of the application, 3 level thresholding has been applied. The level of thresholding depends on image and therefore it is user defined. MMBEHE also gives better result compares to BBHE, DSIHE etc. Table 2 demonstrates the comparison among two well-known quality metrics such as QILV and AMBE. Lower AMBE and higher QILV represent better quality image. Therefore statistical analysis of Table 2 also proves that MTHE is the best for producing the proper enhanced images.

Table 1. Comparison of mean computational time (MCT), Mean Fitness value (Fit_m) and Standard Deviation (Fit_{std}) between Parameterless ABC (PLABC) and traditional ABC (TABC)

Image		2-level thresholding		3-level thresholding		4-level thresholding	
		PLABC	**TABC**	**PLABC**	**TABC**	**PLABC**	**TABC**
Average Over 40 images	*MCT*	**0.6573 sec**	0.8877 sec	**0.8512 sec**	1.1401 sec	**1.7832 sec**	2.5642 sec
	Fit_m	**17.8603**	17.8557	**22.6857**	22.1211	**26.9520**	26.8562
	Fit_{std}	**0**	1.012e-14	**0**	0.001	**2.003e-13**	0.002

Table 2. Comparison of average quality metrics over 40 images

Parameters	HE	BBHE	DSIHE	MMBEBHE	RMSHE	RLBHE	MTHE
Avg. AMBE	45.58	20.96	27.46	1.42	13.73	7.45	**1.34**
Avg. QILV	0.6636	0.8212	0.7993	0.9504	0.8760	0.9506	**0.9714**

Figure 1. Original histopathological images and their histogram with 3-level thresholding points finding by PLABC with entropy as objective function

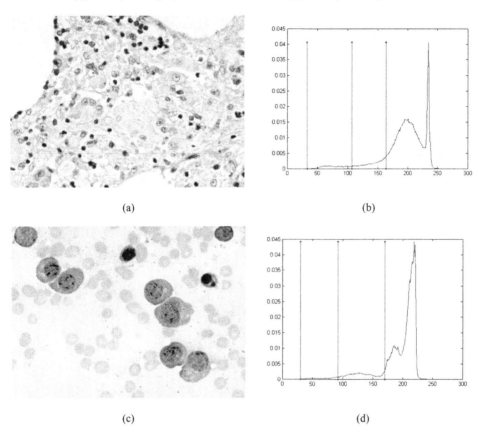

(a) (b)

(c) (d)

In this study, proposed grey level image enhancement methodology i.e. MTHE is also applied in color image enhancement domain. Chien et.al. proposed exact Hue-Saturation-Intensity (eHSI) model to enhance the color images (Chien, C. L., Tseng, D. C. (2011), Chien, C. L., Tsai, W. H. (2014)). Any gray level contrast enhancement method can be successfully employed for color image by using eHSI model. eHSI model is a hue preserving model which has the capability to resolve the out-of-gamut problem i.e. the pixel values of output RGB image always lie within their respective intervals. The color enhanced images using MTHE with eHSI are given as Figure 4.

Figure 2. Enhanced image of figure 1(a) by different methods (a) HE (b) BBHE (c) DSIHE (d) MMBEBHE (e) RMSHE (f) RLBHE (g) MTHE with 3-level thresholding

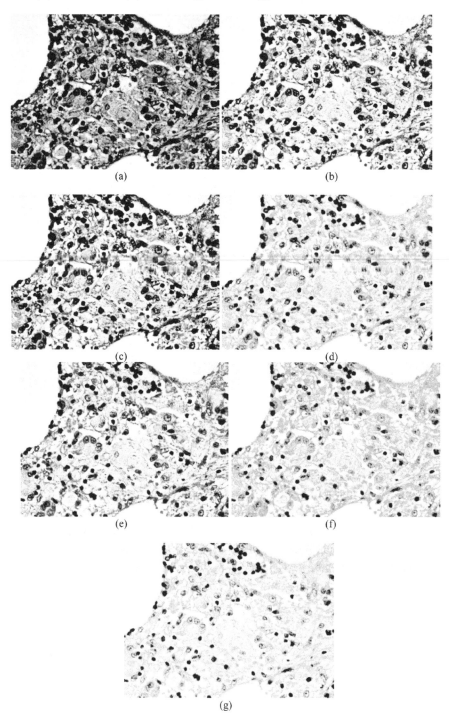

Figure 3. Enhanced image of figure 1(b) by different methods (a) HE (b) BBHE (c) DSIHE (d) MMBEBHE (e) RMSHE (f) RLBHE (g) MTHE with 3-level thresholding

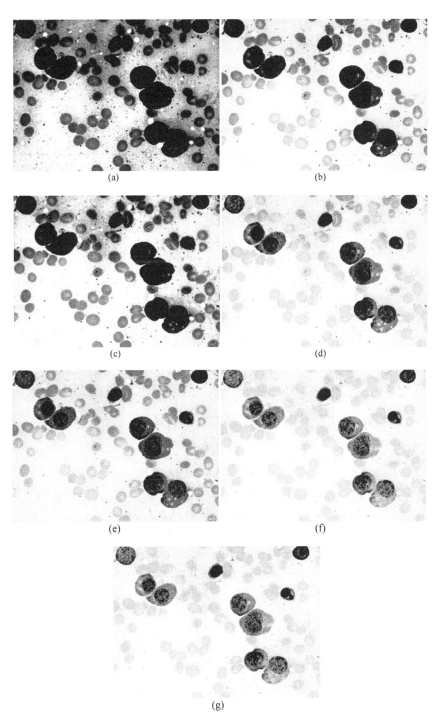

Figure 4. (a) and (c) are the original images, (b) and (d) are the enhanced images using MTHE with eHSI

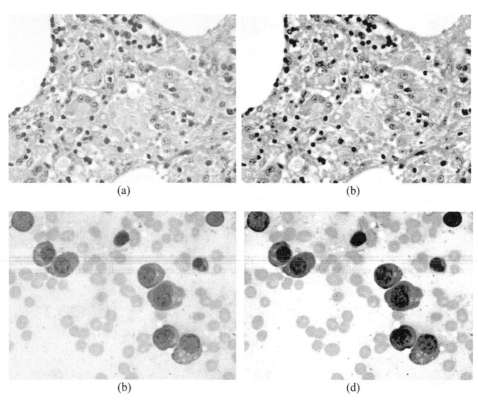

(a) (b)

(b) (d)

*For a more accurate representation see the electronic version.

CONCLUSION

In this paper, one multi-thresholoded Histogram Equalization (MTHE) has been proposed depending on the efficiency of entropic multi-thresholding based segmentation. It is proved here that entropy based multi-separartion of the histogram helps to produce better enhanced grey level images as well as color histopathological images. Visual analysis and values of the quality parameters prove that proposed MTHE significantly performed very well compares to the existing variants of HE. The only problem with the MTHE is the selection of number of threshold level. In the most of histopathological images, 3-level thresholding is sufficient for producing better quality images. To reduce the computational time of multi-thresholding as well as MTHE, one parameterless ABC (PLABC) algorithm has been employed based on chaotic sequence for finding the optimal threshold values. Experimental results state that PLABC has a better convergence rate with the better ability of finding global optima within less computational time compares to traditional ABC. In future, PLABC based image multithresholding model and enhancement could be applied in other kind of image processing domains.

REFERENCES

Abdullah-Al-Wadud, M., Kabir, M. H., Dewan, M. A. A., & Chae, O. (2007). A dynamic histogram equalization for image contrast enhancement. *IEEE Transactions on Consumer Electronics*, *53*(2), 593–600. doi:10.1109/TCE.2007.381734

Caponetto, R., Fortuna, L., Fazzino, S., & Xibilia, M. G. (2003). Chaotic Sequences to Improve the Performance of Evolutionary Algorithms. *IEEE Transactions on Evolutionary Computation*, *7*(3), 289–304. doi:10.1109/TEVC.2003.810069

Chen, S. D., & Ramli, A. R. (2003). Minimum Mean Brightness Error Bi-Histogram Equalization in Contrast Enhancement. *IEEE Transactions on Consumer Electronics*, *49*(4), 1310–1319. doi:10.1109/TCE.2003.1261234

Chen, S. D., & Ramli, A. R. (2003). *Contrast Enhancement using Recursive Mean Separated Histogram Equalization for Scalable Brightness Preservation*. Academic Press.

Chen, S. D., & Ramli, A. R. (2004). Preserving Brightness in histogram equalization based contrast enhancement techniques. *Digital Signal Processing*, *14*(5), 413–428. doi:10.1016/j.dsp.2004.04.001

Cheng, H. D., & Shi, J. (2004). A simple and effective histogram equalization approach to image enhancement. *Digital Signal Processing*, *14*(2), 158–170. doi:10.1016/j.dsp.2003.07.002

Coelho, L. D. S., Sauer, J. G., & Rudek, M. (2009). Differential evolution optimization combined with chaotic sequences for image contrast enhancement. *Chaos, Solitons, and Fractals*, *42*(1), 522–529. doi:10.1016/j.chaos.2009.01.012

Coelho, L. S., & Mariani, V. C. (2008). Use of chaotic sequences in a biologically inspired algorithm for engineering design optimization. *Expert Systems with Applications*, *34*(3), 1905–1913. doi:10.1016/j.eswa.2007.02.002

Dhal, K., G., & Das, S (2015). Diversity Conserved Chaotic Artificial Bee Colony Algorithm based Brightness Preserved Histogram Equalization and Contrast Stretching Method. *International Journal of Natural Computing Research*, *5*, 45-73.

Dhal, K. G., & Das, S. (2017). Combination of histogram segmentation and modification to preserve the original brightness of the image. *Pattern Recognition and Image Analysis, 27*(2), 200-212.

Dhal, K. G., & Das, S. (2017):Colour Retinal images enhancement using Modified Histogram Equalization methods and Firefly Algorithm, Int. Jr. of Biomedical Engineering and Technology (InderScience Publication), (in publication house).

Dhal, K. G., & Das, S. (2017). Cuckoo search with search strategies and proper objective function for brightness preserving image enhancement. *Pattern Recognition and Image Analysis.*

Dhal, K. G., Namtirtha, A., Quraishi, I. M., & Das, S. (2016). Grey level image enhancement using Particle Swarm Optimization with Levy Flight: An Eagle Strategy Approach. *Int. Conf. on Emerging Trends in Computer Sc. And Information* (ETCSIT-2015).

Dhal, K.G, Quraishi, I. M., & Das, S, (2015)·Performance Analysis of Chaotic Lévy Bat Algorithm and Chaotic Cuckoo Search Algorithm for Gray Level Image Enhancement. *Information Systems Design and Intelligent Applications*, 233-244.

Dhal, K. G., Quraishi, I. M., & Das, S. (2015). Development of firefly algorithm via chaotic sequence and population diversity to enhance the image contrast. In Natural Computing (Vol. 14, pp. 1–12). Academic Press.

Dhal, K. G., Quraishi, I. M., & Das, S. (2015). *A Chaotic Lévy flight Approach in Bat and Firefly Algorithm for Gray level image Enhancement. I.J. Image, Graphics and Signal Processing*, 7, 69–76.

Dhal, K.G, Quraishi, I. M., & Das, S. (2015). Performance Enhancement of Differential Evolution by Incorporating Lévy Flight and Chaotic Sequence for the Cases of Satellite Images. *Int. J. of Applied Metaheuristic Computing, 6*, 69-81.

Dhal, K.G, Quraishi, I. M., & Das, S. (2017). An improved cuckoo search based optimal ranged brightness preserved histogram equalization and contrast stretching method. *Int. Jr. of Swarm intelligence Research, 8*, 1-29.

Dhal, K. G., Sen, M., & Das, S. (2017). Cuckoo search based modified Bi-Histogram Equalization method to enhance the cancerous tissues in Mammography images. *International Journal of Medical Engineering and Informatics.*

Dhal, K. G., Sen, S., Sarkar, K., & Das, S. (2016). *Entropy based range optimized brightness preserved histogram equalization for image contrast enhancement* (Vol. 6). Int. Jr. of Computer Vision and Image Processing.

Gonzalez, R. C., & Woods, R. E. (2002). *Digital Image Processing* (2nd ed.). New York: Prentice Hall.

Gorai, A., & Ghosh, A. (2009). Gray-level Image Enhancement By Particle Swarm Optimization. *Proceedings of World Congress on Nature & Biologically Inspired Computing.* doi:10.1109/NABIC.2009.5393603

Hashemi, S., Kiani, S., Noroozi, N., & Moghaddam, M. E. (2010). An image contrast enhancement method based on genetic algorithm. *Pattern Recognition Letters*, *31*(13), 1816–1824. doi:10.1016/j.patrec.2009.12.006

Ibrahim, H., & Kong, N.S.P. (2007). Brightness Preserving Dynamic Histogram Equalization for Image Contrast Enhancement. *IEEE Transactions on Consumer Electronics, 53*(4), 1752-1758.

Kim, Y.T. (1997). Contrast enhancement using brightness preserving bi-histogram equalization. *IEEE Trans. Consum. Electron, 43*(1), 1–8.

Leandro, C. (2009). A novel particle swarm optimization approach using Henon map and implicit filtering local search for economic load dispatch. *Chaos, Solitons, and Fractals*, *39*(2), 510–518. doi:10.1016/j.chaos.2007.01.093

Quraishi, I. M., De, M., Dhal, K.G, Mondal, S., & Das, G. (2013). *Novel hybrid approach to restore historical degraded documents.* IEEE. DOI: 10.1109/ISSP.2013.6526899

Quraishi, I. M., Dhal, K.G, Paul Chowdhury, J., Pattanayak, K., & De, M., (2012). *A novel hybrid approach to enhance low resolution images using particle swarm optimization.* IEEE. DOI: 10.1109/PDGC.2012.6449941

Sarkar, S., Paul, S., Burman, R., Das, S., & Chaudhuri, S. S. (2015). A Fuzzy Entropy Based Multi-Level Image Thresholding Using Differential Evolution. *SEMCCO*, *2014*, 386–395.

Shanmugavadivu, P., Balasubramanian, K., & Muruganandam, A. (2014). Particle swarm optimized bi-histogram equalization for contrast enhancement and brightness preservation of images. *The Visual Computer*, *30*(4), 387–399. doi:10.1007/s00371-013-0863-8

Sheikholeslami, R., & Kaveh, A. (2013). A Survey of Chaos Embedded Meta-Heuristic Algorithms. Int. J. Optim. Civil. *Eng., 3*(4), 617–633.

Sim, K. S., Tso, C. P., & Tan, Y. Y. (2007). Recursive sub-image histogram equalization applied to gray scale image. *Pattern Recognition Letter, 28*, 1209-1221.

Wongsritong, K., Kittayaruasiriwat, K., Cheevasuvit, F., Dejhan, K., & Somboonkaew, A. (1998). Contrast enhancement using multipeak histogram equalization with brightness preserving. *Circuit and System, 1998, IEEE APCCAS 1998, the 1998 IEEE Asia-Pacific Conference on*, 455-458. doi:10.1109/APCCAS.1998.743808

Zuo, C., Chen, Q. & Sui, X. (2013). Range limited Bi-Histogram Equalization for image contrast enhancement. *Optik, 124*, 425-431.

KEY TERMS AND DEFINITIONS

Chaotic Sequence: Chaos defines the complex behavior of non-linear deterministic system which has ergodicity property.

Gamut Problem: The pixels values of the channels of the color space do not lie within their respective intervals.

Hue: Hue represents the kind of color (i.e., the dominant wavelength that exists in a mixture of colors).

Image Enhancement: Image enhancement is the technique of transforming one image into a better quality image according to the requirements.

Segmentation: Image segmentation is a process that subdivides the image in the non-overlapping subset containing similar property, color, intensity, etc.

Chapter 5
Biogeographic Computation as Information Processing in Ecosystems

Rodrigo Pasti
Mackenzie University, Brazil

Alexandre Alberto Politi
Particular, Brazil

Fernando José Von Zuben
State University of Campinas (Unicamp), Brazil

Leandro Nunes de Castro
Mackenzie University, Brazil

ABSTRACT

Assuming nature can be investigated and understood as an information processing system, this chapter aims to explore this hypothesis in the field of ecosystems. Therefore, based on the concepts of biogeography, it further investigates a computational approach called biogeographic computation to the study of ecosystems. The original proposal in the literature is built from fundamental concepts of ecosystems and from a framework called a metamodel that allows the understanding of how information processing occurs. This chapter reproduces part of the content of the original proposal and extends and better formalizes the metamodel, including novel experimental results, particularly exploring the role of information and causality in ecosystems, both being considered essential aspects of ecosystems' evolution.

DOI: 10.4018/978-1-5225-5020-4.ch005

INTRODUCTION

The Natural Computing of Biogeography

By the 1940s Computer Science was engaged in the study of automatic computing. The necessary formalism for computability followed the initial achievements, with emphasis on information processing, Turing machines and computational complexity. Information processing has gained still more evidence in Computer Science lately, considering both natural and artificial processes (Denning P., 2008).

Indeed, information processes have been perceived in the essence of various phenomena in several fields of science. In the book *The Invisible Future* (Denning P. J., The Invisible Future: The Seamless Integration of Thecnology in Everyday Life, 2001), David Baltimore says "Biology is nowadays an information science". However, if computing is concerned with the study of information processing, in what sense nature processes information? A consistent definition is given by Seth Lloyd (Lloyd S., 2002): "all physical system registers information and, by evolving in time, operating in its context, changes information, transforms information or, if you prefer, processes information". Information here is interpreted as a measure of order, organization, a universal measure applicable to any structure, any system (Lloyd, 2006). Understanding nature as an information processing system is the fundamental basis of Natural Computing (de Castro, 2007). Several researchers, in many fields of science, have already studied nature in such context:

- *Immune systems* (Cohen, Real and artificial immune systems: computing the state of the body, Nature Reviews: Immunology, 2009; de Castro & Timmis, Artificial Immune Systems: A New Computational Intelligence Approach, 2002; Hart & Bersini, 2007);
- *Ecosystems* (de Aguiar, Barange, Baptestin, Kaufman, & Bar-Yam, 2009; Pasti, de Castro, & Von Zuben, 2011);
- *Bees* (Lihoreau, Chittka, & Raine, 2010; Maia & de Castro, 2012);
- *Ants* (Dorigo & Maniezzo, 1996; Pratt, Mallon, & Sumpter, 2002; Vittori, Talbot, & Gautrais, 2006);
- *Genes* (Holland, 2000; Kaufman & Ochumba, 1993);
- *Bacteria* (Mehta, Goyal, & Long, 2009; Xavier, Omar, & de Castro, 2011);
- *Basic laws of nature* (Dowek, 2012);
- *All universe* (Lloyd, 2006);
- Among many others, including (Brent & Bruck, 2006; Denning P. J., 2007; de Castro, 2007; Schwenk & Padilla, 2009).

Just as with biogeography, the object of study here are ecosystems: individuals, species and the environment. Ecosystems are highly complex and dynamic environments composed of a large number of interdependent variables defined in space and time (Harel, 2003; Jorgensen, Patten, & Stragkraba, 1992; Kauffman, 1996; Milne, 1998; Provata, Sokolov, & Spagnolo, 2008). They are usually studied by focusing on the interaction of their components, used to explain the emergence of behaviors (Cohen, 2000). The composition of ecosystems obeys physical and chemical laws, but there is no set of fundamental laws that explain how they work (Cohen & Harel, 2007). The application of reductionism for the understanding of how living systems work is widely used, but shows clear limitations when the goal is to extract universal laws to explain these systems (Cohen & Harel, 2007). It is possible to identify a scale of emergence going from simple molecules to a complex organism. Biogeography emphasizes the emergence of societies of living organisms (individuals and species), representing the highest level of Figure 1.

Starting from the premise that nature processes information, the main goal of this chapter is to further investigate ecosystem computing under the perspective of biogeography (Pasti, de Castro, & Von Zuben, 2011).

As a first step towards understanding ecosystem computing, (Pasti, de Castro, & Von Zuben, 2011) formalized the concept of a metamodel, that will be adopted here to demonstrate how information in ecosystems may promote causality. By the mathematical formalism of the metamodel, it will be possible to build dynamic models that represent the spatio-temporal evolution of ecosystems in discrete states, including adaptive radiation, in which biogeographic processes are responsible for state changes.

Figure 1. Emergence of behaviors and objects in different scales. (Based on the paper "Explaining a complex living system: dynamics, multi-scaling and emergence", by Irun R. Cohen, 2007.)

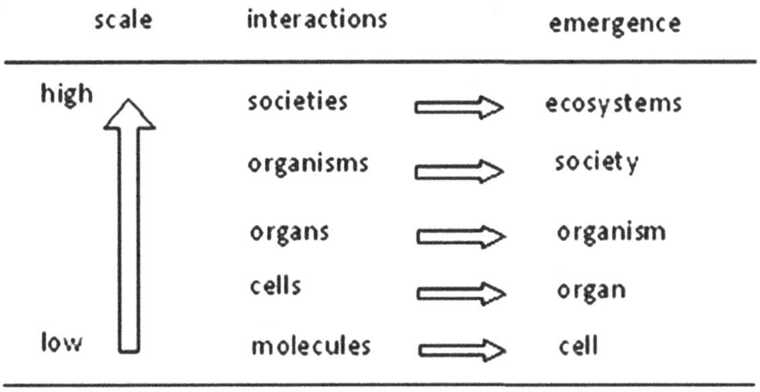

This chapter is organized as follows. Section 2 reviews some elementary concepts for the proposal of Biogeographic Computation and its metamodel. In Section 3, the definition of information in ecosystems is explored and Section 4 briefly revisits and further extends the metamodel. In Section 5, a metamodel application is exemplified by means of nature-inspired biogeographic patterns. After some concluding remarks, Section 6 has a brief discussion on the future perspectives of biogeographic computation.

FUNDAMENTALS OF ECOSYSTEMS AND BIOGEOGRAPHY

Living beings are highly multiform. The diversity of organisms on Earth is overwhelming. It is estimated that there are 50 million species on Earth, including animals, plants and microorganisms (Brown & Lomolino, 2006). In almost all regions of the planet, from the freezing deserts of the Arctic, going through the abyssal of oceans and achieving the hot and humid forests, it is possible to find a large variety of living systems. In all of them, they are adapted to the conditions imposed by the habitats. Heredity is an important aspect related to the diversity of living organisms, given that species often share extinct ancestors. A classic example cited by (Brown & Lomolino, 2006) is that all existing plant species share a common ancestor: green algae that lived approximately 500 million years ago. Therefore, it is possible to define a Biogeography Science, according to (Brown & Lomolino, 2006) Brown and Lomolino:

Biogeography is a science concerned with documenting and understanding special models of biodiversity. It is the study of the distribution of organisms, in the past and in the present, and of the variation patterns that occurred on Earth, related to the number and types of living beings.

The occurrence of patterns in nature implies the existence of some processes. Thus, there is a variation in space and time promoted by them. The abstractions of Biogeographic Computation reside in these patterns and processes.

ECOSYSTEMS

An ecosystem is a set of living beings, the environment that they inhabit and all interactions of these organisms with the environment and with each other. A forest, a river, a lake, a garden and the biosphere are all examples of an ecosystem. The ecosystems present three basic components: the communities of individuals and species (*biota* or *ecological community*); the physical or chemical elements of the environment, and the geographical space (*habitat*). Elements that compose all ecosystems are the *ecological niches* that describe the relational position of a species or population in its ecosystem, defining the way of life of any organism (Brown & Lomolino, 2006). The niches provide answers to the interactions of organisms among each other and with the environment, as in cases of competition by resources or predator-prey interactions (Schoener, 1991). In summary, there are some important concepts to be introduced:

- **Adaptation:** It is intimately related to natural selection, because it complements the notion of graded improvement. The adaptation level to the environment is what determines the path to be followed by natural selection: a response to the selection always occurs when a heritable feature is related with reproductive success; the outcome is an improvement in performance through cumulative generations of reproduction and differentiation.
- **Biological Isolation:** It influences the reproductive capability between two individuals. If there is an isolation, then two individuals cannot reproduce.
- **Ecological Barrier:** It includes any means that prevent a given species from occupying a new habitat; when a species leaves its habitat, its adaptable features may not be sufficient for the survival in the new environment.
- **Geographical Isolation:** It occurs among two or more individuals and species when there are ecological barriers that severely restrict their contact.

There is no consensus on the definition of species (Brown & Lomolino, 2006). In the present chapter, species will be treated in a specific manner, related to the concept of a biological species, which defines a species as a population of organisms that present biological isolation in relation to other populations, thus representing a separate evolutionary lineage (Brown & Lomolino, 2006; Coyne & Orr, 1999). The crossing between species that generated individuals with biological isolation may lead to the emergence of hybrid species.

PROCESSES IN BIOGEOGRAPHY

The biogeographical processes explain geographical, ecological and evolutionary patterns, with the goal of describing and understanding how species occupy habitats, migrate, emerge, disappear, procreate, differentiate and adapt, from the simplest to the most complex ecosystem. All processes are well described and consolidated in the literature (Brown & Lomolino, 2006; Ridley, 2004; Coyne & Orr, 1999;

Rosenzweig, 1995; Myers & Giller, 1991; Hengeveld, 1990; Simmons, 1982) . The processes can be classified based on their type:

- **Geographical Processes:** Related to the Earth surface and spatial distribution of significant phenomena for ecosystems. This includes climate, tectonic and all other phenomena related to environmental changes.
- **Ecological Processes:** Directly related to individuals and species, such as dispersion and interactions.
- **Evolutionary Processes:** Related to the evolution of individuals and species. They can be divided into macro and microevolution.

Basically, the goal is to explain a wide range of spatio-temporal events in an ecosystem. A single species can explore a whole ecosystem, transposing ecological barriers, evolving and giving origin to various descending species that can become completely different genetically from the ancestor species. When expanding its coverage, a species may or may not adapt itself to new environments. If adaptation is necessary, there are several evolutionary processes that lead to an improvement in adaptation. If adaptation is not sufficient, or does not occur at all, a species tends to become extinct. Biogeographical processes are the ones responsible for the theory that explains the diversity of species in space and time, including inter and intraspecific diversity. Thus, it is important not only to understand how the diversity of species emerge, but also how individual diversity can lead to species diversity (Coyne & Orr, 1999; Magurran, 1999). Essentially, it is possible to emphasize the following biogeographical processes:

Geographical Process

- **Environmental Changes:** Includes all processes related to the transformation in geographic spaces and habitats. It can give rise to a series of natural patterns responsible for a great variety of habitats over time. In this context, it is possible to emphasize *vicariance*, which is responsible for habitat fragmentation and the appearance of ecological barriers. For instance, the emergence of an island or the establishment of a terrestrial connection between two pieces of land previously disconnected (Brown & Lomolino, 2006).

Ecological Process

- **Dispersion:** Deals with the displacement of individuals and species throughout the geographical space. Dispersion can be the source of various emergent patterns. Diffusion involves the gradual spread of individuals and species outside their habitats through dispersion. It is a three-stage process: 1) repeated dispersion events that promote the occupation of novel habitats; 2) the establishment, through adaptation, in new environments; and 3) the composition of new populations that can give origin to new species. This process can be viewed as the beginning of dispersion. The definition of dispersion and diffusion gives rise to dispersion routes (Brown & Lomolino, 2006), which correspond to types of habitats in which species can disperse based on their adaptation. There are three dispersion routes: 1) corridors: allow individuals and species to migrate from an original habitat to another without imposing limiting factors; populations remain with a balanced number of individuals; 2) filters: these are dispersion routes more restrictive than corridors; they selectively block the passage of individuals based on their adaptations, as a result, colonizers tend to represent a single subset of their initial population; 3) sweeptake routes: these are rare dispersions, constituting a specific case of filters; a classic example is the colonization of isolated ocean islands. Additionally, when a migratory population fixes on a distant habitat, sufficient to maintain isolation from the other individuals of their species, the result is the founder effect.

Microevolutionary Processes

- **Natural Selection:** The selection of individuals and features favorable to the species. Favorable features that are inherited become more common in successive generations of a population of organisms that reproduce. The natural selection process is responsible for many patterns of evolution that can be found in nature. In a broad sense, it can be considered the force that models the evolutionary dynamics of the biotic components in ecosystems. Obviously, natural selection is a process that depends on many variables and their interaction along time. It is possible to highlight the selective pressure effect, which dictates the survival of a phenotype or genotype in a population. When the selective pressure is intense to the point of considerably reducing the number of individuals in a species along generations, the result is the well-known bottleneck effect.
- **Mutation:** It is defined as any modification in the genetic material of an organism, including the altering, deletion or insertion of a single or many DNA nucleotides, and even a complete rearrangement of a chromosome.
- **Reproduction:** Two individuals, that are not biologically isolated, can reproduce sexually to generate new individuals through their parents' DNA. The individuals that migrate to a new area carry their genes with them and, if they reproduce, they introduce their genes in the local population, promoting the gene or phenotype flow. Reproduction can also occur asexually; that is, without an intercourse and, thus, without the exchange of genetic material.

Macroevolutionary Processes

- **Peripatric Speciation:** It is the simplest and most common speciation process. It occurs when the populations are geographically isolated, such that the gene flow between them is almost completely interrupted. The causes of this type of speciation include the founder effect, by which a population, initially composed of a few colonizer individuals, contains just a small random sample of the alleles present in the ancestor population.
- **Sympatric Speciation:** It occurs due to chromosomal and mutation changes. During fertilization or the developmental process of the embryo, there is a chance that a rearrangement of the genetic material occurs. Individuals that suffered sympatric speciation are mutants in relation to their parents. These new individuals may generate a new species or may still belong to an existing hybrid species.
- **Competitive (or Parapatric) Speciation:** It is the expansion of a species from a single to multiple habitats. When the original species is separated in subgroups, some of them explore the original habitat and the others the new ones. When two or more habitats are occupied, the subgroups tend to diverge after some time, due to the establishment of biological isolation from the ancestor species.
- **Species Extinction:** The differential survival and the proliferation of species in geological time are determined by analogy with the differential survival and reproduction of individuals. Species or groups of species may disappear.

INFORMATION IN ECOSYSTEMS

In Biogeographic Computation, the first step to define information in ecosystems is to contextualize the way information provides functionality. This premise is also present in artificial systems and a specific example is the task performed by a printer: it receives as input paper, ink, and a series of instructions that put it into operation. The printer processes the input through a variety of internal processes, and outputs a paper containing symbols. In other words, the printer has changed the state of matter by systematically applying ink to paper. The input information and its internal processes were causal elements for the printer to operate and produce output. An inspection in this whole process is intrinsically related to the fact that the printer is an artifact that operates in a well-defined functional context: the printing of documents. It was designed for this purpose, and is only in fact fully useful in this context.

In nature, organisms operate in their context without a definite purpose. Consider bacteria (Dyer, 2003) as a case study: they are prokaryote microorganisms that obtain energy and nutrients through metabolic processes. The byproduct of the metabolic processes keeps bacteria alive and functional, as well as changes its environment by eliminating waste products. See, for example, the case of heterotrophic bacteria, such as the species Zymomonas mobilis (Swings & De Ley, 1977). This species processes the matter (molecules) receiving one element, sucrose, and producing two others, alcohol and carbon dioxide. The resulting products have modified the environment, and sucrose can be seen as a causal product for the bacteria. When defined by informational means, this scenario leads to a view that the bacteria are receiving input information that changes their internal state, inducing a series of elements to communicate and perform processing, ultimately producing output information. Thus, as in the case of the printer, matter and energy were the basis for input, processing and output. However, in the case of organisms, the context is emerging and linked to the organism itself, being an emerging product of the matter that composes it and having no definite objective. It is interesting to note that matter and energy continue to give functionality to the system, and if matter and energy are defined as information, then information in nature provides functionality to the organism and changes its state. The same can be verified on an emergency scale above, where societies of living beings emerge. Elements of ecosystems, whether biotic or abiotic, interact by giving functionality to the system, where information plays a fundamental role in the causality of the process. This leads to the following definition:

Definition 1: *Information in ecosystem.* It consists of all elements in an ecosystem that promotes causality.

We may talk about a degree of causality, such that an element may be more or less causal according to the number of other elements it exerts a causal influence. If all elements interact with each other, then one can say that these elements constitute the maximum causality of the information. However, a situation in which some elements interact with only a subset of other elements may be interpreted as promoting a drop in the causality of the information.

INFORMATION PROCESSING IN ECOSYSTEMS BY MEANS OF THE BIOGEOGRAPHIC COMPUTATION METAMODEL

In ecosystems, information is processed and stored in a non-linear and massively parallel manner. Linear input-output behavior and well-defined causal effects are exceptions or even absent events in such systems (Walker & Davies, 2013). What is going to be processed depends not only on the response of a network of information processing elements, but also on the entire internal state of the system and its past states. Aiming at understanding the information processing in ecosystems, it is necessary to employ some type of representation that expresses computationally the existence of such ecosystems and the computation involved. Biogeographic computation models aim to represent ecosystems' elements and to explain how they are interacting and processing information. Therefore, the objects of study of biogeographic computation are computational ecosystems.

Computational ecosystems are abstract universes consisting of basic elements represented by mathematical definitions. Which elements are contained in these ecosystems depends on the computing one wants to reproduce. Formally, defining a computational ecosystem is not an easy task, but one thing is clear: it is possible to describe and manipulate it arbitrarily. The crucial and most important aspect of biogeographic computation is the freedom to manipulate a computational ecosystem. The starting point for this is the definition of the metamodel, which represents an abstract definition of the ecosystem and its biogeographical processes. The metamodel allows the conception of highly complex scenarios, like those found in natural ecosystems. In what follows, we are going to reproduce and further extend the formalism previously proposed in (Pasti, de Castro, & Von Zuben, 2011).

Definitions That Characterize a Computational Ecosystem

In the metamodel, there are three main components that represent an ecosystem: 1) the representational space of the biota elements; 2) the geographical space; 3) and the set of relations. The biota and the geographical space have elements defined in a representational space. On the other hand, relations define how elements of these spaces relate to each other.

Despite the broadness of these spaces, in practical implementations of biogeographic computation only a finite set of elements of the representational spaces will be part of the model. However, for every element considered, it should be possible to define all the relevant relationships that it could establish with other elements of the model.

Definition 2: *Ecosystem.* Defined as a 3-tuple $.E = I,H,R$, where I is the *Biota*, that is, the representational space of individuals; H is the geographical space; and R is the set of relations.

Definition 3: *Biota.* Representational space I that allows characterizing the individuals composing a biota. Consider p as the number of attributes that characterize each individual.

Definition 4: *Individual.* Every individual i_j I, $j=1,..., o$, is described by a set of p attributes.

Definition 5: *Geographical space.* Representational space H that allows characterizing the habitats that compose the geographical space; that is, an environment in which the biota inhabit. Consider r as the number of attributes that characterize each habitat.

Definition 6: *Habitat.* Each habitat h_t H, $t = 1,...,q$, is described by a set of r attributes.

From Definition 1, it is possible to conclude that in the metamodel, biota, individuals, geographical space and habitats represents the causal information of an ecosystem.

Definition 7: *Relations.* Each relation exclusively defines an interaction biota-biota, biota-habitat, or habitat-habitat; that is, a unique interaction of elements of I, or elements of I and H, or elements of H. Relations are directed, e.g., for two individuals, $i_j \rightarrow i_g$, or undirected, denoted by $i_j \leftrightarrow i_g$. They can be binary or take gradual values, e.g., over the interval $[0,1]$. Here are some simple examples, given an arbitrary relation ρ between individuals:

- $i_j \rightarrow i_g$. There is a relation ρ from i_j to i_g.

- $i_j \leftrightarrow i_g$. There is a relation ρ from i_j to i_g and from i_g to i_j (between i_j and i_g).

- $i_j \underline{\rightarrow} i_g$. There is no relation ρ from i_j to i_g.

- $i_j \underline{\leftrightarrow} i_g$. There is no relation ρ from i_j to i_g and from i_g to i_j (between i_j and i_g).

If the relations do not assume binary values, they are defined as follows: $i_j \overset{= x}{\rightarrow} i_g$. To synthesize the representation, it is possible to represent relations of multiple elements in a single expression. Here is an example considering an arbitrary relation ρ among 3 individuals: $\left\{ i_j, i_g \right\} \rightarrow i_t$.

The information about these relations depends on specific criteria relevant to the model. It is possible to use the relations as qualitative and/or quantitative measures of interactions. Relations have an additional effect and can determine if an information, represented by the elements of the ecosystem, is causal or not. For example, an individual can only be a source of causal information to other individuals if they all occupy the same habitat.

Therefore, eight relations are fundamental to the understanding of the metamodel, as follows:

Relation 1: *Habitat occupancy.* Defined as $_{HO}$, given an individual i_j and a habitat h_t , $_{HO}$ provides the relation of occupancy of i_j in h_t : $i_j \xrightarrow{HO} h_t$.

Relation 2: *Adaptation.* Defined as $_A$, given an individual i_j and a habitat h_t , $_A$ provides the adaptation relation of i_j in h_t , allowing to infer the degree of adaptation x of an individual i_j in the habitat h_t : $i_j \xrightarrow{A=x} h_t$.

Relation 3: *Biological isolation.* Defined as $_{BI}$, given two individuals $\{i_j, i_g\}$ I, the relation $_{BI}$ provides the reproduction capability between i_j and i_g . Two individuals can reproduce if and only if $i_j \xleftrightarrow{\overline{BI}} i_g$.

Relation 4: *Habitat neighborhood.* Defined as $_{HN}$, given two habitats $\{h_t, h_u\}$ H, $_{HN}$ provides the relation of neighborhood between two habitats. If $h_t \xleftrightarrow{HN} h_u$ then h_t and h_u are neighbors, i.e., they are continuous habitats.

Relation 5: *Ecological barrier.* Defined as $_{EB}$, given an individual i_j I, three habitats $\{h_t, h_u, h_v\}$ H, where $h_t \xleftrightarrow{HN} h_u$, $h_v \xleftrightarrow{HN} h_u$ and $h_v \xleftrightarrow{HN} h_t$, then h_u is a habitat that separates h_t from h_v . The associated relations $i_j \xrightarrow{HO} h_t$ and $i_j \xrightarrow{\overline{A}} h_u$ imply an ecological barrier of i_j in h_v , leading to $i_j \xrightarrow{EB} h_v$.

Relation 6: *Geographical isolation.* Defined as $_{GI}$, given two individuals $\{i_j, i_g\}$ I and three habitats $\{h_t, h_u, h_v\}$ H, where $h_t \xleftrightarrow{HN} h_u$, $h_v \xleftrightarrow{HN} h_u$ and $h_v \xleftrightarrow{HN} h_t$, h_u is a habitat that separates h_t from h_v , the relations $i_j \xrightarrow{HO} h_t$, $i_g \xrightarrow{HO} h_v$, $i_j \xrightarrow{EB} h_v$ e $i_g \xrightarrow{EB} h_t$ imply the existence of a geographic isolation between i_j and i_g : $i_j \xleftrightarrow{GI} i_g$.

Relation 7: *Trophic Relation.* Defined as $_{TR}$, given two individuals $\{i_j, i_g\}$ I,

where $i_j \overset{BI}{\longleftrightarrow} i_g$, the relation $_{TR}$ provides the trophic relation between i_j and i_g.

If $i_j \overset{TR}{\longrightarrow} i_g$, then i_g feeds from i_j.

Relation 8: *Ancestry relation.* Defined as $_{AR}$, it describes the ancestry relation

between individuals. Given two individuals $\{i_j, i_g\}$ I, i_j is an ancestor of i_g

if $i_j \overset{AR}{\longrightarrow} i_g$. The relation is also defined for subsets that belong to **i**: $\{i_1, ..., i_y\} \overset{AR}{\longrightarrow} i_g$,

or $\{i_1, ..., i_y\} \overset{AR}{\longrightarrow} \{i_1, ..., i_w\}$.

Contextualizing Species

Speciation explains the appearance of new species along time. To understand this process, it is necessary to reason about the concept of species. This is also relevant to biogeographic computation, where the following question can be raised: What are species in computational ecosystems? The answer lies in the relations supported by individuals, which can determine computationally the existence of species.

Definition 9: *Biological species of sexual individuals.* A species S is a set of

individuals, where, for every pair $\{i_j, i_g\}$ I, $j \neq g$, it is true that $i_j \overset{BI}{\longleftrightarrow} i_g$.

The definition of species obtained through the relation $_{BI}$ gives rise to a set of species $S_{BI} = \{S_1, ..., S_m\}$, where $S_l \subseteq$ I, $l = 1, ..., m$, thus characterizing each species as a subset of individuals. Note that Definition 9 allows an individual i_j I to simultaneously belong to two sets of species, leading to the definition of hybrid individuals.

Definition 10: *Hybrid individuals.* Given two species $\{S_f, S_e\}$ S_{BI}, a hybrid

individual between S_f and S_e is an individual that belongs to the set S_f S_e. If S_f $S_e = \varnothing$, then there is no hybrid individual between S_f and S_e. This definition can account for three or more species.

It should be emphasized that other conformations of species sets can be obtained, supported by different definitions of relations between individuals.

Characterizing Ecosystems Computing

The goal of the metamodel is to transpose the computation of biogeographical processes into a discrete spatio-temporal computation. Thus, the state update in a computational ecosystem is provided by the discrete occurrence of processes that are responsible for dynamic events, inserting discrete-time temporal variation in individuals and habitats.

Definition 11: *Processes*. Defined according to the taxonomy of biogeographical processes: ecological (ξ), geographical (φ), microevolutionary (μ) and macroevolutionary (M). Processes ξ, μ and M act upon individuals i_j I, $j=1,...,o$ and process φ acts upon habitats h_t h, $t = 1,..., q$.

The temporal transformation in elements i_j I and h_t H can be represented by the systematic application of processes. Taking individuals i_j and habitats h_t at the time instant k Z^+, results in the extended notation $i_j^{(k)}$ and $h_t^{(k)}$. The application of processes implies updates of these sets in discrete instants of time. Any change in $i_j^{(k)}$ and $h_t^{(k)}$ can lead to changes in their relations. At time instants *k*, relations provide different responses to elements of the ecosystem, then a graph $P^{(k)}$ is the result of a relation R at time *k*. Consequently, a species S_f S_{BI}, may also vary in time: $S_f^{(k)}$.

In the following, the metamodel processes will be presented. Additional definitions, representing causal relations, are also provided.

Process 1: *Dispersion*. Defined as $_D$. Given an individual i_j I, it is considered that a subset of the attribute set represents its spatial location. The process $_D$ applies transformations in this subset of attributes.

During dispersion, different individuals may occupy different habitats and cross ecological barriers, leading to the definition of dispersion routes, diffusion and the founder effect. All these events imply updating and redefinition of relations involving elements of *I*, elements of *I* and *H*, and elements of *H*.

The Effect of a Dispersion Process

- **Dispersion Routes:** Consider an individual i_j I and three habitats $\{h_t, h_u, h_v\}$ H, where $h_t \overset{HN}{\leftrightarrow} h_u$, $h_v \overset{HN}{\leftrightarrow} h_u$ and $h_v \overset{HN}{\leftrightarrow} h_t$. Then, h_u is a habitat that separates h_t from h_v. The existence of different types of dispersion routes can be deduced from the following relations: $i_j \xrightarrow{HO} h_t$ and $i_j \xrightarrow{EB} h_v$. Depending on $_{EB}$, it is possible to define the existence of a corridor, a filter or a sweeptake route if the individual i_j occupies habitat $h_v : i_j \xrightarrow{HO} h_v$ when dispersing.

- **Diffusion:** Occurs gradually by successive dispersions through dispersal routes. Consider a subset of individuals i_j I, $j = 1,..,y$, and a subset of habitats h_u H, $u = 1, ...,w$. Initially, in an instant k Z^+, it is true that $i_j \xrightarrow{HO} h_u$. There are three stages that define the diffusion: (1) successive processes $_D$; (2) occupation of different habitats in future instants: $i_j \xrightarrow{HO} h_t$, where $h_t \not\subset \{h_1, ..., h_w\}$; and finally (3) it must be true that $i_j \xrightarrow{A} h_t$ for every $i_j \xrightarrow{HO} h_t$.

- **Founder Effect:** Occurs gradually by successive dispersions. Assume a species S_f S_{BI}, three habitats $\{h_t, h_u, h_v\}$ H, where $h_t \xleftrightarrow{HN} h_u$, $h_v \xleftrightarrow{HN} h_u$ and $h_v \xleftrightarrow{HN} h_t$. h_u is a habitat that separates h_t from h_v. Given, in an instant k Z^+, a subset $\{i_1, ..., i_y\}$ S_f, assume that $\{i_1, ..., i_y\} \xrightarrow{HO} h_t$. Through successive dispersions, in a future instant of time, the founder effect occurs when $\{i_1, ..., i_y\} \xrightarrow{HO} h_v$ and $\{i_1, ..., i_y\} \xrightarrow{A} h_v$. The subset $\{i_1, ..., i_y\}$ is a founder population.

Process 2: *Environmental changes.* Defined as $_{EC}$. Given a habitat h_t H, the process $_{EC}$ applies transformations in its attributes. It is possible to proceed in changes of abiotic factors and in the topology of h_t. In the second case, there can be a habitat fragmentation of h_t in habitats $h_1, ..., h_y$.

Environmental Changes Effect

- **Vicariance:** Occurs gradually by means of successive environmental changes, resulting in habitat fragmentation of h_t H in $h_1, ..., h_y$. At time instant

$k \ Z^+$, it is true that $i_j \xrightarrow{HO} h_t$ for a subset $i_j \ S_f$, $j = 1,\ldots,m$, $S_f \ S_{BI}$. In a future instant of time, the fragmentation of h_t produces the vicariance condition when, for any pair of individuals $\{i_j, i_g\} \ S_f$, it is true that $i_j \xleftrightarrow{GI} i_g$.

Process 3: *Sexual reproduction.* Defined as $_R$. Given two individuals $\{i_j, i_g\} \ I$, consider $h_t \ H$, where $\{i_j, i_g\} \xrightarrow{HO} h_t$ and $i_j \overline{\xleftrightarrow{BI}} i_g$. The process $_R$ combines attributes i_j and i_g to generate a new individual i_*.

Dispersion and Reproduction Effect

- **Genotypic or Phenotypic Flow:** Initially, at time instant $k \ Z^+$, consider two individuals $\{i_j, i_g\} \ I$ where the following conditions are true: $i_j \xleftrightarrow{GI} i_g$ and $i_j \overline{\xleftrightarrow{BI}} i_g$. In a future time instant, it can be true that $\{i_j, i_g\} \xrightarrow{HO} h_t$. The occurrence of $_R$ between i_j and i_g in this scenario represents a particular case of reproduction: genotypic or phenotypic flow.

Process 4: *Mutation.* Defined as $_M$. Given an individual $i_j \ i$, it is considered that a subset of its attributes represents its genotype. The process $_M$ applies transformations in this subset of attributes, with consequences in the corresponding phenotype.

Process 5: *Natural selection.* Defined as $_{NS}$. Given an individual $i_j \ I$, the process $_{NS}$ determines the survival of i_j. Considering i_j at time instant k, at time $k + 1$, it may happen that i_j ceases to exist. Several factors are crucial in this process, including:

1. *Low adaptation.* Given a habitat $h_t \ h$ where $i_j \xrightarrow{HO} h_t$ and $i_j \overline{\xrightarrow{A}} h_t$.
2. *Intraspecific competition for resources.* Given two individuals $\{i_j, i_g\} \ S_f$, where $S_f \ S_{BI}$, if $\{i_j, i_g\} \xrightarrow{HO} h_t$, then there may exist an intraspecific competition.

3. *Interspecific competition.* Given two individuals $i_j \in S_f$ and $i_g \in S_e$, where $\{S_f, S_e\} \in S_{BI}$ and $\{i_j, i_g\} \xrightarrow{HO} h_t$, this scenario can lead to the existence of competition, determined by specific relations, for example, predator-prey, defined by $i_j \xrightarrow{TR} i_g$.

4. *Selective pressure.* Represents the pressure that an entire ecosystem can exert on individuals and species. There are several factors that should be considered in a selective pressure, all related to the habitat characteristics and relations between individuals and species. In this case, the definition of a selective pressure relation may comprise several factors in a single relation, that will determine the survival of an individual $i_j \in S_f$.

Natural Selection Effect

- **Bottleneck Effect:** Occurs gradually through natural selection. Initially, at time instant $k \in Z^+$, consider a species $S_f = \{i_1, ..., i_y\}$, $S_f \in S_{BI}$. At a future time instant, where $S_f = \{i_1, ..., i_w\}$, if $w \ll y$, then the bottleneck effect occurred.

Process 6: *Extinction.* Defined as $\in_E$. Alters the conformation of the S_{BI} set when a species $S_f \in S_{BI}$ has cardinality $z = 0$, i.e., $S_f = \varnothing$. Under the effect of extinction, S_f ceases to exist.

Process 7: *Sympatric speciation.* Defined as $\in_{SS}$. Alters the conformation of the set S_{BI}, adding a new species S_*. Composed of individuals generated from the following situation: given $\{i_j, i_g\} \in S_f$, the process $\in_R$ generates i_* such that $i_* \xleftrightarrow{BI} i_l$ for every $i_l \in S_f$. By obtaining a set of individuals $\{i_{*1}, ..., i_{*y}\}$ generated by this process, if it is true that for every i_{*j} and $i_{*g} : i_{*j} \xleftrightarrow{BI} i_{*g}$, then $\{i_{*1}, ..., i_{*y}\}$ constitutes a new species $S_* = \{i_{*1}, ..., i_{*y}\}$.

Process 8: *Alopatric speciation.* Defined as $\in_{AS}$. Alters the conformation of the set S_{BI}, adding one or more new species S_*. Through the vicariance process, it is possible to obtain two (or more) subsets (s1,...sn) $\{i_1^{s1}, ..., i_y^{s1}\} \in S_f$ and $\{i_1^{s2}, ..., i_w^{s2}\} \in S_f$, where $\{i_1^{s1}, ..., i_y^{s1}\} \xrightarrow{HO} h_t$, $\{i_1^{s2}, ..., i_w^{s2}\} \xrightarrow{HO} h_u$,

$\left\{ i_1^{s1}, \ldots, i_y^{s1} \right\} \overset{GI}{\leftrightarrow} \left\{ i_1^{s2}, \ldots, i_w^{s2} \right\}$ at time instant $k \; Z^+$. After this isolation, by successive processes $_R$ and $_M$, in a future time instant, subsets $\left\{ i_1^{s3}, \ldots, i_a^{s3} \right\}$ and $\left\{ i_1^{s4}, \ldots, i_b^{s4} \right\}$, where $\left\{ i_1^{s3}, \ldots, i_a^{s3} \right\} \overset{AR}{\rightarrow} \left\{ i_1^{s1}, \ldots, i_y^{s1} \right\}$ and $\left\{ i_1^{s4}, \ldots, i_b^{s4} \right\} \overset{AR}{\rightarrow} \left\{ i_1^{s2}, \ldots, i_w^{s2} \right\}$, individuals may present the following condition: $\left\{ i_1^{s3}, \ldots, i_a^{s3} \right\} \overset{BI}{\leftrightarrow} \left\{ i_1^{s4}, \ldots, i_b^{s4} \right\}$. Additionally, the following condition $\left\{ i_1^{s3}, \ldots, i_a^{s3} \right\} \overset{BI}{\leftrightarrow} \left\{ i_1^{s1}, \ldots, i_y^{s1} \right\}$ and $\left\{ i_1^{s4}, \ldots, i_b^{s4} \right\} \overset{BI}{\leftrightarrow} \left\{ i_1^{s2}, \ldots, i_w^{s2} \right\}$ indicates that it can be considered two new species: $S_{*f} = \left\{ i_1^{s3}, \ldots, i_a^{s3} \right\}$ and $S_{*e} = \left\{ i_1^{s4}, \ldots, i_b^{s4} \right\}$. Otherwise, only a new species S_* can be considered where $S_i = \left\{ i_1^{s3}, \ldots, i_a^{s3} \right\}$ and $S_* = \left\{ i_1^{s4}, \ldots, i_b^{s4} \right\}$ or $S_f = \left\{ i_1^{s4}, \ldots, i_b^{s4} \right\}$ and $S_* = \left\{ i_1^{s3}, \ldots, i_a^{s3} \right\}$.

Process 9: *Peripatric Speciation*. Defined as $_{PS}$. Alters the conformation of the S_{BI} set, adding a new species S_*. By means of dispersion, at a time instant $k \; Z^+$ consider two subsets: $\left\{ i_1^{s1}, \ldots, i_y^{s1} \right\} \; S_f$ and $\left\{ i_1^{s2}, \ldots, i_w^{s2} \right\} \; S_f$, where $\left\{ i_1^{s1}, \ldots, i_y^{s1} \right\} \overset{HO}{\rightarrow} h_t$, $\left\{ i_1^{s2}, \ldots, i_w^{s2} \right\} \overset{HO}{\rightarrow} h_u$, $\left\{ i_1^{s1}, \ldots, i_y^{s1} \right\} \overset{GI}{\leftrightarrow} \left\{ i_1^{s2}, \ldots, i_w^{s2} \right\}$, and $w \ll y$. After this isolation, through successive processes $_R$ and $_M$, in a future time instant, subsets $\left\{ i_1^{s3}, \ldots, i_a^{s3} \right\}$ and $\left\{ i_1^{s4}, \ldots, i_b^{s4} \right\}$, where $\left\{ i_1^{s3}, \ldots, i_a^{s3} \right\} \overset{AR}{\rightarrow} \left\{ i_1^{s1}, \ldots, i_y^{s1} \right\}$ and $\left\{ i_1^{s4}, \ldots, i_b^{s4} \right\} \overset{AR}{\rightarrow} \left\{ i_1^{s2}, \ldots, i_w^{s2} \right\}$, may present the following condition: $\left\{ i_1^{s3}, \ldots, i_a^{s3} \right\} \overset{BI}{\leftrightarrow} \left\{ i_1^{s4}, \ldots, i_b^{s4} \right\}$. The individuals $\left\{ i_1^{s4}, \ldots, i_b^{s4} \right\}$ constitutes a new species S_*.

Process 10: *Competitive speciation*. Defined as $_{CS}$. Alters the conformation of the S_{BI} set, adding a new species S_*. Presents similarities with the process $_{PS}$, where by means of dispersion, at a time instant $k \; Z^+$, consider two subsets: $\left\{ i_1^{s1}, \ldots, i_y^{s1} \right\} \; S_f$ and $\left\{ i_1^{S2}, \ldots, i_w^{s2} \right\} \; S_f$, where $\left\{ i_1^{s1}, \ldots, i_y^{s1} \right\} \overset{HO}{\rightarrow} h_t$, $\left\{ i_1^{s2}, \ldots, i_w^{s2} \right\} \overset{HO}{\rightarrow} h_u$, and $w \ll y$. The difference lies in the relation between populations, where it is true that $\left\{i_1^{s1}, \ldots, i_y^{s1}\right\} \overset{\overline{GI}}{\leftrightarrow} \left\{i_1^{S2}, \ldots, i_w^{s2}\right\}$. It may also be

true that $h_t \overset{HN}{\leftrightarrow} h_u$. Through successive processes $_R$ and $_M$, in a future time

instant, subsets $\left\{i_1^{s3}, \ldots, i_a^{s3}\right\}$ and $\left\{i_1^{s4}, \ldots, i_b^{s4}\right\}$, where

$\left\{i_1^{s3}, \ldots, i_a^{s3}\right\} \overset{AR}{\rightarrow} \left\{i_1^{s1}, \ldots, i_y^{s1}\right\}$ and $\left\{i_1^{s4}, \ldots, i_b^{s4}\right\} \overset{AR}{\rightarrow} \left\{i_1^{s2}, \ldots, i_w^{s2}\right\}$, may present

the following condition: $\left\{i_1^{s3}, \ldots, i_a^{s3}\right\} \overset{BI}{\leftrightarrow} \left\{i_1^{s4}, \ldots, i_b^{s4}\right\}$. The individuals

$\left\{i_1^{s4}, \ldots, i_b^{s4}\right\}$ constitute a new species S_*.

The Role of Information in Ecosystems

Aiming to investigate the role of information in the causality of ecosystems, we are now prepared to conceive a computational ecosystem derived from the metamodel, endowed with the processes of reproduction, natural selection, sympatric speciation and extinction. Individuals and habitats represent the information of the ecosystem, since they are elements that exert mutual causality. In the first case, it is represented by phenotypic attributes and in the second case by ecological opportunities, which are opportunities of adaptation that provide disruptive selection (Cox & Moore, 2010; Brown & Lomolino, 2006; Strecker, 2002) and, therefore, the emergence of new species (Brown & Lomolino, 2006; Bodaly, Clayton, Lindsey, & Vuorinen, 1992; Echelle & Kornfield, 1984). At this point, the principle to be explored arises: the emergence of species is due to biological isolation, that is, it is conditioned to the fact that the information of an individual is not causal for all individuals. The same applies to ecological opportunities that also exert a causality only on subsets of individuals.

Given this principle, this section explores the emergence of adaptive radiation from an informational point of view. By taking the definition of information, it is possible to verify that sympatric speciation can induce a loss of causality, since biological isolation leads to a restriction of interaction between individuals. To verify the role of causality in ecosystems, it is possible to associate uncertainty in predicting the causality of information. In the information theory proposed by Shannon (Shannon, 2001), entropy is associated with the unpredictability (or uncertainty) of information. Shannon's entropy is also applied in studies of ecosystems to investigate biodiversity (Harte, 2011). Here, given an individual randomly selected from the entire population, entropy measures the uncertainty in predicting the individual's species.

Thus, entropy gets higher with an increase in the number of species and also in the uniformity of the distribution of individuals between species. From the point of view of the causality exerted by individuals, it is valid to say that entropy measures uncertainty in causal information and, therefore, quantifies causality. That is, the higher the entropy, the lower the causality of information, and vice versa. The results obtained from the computational dynamics allow us to conclude that entropy patterns that emerge from the adaptive radiation are related to habitat carrying capacity, environmental conditions, variation in ecological opportunities and patterns of speciation and extinction over time, thus positioning the concept of information as the basis for the understanding of the causality present in ecosystems.

A Computational Ecosystem in Adaptive Surfaces

The model presented aims to simulate the adaptive radiation through processes of reproduction, natural selection, sympatric speciation and extinction. Individuals, habitats and opportunities represent ecosystem information. The central point of the proposal lies in the concept of adaptive surfaces (Wright, 1932; Simpson, 1955; Rosenzweig, 1995; Lande, 1985) that represent the degree of adaptation of phenotypes to habitats. Ecological opportunities are defined as attraction basins with the potential of promoting adaptation, which in a surface are represented by adaptive peaks and their surroundings (Pasti, de Castro, & Von Zuben, 2011). By contrast, there are adaptive valleys represented by regions of low adaptation between adaptive zones. Figure 2 shows pictorial examples of adaptive surfaces.

The key concept behind the model lies in the *disruptive selection* (Cox & Moore, 2010; Brown & Lomolino, 2006): when a species occupies a new adaptive zone, it

Figure 2. Adaptive Surfaces. (a) One ecological opportunity. (2) Several ecological opportunities

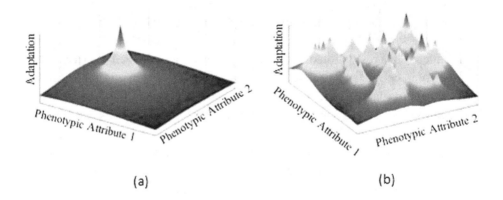

(a)   (b)

tends to diverge and a process of sympatric speciation may occur, due to biological isolation. Multiple sympatric speciation processes, combined with extinction by low adaptation, may guide to adaptive radiation. The following subsections describe the processes involved.

Reproduction (μ_R)

Reproduction processes may generate offspring phenotypes similar to the ones exhibited by their parents or with sufficient differences to occupy new ecological opportunities. The phenotypic variation provided by the reproduction process can be modeled by means of normal distributions (Welch & Waxman, 2002; Limpert, Stahel, & Abbt, 2001; Fear & Price, 1998; Bürger & Lande, 1994). Given two individuals $i_j = \left[i_{j1},\ i_{j2},\ ...,i_{jp}\right]$ and $i_g = \left[i_{g1},\ i_{g2},\ ...,i_{gp}\right]$, a new offspring individual $i_k = \left[i_{k1},\ i_{k2},\ ...,i_{kp}\right]$ will be generated. This is performed *for each* phenotypic attribute applying a random normal distribution N with a standard deviation $_l$ defined as:

$$_l\left(i_{jl},\ i_{gl}\right) = \left|i_{jl}\ i_{gl}\right| + P_{hm}\ U_{ll} \tag{1}$$

where P_{hm} is a controllable parameter that regulates the mutation rate, and U_l is a random number generated by a uniform distribution $U\left(0,1\right)$. Finally, we obtain the value i_{k1} by using Equation 2:

$$i_{k1} = i_{j1} + N\left(\alpha_l\right) \tag{2}$$

Natural Selection (μ_{NS})

There are many variables that will dictate whether an individual or species will survive in an ecosystem and pass their phenotypic attributes forward. These variables depend on intra-species, interspecies and species-environment relationships (Schoener, 1991). Thus, the natural selection process will be derived from the calculation of the selective pressure (*sp*) applied to each individual that compose the set S_{BI}. Calculating the selective pressure of each individual is performed by using a logistic function and the following three parameters: $\sigma_{inter}, \rho_{inter}, \rho_{intra}$.

Parameters σ_{inter} and ρ_{inter} are called the interspecies selective pressure intensity, and correspond to the competition level among all species of the set S_{BI}. Figure 4 presents the logistic function and the influence of these two parameters.

Figure 4 shows the influence of the two parameters σ_{inter} and ρ_{inter} that correspond to the slope of the logistic curve and the and the starting point on the x-axis where the logistic curve will be evaluated, respectively.

To calculate the selective pressure, it is necessary to rank the most adapted individual of each species i^*. The individual that represents the most adapted species is positioned in the ρ_{inter} of the x-axis of the logistic function; and the individual representing the least adapted species is placed in position 1 of the x-axis. Individuals representing the intermediate species are placed between ρ_{inter} and 1, keeping equal steps. Then, for each position of individuals i^*, it is associated a corresponding value for $f(x)$, which will represent the selective pressure of that species. This way we are able to associate to each species a corresponding selective pressure value

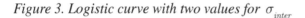

Figure 3. Logistic curve with two values for σ_{inter}

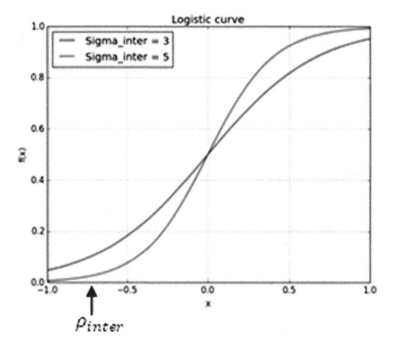

For a more accurate representation see the electronic version.

Figure 4. Examples of adaptive surfaces with A = 11 sampling points and A−1 intervals. (a) Surface without adaptive valley crossing. (b) Surface with an adaptive valley crossing

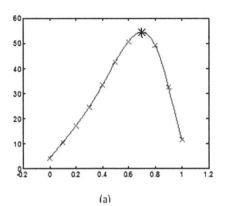 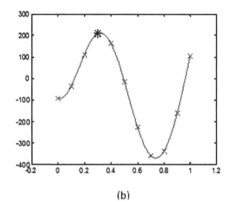

(a)   (b)

and with the value ρ_{intra} parametrized at the beginning, we can now calculate the selective pressure applied to each individual of a given species.

The calculation of the selective pressure for each individual is done in a similar way, also using a logistic function, but now each species has a characteristic curve determined by its σ_{intra}. Equation 3 depicts the logistic function used.

$$f(x) = \frac{1}{1 + e^{-\sigma * n * x}} \tag{3}$$

where σ corresponds to σ_{inter} or σ_{intra}, and n corresponds to the number of species or the number of individuals of the corresponding species. Now that we have access to the selective pressure for each individual i, it is possible to determine whether i will remain alive or not, as follows:

- Given the selective pressure value of individual i_j, $SP(i_j)$, and a number $U(0,1)$ coming from a uniform distribution;

- If $SP(i_j)$ is greater than $U(0,1)$, then the individual i_j dies.

Sympatric Speciation (μ_{SS})

Given two individuals i_j and i_g, ρ_{BI} is the biological isolation relation between them. When two individuals are biologically isolated there is one or more adaptive valleys between them, characterizing the occupation of different ecological opportunities (they form distinct species).Whenever biological isolation is observed between two individuals, a new process of sympatric speciation has occurred. To be able to implement the dynamics of the computational ecosystem, it will be proposed a method to detect adaptive valleys on adaptive surfaces. Consider the following elements:

P: set of surface samples between individuals i_j and i_g ;

A: cardinality of the P set;

$i_{a_{max}} = \arg\max\limits_{i_a\,P\,A} \left(i_a \right)$: represents the maximum sample value for ρ_A .

By adopting quasi-concave adaptive zones as references, consider initially i_j , i_g, P and $i_{a_{max}}$. Starting from i_j towards $i_{a_{max}}$, it is possible to obtain scalars $_i$ $i = 1,...,A1$, which represent intervals of adaptation, determined by the differences $_A\left(i_a\right)$ and $_A\left(i_{a+1}\right)$ from $a = 1$ to $a = a_{max}$, and in the opposite direction, from i_y to $i_{a_{max}}$ composing differences among $_A\left(i_a\right)$ and $_A\left(i_{al}\right)$, from $a = A$ to $a = a_{max}$. If $a_{max} = 1$, only the differences from i_g to $i_{a_{max}}$ are considered, and when $a_{max} = A$ only the differences from i_j towards $i_{a_{max}}$ are considered. Figure 4 illustrates the sampling of points in two examples of adaptation curves and the identification of $_i$. In Figure 4(a), there is no biological isolation between individuals i_j and i_g . In Figure 4(b), there is biological isolation between individuals i_j and i_g . The symbol $\times$ represents the sampled points $\left(i_a\right)$.

The sympatric speciation process detects the occupation of a new ecological opportunity and promotes the change of the set S_{BI} , adding a new species. Given two individuals i_j and i_g belonging to the same species, by means of the process μ_R , a new individual i_k is generated. Using the computational definition of biological isolation, it is necessary to verify if the new individual i_k has biological isolation with all the other individuals of the set S_{BI} . If this happens, a new species is counted in the set S_{BI} .

Extinction (μ_{EX})

Let $S_f \in S_{BI}$ be a species at iteration ω. If after the application of the natural selection process μ_{NS} the number of individuals in species S_f equals to zero, then species S_f becomes extinct at iteration $\omega + 1$.

Pseudocode of the Computational Ecosystem

To obtain the dynamics of the computational ecosystem, from the proposed processes, it is introduced the following pseudocode (Box 1).

EXPERIMENTAL METHODOLOGY

To assess the proposed ecosystem, some experiments were conducted in two different scenarios varying the habitat type: (1) Dynamic ecological opportunities

Box 1.

Pseudocode representing the dynamics of the proposed ecosystem
Given an initial generation of individuals in iteration $\omega = 1$ and a set of species S_{BI}, repeat the steps below until a stopping criterion is met.
1. For every individual $i_j^{(f)} \in S_f$ and every specie $S_f \in S_{BI}$, randomly choose a second individual $i_g^{(f)}$ and execute the process μ_R for $i_j^{(f)}$ and $i_g^{(f)}$, keeping the new individual i_k in a matrix I_k.
2. For every individual $i_k \in I_k$ do: i. Examine the biological isolation relation ρ_{BI} of i_k with the most adapted individual of each species $S_f \in S_{BI}$.   ii. Perform the μ_{SS} process.   iii. Check for the extinction of species.
3. For every individual $i_j^{(f)} \in S_f$ and every species $S_f \in S_{BI}$, perform the μ_{NS} process.

are time-varying and there is no emergence and disappearance of opportunities; (2) Ecological opportunities arise and disappear over time. These two scenarios allowed to investigate the influence of different environmental conditions for adaptive radiation and the entropy of the information produced.

Each scenario was run for 2,000 iterations, with the adaptive surface dynamics being triggered at iteration 500, and with changes being applied every twenty iterations (after triggered). This hypothesis allowed the ecosystem to evolve in a way that species would occupy different ecological opportunities, and from that point on, environmental changes had an effect on the ecosystem. Additionally, for all experiments, the following methodology was adopted:

1. Dynamic adaptive surfaces obtained from the set of functions *moving peaks* (Branke, 2007) with the following characteristics:
    a. Number of ecological opportunities $= 10$;
    b. Height of the adaptive peaks $= 50$;
2. Phenotypic domain $= |-100,100|$.
3. Initial condition of the ecosystem: a species with an initial number of individuals equals to 2.
4. Selective pressure parameters: $[\sigma_{inter}, \rho_{inter}, \rho_{intra}] = [0.07, 0.7, 0.1]$.
5. The results were obtained from 10 runs for each scenario.

Finally, the Shannon entropy is calculated as follows:

$$E = -\sum_{f=1}^{m} p_f * \ln\left(\frac{o_f}{\sum_{f=1}^{m} o_f}\right) \tag{4}$$

where o_f is the number of individuals in species f and m is the number of species.

In (Pasti, de Castro, & Von Zuben, 2011) the authors performed the study of a model in static habitats. The main objective of the proposed methodology is to observe the behavior of the model in time-varying ecosystems. The objective is to compare the behavior of the ecosystem in the two proposed scenarios of temporal variation. Real ecosystems are not static, so a more coherent model with reality must incorporate temporal variations in habitat.

Computational Experiments

The computational experiments conducted were aimed at investigating the relationship of information that emerges from adaptive radiation with causality in ecosystems. As a consequence, it is possible to show the causal relationship, in the form of entropy, with the emerging patterns associated with the dynamics of ecosystems. The starting point to understand the results lies in the two scenarios depicted in Figure 5, which presents time series produced by the iterations of the computational ecosystem. The time series correspond to the evolution over time of entropy, number of species, number of accumulated species and extinctions for scenarios 1 and 2. Table 1 presents the average values after 10 executions. Drawing a parallel with specific emerging patterns, it is possible to conclude the following:

- **Population Equilibrium:** The concept of habitat carrying capacity is related to the amount of resources that can sustain the population of individuals. When the population reaches a peak of consumption, the trend then is that of a population cycle, where the mean represents a population equilibrium (Ginzburg & Colyvan, 2004; Berryman, 2002). In the experiments conducted it is possible to observe the existence of a balance in the number of species and the carrying capacity that emerges due to the number of ecological opportunities. The same happens with entropy, that is, there is a balance in the causality of the ecosystem. It is possible to observe that amplitude and variation of entropy is related to the fact that the ecosystem reaches its capacity limit. While the equilibrium is not reached, the number of species tends to increase and the entropy variation is larger, having some peaks of low entropy that can be translated into a high causality provided by the population increase in some specific species. When the population achieve equilibrium, the tendency is to increase entropy and decrease its amplitude, which means that the ecosystem has entered into a causal equilibrium of information exchange. This is evidenced by Scenario 1, and Figures 5(a). However, when the emergence and disappearance of new ecological opportunities is

Table 1. Average measures and standard deviation obtained from 10 runs of scenarios 1 and 2

	Entropy	**Nr. of Species**	**Final Nr. of Species**	**Nr. of Extinctions**
Scenario 1	2.26±0.14	12.47±0.85	73.10±17.47	61.10±17.39
Scenario 2	2.40±0.02	14.59±0.33	128.50±8.95	114.60±9.37

Figure 5. Results obtained by the two different scenarios

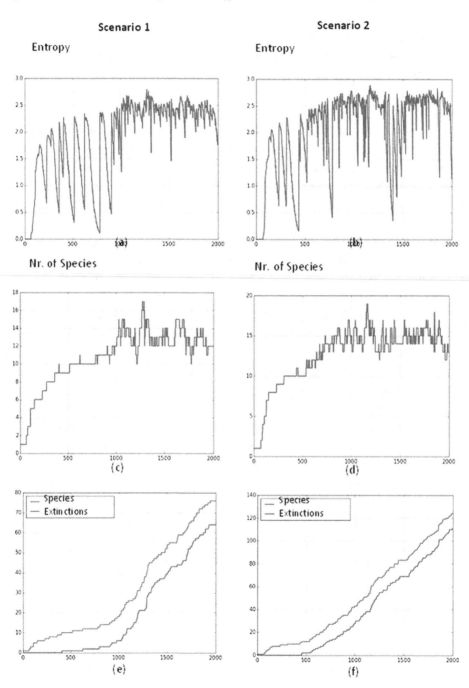

For a more accurate representation see the electronic version.

allowed, as in Scenario 2, an increase in the entropy variation during the species equilibrium is observed, maintaining low peaks. It is possible to see that environmental changes that lead to the emergence and disappearance of ecological opportunities also bring about possible increases in causation leading the ecosystem back into equilibrium. No matter how abrupt and what are the conditions of environmental changes, the ecosystem finds a causality equilibrium.

- **Environmental Conditions:** As expected, the emergence of ecological opportunities favored an increase in the number of species over time, as the disappearance of ecological opportunities led to an increase in the number of extinctions. This can be seen in Figures 5(c) and (d), as well as in the mean value of the simulations shown in Table 1. Although the variation in the existence of ecological opportunities implies low entropy and high causality peaks, the mean value of entropy for Scenario 1 was lower than for Scenario 2 (Table 1). These results show that increased causality may take the ecosystem back to equilibrium. The higher the variation, the higher the entropy, and therefore the less causation is necessary to maintain equilibrium.

- **Adaptive Radiation:** It is generally concluded that the increase of entropy and, therefore, a decrease in the causality, implies the favoring of the adaptive radiation, when the ecosystem enters in balance. When the variation in habitat is due to the emergence and disappearance of ecological opportunities, this fact is evidenced, where scenario 2 presented a larger number of species and accumulated extinctions, together with a larger average number, when compared to scenario 1 (see Table 1). This can be seen in Figures 5 (d) and (e). Patterns of rapid bursts of adaptive radiation are largely found in fossil and geological records, with the classic case of the extinction of dinosaurs that supposedly allowed mammals to ascend (Lillegraven, 1972; Kaufman & Ochumba, 1993). This leads to the conclusion that there is a tendency that when the entropy is larger, and, therefore, the causality between the elements of the ecosystem is smaller, the adaptive radiation is capable of producing a higher number of species and extinctions.

CONCLUSION

This chapter follows the hypothesis that elements of ecosystems can be viewed as information processors. There are unique features inherent to ecosystems, such as diversity of species and habitats, which motivate the study and application of biogeographic computation in several contexts.

Being a conceptual chapter founded on a well-established theory, the relevance of the extended metamodel can be supported by two main reasons: (*i*) The absence of such a general and complete biogeographic computation formalism in the current literature; (*ii*) The maturity of the Biogeography research field, with convincing explanations for a wide range of spatio-temporal phenomena in ecosystems. The metamodel further extended in this chapter may thus represent a proper framework to favor two avenues of research:

1. The theoretical investigation into novel models aimed at understanding ecosystems under the viewpoint of information processing, helping the validation of theories and propositions within Biogeography;
2. The development of innovative computational tools based on computational ecosystems for solving complex problems.

Both avenues are yet to be explored and there are distinct aspects in the conceptual framework of Biogeographic Computation that may guide to spatio-temporal emergent phenomena not properly addressed in alternative views of the study of ecosystems.

ACKNOWLEDGMENT

The authors would like to thank Fapesp, CNPq, Capes and MackPesquisa for the financial support. As a Machine Learning Center of Excellence by Intel, special thanks also goes to Intel for all its support.

REFERENCES

Berryman, A. (2002). *Population Cycles: The Case for Trophic Interactions*. Oxford, UK: Oxford University Press.

Bodaly, R. A., Clayton, J. W., Lindsey, C. C., & Vuorinen, J. (1992). Evolution of Lake Whitefish (Coregonus clupeaformis) in North America during the Pleistocene: Genetic Differentiation between Sympatric Populations. *Canadian Journal of Fisheries and Aquatic Sciences*, *49*(4), 769–779. doi:10.1139/f92-086

BrankeJ. (2007). *KIT*. Retrieved from http://www.aifb.uni-karlsruhe.de/ ~jbr/ MovPeaks/

Brent, R., & Bruck, J. (2006). Can computers help to explain biology? *Nature*, *440*(7083), 416–417. doi:10.1038/440416a PMID:16554784

Brown, J. H., & Lomolino, M. V. (2006). *Biogeography*. Sinauer Associates.

Bürger, R., & Lande, R. (1994). On the distribution of the mean and variance of a quantitative trait under mutation-selection-drift balance. *Genetics*, *138*, 901–912. PMID:7851784

Cohen, I. R. (2000). *Tending Adam's garden: evolving the cognitive immune self.* London, UK: Academic Press.

Cohen, I. R. (2009). Real and artificial immune systems: computing the state of the body, Nature Reviews: Immunology. *Nature Reviews. Immunology*, *7*(07), 569–574. doi:10.1038/nri2102 PMID:17558422

Cohen, I. R., & Harel, D. (2007). Explaining a complex living system: Dynamics, multi-scaling and emergence. *Journal of the Royal Society, Interface*, *4*(13), 175–182. doi:10.1098/rsif.2006.0173 PMID:17251153

Cox, C. B., & Moore, P. D. (2010). *Biogeography - An Ecological and Evolutionary Approach*. Wiley.

Coyne, J. A., & Orr, H. A. (1999). The evolutionary genetics of speciation. In A. E. Magurran & R. M. May (Eds.), *Evolution of Biological Diversity*. Oxford University Press.

de Aguiar, M., Barange, M., Baptestin, M., Kaufman, L., & Bar-Yam, Y. (2009). Global patterns of speciation and diversity. *Nature*, *460*(16), 384–387. doi:10.1038/nature08168 PMID:19606148

de Castro, L. N. (2007). Fundamentals of natural computing: An overview. *Physics of Life Reviews*, *4*(1), 1–36. doi:10.1016/j.plrev.2006.10.002

de Castro, L. N., & Timmis, J. (2002). *Artificial Immune Systems: A New Computational Intelligence Approach*. Springer-Verlag.

Denning, P. (2008). The computing field: Structure. In *Encyclopedia of Computer Science and Engineering* (pp. 615–623). Wiley Interscience.

Denning, P. J. (2001). *The Invisible Future: The Seamless Integration of Thecnology in Everyday Life*. McGraw-Hill.

Denning, P. J. (2007). Computing is a natural science. *Communications of the ACM*, *50*(7), 13–18. doi:10.1145/1272516.1272529

Dorigo, M., Maniezzo, V., & Colorni, A. (1996). The Ant System: Optimization by a Colony of Cooperating Agents. *IEEE Transactions on Systems, Man, and Cybernetics*, *26*(1), 29–41. doi:10.1109/3477.484436 PMID:18263004

Dowek, G. (2012). The physical Church Thesis as an explanation of the Galileo Thesis. *Natural Computing, 11*, 247-251.

Dyer, B. D. (2003). *A Field Guide to Bacteria*. Comstock Publishing.

Echelle, A., & Kornfield, I. (1984). *Evolution of Fish Species Flocks*. University of Maine Press.

Fear, K., & Price, T. (1998). The adaptive surface in ecology. *Oikos*, *82*(3), 440–448. doi:10.2307/3546365

Gavrilets, S., & Losos, J. (2009). Adaptive Radiation: Contrasting Theory with Data. *Science*, 323. PMID:19197052

Gavrilets, S., & Vose, A. (2005). Dynamic patterns of adaptive radiation. *PNAS*, *12*(50), 18040-18045.

Ginzburg, L. R., & Colyvan, M. (2004). *Ecological Orbits: How Planets Move and Populations Grow*. New York: Oxford University Press.

Harel, D. (2003). A grand challenge for computing: Full reactive modeling of a multi-cellular anima. *Bull. EATCS*, *81*, 226–235.

Hart, E., Bersini, H., & Santos, F. C. (2007). How affinity influences tolerance in an idiotypic network. *Journal of Theoretical Biology*, *249*(3), 422–436. doi:10.1016/j.jtbi.2007.07.019 PMID:17904580

Harte, J. (2011). *Maximum Entropy and Ecology: A Theory of Abundance, Distribution, and Energetics*. Oxford University Press. doi:10.1093/acprof:oso/9780199593415.001.0001

Hengeveld, R. (1990). *Dynamic Biogeography*. Cambridge University Press.

Holland. (2000). Building blocks, cohort genetic algorithms, and hyperplane-defined functions. *Evolutionary Computation*, 373-391.

Jorgensen, S. E., Patten, B. C., & Stragkraba, M. (1992). Ecosystems emerging: Toward an ecology of complex systems in a complex future. *Ecological Modelling*, *62*(1-3), 1–27. doi:10.1016/0304-3800(92)90080-X

Kauffman, S. (1996). *The Origins of Order: Self-Organization and Selection in Evolution*. Oxford University Press.

Kaufman, L., & Ochumba, P. (1993). Evolutinary and conservation biology of cichlid fishes as revealed by faunal remnants in northern Lake Victoria. *Conservation Biology, 7*(3), 719–730. doi:10.1046/j.1523-1739.1993.07030719.x

Lande, R. (1985). Genetic variation and phenotypic evolution during allopatric speciation. *American Naturalist, 116*(4), 463–479. doi:10.1086/283642

Lihoreau, M., Chittka, L., & Raine, N. (2010). Travel Optimization by Foraging Bumblebees through Readjustments of Traplines after Discovery of New Feeding Locations. *American Naturalist, 176*(6), 744–757. doi:10.1086/657042 PMID:20973670

Lillegraven, J. A. (1972). Ordinal and familial diversity in Cenozoic mammals. *Taxon, 21*(2/3), 261–274. doi:10.2307/1218194

Limpert, E., Stahel, W., & Abbt, M. (2001). Log-normal distributions across the sciences: Keys and clues. *Bioscience, 51*(5), 342–352. doi:10.1641/0006-3568(2001)051[0341:LNDATS]2.0.CO;2

LloydS. (2002). Retrieved from http://edge.org/conversation/the-computational-universe

Lloyd. (2006). *Programming the Universe: A Quantum Computer Scientist Takes On the Cosmos*. Knopf.

Magurran, A. (1999). Population differentiation without speciation. In A. Magurran & R. M. May (Eds.), *Evolution of Biological Diversity*. Oxford, UK: Oxford University Press.

Maia, R., & de Castro, L. N. (2012). Bee Colonies as Model for Multimodal Continuous Optimization: The OptBees Algorithm. *Proceedings of the IEEE Congress on Evolutionary Computation*, (pp. 1-8). doi:10.1109/CEC.2012.6252975

Mehta, P., Goyal, S., & Long, T. (2009). Information processing and signal integration in bacterial quorum sensing. Molecular Systems Biology, 5.

Milne, B. T. (1998). Motivation and Benefits of Complex Systems Approaches in Ecology. *Ecosystems (New York, N.Y.), 1*(5), 449–456. doi:10.1007/s100219900040

Myers, A. A., & Giller, P. S. (1991). *Analytical Biogeography*. Chapman & Hall.

Pasti, R., de Castro, L. N., & Von Zuben, F. J. (2011). Ecosystems Computing. *International Journal of Natural Computing Research*, *2*(4), 47–67. doi:10.4018/jncr.2011100104

Pratt, S. C., Mallon, E. B., Sumpter, D. J., & Franks, N. (2002). Quorum sensing, recruitment, and collective decision-making during colony emigration by the ant Leptothorax albipennis. *Behavioral Ecology and Sociobiology*, *52*(2), 117–12. doi:10.1007/s00265-002-0487-x

Provata, A., Sokolov, I. M., & Spagnolo, B. (2008). Ecological Complex Systems. *European Physical Journal. B, Condensed Matter and Complex Systems*, *65*(3), 304–314. doi:10.1140/epjb/e2008-00380-9

Ridley, M. (2004). *Evolution* (3rd ed.). Wiley-Blackwell.

Rosenzweig, M. (1995). *Species Diversity in Space and Time*. Cambridge University Press. doi:10.1017/CBO9780511623387

Schoener, T. W. (1991). Ecological interactions. In A. A. Myers & P. S. Giller (Eds.), Analytical Biogeography (pp. 255-295). Chapman & Hall.

Schwenk, G., Padilla, D. G., Bakken, G. S., & Full, R. J. (2009). Grand challenges in organismal biology. *Integrative and Comparative Biology*, *49*(1), 7–14. doi:10.1093/icb/icp034 PMID:21669841

Shannon, C. E. (2001, January). A mathematical theory of communication. ACM SIGMOBILE Mobile Computing and Communications Review, 3-55.

Simmons, I. (1982). *Biogeographical Processes*. Allen & Unwin.

Simpson, G. G. (1955). *The Major Features of Evolution*. New York: Columbia University.

Strecker, U. (2002). Cyprinodon esconditus, a new pupfish from Laguna Chichancanab, Yucatan, Mexico (Cyprinodontidae). *Cybium*, *26*, 301–307.

Swings, J., & De Ley, J. (1977). The biology of Zymomonas. *Bacteriological Reviews*, *41*, 1–46. PMID:16585

Vittori, G., Talbot, G., Gautrais, J., Fourcassié, V., Araújo, A. F. R., & Theraulaz, G. (2006). Path Efficiency of Ant Foraging Trails in an Artificial Network. *Journal of Theoretical Biology*, *239*(4), 507–515. doi:10.1016/j.jtbi.2005.08.017 PMID:16199059

Walker, S. I., & Davies, P. C. (2013). The algorithmic origins of life. *Journal of the Royal Society, Interface*, *10*. PMID:23235265

Welch, J. J., & Waxman, D. (2002). Nonequivalent Loci and the Distribution of Mutant Effects. *Genetics*, *161*, 897–904. PMID:12072483

Wright, S. (1932). The roles of mutation, inbreeding, crossbreeding, and selection in evolution. *Proceedings of VI International Congress of Genetics*, 356-366.

Xavier, R., Omar, N., & de Castro, L. N. (2011). Bacterial Colony: Information Processing and Computational Behavior. *Proceedings of Third World Congress on Nature and Biologically Inspired Computing*, 439-443. doi:10.1109/NaBIC.2011.6089627

KEY TERMS AND DEFINITIONS

Adaptive Radiation: Dynamics of emergence and extinction of species over time, from a single ancestral species.

Biogeography: Field of biology that aims to study the space-time dynamics of an ecosystem.

Biogeograpic Processes: Events that provide the dynamics of an ecosystem, changing its conformation between a certain time t and another t'.

Causality: Capacity of an ecosystem element in influencing another element.

Information in Ecosystem: It consists of all elements in an ecosystem that promote causality.

Metamodel: Structure that allows computational representation of the elements of an ecosystem, their interrelations, and biogeographic processes.

Relation: Define how elements of the geographical space relate to each other.

Chapter 6

Evolutionary Approaches to Test Data Generation for Object–Oriented Software:
Overview of Techniques and Tools

Ana Filipa Nogueira
University of Coimbra, Portugal

José Carlos Bregieiro Ribeiro
Polytechnic Institute of Leiria, Portugal

Francisco Fernández de Vega
University of Extremadura, Spain

Mário Alberto Zenha-Rela
University of Coimbra, Portugal

ABSTRACT

In object-oriented evolutionary testing, metaheuristics are employed to select or generate test data for object-oriented software. Techniques that analyse program structures are predominant among the panoply of studies available in current literature. For object-oriented evolutionary testing, the common objective is to reach some coverage criteria, usually in the form of statement or branch coverage. This chapter explores, reviews, and contextualizes relevant literature, tools, and techniques in this area, while identifying open problems and setting ground for future work.

INTRODUCTION

Search-Based Software Engineering (SBSE) seeks to reformulate Software Engineering (SE) problems as search-based optimisation problems. It has been applied to a wide variety of SE areas, including requirements engineering, project

DOI: 10.4018/978-1-5225-5020-4.ch006

planning and cost estimation, automated maintenance, service-oriented software engineering, compiler optimisation and quality assessment (Harman, 2007). Most of the overall literature (an estimated 59%) in the SBSE area is, however, concerned with Software Testing (ST) related applications, with structural test data generation being the most studied sub-topic (Harman, Mansouri, & Zhang, 2009).

The application of Evolutionary Algorithms (EAs) to test data generation or selection is often referred to as *Evolutionary Testing (ET)* (Tonella, 2004b; Wappler & Wegener, 2006b) or *Search-Based Test Data Generation (SBTDG)* (McMinn, 2004). ET consists of exploring the space of test programs by using metaheuristic techniques that direct the search towards the potentially most promising areas of the input space (Bertolino, 2007); its foremost objective is usually that of searching for a set of test programs that satisfies a predefined test criterion.

EAs have already been applied, with significant success, to the search for test data; the first application of heuristic optimisation techniques to test data generation was presented in 1992 (Xanthakis, Ellis, Skourlas, Gall, & K. Karapoulios, 1992). However, research has been mainly geared towards generating test data for procedural software, and traditional methods – despite their effectiveness and efficiency – cannot be applied without adaptation to Object-Oriented (OO) systems.

The application of search-based strategies to unit testing of OO programs is, in fact, fairly recent – the first approach was presented in 2004 (Tonella, 2004b) – and is yet to be investigated comprehensively (Harman, Hassoun, Lakhotia, McMinn, & Wegener, 2007). Interesting review articles on the topic of SBSE, and Search-Based Software Testing (SBST) in particular, include: (McMinn, 2004; Mantere & Alander, 2005; Xiao, El-Attar, Reformat & Miller, 2007; Afzal, Torkar, & Feldt, 2009; Ali, Briand, Hemmati, & Panesar-Walawege, 2009; Harman et al., 2009; Harman & McMinn, 2010; Maragathavalli, 2011; McMinn, 2011; Harman, Mansouri, & Zhang, 2012; Varshney & Mehrotra, 2013; Anand *et al.*, 2013). McMinn surveys the use of metaheuristic search techniques for the automatic generation of test data (McMinn, 2004); because the work on SBST had, thus far (2004), been largely restricted to programs of a procedural nature, these are the main subject of this review. In (Mantere & Alander, 2005), a review of the application of Genetic Algorithm (GA)-based optimisation methods to ST is presented; the authors stress out that all the researchers in this area report good (or, at least, encouraging) results regarding their use. Xiao *et al.* reported the experimental results regarding the effectiveness of five different optimisation techniques over five different C/C++ programs (Xiao *et al.*, 2007). The results show that the GA-based approach outperformed the remaining techniques – e.g., Simulated Annealing (SA), Genetic Simulated Annealing (GSA), Simulated Annealing with Advanced Adaptive Neighborhood (SA/ANN) and Random Testing – achieving the best overall performance.

The work proposed in (Afzal *et al.*, 2009) builds on on McMinn's research (McMinn, 2004) and presented a review on how search-based techniques are used to test non-functional properties of the software, focusing on: the properties studied, the fitness functions implemented and the constraints and limitations found when testing each property. The set of non-functional properties identified include (listed in descending order of the number of papers that investigate it): execution time, security, usability, safety and quality of service. A systematic review on the way SBST techniques have been empirically assessed is presented in (Ali *et al.*, 2009). In (Harman et al., 2009, 2012) a thorough index and classification of SBSE-related literature is provided, supported by an online repository. Local search, SA, GAs and Genetic Programming (GP) are identified as the most widely used optimisation and search techniques. Harman and McMinn conducted a theoretical and empirical study on the SBST field with the purposes of predicting the scenarios in which ET should perform properly and of justifying the reasons why a specific technique suited a particular situation (Harman & McMinn, 2010). The predictions were supported by empirical studies which showed that sometimes a simpler solution can be more suitable than a more sophisticated one, and it was theoretically and empirically proved that an evolutionary approach is suitable for several scenarios.

Maragathavalli also performed an overview of the current SBST techniques, and pointed out that for programs in which the complexity of the input domain grows, the efficacy of GA is quite significant when compared to random testing (Maragathavalli, 2011). (Varshney & Mehrotra, 2013) overviews the SBST techniques employed to automatically generate structural test data. The authors point out that control-flow based coverage criteria are the most often used to assess the effectiveness of the SBST techniques. In particular, the branch coverage metric is the most used by the researchers. Possible future research directions are also present, and are in accordance with the open problems discussed in (McMinn, 2011). In (Anand *et al.*, 2013), an orchestrated survey on the most prominent techniques for automatic test case generation was conducted, in which SBST is included. The survey focuses on several SBST emerging areas including: (i) the combination of SBST with other techniques – e.g., dynamic symbolic execution; (ii) the oracle problem; (iii) the co-evolutionary computation paradigm; (iv) the use of hyper-heuristics to combine different SE activities; and (v) the optimisation and better understanding of failures. Nevertheless, none of these surveys is devoted to the specific topic of Object-Oriented Evolutionary Testing (OOET). This paper extends previous work by the authors (Nogueira, Ribeiro, Fernández de Vega, & Zenha-Rela, 2014) with the latest advances in the field; and its goal is precisely that of overviewing current literature in the area while providing a primer to newcomers to this field of study.

Relevant literature was retrieved from three main sources: (i) the *Repository of Publications on Search Based Software Engineering (Centre For Research on*

Evolution, Search And Testing (CREST), 2008), a page maintained by the CREST which provides a complete collection of the literature addressing SE problems using metaheuristic search techniques. Only those papers belonging to the "Testing and Debugging" category were considered; (ii) the Google Scholar (Google, 2004) search engine, which allowed us to retrieve other studies, including some *grey literature* that may otherwise be missing (the following search terms were used: *"search based software testing"*, *"search based test data generation"*, *"evolutionary testing"*, and *"search based software engineering"*); and (iii) the bibliography sections of previously analysed relevant literature and surveys.

This paper is organized as follows. The next Section starts by providing background information on Object-Oriented Evolutionary Testing; relevant literature and research is explored, reviewed and contextualized in the following Section; and finally, in the concluding Section, achievements and open problems in the area are summarized and discussed.

BACKGROUND

This Section provides background on the most relevant aspects related with the interdisciplinary area of OOET. The OO paradigm is overviewed in the following Subsection. Then, key ST concepts are reviewed, and Metaheuristics and EAs are explored in the subsequent Subsections. The final Subsection introduces the reader to the ET area.

Object-Orientation

The use of OO technology is not restricted to any particular language; rather, it applies to a wide spectrum of programming languages, such as C++, Java, C# and Visual Basic. A language is considered OO if it directly supports data abstraction and classes, and also encapsulation, inheritance, and polymorphism (Booch *et al.*, 2007).

An *Object* is a software bundle of related state and behaviour. This is the key difference between OO and procedural programming methodologies: in OO design, the state and behaviour are contained within a single object, whereas in procedural (or structured) design they are normally separated, with data being placed into totally distinct functions or procedures. With the procedural paradigm, procedures ideally become "black boxes", where inputs go in and outputs come out. Also, the data is occasionally global, so it is easy to modify data that is outside the scope of the code, this means that access to data is uncontrolled.

Hiding internal state and requiring all interaction to be performed through an object's methods is known as data *encapsulation* – a fundamental principle of OO programming. The most important reason underlying the usage of encapsulation is that of separating the interface from the implementation (Eckel, 2002); this allows establishing boundaries within a data type and hiding its internal mechanism, and prevents client programmers from accidentally treating the internals of an object as part of the interface that they should be using.

OO programming allows classes to inherit commonly used state and behaviour from other classes. *Inheritance* expresses this similarity between classes by using the concept of *base classes* and *derived classes*: a base class contains all of the characteristics and behaviours that are shared among the classes derived from it. Semantically, inheritance denotes an "is a" relationship; inheritance thus implies a generalization/specialization hierarchy, wherein a subclass specialises the more general structure or behaviour of its superclass.

Polymorphism means "different forms" and it represents a concept in type theory in which a single name (such as a variable declaration) may denote objects of many different classes that are related by a common superclass. Any object denoted by this name is therefore able to respond to some common set of operations; distinction is expressed through differences in behaviour of the methods that can be called through the base class.

Testing OO software is particularly challenging: in an OO system, the basic test unit is a class instead of a subprogram, and testing should hence focus on classes and objects. While a test program for procedural software typically consists of a sequence of input values to be passed to a procedure upon execution, test programs for class methods must also account for the state of the objects involved in the methods' calls. This *state problem* (McMinn & Holcombe, 2003) is, in fact, one of the main hindrances posed to search-based approaches to test data generation, and one of the main reasons why procedural testing techniques cannot be applied directly to OO programs.

Software Testing

Software Testing (ST) is the process of exercising an application to detect errors and to verify that it satisfies the specified requirements. The general aim of testing is to affirm the quality of software systems by systematically exercising the software in carefully controlled circumstances (Marciniak, 1994). Despite advances in formal methods and verification techniques, a program still needs to be tested before it is used; testing remains the truly effective means to assure the quality of a software system of non-trivial complexity.

"Test early, test often" is the mantra of experienced programmers; however, developing conformance testing code can be more time consuming and expensive than developing the standard or product that will be tested (Tassey, 2002). Automating the testing process is, thus, key to improve the quality of complex software systems that are becoming the norm of modern society (Bertolino, 2007).

Although testing is involved in every stage of the software life-cycle, the testing done at each level of software development differs in terms of its nature and objectives, and normally targets specific types of faults. It is, nevertheless, clear that most errors are introduced at the coding/unit stage, and that the cost of repairing these errors increases significantly if they are dealt with at later stages of software development (Marciniak, 1994; Tassey, 2002). *Unit testing* thus plays a major role in the total testing efforts: it can be defined as the process of testing the individual subprograms, subroutines, procedures or methods in a program (Beizer, 1990), and is typically performed by executing the unit – i.e., the smallest testable piece of software – in different scenarios, using a set of relevant and interesting test programs.

To gain sufficient confidence that most faults are detected, testing should ideally be exhaustive; since in practice this is not possible, testers resort to test models and adequacy/coverage criteria to define systematic and effective test strategies that are fault revealing. Distinct test strategies include: *functional (or black-box) testing*, which is concerned with showing the consistency between the implementation and its requirements or functional specification; and *structural (or white-box) testing*, in which test program design is performed with basis on the internal structure of the software entity under test, with the basic idea being to ensure that all of the control elements in a program are executed by a given *test set* providing evidence of the quality of the testing activity. As will be made clear in subsequent sections, most SBTDG approaches rely on structural testing – not only because a formal specification of the test object is seldom available but also, and most importantly, because it is problematic to guide the search towards the definition of pertinent test scenarios with basis on the specification alone.

Evolutionary Algorithms

Computing optimal solutions for many problems of industrial and scientific importance is often difficult and sometimes impossible; automating the *test data generation process* is a paradigmatic example. Unlike exact methods, metaheuristics allow solving hard and complex problem instances by delivering satisfactory solutions in a reasonable time.

Evolutionary Algorithms (EAs) are the most studied metaheuristics; they are stochastic algorithms, which use simulated evolution as a search strategy to iteratively evolve candidate solutions, using operators inspired by genetics and natural selection (Michalewicz, 1994). They draw their inspiration from the works of Mendel on heredity and from Darwin's studies on the evolution of species. *Genetic Algorithms (GAs)* are the most well-known form of EAs (Holland, 1962*)*. The term "Genetic

Algorithm" comes from the analogy between the encoding of candidate solutions as a sequence of simple components and the genetic structure of a chromosome. Like other EAs, GAs are based on the notion of competition: they maintain a population of solutions rather than just one current solution. In consequence, the search is afforded many starting points, and the chance to sample more of the search space than local searches. The population is iteratively recombined and mutated to evolve successive populations, known as *generations*. Various selection mechanisms can be used to decide which individuals should be used to create offspring for the next generation. Key to this is the concept of the *fitness* of individuals – the idea of selection is to favour the fitter individuals, in the hope of breeding better offspring.

Genetic Programming (GP) is a type of EA usually associated with the evolution of tree structures; it focuses on automatically creating computer programs by means of evolution (Koza, 1992). Fitness evaluation is typically performed by executing the individuals and assessing their behaviour; GP is generally interested in the space where there are many possible programs, but it is not clear which ones outperform the others and to what degree. In most GP approaches, the programs are represented using variable-sized tree genomes. The leaf nodes are called *terminals*, whereas the non-leaf nodes are called *non-terminals* or *functions*. The *function set* is the set of functions from which the GP system can choose when constructing trees; GP builds new trees by repeatedly selecting nodes from a function set and putting them together. The individuals in the initial population are typically randomly generated. The specification of the control parameters in a run is a mandatory preparatory step. There are several parameters, which some of the most important being: i) the population size; ii) the probabilities of performing the genetic operations; iii) the minimum and maximum tree sizes; and iv) the stopping criteria. It is impossible to define general guidelines for setting optimal parameter values, as these depend greatly on the details of the application. Nevertheless, GP is in practice robust, and it is likely that many different parameter values will work (Poli, Langdon, & Mcphee, 2008). When applied to testing, GP trees are representations of the test programs that exercise the software under test.

The nodes of a GP tree are usually not typed – i.e., all the functions are able to accept every conceivable argument. *Type consistency* (Koza, 1994) ensures that operators will always produce legal offspring – i.e., *crossover* is not able to attempt incompatible connections between nodes, and *mutation* does not produce illegal programs. An implicit assumption underlying *type consistency* is that all combinations of structures are equally likely to be useful; in many cases, however, it is known in advance that there are constraints on the structure of the potential solutions. What's more, the nonexistence of types may lead to the generation of syntactically incorrect parse trees; specifically, non-typed GP approaches are unsuitable for representing OO programs (Haynes, Schoenefeld, & Wainwright,

1996). *Strongly-Typed Genetic Programming (STGP)* (Montana, 1993) is arguably the most natural approach to incorporate types and their constraints into GP (Poli *et al.,* 2008), since constraints are often expressed using a type system. Variables, constants, arguments and returned values can be of any data type, with the provision that the data type for each such value is specified beforehand in the function set. The STGP search space is the set of all legal parse trees and is thus particularly suited for representing OO programs, as it enables the reduction of the search space to the set of *compilable*, i.e., formally *feasible* (Wappler, 2007), programs by allowing the definition of constraints that eliminate invalid combinations of operations. In addition, STGP has already been extended to support more complex type systems, including simple generics (Montana, 1995), inheritance (Haynes et al., 1996), and polymorphism (Olsson, 1994; Yu, 2001).

Object-Oriented Evolutionary Testing

Software Testing can benefit from OO technology, for instance, by capitalising on the fact that a superclass has already been tested, and by decreasing the effort to test derived classes, which reduces the cost of testing in comparison with a flat class structure. However, the myth that the enhanced modularity and reuse brought forward by the OO programming paradigm could prevent the need for testing has long been rejected (Bertolino, 2007). In fact, the OO paradigm poses several hindrances to testing due to some aspects of its very nature (Barbey & Strohmeier, 1994): (i) inheritance opens the issue of retesting (*should operations inherited from ancestor classes be retested in the context of the descendant class?*); (ii) polymorphism and dynamic binding call for new coverage models, and induce difficulties because they introduce *undecidability* in program-based testing. The hidden state, in particular, poses a serious barrier to the OO software testing. This issue – usually referred to as the *state problem* (McMinn & Holcombe, 2003) – is related with the fact that, due to the encapsulation principle of the OO paradigm, the state of an object is accessible only through an interface of public methods. As such:

- The only way to change the state of an object is through the execution of a series of method calls (i.e., it is not possible to directly manipulate the object's attributes);
- And the only way to observe the state of an object is through its operations, which hinders the task of accurately measuring the quality of a candidate test program.

The term *OOET* usually refers to the search-based unit test generation for OO software (Harman *et al.*, 2009), and involves the search for unit test programs that define interesting state scenarios for the objects involved in the call to the *Method Under Test (MUT)*. During test program execution, all participating objects must be created and put into particular states by calling several instance methods on these objects. The search space thus encompasses the set of all possible inputs – and their states – to the public methods of a particular *Class Under Test (CUT)*, including the implicit parameter (i.e., the *this* parameter) and all the explicit parameters.

A test program for OO software typically consists of a Method Call Sequence (MCS), which represents the test scenario. In general, a MCS is a sequence of method calls, constructor calls and value attributions, when assuming that no decision or repetition structures are present (Wappler, 2007). Given that each MCS usually focuses on the execution of one particular method (the MUT), at least one method call must refer to that method – in general, the last element of the sequence. Also, it is usually not possible to test a single class in isolation; other data types may be necessary for calling the CUT's public methods. The set of classes which are relevant for testing a particular class is called the *Test Cluster* (Wappler & Wegener, 2006a).

Let us consider the search method of the *Stack* class of Java Development Kit (JDK) 1.4 for illustration purposes. The *Stack* container class represents a *last-in-first-out* stack of objects; and the *search* method returns the 1-based position (i.e., the distance from the top) where an object is on the stack.

The behaviour of the *search* method differs depending on both the state of the stack on which the method call is issued (i.e., empty or containing elements) and on the properties of the *Object* instance passed to the method as an argument (i.e., the stack instance may either contain it or not). Modifying and "tuning" the state of the *Stack* and *Object* instances, however, is not trivial. The state of the *Stack* can only be modified by calling one of the 5 public methods made available by its public interface (*push, pop, empty, peek* and *search*), and these methods have method call dependencies themselves (e.g., an *Object* instance must be created and passed to the *push* method in order to issue a method call).

Table 1 depicts an example test program for OO software. The MUT is the *search* method of the *Stack* class. In this program, instructions 1, 3 and 5 instantiate new objects, whereas instructions 2 and 4 aim to change the state of the *stack1* instance

Table 1. Example unit test program for Object-Oriented Java Software

```
1 Stack stack1 = new Stack();
2 stack1.peek();
3 Object object2 = new Object();
4 stack1.push(object2);
5 Object object3 = new Object();
6 stack1.search(object3);
```

Source: adapted from Ribeiro, 2010

variable that will be used, as the implicit parameter, in the call to the MUT at instruction 6.

It should be noted that syntactically correct and *compilable* test programs may still abort prematurely, if a *runtime* exception is thrown during execution (Wappler & Wegener, 2006a). In the example test program shown in Table 1, instruction 2 will throw a *runtime* exception (an *EmptyStackException*), rendering the test program *unfeasible*; when this happens, it is not possible to assess the quality of the test program because the final instruction (i.e., the call to the MUT) is not reached. Test programs can thus be separated in two classes: (i) *feasible* test programs that are effectively executed, and terminate with a call to the MUT; and (ii) *unfeasible* test programs which terminate prematurely because a *runtime* exception is thrown by an instruction of the MCS.

METHODOLOGIES AND TECHNIQUES FOR OBJECT-ORIENTED EVOLUTIONARY TESTING

In this Section, the existing literature on Object-Oriented Evolutionary Testing (OOET) is explored. Firstly, GA-based techniques are described; a discussion on methodologies which employ the GP technique follows; and finally, special attention is paid to approaches that employ other metaheuristic strategies.

Genetic Algorithms-Based Approaches

The first approach to the field of OOET was presented in (Tonella, 2004b), and proposes a technique for automatically generating input sequences for the structural unit testing of Java classes by means of GA. Possible solutions are represented as chromosomes, which consist of the input values to use in test program execution; the creation of objects is also accounted for. Because the GA performs on chromosomes with a specific organization, the standard evolutionary operators cannot be applied; special mutation operators (for replacing input values, changing constructors, and inserting/removing method invocations) and a one-point crossover operator are defined. A population of test programs is evolved in order to increase a measure of fitness accounting for their ability to satisfy a branch coverage criterion; new test programs are generated as long as there are targets to be covered or a maximum execution time is reached. The *eToc* framework for the evolutionary testing of OO software was implemented and made available as a result of this research.

Experimental studies were performed on 6 Java classes; full branch coverage was not achieved in all of them, but the only branches remaining corresponded to non-traversable portions of code. Even though several ET-related problems were not addressed on this work (e.g., the usage of universal EAs, encapsulation, complex state problems, test program feasibility, search guidance, MCS minimisation), it was able to prove the applicability of EAs to test data generation. Several approaches built on Tonella's experiments with GAs in the following years.

Wappler and Lammermann defined a grammar-based encoding for test programs which enabled the application of any given universal EAs (e.g., Hill Climbing or SA) to OOET. Unlike Tonella's previous approach, this methodology allows an effortless change of the evolutionary strategy employed (Wappler & Lammermann, 2005). Objective functions based on the distance-oriented approach, which guide the evolutionary search in cases of conditions that are hard to meet by random, are also defined. However, the technique proposed permits the generation of individuals that cannot be decoded into test programs without errors; this hindrance is circumvented by the definition of a fitness function which penalises invalid sequences. Experiments were performed on a custom-made Java class; even though coverage metrics were not provided, relevant results included the observation that the number of inconvertible individuals visibly decreased constantly over the generations.

In (Cheon, Kim, & Perumandla, 2005), the authors combined the Java Modelling Language (JML) and GAs in order to automate test data generation for Java programs. JML is used both as a tool for describing test oracles and as a basis for generating test data; each class to be tested is assumed to be annotated with JML assertions. A proof-of-concept tool is briefly described with basis on a custom-made example. In (Cheon & Kim, 2006), a specification-based fitness function for evaluating *boolean* methods of OO programs was presented, with an example being provided for illustration and experimentation purposes. The evolutionary search's efficiency was reported to improve from 300% up to 800% as a result of application of the fitness function.

In (Inkumsah & Xie, 2007), a technique that merges *Concolic Testing* (a combination of concrete and symbolic testing techniques) and ET was introduced; this approach was implemented into the *Evacon* framework, which integrated Tonella's *eToc* ET tool and the *jCUTE* concolic testing tool (which tests Java classes using the dynamic symbolic execution technique). ET is used to search for desirable method sequences, while concolic testing is employed to generate desirable method arguments. The inclusion of concolic testing into the process was supported by the perception that typical ET tools do not use program structure or semantic knowledge to directly guide test generation, nor provide effective support for generating desirable primitive method arguments. Empirical studies were conducted on 6 Java classes, with the results showing that the tests generated using *Evacon* achieved higher branch coverage than ET or concolic testing alone.

The *Evacon* tool is described with further detail in (Inkumsah & Xie, 2008). Additionally, *Evacon* is empirically compared to *eToc*, *jCUTE*, *JUnit Factory* (an industrial test generation tool developed by *AgitarLabs*), and *Randoop* (a random testing tool). *Evacon* is reported to achieve higher branch coverage than any of the aforementioned tools for the 13 Java classes tested. The *Evacon* framework includes 4 components: evolutionary testing, symbolic execution, argument transformation (for bridging from ET to symbolic execution), and chromosome construction (for bridging from symbolic execution to ET). In a short position paper (Xie, Tillmann, Halleux, & Schulte, 2008), the authors briefly describe an additional tool for the generation of method sequences with a demand-driven mechanism and a heuristic-guided mechanism, which is incorporated into *Pex* (a test data generation framework for .NET).

In (Dharsana, Jennifer, Askarunisha, & Ramaraj, 2007), a GA-based tool for generating test cases for Java programs is briefly described. Experiments were performed on 3 JDK classes and 2 custom-made programs, but no details were provided on the setup or results.

The work described in (Ferrer, Chicano, & Alba, 2009) proposes dealing with the inheritance feature of OO programs by focusing on the Java *instanceof* operator. The main motivation is that of providing guidance for an automatic test case generator in the presence of conditions containing the aforementioned operator, and is supported by the fact that it appears in 2700 of the 13000 classes of the JDK 1.6 class hierarchy. Two *mutation* operators, which change the solutions based on a distance measure that computes the branch distance in the presence of the *instanceof* operator, were proposed. Experiments were performed on 9 custom-made test programs, each consisting of 1 method with 6 conditions; the mutation operators proposed were reported to behave well when used in place of a simpler mutation operator, and when compared to random search.

Genetic Programming-Based Approaches

GP emerges as a natural candidate to address OOET problems, for reasons which include: (i) the fact that GP is usually associated with the evolution of tree structures and is thus particularly suited for representing and evolving test programs; (ii) the existence of a number of typing mechanisms (most notably STGP) which facilitate the encoding of OO programs using GP; (iii) the possibility of having a tree vary in length throughout the run, thus allowing experimenting with different sized test programs; and (iv) the possibility of evolving active structures, enabling the solutions to be executed without post-processing. The first GP-based approaches to OOET were presented in 2006 in (Wappler & Wegener, 2006a, 2006b), and in (Seesing, 2006; Seesing & Gross, 2006).

The encoding of potential solutions using the STGP technique was first proposed in (Wappler & Wegener, 2006b). Test programs are represented as STGP trees, which are able to express the call dependencies of the methods that are relevant for a given test object. In contrast with previous approaches in this area, neither repair of individuals nor penalty mechanisms are required in order to achieve sequence validity; the usage of STGP preserves validity throughout the entire search process (i.e., only *compilable* test programs are generated by tree builders and genetic operators). To account for polymorphic relationships which exist due to inheritance relations, the STGP types used by the function set are specified in correspondence to the type hierarchy of the test cluster classes: the function set is derived from the signatures of the methods of the test cluster classes, and the type set is derived from the inheritance relations of the test cluster classes. *Runtime* exceptions are dealt with by means of a distance-based fitness function. Experiments were performed on 4 JDK classes, with full structural coverage being achieved in all cases.

Wappler and Wegener extended their previous work and focused on dealing with unfeasible test programs; unlike previous approaches, the search is guided in case of uncaught *runtime* exceptions (Wappler & Wegener, 2006a). They propose a minimising distance-based fitness function in order to assess and differentiate the test programs generated during the evolutionary search, which rates them according to their distance to the given test goal (i.e., the program element to be covered). The aim of each individual search is therefore to generate a test program that covers a particular branch of the CUT. This fitness function makes use of a distance metric that is based on the number of non-executed methods of a test program if a *runtime* exception occurs. The *EvoUnit* framework, which implements the concepts proposed in (Wappler & Wegener, 2006a, 2006b), is also described; unfortunately the tool is proprietary and is thus not openly available. Experiments were performed on a custom-made test cluster with full branch coverage being achieved.

An improvement to the aforementioned ET approach was suggested in (Wappler & Schieferdecker, 2007), which particularly addresses the test of non-public methods. The existing objective functions are extended by an additional component that accounts for encapsulation; candidate test programs are rewarded if they cover calls to specific non-public methods. Experiments performed on 6 Java classes yield better branch coverage for non-public methods in comparison with random search and with their previous approach.

In his Ph.D. Thesis, Wappler provides a thorough explanation of his approach to automatic test data generation for OO software, and compares it to other testing techniques, e.g., symbolic execution and constraint solving (Wappler, 2007). An empirical investigation also demonstrated the effectiveness of the methodology; it outperformed random testing and 2 commercial test sequence generators (*CodePro* and *Jtest*) when being allocated the same resources. Limitations on the current stage of development of the approach were also pinpointed: the efficiency level of the approach decreases as the test cluster (and, in consequence, the function set) increases in size; and the test sequences might include unnecessary method calls.

Ribeiro *et al.* also employed STGP for representing test programs, and presented a series of studies on defining strategies for addressing the challenges posed by the OO paradigm, which include methodologies for: (i) systematizing both the test object analysis (Ribeiro, Vega, & Zenha-Rela, 2007; Ribeiro, Zenha-Rela, & Vega, 2007) and the test data generation (Ribeiro et al., 2007; Ribeiro, 2008) processes; (ii) introducing an *input domain reduction* methodology, based on the concept of *purity analysis*, which allows the identification and removal of entries that are irrelevant to the search problem because they do not contribute to the definition of relevant test scenarios (Ribeiro, Zenha-Rela, & Vega, 2008; Ribeiro, Zenha-Rela, & Vega, 2009); (iii) proposing an adaptive strategy for promoting the introduction of relevant instructions into the generated test cases by means of *mutation*, which utilizes Adaptive EAs (Ribeiro, Zenha-Rela, & Vega, 2010a); and (iv) defining an *object reuse* methodology for GP-based approaches to ET, which allows one object instance can be passed to multiple methods as an argument (or multiple times to the same method as arguments) and enables the generation of test programs that exercise structures of the software under test that would not be reachable otherwise (Ribeiro, Zenha-Rela, & Vega, 2010b).

Ribeiro elaborates on these topics in his Ph.D. Thesis (Ribeiro, 2010) and provides a thorough description of the authors' technical approach, embodied by the *eCrash* OOET tool. Special attention is put on bridging and automating the static test object analysis and the iterative test data generation processes; the function set is computed automatically with basis on the test cluster, and the test programs are evolved iteratively solely with basis on function set information. Experiments were performed on JDK 1.4 container classes; the results demonstrated the pertinence of the approach and the applicability of STGP as a basis for developing an automated, general-purpose test data generation tool for OO software.

Seesing and Gross proposed a distinct typed GP mechanism for creating test data for OO systems; in (Seesing & Gross, 2006), the advantages of employing a tree-shaped data structure (which can be mapped instantly to the abstract syntax trees commonly used in computer languages) for representing test programs is discussed, and the proposed GP methodology is compared to previous GA-based approaches (Tonella, 2004b; Wappler & Lammermann, 2005). A custom-made encoding of OO test programs is presented, and mutation operators for method introduction, method removal, and variable introduction are described. Experiments were performed on 5 Java classes; the results demonstrated the advantage of GP over random search, with much higher structural coverage being achieved. In (Seesing, 2006), the author elaborates on the approach and describes the *EvoTest* test case generation and software analysis framework.

Arcuri and Yao employed STGP in a different scenario. (Arcuri & Yao, 2007a) introduces the idea of employing Co-Evolution (Hillis, 1990) for automatically generating OO programs from their specification; STGP is used to evolve these programs and, at the same time, the specifications are exploited in order to co-evolve a set of unit tests. More specifically, given a specification of a program, the goal is to evolve a program that satisfies it; at each step of the evolutionary process, each program is evaluated against a set of unit tests that also depends on the specification. The more unit tests a program is able to pass, the higher its fitness will be; similarly, unit tests are rewarded on how many programs they make fail. The experiments performed on 4 array-related problems achieved successful results. In (Arcuri, 2008; Arcuri & Yao, 2008a), the authors elaborate on the topic and provide further details on the approach, and in (Arcuri, White, Clark, & Yao, 2008) they present a related co-evolution approach to optimising software, which also involves Multi-Objective Optimisation; still, and even though it is argued that it possible to apply the methodology proposed to any problem that can be defined with a formal specification, its application to the OO software was not the subject of the latter study.

Cody-Kenny *et al.* (Cody-Kenny, Galván-López, & Barrett, 2015) presented a GP system for improving the performance of Java programs named *locoGP*. Program performance is measured by: counting the number of instructions taken to execute a program; and problem-specific functions for counting functionality errors. Experiments were performed on a number of sort algorithms; results showed improvements, encouraging further studies on larger programs.

Other Metaheuristics and Hybrid-Based Approaches

Even though the majority of the OO literature is devoted to the study of either GAs or GP, there are several studies that focus on distinct evolutionary techniques. In fact, as stated in (Arcuri & Yao, 2007c), other metaheuristic techniques have the potential to achieve promising results in this area.

An approach which employed a hybrid of Ant Colony Optimisation and Multi-Agent GAs was the subject of the work described in (Liu, Wang, & Liu, 2005). The focus was on the generation of the shortest MCS for a given test goal, under the constraint of state dependent behaviour and without violating encapsulation. This hybrid algorithm was reported to yield encouraging results on the experiments performed.

In (Sagarna, Arcuri, & Yao, 2007), the authors addressed the OOET problem using Estimation of Distribution Algorithms (EDAs). EDAs only differ from GAs in the procedure to generate new individuals; instead of using the typical breeding operators, EDAs perform this task by sampling a probability distribution previously built from the set of selected individuals. The focus was put on generating test data for Java container classes. Relevant conclusions include the observations that the positions at which methods are called in the test program are (considering the particular conditions of the approach) independent of each other, and that coverage grows as the length of the MCS increases.

In (Liaskos & Roper, 2008), the authors investigated whether the properties of the Clonal Selection (CS) algorithm (memory, combination of local and global search) could help tackling the hindrances posed by OOET. CS is one of the most popular population-based Artificial Immune Systems (AIS) algorithms (computational systems inspired by theoretical immunology and observed immune functions). Despite employing mutation to generate new populations, and unlike GAs, CS performs mutation on the selected solutions with a rate that is inversely proportionate to their fitness, and does not use crossover; also, high quality solutions are stored for future use, leading to a faster immune response. The encoding of solutions is identical to the one used by the GAs (test programs are encoded as chromosomes), and the goal is to minimise the distance between "*receptors*" (i.e., the executed paths) and "*antigens*" (i.e., the test targets). Comparative experiments were performed on 6 Java classes to assess the behaviour of the hybridisation of a GA with both AIS and Local Search. The results suggested that hybridised approaches usually outperform the GA; however, there are scenarios for which the hybridisation with Local Search is more suited than the more sophisticated CS algorithm. This paper extended the authors' previous works (Liaskos & Roper, 2007; Liaskos, Roper, & Wood, 2007), which also addressed the problem of automated testing with data-flow as the adopted coverage criterion.

Arcuri *et al.* performed extensive research on the application of distinct search algorithms to the test data generation for container classes (i.e., classes designed to store any arbitrary type of data). This is precisely the topic of (Arcuri & Yao, 2007b). Hill Climbing, GAs and Memetic Algorithms were the evolutionary approaches used and compared (extending their previous work presented in (Arcuri & Yao, 2007d)). While GAs are global metaheuristics and Hill Climbing is a local search metaheuristic, Memetic Algorithms can approximately be described as a population-based metaheuristics in which, whenever an offspring is generated, a local search is applied to it until it reaches a local optimum. Case studies conducted on 5 Java container classes showed that the Memetic Algorithm outperforms the other algorithms; also, novel search operators and a search space reduction technique were able to increase its performance. In (Arcuri & Yao, 2008b), the authors elaborate on their previous studies, and focused on the difficulties of testing OO container classes with metaheuristic search algorithms. The performance of five search algorithms (Random Search, Hill Climbing, SA, GAs and Memetic Algorithms) was compared on 10 Java classes. The experimental studies revealed

TreeMap (an implementation of Red-Black Tree) as the most difficult container to test, with Memetic Algorithms arising as the best technique for the problem. Also interestingly, Hill Climbing performed better than GAs (Local Search algorithms are generally supposed to behave worse in these situations (Wegener, Baresel, & Sthamer, 2001)), and Random Search behaved poorly especially on more complicated problems. In his Ph.D. Thesis (Arcuri, 2009), the author compiles and elaborates on his previous proposals. Relevant contributions to the SBSE area include: theoretical analyses of search algorithms applied to test data generation (and, in particular, to OOET); and the proposal of methodologies for (i) automatic refinement – i.e., automating implementation with basis on a formal specification, (ii) fault correction – i.e., automatically evolving the input program to make it able to pass a set of test cases, (iii) improving non-functional criteria – e.g., execution time and power consumption, and (iv) reverse engineering – i.e., automatically deriving source code from bytecode or assembly code. Test suites targeting branch coverage, for real Java classes, were generated by employing GA and Random techniques and compared in the empirical study conducted by Shamshiri et al. (Shamshiri, Rojas, Fraser, & McMinn, 2015); it included 1000 classes randomly selected from SF110 corpus of open projects (Fraser & Arcuri, 2014). In this study, for the majority of the classes, the behaviour observed was quite similar; most notably when optimisation techniques were applied (e.g., seeding). The authors arguemented that one reason for the unexpected similarity between algorithms resides on the fact that there are a huge number of branches that don't provide any type of guidance (when compared with the ones that provide guidance that can be leveraged by GA algorithms); as a consequence, low coverage values for the GA algorithms were observed in large classes containing these type of branches (no guidance), and better results were observed by randomly generated test suites..

Miraz *et al.* proposed a holistic incremental approach to the generation of test data for OO software, as the internal states reached with previous test programs are used as starting points to subsequent individuals (Miraz, Lanzi, & Baresi, 2009; Baresi, Lanzi, & Miraz, 2010; Baresi & Miraz, 2010). Strategies for enhancing the efficiency of the approach include: (i) local search – integrating the global evolutionary search in order to form a hybrid approach; (ii) seeding – providing an initial population so as to speed up the start of the evolutionary process; and (iii) fitness inheritance – replacing the evaluation of the fitness function by replacing the fitness of some individuals with estimated fitness inherited from their parents. A multi-objective approach is used to combine coverage and length criteria. Test program quality is evaluated with a technique which merges black-box analysis (to evaluate the behaviours of tested classes and reward test programs accordingly) and white-box analysis (which utilises coverage criteria). These techniques were implemented in the *Testful* tool.

EvoSuite, which was presented in (Fraser & Arcuri, 2011a), is a tool that applies a hybrid approach – integrating hybrid search, dynamic symbolic execution and testability transformation – for generating and optimizing test suites, while suggesting possible oracles by adding assertions that concisely summarize the current behaviour. *EvoSuite* implements a "whole test suite" (Fraser & Arcuri, 2011c) approach towards evolving test data, meaning that optimisation is performed with respect to a coverage criterion, rather than individual coverage goals. The rationale for this methodology is related with the observation that coverage goals are not independent nor equally difficult, and are sometimes infeasible; test suites are thus evolved with the aim of covering all coverage goals at the same time, while keeping the total size as small as possible. In (Fraser & Arcuri, 2013), the authors evaluated the approach on open source libraries and an industrial case study for a total of 1,741 classes, showing that *EvoSuite* achieved up to 188 times the branch coverage of a traditional approach targeting single branches, with up to 62% smaller test suites.

The *EvoSuite* tool was extended and utilised as a platform for experimentation. Pavlov and Fraser presented a semi-automatic test generation approach based on *EvoSuite* in (Pavlov & Fraser, 2012); a human tester is included in the test generation process, with the tester being given the opportunity to improve the current solution (an editor window is presented to the user with a pre-processed version of the current best individual) if and when the search stagnates, under the assumption that where the search algorithm struggles, a human tester with domain knowledge can often produce solutions easily. Another prototype that extends *Evosuite* was presented in (Gross, Fraser, & Zeller, 2012): *EXSYST* is a test generator for interactive Java programs, which operates at system-level; it synthesizes input actions in order to test a program through its Graphical User Interface. The maximization of coverage is the main goal of the tool, and it uses *Evosuite* as the mechanism to incorporate search-based techniques that aim to reach the maximum of coverage possible. A major advantage of this approach is the fact that every reported failure is a real failure, as each one is a consequence of sequences of input events. (Gross et al., 2012) also reports the study conducted on five study subjects, for which *EXSYST* has revealed errors that were in fact real errors of the programs being tested.

In (Fraser, Arcuri, & McMinn, 2013), the authors addressed the issue of *primitive value* (e.g., numbers and strings) optimisation by extending the global search applied in *EvoSuite* with local search on the individual statements of method sequences: at regular intervals, the search inspects the primitive variables and tries to improve them. The Memetic Algorithm described achieved up to a 32% higher branch coverage than the standard GA; still, the authors identify the need for future work to make the local search adaptive, so as to make it less dependent of a specific parameter configuration. (Goffi, Gorla, Mattavelli, Pezzè, & Tonella, 2014) propose a search-based technique (the prototype implementation uses *EvoSuite*) to synthesize sequences of method invocations that are equivalent to a target method within a finite set of execution scenarios (e.g., the method *pop()* of the *Stack* class is equivalent to the method sequence *remove(size()-1)*), with the goal of achieving a higher level of redundancy and thus increase code reusability. Experiments performed on 47 methods of 7 classes taken automatically synthesized 123 equivalent method sequences, which represent more than 87% of the 141 sequences manually identified.

Evosuite - MOSA (Panichella, Kifetew, & Tonella, 2015a) is an extension of *Evosuite* tool (search-based testing) which incorporates an additional technique referred as Many-Objective Sorting Algorithm (MOSA) -- a many-objective GA. Similarly to several search-based testing tools, its uses branch coverage as criteria; however, in MOSA, branch coverage is addressed as a many-objective problem, in which different branches pose as different optimization problems/goals. The MOSA considers a search population composed by test cases generated randomly; it uses the traditional operators in each generation (crossover and mutation), and for each generation, the selection of the fittest individuals takes into account the sort algorithm. This sort algorithm attributes higher survival probability to test cases that are closest to at least one of the uncovered branches (many-objective optimization problem). In a search-based testing tool competition (Panichella, Kifetew, & Tonella, 2015b) *Evosuite-MOSA* was able to reach better coverage results, for a set of 63 classes, when compared with its competitors; however, it was penalised by the execution time. Limitations of this tool include the ones belonging to *Evosuite* version used, for instance: issues with non-deterministic code and code that uses external/environmental dependencies.

(Boussaa, Barais, Sunye, & Baudry, 2015) introduced the Novelty Search (NS) algorithm to address the test data generation problem for Java programs, with focus on the statement-coverage criteria; this algorithm aims to explore the search space without an objective, i.e. a fitness-based function. Instead, the selection is done with basis on how different individuals are from the solutions evaluated until that moment. The authors presented the concept of *archive* which stores, as a memory, the set of test cases generated; the *archive* is then used as a means to measure an individual's novelty degree; and if a new level of novelty is reached (higher than a specified threshold *T*) then the test case is included in the *archive*. Typical EA operators (crossover and mutation) are then applied to the test cases with the purpose of generating offspring that will settle the next population. The aim of the authors was to promote the variety among the solutions found by the generation process; and measures of statement coverage are kept during the generation process so that at the end, the best test cases are selected. Finally, the generation process ends when a certain criteria is reached (e.g., number of iterations). The concept of novel search/ behaviour as alternative to fitness functions was also addressed in a previous work from Lehman and Stanley (Lehman & Stanley, 2010).

An empirical study was conducted on 100 Java Classes by Rojas et al. (Rojas, Vivanti, Arcuri, & Fraser, 2016) with the purpose of comparing the whole test suite approach employed by *Evosuite*, which searches for tests that cover all goals at the same time, with approaches that target specific individual goals (branch coverage, for instance). The individual test goals addressed in this paper were: line coverage, branch coverage and weak mutation, and the authors concluded that traditional approaches can be best to cover a few and specific set of individual testing goals -- a very rare occurrence (if we compare those with the cases for which only *Evosuite* is able to cover the criteria goals). This work is an extended version of the research presented by Arcuri and Fraser (Arcuri & Fraser, 2014) and it includes an impact analysis focusing the usage of a test *archive*: by analysing the results, the average performance was improved but some negative side-effects were also observed due to the necessity of having specialized search operators that are able to handle the test *archive* concept.

SBES (Search-Based Equivalent Synthesis) is a Java prototype that utilises a search search-based technique to automatically synthesize and validate sequences functionally equivalent to sequences of method calls (Goffi et al., 2014). If we consider the method *put(<key>, <value>)* as an example which is available in collections' objects (and inserts the pair in a collection object), the technique proposed in SBES would be able to generate an "equivalent" set of instructions that would test the put method, example: *m=new Multimap(); m.putAll(key, new List().add(value))* (adapted from (Mattavelli, Goffi, & Gorla, 2015)). The equivalence notion proposed by the authors is based on the notion defined by De Nicola and Hennessy (De Nicola & Hennessy, 1984). The search-based engine used by SBES is a custom version of *Evosuite*; the exclusive goal to be covered is the "TRUE" branch of the MUT. In (Mattavelli et al., 2015) the authors reported an improvement of the tool by implementing means to handle a language feature that was not originally supported -- Java generics. (Mattavelli et al., 2015) reports an experiment using Google Guava library as the case study which, according to the authors, present a large search space mainly due to the high number of classes, methods and parameter values. Memetic algorithms were used to address the specificities of such search space. A total of 220 methods from 16 classes belonging to the Google Guava collections library were evaluated by SBES, and the new prototype that includes generics support and memetic algorithms is able to "find 86% more true functionally equivalent method sequences."

In (He, Zhao, & Zhu, 2015), the authors propose to integrate Reinforcement Learning into OO Evolutionary Testing; GP is used to evolve candidate method call sequences in ET, and Reinforcement Learning to steer search towards pertinent individuals -- namely, by replacing method calls with others that return subclasses of the original type, and public method with others that can call specific non-public methods. The aim is to tackle the hindrances posed by the inheritance and encapsulation properties of the OO paradigm. Empirical studies conducted on the proposed *EvoQ* prototype showed encouraging results in comparison with *eToc* and *Randoop*.

(Chawla, Chana, & Rana, 2015; He et al., 2015) presents a hybrid Particle Swarm Optimization and GA methodology for the automatic generation of test suites, with the objective of making use of the diversity of GA and fast convergence rate of Particle Swarm Optimization. Empirical studies yielded positive results for the container classes used as Test Objects, although it was stated that further experiments were required in order to extend the conclusions to generic OO software.

CONCLUSION

Test data generation by means of EAs requires the definition of a suitable representation of OO test programs. Even though it is still a relatively young field of study and no definitive conclusions have been reached on deciding the best search algorithm to apply for this purpose, existing OOET approaches have mainly used GAs and GP.

An analysis of the current literature on OOET allows making some observations: nearly all studies have been developed with basis on the program's structure, with the objective being that of attaining a coverage criterion (usually statement or branch coverage). Java is clearly the programming language of choice for the purposes of implementation and experimentation; and even though several test objects have considered for experimentation purposes, nearly all works (and, in particular, those that do not use custom-made classes) employ container classes (e.g., Stack, BitSet, Vector, TreeMap) as a basis for their studies, mostly due to the lack of a common benchmark which can be used by researchers to test and compare their techniques (Arcuri & Yao, 2007c).

Even though several OOET techniques have been proposed, the test data generation frameworks developed are seldom publicly available, with the only exceptions known to the authors being *eToc* (Tonella, 2004a), *Testful* (Miraz, Lanzi, & Baresi, 2011), *EvoSuite* (Fraser & Arcuri, 2011b), *EvoSuite-MOSA* (Panichella, Kifetew, & Tonella, 2015a) and *eCrash* (Ribeiro, Nogueira, Vega, & Zenha-Rela, 2013). This makes it difficult for researchers to experiment and compare their approaches; as such, comparisons are usually performed against Random Search, e.g., (Gupta & Rohil, 2008; Ribeiro et al., 2010b; Seesing & Gross, 2006; Wappler & Schieferdecker, 2007). A recent study (Nogueira, Ribeiro, Vega, & Zenha-Rela, 2013) compared the performance of three test data generation tools – the *Randoop* (Pacheco & Ernst, 2007) random testing tool, and the *EvoSuite* and *eCrash* ET tools – when applied to a complex software product – the Apache Ant project (The Apache

Software Foundation, 2012) release 1.8.4. The results provided solid indicators of the effectiveness and efficiency of the ET tools, and allowed pinpointing some limitations and hindrances to be addressed in future work, including the difficulty of generating tests for some instance methods that enter infinite loops, for some static methods in classes that are not able to provide instances of that data type (namely, when public constructors are not defined), and for specific problematic methods (e.g., class loaders; input handlers; task and thread handlers; file and folder managers; compilers; audio and image processors; and encapsulators of Unix commands). The difficulty in testing classes related to certain system's features and functionalities had, in fact, already been reported in the literature (Fraser & Arcuri, 2012). In (Shamshiri, Just, et al., 2015) three generation tools for Java (*Randoop*, *EvoSuite*, and *Agitar*) were employed to empirically evaluate automatic unit test generation; the goal was that of investigating whether the resulting test suites could find faults. Results indicated that any individual tool on a given software project is far from providing confidence about finding faults, providing basis for concluding that code coverage remains a major problem and that improved techniques to achieve fault propagation and generation of assertions are still required.

It is, nevertheless, clear that significant success has been achieved by applying metaheuristics to automate the generation of test data for OO software. In fact, nature-inspired algorithms seem to perform better than "traditional" techniques (Arcuri & Yao, 2008b) (e.g., based on symbolic execution and state matching) as they seem able to solve more complex test problems in less time. Still, several open problems exist in the field of OOET, mostly arising from the challenges posed by the three cornerstones of OO programming: encapsulation, inheritance, and polymorphism. The *Search Space Sampling* issue is particularly pertinent; it deals with the inclusion of all the relevant variables to a given test object into the test data generation problem, so as to enable the coverage of the entire search space whenever possible and improve the effectiveness the approach. Because the test cluster cannot possibly include all the subclasses that may override the behaviours of the classes which are relevant for the test object, adequate strategies for search space sampling – which take the commonality among classes and their relationships with each other into account – are of paramount importance.

Future research should also involve addressing the *Oracle Generation* problem; although it is possible to generate inputs for certain classes of programs using search-based techniques, automatically determining whether the corresponding outputs are correct also remains a significant problem; one that is not limited to ET, but is orthogonal to the entire field of ST. This is because an *oracle* (i.e., a mechanism for checking that the output of a program is correct given some input), is seldom available. In (Davis & Weyuker, 1981), the authors proposed the use of a "pseudo-oracle" to alleviate this problem. A pseudo-oracle is a program that has been produced to perform the same task as its original counterpart. The two programs, the original and its pseudo-oracle, are run using the same input and their respective outputs compared; any discrepancy may represent a failure on the part of the original program or its pseudo-oracle. In (Tonella, 2004b), the oracle problem is handled by manually adding assertions; Tonella reported that the test suites produced by the ET method proposed were quite compact, and that augmenting them with assertions would thus be expected to require a minor effort. McMinn introduced testability transformations (i.e., techniques that change a program in order to make it more "testable") to automatically generate pseudo-oracles from certain classes of OO programs (McMinn, 2009). *EvoSuite* suggests possible oracles by adding assertions that concisely summarize the current behaviour, utilising a mutation testing approach; still, the authors state that they are investigating strategies to support the developer by automatically producing effective assertions (Fraser & Arcuri, 2011a) and by increasing the readability of the produced test cases (Fraser & Zeller, 2011).

REFERENCES

Afzal, W., Torkar, R., & Feldt, R. (2009). A systematic review of search-based testing for non-functional system properties. *Information and Software Technology*, *51*(6), 957–976. doi:10.1016/j.infsof.2008.12.005

Ali, S., Briand, L. C., Hemmati, H., & Panesar-Walawege, R. K. (2009). A systematic review of the application and empirical investigation of search-based test-case generation. *IEEE Transactions on Software Engineering*, *99*(1).

Anand, S., Burke, E. K., Chen, T. Y., Clark, J., Cohen, M. B., Grieskamp, W., ... Mcminn, P. (2013). An orchestrated survey of methodologies for automated software test case generation. *Journal of Systems and Software*, *86*(8), 1978–2001. doi:10.1016/j.jss.2013.02.061

Arcuri, A. (2008). On the automation of fixing software bugs. In *ICSE companion '08: Companion of the 30th international conference on software engineering* (pp. 1003–1006). New York, NY: ACM. doi:10.1145/1370175.1370223

Arcuri, A. (2009). *Automatic software generation and improvement through search based techniques* (Doctoral dissertation). University of Birmingham.

Arcuri, A., & Fraser, G. (2014). On the Effectiveness of Whole Test Suite Generation. In Lecture Notes in Computer Science (pp. 1–15). Academic Press. doi:10.1007/978-3-319-09940-8_1

Arcuri, A., White, D. R., Clark, J., & Yao, X. (2008). Multi-objective improvement of software using co-evolution and smart seeding. In *Proceedings of the 7th international conference on simulated evolution and learning (seal '08)* (p. 61-70). Springer. doi:10.1007/978-3-540-89694-4_7

Arcuri, A., & Yao, X. (2007a). Coevolving programs and unit tests from their specification. In *ASE '07: Proceedings of the twenty-second IEEE/ACM international conference on automated software engineering* (pp. 397–400). New York, NY: ACM. doi:10.1145/1321631.1321693

Arcuri, A., & Yao, X. (2007b). A memetic algorithm for test data generation of object-oriented software. In *Proceedings of the 2007 ieee congress on evolutionary computation (CEC)* (p. 2048-2055). IEEE. doi:10.1109/CEC.2007.4424725

Arcuri, A., & Yao, X. (2007c). On test data generation of object-oriented software. In *Taicpart-mutation '07: Proceedings of the testing: Academic and industrial conference practice and research techniques - mutation* (pp. 72–76). Washington, DC: IEEE Computer Society. doi:10.1109/TAIC.PART.2007.11

Arcuri, A., & Yao, X. (2007d). *Search based testing of containers for object-oriented software* (Tech. Rep. No. CSR-07-3). University of Birmingham, School of Computer Science.

Arcuri, A., & Yao, X. (2008a). A novel co-evolutionary approach to automatic software bug fixing. In *Proceedings of the IEEE congress on evolutionary computation (CEC '08)* (p. 162-168). IEEE Computer Society. doi:10.1109/CEC.2008.4630793

Arcuri, A., & Yao, X. (2008b). Search based software testing of object-oriented containers. *Information Sciences, 178*(15), 3075–3095. doi:10.1016/j.ins.2007.11.024

Barbey, S., & Strohmeier, A. (1994). The problematics of testing object-oriented software. In M. Ross, C. A. Brebbia, G. Staples, & J. Stapleton (Eds.), *SQM '94 second conference on software quality management* (Vol. 2, pp. 411–426). Academic Press.

Baresi, L., Lanzi, P. L., & Miraz, M. (2010). Testful: An evolutionary test approach for java. In *Proceedings of the 2010 third international conference on software testing, verification and validation* (pp. 185–194). Washington, DC: IEEE Computer Society. doi:10.1109/ICST.2010.54

Baresi, L., & Miraz, M. (2010). Testful: automatic unit-test generation for java classes. In *Proceedings of the 32nd ACM/IEEE international conference on software engineering - volume 2* (pp. 281–284). New York, NY: ACM. doi:10.1145/1810295.1810353

Beizer, B. (1990). *Software testing techniques*. New York: John Wiley & Sons, Inc.

Bertolino, A. (2007). Software testing research: Achievements, challenges, dreams. In *Fose '07: 2007 future of software engineering* (pp. 85–103). Washington, DC: IEEE Computer Society.

Booch, G., Maksimchuk, R. A., Engel, M. W., Young, B. J., Conallen, J., & Houston, K. A. (2007). *Object-oriented analysis and design with applications* (3rd ed.). Addison-Wesley Professional.

Boussaa, M., Barais, O., Sunye, G., & Baudry, B. (2015). A Novelty Search Approach for Automatic Test Data Generation. *2015 IEEE/ACM 8th International Workshop on Search-Based Software Testing*. doi:10.1109/SBST.2015.17

Chawla, P., Chana, I., & Rana, A. (2015). A novel strategy for automatic test data generation using soft computing technique. *Frontiers of Computer Science*, *9*(3), 346–363. doi:10.1007/s11704-014-3496-9

Cheon, Y., & Kim, M. (2006). A specification-based fitness function for evolutionary testing of object-oriented programs. In *Gecco '06: Proceedings of the 8th annual conference on genetic and evolutionary computation* (pp. 1953–1954). New York: ACM. doi:10.1145/1143997.1144322

Cheon, Y., Kim, M., & Perumandla, A. (2005). A complete automation of unit testing for java programs. In H. R. Arabnia & H. Reza (Eds.), *Proceedings of the international conference on software engineering research and practice, SERP 2005* (vol. 1, pp. 290–295). CSREA Press.

Cody-Kenny, B., Galván-López, E., & Barrett, S. (2015). locoGP: Improving Performance by Genetic Programming Java Source Code. In *Proceedings of the Companion Publication of the 2015 on Genetic and Evolutionary Computation Conference - GECCO Companion '15* (pp. 811–818). New York: ACM Press.

Davis, M. D., & Weyuker, E. J. (1981). Pseudo-oracles for non-testable programs. In *ACM 81: Proceedings of the Acm '81 conference* (pp. 254–257). New York: ACM. doi:10.1145/800175.809889

De Nicola, R., & Hennessy, M. C. B. (1984). Testing equivalences for processes. *Theoretical Computer Science*, *34*(1-2), 83–133. doi:10.1016/0304-3975(84)90113-0

Dharsana, C. S. S., Jennifer, D. N., Askarunisha, A., & Ramaraj, N. (2007). Java based test case generation and optimization using evolutionary testing. In *ICCIMA '07: Proceedings of the international conference on computational intelligence and multimedia applications (ICCIMA 2007)* (pp. 44–49). Washington, DC: IEEE Computer Society. doi:10.1109/ICCIMA.2007.445

Eckel, B. (2002). *Thinking in java*. Prentice Hall Professional Technical Reference.

Ferrer, J., Chicano, F., & Alba, E. (2009). Dealing with inheritance in oo evolutionary testing. In *Gecco '09: Proceedings of the 11th annual conference on genetic and evolutionary computation* (pp. 1665–1672). New York: ACM. doi:10.1145/1569901.1570124

Fraser, G., & Arcuri, A. (2011a). Evosuite: automatic test suite generation for object-oriented software. In *Proceedings of the 19th ACM SIGSOFT symposium and the 13th European conference on foundations of software engineering* (pp. 416–419). New York: ACM. doi:10.1145/2025113.2025179

Fraser, G., & Arcuri, A. (2011b). *Evosuite – automatic test suite generation for java*. Available from http://www.evosuite.org/

Fraser, G., & Arcuri, A. (2011c). Evolutionary generation of whole test suites. In *Proceedings of the 2011 11th international conference on quality software* (pp. 31–40). Washington, DC: IEEE Computer Society. doi:10.1109/QSIC.2011.19

Fraser, G., & Arcuri, A. (2012). Sound empirical evidence in software testing. In *34th international conference on software engineering, ICSE 2012* (pp. 178–188). IEEE. doi:10.1109/ICSE.2012.6227195

Fraser, G., & Arcuri, A. (2013). Whole test suite generation. *IEEE Transactions on Software Engineering*, *39*(2), 276–291. doi:10.1109/TSE.2012.14

Fraser, G., & Arcuri, A. (2014). A Large-Scale Evaluation of Automated Unit Test Generation Using EvoSuite. *ACM Transactions on Software Engineering and Methodology*, *24*(2), 1–42. doi:10.1145/2685612

Fraser, G., Arcuri, A., & McMinn, P. (2013). Test suite generation with memetic algorithms. In *Proceeding of the fifteenth annual conference on genetic and evolutionary computation conference* (pp. 1437–1444). New York: ACM. doi:10.1145/2463372.2463548

Fraser, G., & Zeller, A. (2011). Exploiting common object usage in test case generation. In *Proceedings of the 2011 fourth ieee international conference on software testing, verification and validation* (pp. 80–89). Washington, DC: IEEE Computer Society. doi:10.1109/ICST.2011.53

Goffi, A., Gorla, A., Mattavelli, A., Pezzè, M., & Tonella, P. (2014). Search-based synthesis of equivalent method sequences. *Proceedings of the 22nd ACM SIGSOFT International Symposium on Foundations of Software Engineering - FSE 2014*. doi:10.1145/2635868.2635888

Google. (2004). *Google scholar*. Available from http://scholar.google.com/

Gross, F., Fraser, G., & Zeller, A. (2012). Search-based system testing: high coverage, no false alarms. *Proceedings of the 2012 International Symposium on Software Testing and Analysis - ISSTA 2012*. doi:10.1145/2338965.2336762

Gupta, N. K., & Rohil, M. K. (2008). Using genetic algorithm for unit testing of object oriented software. In *ICETET '08: Proceedings of the 2008 first international conference on emerging trends in engineering and technology* (pp. 308–313). Washington, DC: IEEE Computer Society. doi:10.1109/ICETET.2008.137

Harman, M. (2007). The current state and future of search based software engineering. In *FOSE '07: 2007 future of software engineering* (pp. 342–357). Washington, DC: IEEE Computer Society. doi:10.1109/FOSE.2007.29

Harman, M., Hassoun, Y., Lakhotia, K., McMinn, P., & Wegener, J. (2007). The impact of input domain reduction on search-based test data generation. In *Esec-fse '07: Proceedings of the 6th joint meeting of the European software engineering conference and the ACM SIGSOFT symposium on the foundations of software engineering* (pp. 155–164). New York: ACM Press. doi:10.1145/1287624.1287647

Harman, M., Mansouri, S. A., & Zhang, Y. (2009). *Search based software engineering: A comprehensive analysis and review of trends techniques and applications* (Tech. Rep. No. TR-09-03). Academic Press.

Harman, M., Mansouri, S. A., & Zhang, Y. (2012). Search-based software engineering: Trends, techniques and applications. *ACM Comput. Surv., 45*(1), 11:1–11:61.

Harman, M., & McMinn, P. (2010). A theoretical and empirical study of search-based testing: Local, global, and hybrid search. *Software Engineering. IEEE Transactions on, 36*(2), 226–247.

Haynes, T. D., Schoenefeld, D. A., & Wainwright, R. L. (1996). Type inheritance in strongly typed genetic programming. In P. J. Angeline & K. E. Kinnear Jr., (Eds.), *Advances in genetic programming 2* (pp. 359–376). Cambridge, MA: MIT Press.

He, W., Zhao, R., & Zhu, Q. (2015). Integrating Evolutionary Testing with Reinforcement Learning for Automated Test Generation of Object-Oriented Software. *Liangzi Dianzi Xuebao. Liangzi Dianzi Xuebao, 24*(1), 38–45.

Hillis, W. D. (1990). Co-evolving parasites improve simulated evolution as an optimization procedure. *Physica D. Nonlinear Phenomena, 42*(1-3), 228–234. doi:10.1016/0167-2789(90)90076-2

Holland, J. H. (1962). Outline for a logical theory of adaptive systems. *Journal of the Association for Computing Machinery*, *9*(3), 297–314. doi:10.1145/321127.321128

Inkumsah, K., & Xie, T. (2007). Evacon: A framework for integrating evolutionary and concolic testing for object-oriented programs. In *Proc. 22nd IEEE/ACM international conference on automated software engineering (ase 2007)* (pp. 425–428). IEEE. doi:10.1145/1321631.1321700

Inkumsah, K., & Xie, T. (2008). Improving structural testing of object-oriented programs via integrating evolutionary testing and symbolic execution. *Proc. 23rd ieee/acm international conference on automated software engineering (ASE 2008)*. doi:10.1109/ASE.2008.40

Koza, J. R. (1992). *Genetic programming: On the programming of computers by means of natural selection (complex adaptive systems)*. The MIT Press.

Koza, J. R. (1994). *Genetic programming II: Automatic discovery of reusable programs*. Cambridge, MA: The MIT Press.

Lehman, J., & Stanley, K. O. (2010). Efficiently evolving programs through the search for novelty. *Proceedings of the 12th annual conference on Genetic and evolutionary computation - GECCO '10*. doi:10.1145/1830483.1830638

Liaskos, K., & Roper, M. (2007, September). *Automatic test-data generation: An immunological approach*. IEEE Computer Society.

Liaskos, K., & Roper, M. (2008). Hybridizing evolutionary testing with artificial immune systems and local search. In *ICSTW '08: Proceedings of the 2008 IEEE international conference on software testing verification and validation workshop* (pp. 211–220). Washington, DC: IEEE Computer Society. doi:10.1109/ICSTW.2008.21

Liaskos, K., Roper, M., & Wood, M. (2007). Investigating data-flow coverage of classes using evolutionary algorithms. In *GECCO '07: Proceedings of the 9th annual conference on genetic and evolutionary computation* (pp. 1140–1140). New York: ACM. doi:10.1145/1276958.1277183

Liu, X., Wang, B., & Liu, H. (2005). Evolutionary search in the context of object-oriented programs. *Mic'05: Proceedings of the sixth metaheuristics international conference*.

Mantere, T., & Alander, J. T. (2005). Evolutionary software engineering, a review. *Applied Soft Computing*, *5*(3), 315–331. doi:10.1016/j.asoc.2004.08.004

Maragathavalli, P. (2011). *Search-based software test data generation using evolutionary computation.* CoRR, abs/1103.0125

J. J. Marciniak (Ed.). (1994). *Encyclopedia of software engineering.* New York: Wiley-Interscience.

Mattavelli, A., Goffi, A., & Gorla, A. (2015). Synthesis of Equivalent Method Calls in Guava. In Lecture Notes in Computer Science (pp. 248–254). Academic Press. doi:10.1007/978-3-319-22183-0_19

McMinn, P. (2004). Search-based software test data generation: A survey. *Software Testing, Verification & Reliability, 14*(2), 105–156. doi:10.1002/stvr.294

McMinn, P. (2009). Search-based failure discovery using testability transformations to generate pseudo-oracles. In *GECCO '09: Proceedings of the 11th annual conference on genetic and evolutionary computation* (pp. 1689–1696). New York: ACM. doi:10.1145/1569901.1570127

McMinn, P. (2011). Search-based software testing: Past, present and future. In *Software testing, verification and validation workshops (ICSTW), 2011 IEEE fourth international conference on* (p. 153-163). IEEE.

McMinn, P., & Holcombe, M. (2003). *The state problem for evolutionary testing.* Available from citeseer.ist.psu.edu/mcminn03state.html

Michalewicz, Z. (1994). Genetic algorithms + data structures = evolution programs (2nd ed.). New York: Springer-Verlag New York, Inc.

Miraz, M., Lanzi, P. L., & Baresi, L. (2009). Testful: using a hybrid evolutionary algorithm for testing stateful systems. In *Proceedings of the 11th annual conference on genetic and evolutionary computation* (pp. 1947–1948). New York: ACM. doi:10.1145/1569901.1570252

Miraz, M., Lanzi, P. L., & Baresi, L. (2011). *Testful – an evolutionary testing framework for java.* Available from https://code.google.com/p/testful/

Montana, D. J. (1993). Strongly typed genetic programming (Tech. Rep. No. #7866). Academic Press.

Montana, D. J. (1995). Strongly typed genetic programming. *Evolutionary Computation, 3*(2), 199–230. doi:10.1162/evco.1995.3.2.199

Myers, G. J., & Sandler, C. (2004). *The art of software testing.* John Wiley & Sons.

Nogueira, A. F., Ribeiro, J. C. B., de Vega, F. F., & Zenha-Rela, M. A. (2013). ecrash: An empirical study on the apache ant project. In *Proceedings of the 5th international symposium on search based software engineering (SSBSE '13)* (Vol. 8084). St. Petersburg, Russia: Springer. doi:10.1007/978-3-642-39742-4_25

Nogueira, A. F., Ribeiro, J. C. B., Fernández de Vega, F., & Zenha-Rela, M. A. (2014). Object-Oriented Evolutionary Testing: A Review of Evolutionary Approaches to the Generation of Test Data for Object-Oriented Software. *International Journal of Natural Computing Research*, 4(4), 15–35. doi:10.4018/ijncr.2014100102

Olsson, J. R. (1994). *Inductive functional programming using incremental program transformation and execution of logic programs by iterative-deepening a* sld-tree search* (research report No. 189). University of Oslo.

Pacheco, C., & Ernst, M. D. (2007). Randoop: feedback-directed random testing for java. In *Oopsla '07: Companion to the 22nd ACM SIGPLAN conference on object-oriented programming systems and applications companion* (pp. 815–816). New York: ACM. doi:10.1145/1297846.1297902

Panichella, A., Kifetew, F. M., & Tonella, P. (2015a). Reformulating Branch Coverage as a Many-Objective Optimization Problem. In *2015 IEEE 8th International Conference on Software Testing, Verification and Validation (ICST)*. IEEE. doi:10.1109/ICST.2015.7102604

Panichella, A., Kifetew, F. M., & Tonella, P. (2015b). Results for EvoSuite -- MOSA at the Third Unit Testing Tool Competition. In *2015 IEEE/ACM 8th International Workshop on Search-Based Software Testing*. IEEE. doi:10.1109/sbst.2015.14

Pavlov, Y., & Fraser, G. (2012). Semi-automatic search-based test generation. In *Proceedings of the 2012 ieee fifth international conference on software testing, verification and validation* (pp. 777–784). Washington, DC: IEEE Computer Society. doi:10.1109/ICST.2012.176

Poli, R., Langdon, W. B., & Mcphee, N. F. (2008). *A field guide to genetic programming. Lulu Enterprises*. UK Ltd.

Ribeiro, J. C. B. (2008). Search-based test case generation for object-oriented java software using strongly-typed genetic programming. In *GECCO '08: Proceedings of the 2008 gecco conference companion on genetic and evolutionary computation* (pp. 1819–1822). New York: ACM. doi:10.1145/1388969.1388979

Ribeiro, J. C. B. (2010). *Contributions for improving genetic programming-based approaches to the evolutionary testing of object-oriented software* (Doctoral dissertation). Universidad de Extremadura, España.

Ribeiro, J. C. B., de Vega, F. F., & Zenha-Rela, M. (2007). Using dynamic analysis of java bytecode for evolutionary object-oriented unit testing. In *Sbrc wtf 2007: Proceedings of the 8th workshop on testing and fault tolerance at the 25th Brazilian symposium on computer networks and distributed systems* (pp. 143–156). Brazilian Computer Society (SBC).

Ribeiro, J. C. B., Nogueira, A. F., de Vega, F. F., & Zenha-Rela, M. A. (2013). *eCrash – evolutionary testing for object-oriented software*. Available from http://sourceforge.net/projects/ecrashtesting/

Ribeiro, J. C. B., Zenha-Rela, M., & de Vega, F. F. (2007). ecrash: a framework for performing evolutionary testing on third-party java components. In *Cedi jaem'07: Proceedings of the i jornadas sobre algoritmos evolutivos y metaheuristicas at the ii congreso español de informática* (pp. 137–144). Academic Press.

Ribeiro, J. C. B., Zenha-Rela, M. A., & de Vega, F. F. (2008). Strongly-typed genetic programming and purity analysis: input domain reduction for evolutionary testing problems. In *Gecco '08: Proceedings of the 10th annual conference on genetic and evolutionary computation* (pp. 1783–1784). New York: ACM. doi:10.1145/1389095.1389439

Ribeiro, J. C. B., Zenha-Rela, M. A., & de Vega, F. F. (2010a). Adaptive evolutionary testing: an adaptive approach to search-based test case generation for object-oriented software. In Nicso 2010 - international workshop on nature inspired cooperative strategies for optimization. Springer. doi:10.1007/978-3-642-12538-6_16

Ribeiro, J. C. B., Zenha-Rela, M. A., & de Vega, F. F. (2010b). Enabling object reuse on genetic programming-based approaches to object-oriented evolutionary testing. In *Eurogp 2010 - 13th european conference on genetic programming*. Springer. doi:10.1007/978-3-642-12148-7_19

Ribeiro, J. C. B., Zenha-Rela, M. A., & Vega, F. (2009). Test case evaluation and input domain reduction strategies for the evolutionary testing of object-oriented software. *Information and Software Technology, 51*(11), 1534–1548. doi:10.1016/j.infsof.2009.06.009

Rojas, J. M., Vivanti, M., Arcuri, A., & Fraser, G. (2016). A detailed investigation of the effectiveness of whole test suite generation. *Empirical Software Engineering, 22*(2), 852–893. doi:10.1007/s10664-015-9424-2

Sagarna, R., Arcuri, A., & Yao, X. (2007). Estimation of distribution algorithms for testing object oriented software. In D. Srinivasan & L. Wang (Eds.), 2007 IEEE congress on evolutionary computation. Singapore: IEEE Press. doi:10.1109/CEC.2007.4424504

Seesing, A. (2006). *Evotest: Test case generation using genetic programming and software analysis* (Master's thesis). Delft University of Technology.

Seesing, A., & Gross, H.-G. (2006). A genetic programming approach to automated test generation for object-oriented software. *International Transactions on System Science and Applications*, *1*(2), 127–134.

Shamshiri, S., Just, R., Rojas, J. M., Fraser, G., McMinn, P., & Arcuri, A. (2015). Do Automatically Generated Unit Tests Find Real Faults? An Empirical Study of Effectiveness and Challenges (T). In *2015 30th IEEE/ACM International Conference on Automated Software Engineering (ASE)*. IEEE. doi:10.1109/ase.2015.86

Shamshiri, S., Rojas, J. M., Fraser, G., & McMinn, P. (2015). Random or Genetic Algorithm Search for Object-Oriented Test Suite Generation? *Proceedings of the 2015 on Genetic and Evolutionary Computation Conference - GECCO '15*. doi:10.1145/2739480.2754696

Tassey, G. (2002). *The economic impacts of inadequate infrastructure for software testing (Tech. Rep.)*. National Institute of Standards and Technology.

The Apache Software Foundation. (2012). *The apache ant project, release 1.8.4*. Available from http://ant.apache.org/

Tonella, P. (2004a). *eToc – evolutionary testing of classes*. Available from http://star.fbk.eu/etoc/

Tonella, P. (2004b). Evolutionary testing of classes. In *Issta '04: Proceedings of the 2004 acm sigsoft international symposium on software testing and analysis* (pp. 119–128). New York: ACM Press. doi:10.1145/1007512.1007528

Varshney, S., & Mehrotra, M. (2013). Search based software test data generation for structural testing: A perspective. *SIGSOFT Softw. Eng. Notes*, *38*(4), 1–6. doi:10.1145/2492248.2492277

Wappler, S. (2007). *Automatic generation of object-oriented unit tests using genetic programming* (Doctoral dissertation). Technischen Universitat Berlin.

Wappler, S., & Lammermann, F. (2005). Using evolutionary algorithms for the unit testing of object-oriented software. In *Gecco '05: Proceedings of the 2005 conference on genetic and evolutionary computation* (pp. 1053–1060). New York: ACM Press. doi:10.1145/1068009.1068187

Wappler, S., & Schieferdecker, I. (2007). Improving evolutionary class testing in the presence of non-public methods. In *Ase '07: Proceedings of the twenty-second ieee/ acm international conference on automated software engineering* (pp. 381–384). New York: ACM. doi:10.1145/1321631.1321689

Wappler, S., & Wegener, J. (2006a). Evolutionary unit testing of object-oriented software using a hybrid evolutionary algorithm. In *Cec'06: Proceedings of the 2006 ieee congress on evolutionary computation* (pp. 851–858). IEEE. doi:10.1109/CEC.2006.1688400

Wappler, S., & Wegener, J. (2006b). Evolutionary unit testing of object-oriented software using strongly-typed genetic programming. In *Gecco '06: Proceedings of the 8th annual conference on genetic and evolutionary computation* (pp. 1925–1932). New York: ACM Press. doi:10.1145/1143997.1144317

Wegener, J., Baresel, A., & Sthamer, H. (2001). Evolutionary test environment for automatic structural testing. *Information and Software Technology, 43*(14), 841-854.

Xanthakis, S., Ellis, C., Skourlas, C., Gall, A. L., & Karapoulios, K. (1992). Application of genetic algorithms to software testing [application des algorithmes génétiques au test des logiciels]. In *Proceedings of the 5th international conference on software engineering* (pp. 625–636). Academic Press.

Xiao, M., El-Attar, M., Reformat, M., & Miller, J. (2007). Empirical evaluation of optimization algorithms when used in goal-oriented automated test data generation techniques. *Empirical Software Engineering, 12*(2), 183–239. doi:10.1007/s10664-006-9026-0

Xie, T., Tillmann, N., de Halleux, J., & Schulte, W. (2008). Method-sequence exploration for automated unit testing of object-oriented programs. *Proc. workshop on state-space exploration for automated testing (sseat 2008).*

Yu, T. (2001). Hierachical processing for evolving recursive and modular programs using higher order functions and lambda abstractions. *Genetic Programming and Evolvable Machines, 2*(4), 345–380. doi:10.1023/A:1012926821302

Chapter 7
Evolutionary Control Systems

Jesús-Antonio Hernández-Riveros
Universidad Nacional de Colombia, Colombia

Jorge Humberto Urrea-Quintero
Universidad de Antioquia, Colombia

Cindy Vanessa Carmona-Cadavid
Universidad Pontificia Bolivariana, Colombia

ABSTRACT

In control systems, the actual output is compared with the desired value so a corrective action maintains an established behavior. The industrial controller most widely used is the proportional integral derivative (PID). For PIDs, the process is represented in a transfer function. The linear quadratic regulator (LQR) controller needs a state space model. The process behavior depends on the setting of the controller parameters. Current trends in estimating those parameters optimize an integral performance criterion. In this chapter, a unified tuning method for controllers is presented, the evolutionary algorithm MAGO optimizes the parameters of several controllers minimizing the ITAE index, applied on benchmark plants, operating on servo and regulator modes, and representing the system in both transfer functions and differential equation systems. The evolutionary approach gets a better overall performance comparing with traditional methods. The evolutionary method is indeed better than the classical, eliminating the uncertainty in the controller parameters. Better results are yielded with MAGO algorithm than with optimal PID, optimal-robust PID, and LQR.

INTRODUCTION

Optimal control is a branch of modern control theory (Hull, 2003) that focuses on those properties of the control strategies that provide solutions to problems by minimizing an objective function, or otherwise, a function depending on the

DOI: 10.4018/978-1-5225-5020-4.ch007

performance of a system variable. Those indices or performance functions may include a measurement error, the control effort or some other important characteristic from the control system; performance indices most commonly used in control loops are IAE, ITAE, IE and ISE (Åström and Hägglund, 1995). So, when minimizing some of these performance indices in conjunction with the controllers tuning, is a situation that can be formulated as an optimization case. A problem with this approach is that the controller and the plant are loosely coupled, yielding multiple kinds of uncertainty. Addressing this uncertainty, when tuning optimal controllers via an evolutionary algorithm, is one of the purposes of this Chapter.

One of the trends in the tuning of controllers is the use of Evolutionary Algorithms (EA) to determine the optimal parameters of the controller. EA have been used in various fields of engineering (Fleming and Purshouse, 2002), LQR tuning (Ghoreishi et al., 2011; Tijani et al, 2013; Hassani 2014), drivers in tuning PID controllers (Li et al., 2006; Hernández-Riveros et al, 2014), showing successful solutions in each case applied. It has been found in the literature reviewing that EA are applied to the tuning of controllers on particular cases and not in the general cases, as in this chapter. Nor are compared with traditional methods that minimize some tuning performance index (Chang & Yan, 2004; Fan & Joo, 2009; Junli et all, 2011; Saad et al, 2012a; Saad et al, 2012b). There are alternatives to the traditional rules of tuning, but there is not yet a study showing that the use of heuristic algorithms it is indeed better than using the traditional rules of optimal tuning. Hence, this matter is addressed.

EA are widely studied as a heuristic tool for solving nonlinear systems, continuous, discontinuous, convex and not convex optimization problems where traditional methods are not effective, and in many cases, to support successful solutions. EA are based on biological or natural principles for the study and design of human-made systems (Yu and Gen, 2010), such as the theory of natural selection (Darwin, 1859), heredity (Ayala and Kiger, 1984) and population genetics (Fisher, 1930).

In this chapter, the use of the evolutionary algorithm MAGO (Hernández and Ospina, 2010) as a tool to minimize a characteristic performance index in a control loop to thereby obtaining optimal values of the controller parameters is presented.

MAGO (Multi dynamics Algorithm for Global Optimization) works with statistics from the evolution of the population (Hernandez and Ospina, 2010). MAGO is a heuristic algorithm resulting from the combination of multidimensional unconstrained optimization without derivatives, Statistical Control and Estimation of Distribution. MAGO has shown to be an efficient and effective tool to solve problems whose search space is complex (Hernandez and Villada, 2012) and works with a real-valued representation. Additionally, MAGO only requires two parameters provided by the analyst: the number of generations and the population size; features that facilitate its use. Setting a classic evolutionary algorithm is itself a difficult optimization problem; the analyst must test with probabilities of crossover, mutation, replication, operator forms, legal individuals, loss of diversity, etc. For its part, the Estimation Distribution Algorithms require specialized knowledge as the formulation of simultaneous complex distributions or the Bayesian networks structure. Because of those difficulties, MAGO becomes a good choice as a tool for solving controller tuning as an optimization problem. MAGO divides autonomously the population in three subgroups, each one with its own dynamics. The first group shapes the promising region displacing the fittest individuals toward the best. The Second explores the potential regions through a uniform distribution with varying limits upon the actual population. The third, keeps diversity via a uniform distribution over the whole space.

Control could be divided in two major fields. On the one hand, classic control that is based mostly on the transfer function as mathematical representation of the process and PID controller as most successfully closed-loop control strategy for SISO applications. On the other hand, modern control that is based on the state space paradigm as mathematical process representation and LQR control structure as an extension of the feedback principle to MIMO applications. This chapter attempts for both control approaches, but controller parameters are tuned solving an optimization problem instead of using any tuning rules. Notwithstanding, some tuning rules are adopted as references to evaluate the optimization-based controllers performance.

In case of the PI/PID controllers, the selection of the tuning rule is based on the required performance and the desired robustness. 90% of the tuning rules developed to date are based on a model of first and second order plus time delay. The controller tuning rules most frequently used are not based on an integral performance criterion. The optimal tuning rules based on second-order models are just 14 of the 84 reported by O'Dwyer (2009).

A comparative study of performance of different tuning classical methods for PI and PID controllers is achieved in (Desanti, 2004). This study concludes that tuning methods that require a *Second Order System Plus Time Delay* (SOSPD) model perform better than those that require a *First Order Lag Plus Time Delay* (FOLPD) model. This is the reason why SOSPD model is dealt in this chapter. SOSPD model was selected as representing the plants in order to compare the performance of a heuristic algorithm with the "best" techniques developed for PID controllers optimal tuning. For SOSPD models represented by equations (1) and (2), 147 tuning rules have been defined based on the ideal structure of a controller PI/PID (O'Dwyer, 2009). In general, those rules are based on several relationships and/or conditions of the parameters defining the process model.

$$G(s) = \frac{K_p e^{-\tau_m s}}{T_{m1}^2 s^2 + 2\xi_m T_{m1} s + 1} \tag{1}$$

$$G(s) = \frac{K_p e^{-\tau_m s}}{(1 + T_{m1} s)(1 + T_{m2} s)} \tag{2}$$

In equations (1) and (2), K_p: Plant Gain; τ_m: Time Delay; T_{m1}, T_{m2}: Time constants of the plant; ξ: Damping factor of the plant.

The performance and robustness of some tuning rules have been evaluated, and a complete analysis of the methods of tuning controllers based on SOSPD has been made in (Mora, 2004; and Solera, 2006).

Each of the developed tuning rules for PI/PID controllers is only applied to a certain group of processes. Alternative methodologies, such as design based on the root locus, tuning by pole-zero cancellation, tuning by the location of the closed-loop poles, among others, require cumbersome procedures and specialized knowledge in control theory. Additionally, most methods for optimal tuning of SOSPD systems require additional system information from experiments carried out directly on the plant; activities that are not recommended, and are not always possible to perform, because the presence of extreme stresses and oscillations which may create instability and damage to the system.

However, the tuning of controllers that minimize an integral performance criterion can be established as an optimization problem that consists of minimizing an objective function. The minimum is the result of obtaining a suitable combination of the three parameters required by the PID controller. The use of the MAGO for the tuning of PID controllers acting on processes represented by SOSPD models optimizing the ITAE (Integral of Time multiplied by Absolute Error) and not requiring additional system information is developed in this chapter.

The LQR (Linear Quadratic Regulator) is a control strategy well known in the modern theory of optimal control, for systems represented in state space. This strategy ensures certain characteristics of robustness in closed loop. LQR has been used in various fields of engineering (Lewis and Syrmos, 1995). This control strategy is based on developing a law of control, optimal and robust, that minimizes the sum of control efforts and the deviation of the output signal (state) from the desired value (set point), giving a weighting to each of these through the matrices R and Q respectively. To generate or give value to these matrices are available for selection, the method of Bryson, pole allocation and the trial and proof method (Brynson, 1987), where the latter is the most used.

The results obtained for adjusting the weights of the Q and R matrices in the LQR controller are compared with LQR tuned by trial and proof (since this is one of the most used methods) and two PID strategies (optimum PID and optimum-robust PID) (Hernández-Riveros and Carmona-Cadavid, 2016). These last strategies are also tuned with MAGO because they have better performance when compared with traditional methods for tuning PID controllers optimizing some criterion of overall performance (Hernández-Riveros et al, 2016-a). PID strategies as comparative method are applied because they are one of the control strategies most used in the industry. The results obtained by the evolutionary algorithm overcome those from the traditional methods of optimal tuning.

This chapter is organized as follows: the problem of process representation, an introduction of controllers, their parameters estimation and performance index calculation. The tuning of PID controllers on SOSPD models using the traditional methods and the evolutionary algorithm MAGO follows. Next section includes the description of LQR and PID controllers, evolutionary calculation of the matrices Q and R. An analysis of results comes after and the chapter finishes with some conclusions.

CONTROLLERS

A controller is a device that operates automatically to handle a predetermined variable. It aims to ensure the balance of the system around an operating point. To do this, the current value $Y(s)$ of the controlled variable is compared to its desired value $R(s)$ to obtain an error signal $E(s)$ (feedback). This error is processed by the controller to calculate the necessary change in the manipulated variable, $U(s)$, (control action). The controllers' modes most commonly used in industry are the PI (proportional-integral) and PID (proportional-integral-derivative).

The proportional mode P provides to the controller an output proportional to the error. The integral mode I produces a signal proportional to the integral of the error. The integration time Ti is the time that must elapse before the integral action reaches the magnitude of the proportional action. A controller takes a time before noticing a change in the controlled variable. The derivative action anticipates this change in the controlled variable. PID controllers consist of the three modes. The control policy of an ideal PID controller with one input and one output process (SISO) is expressed in the frequency domain by the equation (3), where $(R(s) - Y(s))$ is the error $E(s)$.

$$U(s) = K_c \left[1 + \frac{1}{T_i s} + T_d s \right] E(s) \tag{3}$$

Process Representation

A model is characterized by a structure that represents the formalization or abstraction of a given study process. At present, there are different applications for models and therefore several analytical approaches have yielded different structures or forms of models, such as those based on data (deterministic, stochastic), based on time (continuous, discrete), symbolic (mathematical, conceptual), etc.; these representations will be used upon the design criterion.

It should be remembered when achieving the objective of modeling, that the model should not be too complex, however, it should give a sufficient description of the system. That is, every model has a degree of uncertainty, either by lack of information or structural uncertainty, or by the approximation or parametric uncertainty (Roffel and Betlem, 2007).

For the design of controllers are used two typical representations of a system, they are state space and transfer function. These representations depend on the selected control structure. Currently, it is a fact that these two approaches, input-output and state space, complement each other, offering a much wider range for control systems.

State-Space Model

Kalman in the early 1960s proposed the concept of state, and initiates what is known as modern control. Modern control refers to the control in state space. Its analysis is focused on three types of variables in the dynamic system: input variables, output variables and state variables. Their general representation is given in equations (4) and (5). Where (4) is the equation of the state of the system and (5) is the equation of system outputs.

$$\dot{x}(t) = f(x, u, t) \tag{4}$$

$$y(t) = g(x, u, t) \tag{5}$$

The time-invariant equations (6) and (7) are obtained after linearizing equations (4) and (5) around an operation point. Where $A \in \Re^{nxn}$ is a matrix of the system states, $B \in \Re^{nxm}$ is an input matrix, $C \in \Re^{kxn}$ is an output matrix and $D \in \Re^{kxm}$ is a direct transmission matrix.

$$\dot{x}(t) = Ax(t) + Bu(t) \tag{6}$$

$$y(t) = Cx(t) + Du(t) \tag{7}$$

Transfer Function Model

The representation of the process in transfer function and block diagrams is widely used for the control systems analysis and design. The approximation in transfer function is very useful for analysis of the system in open- and closed-loop around an operating point, although most processes are highly nonlinear (Ogunnaike and Harmon, 1994). Equation (8) gives its general form of representation. Where, $G(s)$ represents the "transfer" of the input $U(s)$ to the output $Y(s)$ of the process. Thus, an input-output structure of the system to be analyzed is obtained.

$$Y(s) = G(s)U(s) \tag{8}$$

PID CONTROLLERS TUNING: STATEMENT OF THE PROBLEM

Figure 1 represents a conventional closed-loop control, where the controller is PID type. $r(t)$ is the reference signal; $u(t)$ is the control action, resulting from the necessary compensation applied to the system to lead it to the desired operating value; $y(t)$ output of the system; $e(t)$ is the error measured as the difference between the system output and the reference signal.

There are two types of controller operation. One is a regulator (Alfaro and Vilanova, 2012) when the reference value $r(t)$ remains constant (a system behavior insensitive to disturbances is preferred) (See Figure 2). The other one is a servomechanism (Alfaro and Vilanova, 2012) when the reference $r(t)$ may change over time (therefore good tracking is expected) (See Figure 3). For a process matching

Figure 1. Block diagram of the closed loop system

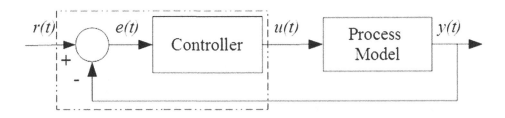

Figure 2. Error measurement in a system operating as servomechanims

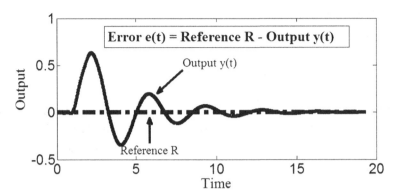

Figure 3. Error measurement in a system operating as regulator

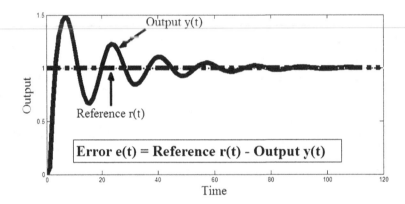

some predetermined design specifications and robustness according with a performance criteria, the controller tuning based on PID structure consists on setting their parameters K_C, T_i and T_d, representing the proportional, integral and derivative criteria, respectively.

Performance Criteria of Controllers

The criterion used for tuning a controller is directly related to the expected performance of the control loop. It can be based on desired characteristics of the response, in time or frequency. Searching for a way to quantify the behavior of control loops led to the establishment of performance indexes based on the error signal $e(t)$. Of these, the best known are the so-called integral criteria (Aström and Hägglund, 1995), defined in equations (4), (5).

Integral of Absolute Error (IAE)

$$IAE = \int_0^\infty |e(t)|dt \tag{9}$$

Integral of Time Multiplied by Absolute Error (ITAE)

$$ITAE = \int_0^\infty t\,|e(t)|dt \tag{10}$$

For a system, the objective is to determine the controller setting that minimizes the chosen cost function; the parameters are optimal under fixed performance criteria.

Tuning Methods of PID Controllers

Tuning controllers consists in determining the best values of a set of parameters to drive the selected control strategy ensuring that the process behavior meets design specifications. The tuning may be also optimal under some performance criterion.

There are different methods for tuning controllers, such as the design based on the locus of the roots, tuning by pole-zero cancellation, by the location of the closed-loop poles, among others. Furthermore, some rules of tuning controllers are based on critical system information, on reaction curves and on closed-loop tests (Aström and Hägglund, 1995). This part of the chapter is concerned to PID controllers for processes modeled as SOSPD, optimizing the ITAE and not requiring additional system information.

In (O'Dwyer, 2009), it is indicated that 20.7% of the rules of tuning PID controllers have been developed from SOSPD models (with or without a zero in the numerator). This implies 84 tuning rules, 66 of them do not include the zero in the numerator. However, of these, only 14 optimize an integral performance criterion, from which 4 rules propose selecting controller parameters by means of tables and other 6 require additional system information (ultimate gain, Ku; ultimate frequency, Tu). Therefore, there are only 4 tuning rules that optimize an integral performance criterion and the controller parameters are only function of the SOSPD model parameters. These rules are for regulators: Bohl and McAvoy, Minimum ITAE - Hassan, Minimum ITAE - Sung; for servomechanisms: Minimum ITAE - Sung. Table 1 shows the summary of the study, the chosen rules are not shadowed. The equations for the calculation of all parameters K_C, T_i and T_d can be consulted in (Bohl & McAvoy, 1976; Hassan, 1993; Sung, 1996; Lagunas, 2006).

Table 1. Tuning PID controllers methods that only require SOPDT system parameters and minimize an integral performance criterion

Tuning Methods for PID Controllers Optimizing an Integral Criterion on SOMTM					
Method	Type of Operation	Performance Criterion	Type of Plant	Range of Pertinence	Observation
Minimum IAE - Wills	Regulator	IAE	2	Tm2 = τ = 0.1Tm1	Requires critical system information (Ku, Tu).
Minimum IAE - López	Regulator	IAE	1	0.5 < ξ < 4 , 0.1 < τ/Tm1 < 10	Tuning rule based on tables.
Minimum IAE - Shinskey	Regulator	IAE	2	Tm2/(Tm2+τ) = 0.25, 0.5, 0.75	Requires critical system information (Ku, Tu).
Minimum IAE - Kang	Regulator	IAE	2	τ/Tm1, Tm2/Tm1	Tuning rule based on tables
Minimum ITAE - López	Regulator	ITAE	1	0.5 < ξ < 4 , 0.1 < τ/Tm1 < 1	Tuning rule based on tables
Bohl and McAvoy	**Regulator**	**ITAE**	**2**	**0.12 < Tm1/Tm2 < 0.9, 0.1<τ/Tm1<0.5**	**Tuning Rule requiring only SOMTM model parameters.**
Minimum ITAE - Hassan	**Regulator**	**ITAE**	**1**	**0.5 < ξ < 2 , 0.1 < τ/Tm1 < 4**	**Tuning Rule requiring only SOMTM model parameters.**
Minimum ITAE - Sung	**Regulator**	**ITAE**	**1**	**0.05 < τ/Tm1 < 2**	**Tuning Rule requiring only SOMTM model parameters.**
Nearly minimum IAE, ISE, ITAE - Hwang	Regulator	IAE, ISE, ITAE	1	0.6 < ξ < 4.2 , 0.2 < τ/Tm1 < 2	Requires critical system information (Ku, Tu).
Minimun IAE - Wills	Servomechanism	IAE	2	Tm2 = τ = 0.1Tm1	Requires critical system information (Ku, Tu).
Minimum IAE - Gallier and Otto	Servomechanism	IAE	1 & 2	0.05 < τ/2Tm1 < 4	Tuning rule based on tables
Minimum ITAE - Wills	Servomechanism	ITAE	2	Tm1 = Tm2; τ = 0.1Tm1	Requires critical system information (Ku, Tu).
Minimum ITAE - Sung	**Servomechanism**	**ITAE**	**1**	**0.05 < τ/Tm1 < 2**	**Tuning Rule requiring only SOMTM model parameters.**
Nearly minimum IAE, ISE, ITAE - Hwang	Servomechanism	IAE, ISE, ITAE	1	0.6 < ξ < 4.2 , 0.2 < τ/Tm1 < 2	Requires critical system information (Ku, Tu).

Table 2. Transfer Functions of Plants in equations (1) and (2) for the tuning of PID controllers

Plants given by Equation (1)	Plants given by Equation (2)
$G_{p1\_servo1}(s) = G_{p1\_reg1}(s) = \dfrac{e^{-s}}{s^2 + 2s + 1}$	$G(s)_{p2\_servo1} = G(s)_{p2\_reg1} = \dfrac{e^{-s}}{(1+s)(1+0.1s)}$
$G_{p1\_servo2}(s) = G_{p1\_reg3}(s) = \dfrac{e^{-s}}{100s^2 + 20s + 1}$	$G(s)_{p2\_servo2} = G(s)_{p2\_reg2} = \dfrac{e^{-s}}{(1+s)(1+0.5s)}$
$G_{p1\_servo3}(s) = G_{p1\_reg5}(s) = \dfrac{e^{-s}}{400s^2 + 40s + 1}$	$G(s)_{p2\_servo3} = G(s)_{p2\_reg3} = \dfrac{e^{-s}}{(1+s)(1+s)}$

To compare the performance of the studied controllers it is necessary to tune them with the same plants. Plant models used are given in equations (1) and (2). The following considerations are taken for plant (1): $K_p = 1$, $\tau_m = 1$, $\xi = 1$ and T_{m1} ranging from 1, 10 and 20. For plant (2), the following considerations are taken: $K_p = 1$, $\tau_m = 1$, $T_{m1} = 1$ y $T_{m2} = aTm1$, where $a \leq 1$. Table 2 presents a set of transfer functions according to the parameter values of each plant given by equations (1) and (2).

Table 3. Equations for calculating the parameters for PID controllers

Bohl and McAvoy: Regulator Tuning Method
$K_C = \dfrac{10.9507}{Kp}\left[\left(\dfrac{10\tau_m}{T_{m1}}\right)^{-1.2096+0.1760\ln\left(\frac{10\tau_m}{T_{m1}}\right)}\right]\left[\left(\dfrac{10T_{m2}}{T'_{m1}}\right)^{0.1044+0.1806\ln\left(\frac{10T_{m2}}{T_{m1}}\right)-0.2071\ln\left(\frac{10\tau_m}{T_{m1}}\right)}\right]$
$T_i = 0.2979T_{m1}\left[\left(\dfrac{10\tau_m}{T_{m1}}\right)^{0.7750-0.1026\ln\left(\frac{10\tau_m}{T_{m1}}\right)}\right]\left[\left(\dfrac{10T_{m2}}{T_{m1}}\right)^{0.1701+0.0092\ln\left(\frac{10T_{m2}}{T_{m1}}\right)+0.0081\ln\left(\frac{10\tau_m}{T_{m1}}\right)}\right]$
$T_d = 0.1075T_{m1}\left[\left(\dfrac{10\tau_m}{T_{m1}}\right)^{0.6025-0.0624\ln\left(\frac{10\tau_m}{T_{m1}}\right)}\right]\left[\left(\dfrac{10T_{m2}}{T_{m1}}\right)^{0.4531+0.0479\ln\left(\frac{10T_{m2}}{T_{m1}}\right)+0.0128\ln\left(\frac{10\tau_m}{T_{m1}}\right)}\right]$
Minimum ITAE – Sung: Regulator Tuning Method
$K_C = \dfrac{1}{K_p}\left[-0.67+0.297\left(\dfrac{T_{m1}}{\tau_m}\right)^{2.001}+2.189\left(\dfrac{T_{m1}}{\tau_m}\right)^{0.766}\xi\right]$ $si\ \dfrac{T_{m1}}{\tau_m}<0.9$
$K_C = \dfrac{1}{K_p}\left[-0.365+0.260\left(\dfrac{\tau_m}{T_{m1}}-1.4\right)^{2}+2.189\left(\dfrac{T_{m1}}{\tau_m}\right)^{0.766}\xi\right]$ $si\ \dfrac{T_{m1}}{\tau_m}\geq0.9$
$T_i = T_{m1}\left[2.212\left(\dfrac{\tau_m}{T_{m1}}\right)^{0.520}-0.3\right]$ $si\ \dfrac{\tau_m}{T_{m1}}<0.4$

continued on following page

Table 3. Continued

$$T_i = T_{m1} \left[-0.975 + 0.910 \left(\frac{\tau_m}{T_{m1}} - 1.845 \right)^2 + x_1 \right]$$

$$x_1 = \left[1 - e^{-\frac{\xi}{0.15 + 0.33 \frac{\tau_m}{T_{m1}}}} \right] \left[5.25 - 0.88 \left(\frac{\tau_m}{T_{m1}} - 2.8 \right)^2 \right]$$

$$si \frac{\tau_m}{T_{m1}} \geq 0.4$$

$$T_d = \frac{T_{m1}}{\left[1 - e^{-\frac{\xi}{-0.15 + 0.939 \left(\frac{T_{m1}}{\tau_m} \right)^{1.121}}} \right] \left[1.45 + 0.969 \left(\frac{T_{m1}}{\tau_m} \right)^{1.171} \right] - 1.9 + 1.576 \left(\frac{T_{m1}}{\tau_m} \right)^{0.530}}$$

Minimum ITAE – Sung: Servo Tuning Method	
$K_C = \frac{1}{K_p} \left[-0.04 + \left[0.333 + 0.949 \left(\frac{T_{m1}}{\tau_m} \right)^{-0.983} \right] \xi \right]$	$si \frac{T_{m1}}{\tau_m} \leq 0.9$
$K_C = \frac{1}{K_p} \left[-0.544 + 0.308 \frac{\tau_m}{T_{m1}} + 1.408 \left(\frac{T_{m1}}{\tau_m} \right)^{-0.832} \xi \right]$	$si \frac{T_{m1}}{\tau_m} \geq 0.9$
$T_i = T_{m1} \left[2.055 + 0.072 \left(\frac{\tau_m}{T_{m1}} \right) \right] \xi$	$si \frac{\tau_m}{T_{m1}} \leq 1$
$T_i = T_{m1} \left[1.768 + 0.329 \left(\frac{\tau_m}{T_{m1}} \right) \right] \xi$	$si \frac{\tau_m}{T_{m1}} > 1$
$T_d = \dfrac{T_{m1}}{\left[1 - e^{-\frac{\left(\frac{\tau_m}{T_{m1}} \right)^{1.060} \xi}{0.870}} \right] \left[0.55 + 1.683 \left(\frac{T_{m1}}{\tau_m} \right)^{1.090} \right]}$	

continued on following page

Table 3. Continued

<table>
<tr><td colspan="1">Minimum ITAE – Hassan: Regulator Tuning Method</td></tr>
<tr><td>

$$\log[K_p K_C] = 1.9763 - 0.6436\xi - 5.1887\frac{\tau_m}{T_{m1}} + 0.4375\xi^2 + 2.9005\left(\frac{\tau_m}{T_{m1}}\right)^2 + 3.1468\xi\frac{\tau_m}{T_{m1}}$$

$$-0.1697\xi^2\left(\frac{\tau_m}{T_{m1}}\right)^2 - 0.8162\xi\left(\frac{\tau_m}{T_{m1}}\right)^2 - 1.2048\xi^2\frac{\tau_m}{T_{m1}} - 0.0810\xi^3 - 0.4444\left(\frac{\tau_m}{T_{m1}}\right)^3 + 0.0319\xi\left(\frac{\tau_m}{T_{m1}}\right)^3$$

$$+0.1054\xi^2\left(\frac{\tau_m}{T_{m1}}\right)^2 + 0.1653\xi^3\frac{\tau_m}{T_{m1}} + 0.1176\xi^3\left(\frac{\tau_m}{T_{m1}}\right)^2 - 0.0375\xi^3\left(\frac{\tau_m}{T_{m1}}\right)^3$$

</td></tr>
<tr><td>

$$\log\left[\frac{T_i}{T_{m1}}\right] = -0.7866 - 0.6797\xi + 2.1891\frac{\tau_m}{T_{m1}} - 0.3471\xi^2 - 1.9004\left(\frac{\tau_m}{T_{m1}}\right)^2 - 0.7007\xi\frac{\tau_m}{T_{m1}}$$

$$+0.3078\xi^2\left(\frac{\tau_m}{T_{m1}}\right)^2 + 0.8567\xi\left(\frac{\tau_m}{T_{m1}}\right)^2 - 0.2535\xi^2\frac{\tau_m}{T_{m1}} + 0.0413\xi^3 + 0.3484\left(\frac{\tau_m}{T_{m1}}\right)^3 - 0.1626\xi\left(\frac{\tau_m}{T_{m1}}\right)^3$$

$$0.0662\xi^2\left(\frac{\tau_m}{T_{m1}}\right)^2 + 0.2248\xi^3\frac{\tau_m}{T_{m1}} \quad 0.2470\xi^3\left(\frac{\tau_m}{T_{m1}}\right)^2 + 0.0493\xi^3\left(\frac{\tau_m}{T_{m1}}\right)^3$$

</td></tr>
<tr><td>

$$\log\left[\frac{T_d}{T_{m1}}\right] = -0.6727 - 0.2072\xi + 2.6826\frac{\tau_m}{T_{m1}} + 0.0807\xi^2 - 1.7707\left(\frac{\tau_m}{T_{m1}}\right)^2 - 1.6685\xi\frac{\tau_m}{T_{m1}}$$

$$+0.0846\xi^2\left(\frac{\tau_m}{T_{m1}}\right)^2 + 0.7159\xi\left(\frac{\tau_m}{T_{m1}}\right)^2 + 0.5631\xi^2\frac{\tau_m}{T_{m1}} - 0.0225\xi^3 + 0.2822\left(\frac{\tau_m}{T_{m1}}\right)^3 - 0.0616\xi\left(\frac{\tau_m}{T_{m1}}\right)^3$$

$$-0.0627\xi^2\left(\frac{\tau_m}{T_{m1}}\right)^2 - 0.0373\xi^3\frac{\tau_m}{T_{m1}} - 0.0948\xi^3\left(\frac{\tau_m}{T_{m1}}\right)^2 + 0.0272\xi^3\left(\frac{\tau_m}{T_{m1}}\right)^3$$

</td></tr>
</table>

Table 3 shows their corresponding equations for calculating the parameters K_C, T_i and T_d of a PID controller for processes modeled as SOSPD and not requiring additional system information. These equations are shown to illustrate how uneconomical it is to calculate the parameters of PID controller with these rules. Note that each of these tuning rules defines restrictions on the behavior of the system, expressed in the range of validity.

TUNING OF PID CONTROLLERS USING AN EVOLUTIONARY ALGORITHM

Different solutions there may exist in optimization problems, therefore a criterion for discriminating between them, and finding the best one, is required. The tuning of controllers that minimize an integral performance criterion can be seen as an optimization problem, in as much as the ultimate goal is to find the combination of parameters K_C, T_i and T_d, such that the value of the integration of a variable of interest is minimal (i.e. error between the actual output of the plant and the desired value). The problem consists of minimizing an objective function, where the minimum is the result of obtaining a suitable combination of the three parameters required by the PID controller.

Evolutionary Algorithms

Evolutionary Algorithms (EA) emulate the synthetic theory of evolution or neo-Darwinian theory of natural selection, which merge the theory of natural selection (Darwin, 1859), heredity (Ayala and Kiger, 1984) and genetic population (Fisher, 1930). The evolution can be seen as the change in the genetic characteristics in a population. In every species there are variations that are inherited and inheritable and others are modified due to the environment. Hereditary variations (caused by mutations) occurring randomly in all organisms are the raw material of evolution acting the natural selection on them. Synthetic theory of evolution says that mutation and natural selection complement each other, and none of these processes, by itself, can lead to evolutionary change.

As natural evolution begins with an initial population of individuals, an evolutionary algorithm begins with the selection of an initial set of potential solutions to a particular problem; this set can be selected randomly or using prior information of the problem. EA include operators to select and create a sequence of new individuals. These operators are crossover and mutation. The crossover operator performs an exchange of genetic material between "parents" to generate new "spring" and the mutation operator makes small variations in the "parents". Once a new set of possible solutions is generated, it is evaluated using a "fitness" function. The best individuals are favored "survival of the fittest", leaving these as new parents and the process is cyclically repeated to find the best solution in a delimited search space.

Multidynamics Algorithm for Global Optimization (MAGO)

Evolutionary algorithms are a proven tool for solving nonlinear systems and optimization problems. Regardless of which of its many variants are applied, the weaknesses of these algorithms are in the large number of control parameters of the same algorithm to be determined by the analyst (Whitley, 2001). To address these weaknesses, the Estimation of Distribution Algorithms (Lozano, 2006) surged. These algorithms do not use genetic operators, but are based on statistics calculated on samples of the population, which is constantly evolving. This variant when introducing statistics operators provides a strong way to demonstrate the evolution. Nevertheless, Estimation of Distribution Algorithms are difficult to manage and does not eliminate the large number of control parameters of classical evolutionary algorithms.

Evolutionary algorithms (EA) are widely studied as a heuristic tool for solving optimization problems. They have shown to be effective in problems that exhibit noise, random variation and multimodality. Genetic algorithms, for example, have proven to be valuable in both obtaining the optimal values of the PID controller parameters, and in the computational cost (Lagunas, 2004).

The Multidynamics Algorithm for Global Optimization (MAGO, by acronym) is an evolutionary heuristic method that transforms groups of individuals to achieve a goal, resembling their behavior to the process of evolution of species. Formally presented in (Hernandez and Ospina, 2010), MAGO was born of a hybrid among estimation distribution algorithms, statistical control of quality and multidimensional unconstrained optimization without derivatives. MAGO is autonomous in the sense that it regulates its own behavior and does not need human intervention. MAGO has only two parameters, which could be removed but they remain because in real situations the user upon the context of the problem handles the population size and the number of generations. MAGO takes advantage of the concept of control limits (Montgomery, 2008) to produce individuals on each generation simultaneously from three distinct subgroups, each one with different dynamics. The size of the whole population is fixed, but the cardinality of each sub-group changes in each generation according to the first, second and third deviation of the actual population, respectively. The exploration is performed by creating new individuals from these three sub-populations. For the exploitation, MAGO uses a greedy criterion in one subset looking for the goal.

As in EA, MAGO begins with a population of possible solutions randomly distributed throughout the search space. The population is divided autonomously by the algorithm in three subgroups, each with its own evolution. In every generation, the actual entire population is observed as having a normal distribution, with the aim of establish according to the different levels of standard deviation how many individuals will belong to each subgroup. In every generation, the average location and the first, second and third dispersion of the whole population are calculated to form the groups. The exploration is done by creating new individuals that are governed by any of these subgroups or Dynamics. The cardinality of these subgroups changes autonomously in each generation, according to a rule inspired by methods of statistical control. MAGO uses the covariance matrix of the population of each generation, to establish a distribution of exploration and create three dynamics making the whole individuals in each generation. The subgroup named Emerging Dynamics (G1) creates a small group of individuals around the individual with better genetic characteristics; this group is the evolutionary elite of each generation, i.e. fittest individuals to contribute with their genes to the next generation. The Crowd Dynamics (G2) follows a similar process, around the current population mean. This dynamic is applied to a largest portion of the population and is always close to the emerging dynamics, but never close enough to be confused. Only until there are sufficient and necessary conditions to ensure full exploration of the search space, these two dynamics could be merged within a territory, usually at the end of the evolutionary process. The Accidental dynamics (G3) is a quantum speciation. It is established in isolation from individuals of the other dynamics in generation by generation. This portion of the population is always formed spontaneously and contains a number of entirely new individuals. This way the main diagonal of the covariance matrix is different from zero, ensuring numerical stability of the evolutionary process. G1, G2 and G3 cannot interbreed.

The Emerging Dynamics is created with the N1 individuals being better in the generation. This number of the fittest individuals moves towards the best of the entire population. The Emerging Dynamics seeks solutions in a neighborhood near the best of all the current individuals. The N1 fittest individuals within one standard deviation of the average location of the current population of individuals are displaced in a line toward the best of all, suffering a mutation that incorporates information from the best one. The mutation is a simplex search method (Nelder and Mead, 1965) but only two individuals are used, the best one and the trial one. A movement in a line of a fit individual toward the best one occurs. If this movement generates a better individual, this one passes to the next generation; otherwise, its predecessor passes on with no changes. This method does not require gradient information.

For every individual, i, in the generation, j, $x_i^{(j)}$, a test individual, t, is created according to the rule presented in equation (11).

$$x_t^{(j)} = x_i^{(j)} + F^{(j)}(x_B^{(j)} - x_m^{(j)})$$
(11)

Where $x_B^{(j)}$ is the best of all individuals in the generation j, and $x_m^{(j)}$ is the same tested individual $x_i^{(j)}$. To incorporate information of the current relations among the variables, the factor $F^{(j)}$, depending on the covariance matrix, is chosen in each generation, as defined in equation (12). Where, $S^{(j)}$ is the simple covariance matrix of the populations of individuals in generation j.

$$F^{(j)} = S^{(j)} / \left\| S^{(j)} \right\|$$
(12)

This procedure compiles the differences among the best individuals and the very best one. The covariance matrix of the current population takes into account the effect of the evolution. This information is propagated on new individuals.

The Crowd Dynamics is created with N2 individuals from a uniform distribution, determined by the upper and lower limits $[LB^{(j)} \quad UB^{(j)}]$ of the second dispersion and the average location of the current population of individuals. This subgroup seeks possible solutions in a neighborhood close to the population mean. At first, the neighborhood around the mean can be large, but as evolution proceeds this neighborhood is reduced, so that across the search space the population mean is getting closer to the optimal.

For its part, the Accidental Dynamics is the smaller one in relation to its operation on the population. N3 new individuals are created from a uniform distribution over the whole search space, as in the initial population. This dynamic has two basic functions: maintaining the diversity of the population, and ensuring numerical stability of the algorithm. Thus, the dispersion of the population and diversity are always guaranteed even if the other two groups already have converged.

The covariance matrix of the population, $S^{(j)}$, and its diagonal $diag(S^{(j)})$ are considered for the cardinality of each dynamics in the generation j. If $Pob^{(j)}$ is the set of possible solutions under consideration in the generation j the three groups can be defined as in equation (13). If N1, N2 and N3 are the cardinalities of the sets G1, G2 and G3, then the cardinality of the Emerging Dynamics, Crowd Dynamics and Accidental Dynamics are set, respectively. This way of defining the elements of each group is dynamical in nature and autonomous in MAGO. Cardinalities depend on the dispersion of the whole population in generating j. Where, $XM^{(j)}$ is the mean of the actual population and $Pob^{(j)} = G1 \cup G2 \cup G3$.

$$G_1 = \left\{ \left. x \in Pob(j) \middle/ \begin{array}{c} XM(j) - \sqrt{diag(S(j))} <= x \\ <= XM(j) + \sqrt{diag(S(j))} \end{array} \right. \right\}$$

$$G_2 = \left\{ \left. x \in Pob(j) \middle/ \begin{array}{c} XM(j) - 2\sqrt{diag(S(j))} < x \\ <= XM(j) + \sqrt{diag(S(j))}, or, \\ XM(j) + \sqrt{diag(S(j))} <= x \\ < XM(j) + 2\sqrt{diag(S(j))} \end{array} \right. \right\} \qquad (13)$$

$$G_3 = \left\{ \left. x \in Pob(j) \middle/ \begin{array}{c} x <= XM(j) - 2\sqrt{diag(S(j))}, or, \\ x >= XM(j) + 2\sqrt{diag(S(j))} \end{array} \right. \right\}$$

Emergent Dynamics tends to concentrate N1 individuals around the best one as MAGO iterates. The Crowd Dynamics tends to concentrate N2 individuals around the mean of the actual population. The Accidental Dynamics, with N3 individuals, keeps the population dispersion at an adequate level. The locus of the best individual is different from the population's mean. As the evolution advances, the location of the best individual and of the population's mean could be closer between themselves. This is used to self-control the population diversity. The Island Model Genetic Algorithm also works with subpopulations (Skolicki, 2005). However, in the Island model, more parameters are added to the genetic algorithm: number of islands, migration size, migration interval, which island to migrate, how migrants are selected and how to replace individuals. Instead, in MAGO only two parameters are needed: number of generations and population size. On another hand, the use of a covariance matrix to set an exploring distribution can also be found in (Hansen, 2006), where new individuals are created in only one dynamics to explore the promising region, sampling from a Gaussian distribution with an intricate adapted covariance matrix. In MAGO, a simpler distribution is used. Following, the pseudo code of MAGO is presented.

Evolutionary Design of a PID Controller

EA represent a reliable approach when controllers tuning is proposed as an optimization problem (Fleming and Purshouse, 2002). Given their nature of global optimizers, EA face non-convex, nonlinear and highly restrictive optimization problems (Herreros et al, 2002; Tavakoli et al, 2007; Iruthayarajan and Baskar, 2009). It has been shown that MAGO is a very efficient and effective instrument to solve problems in continuous domain (Hernandez and Villada, 2012).

Thus, MAGO is proposed as a tool for estimating the parameters of a controller that minimizes an integral performance index. The optimization problem for PID controllers is defined in equation (14). The error in equation (14) is calculated as the difference between the system output and the reference signal as follows $e(t_k) = y(t_k) - y_{sp}(t_k)$. The error is calculated for each point of time throughout the measurement horizon. t_k is the time discretization.

Table 4. MAGO Pseudocode

1: j:= 0, Random initial population generation uniformly distributed over the search space.
2: repeat
   3: Evaluate each individual with the objective function.
   4: Calculate the population covariance matrix and the first, second and third dispersion.
   5: Calculate the cardinalities N1, N2 and N3 of the groups G1, G2 and G3.
   6: Select N1 best individuals, modify them according to equation (7), make them compete and translate the winners towards the best one. Pass the fittest to the next generation j + 1.
   7: Sample from a uniform distribution in hyper rectangle [LB(j), UB(j)] N2 individuals and pass them to generation j + 1.
   8: Sample from a uniform distribution over the whole search space N3 individuals and pass them to generation j + 1.
   9: j = j + 1
10: until an ending criterion is satisfied.

Figure 4. General scheme of MAGO

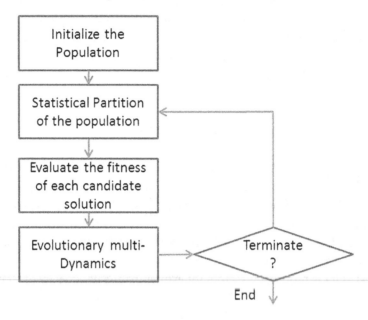

$$\min_{K_C, T_i, T_d} \sum_{t_k=0}^{t_{k_f}} k \left| e(t_k) \right|$$

$s.t.$

$eq.(1) \quad or \quad eq.(2)$

$$u(t_k) = K_C e(t_k) + \frac{K_C}{T_i} \sum_{t_k=0}^{t_k} e(t_k) + K_C T_d \frac{\Delta e(t_k)}{\Delta k} \qquad (14)$$

$$K_{C_{\min}} \leq K_C \leq K_{C_{\max}}$$

$$T_{i_{\min}} \leq T_i \leq T_{i_{\max}}$$

$$T_{d_{\min}} \leq T_d \leq T_{d_{\max}}$$

MAGO does not use genetic operators as crossover or mutation. The adaptation of the population is based on moving N1 individuals to the best one with a Simplex Search; creating N2 individuals through a normal distribution over the average location of the actual population, and creating N3 individuals through a uniform distribution over the whole search space, as previously discussed. Further ahead, the LQR case will be defined.

Evolutionary SOSPD Controllers Tuning

The controller design is made for the closed-loop modes servo and regulator. For the servo, a change in a unit step reference is applied. For the regulator, the same change is applied but as a unit step disturbance to the second-order plant. The controllers are tuned for the six plants defined in Table 3. The only two parameters of MAGO: number of generations (ng) and number of individuals (n), are very low and fixed for all cases ($ng = 150, n = 100$).

MAGO is a real-valued evolutionary algorithm, so that the representation of an individual is a vector containing the controller parameters. The parameters are positive values in a continuous domain. See Table 5. The fitness function is the same as Equation (14).

PID Controller Parameters and Performance Index Calculation

The values of the PID controller parameters for each one of the selected tuning rules are presented on Table 5. The parameters are calculated according to the formulas proposed for each kind of plant. The selected methods for tuning controllers minimize the integral performance criterion, ITAE. The ITAE is calculated in all cases using the commercial software MATLAB function "trapz". Table 6 shows the values of the PID controller parameters calculated by the MAGO; these values minimize the ITAE. For the Hassan method, the controller parameter values are not reported because there was no convergence in the closed loop system response for the selected plants given by equation (1), operating as regulator. The comparison between the parameter values obtained with the traditional tuning rules and the proposed algorithm are shown. Figure 5 illustrates the time response, in closed-loop, for the plants given in Table 3. Figure 6 illustrates the time response of the plants defined by equation 2, given in Table 3. It is possible to find controller parameters that minimize the ITAE, without additional information and regardless of the operating mode. However, for this last mode of operation, in the literature reviewed, no tuning rule has been found that could compute the PID controller parameters requiring only the parameters of the plant. Here, the closed-loop system simulations of which the controller was tuned using the MAGO are presented.

Table 5. Structure of the evolutionary individual

$K_C \in \Re$	$T_i \in \Re$	$T_d \in \Re$

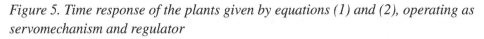

Figure 5. Time response of the plants given by equations (1) and (2), operating as servomechanism and regulator

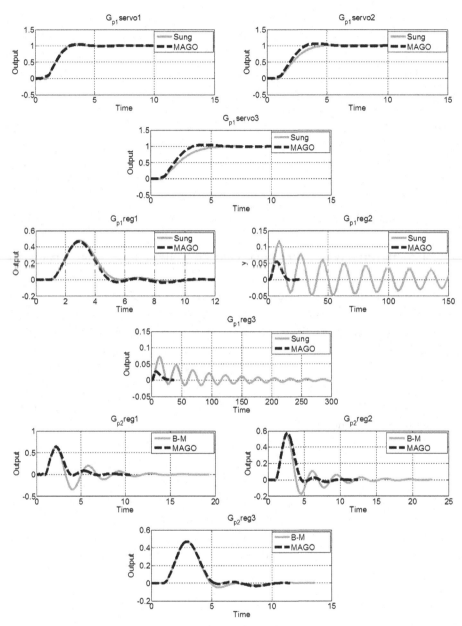

RESULTS FOR SOSPD CONTROLLERS
TUNING ON BENCHMARK PLANTS

The study of traditional tuning methods showed that despite the large amount of available tuning rules, there is no one that is effective for the solution of all control problems based on SISO systems. It is evident that a single tuning rule applies only to a small number of problems. A tendency to develop new methods for tuning PID controllers (Tavakoli, Griffin & Fleming, 2007; Iruthayarajan & Baskar, 2009; Solera, 2005; Liu & Daley, 2001) has been noticed. The most recent are focused on controller's parameter calculation achieving a desired performance, where this index is one of those mentioned before (IAE, ITAE). Table 6 shows the results when tuning PID controllers for different plant models based on equations (1) and (2). The parameters obtained minimize the ITAE criterion.

*Table 6. PID Controller Parameters Controller (N C * = Not converged)*

| Plant (2) | PID Operating as Regulator | | | | | | ITAE | |
| | Kc | | Ti | | Td | | | |
	B&M	MAGO	B&M	MAGO	B&M	MAGO	B&M	MAGO
$G(s)_{p2\_reg1}$	1.7183	1.4296	1.8978	1.5433	1.8988	0.3341	7.7760	3.1052
$G(s)_{p2\_reg2}$	1.0300	1.4656	1.4164	1.5552	1.6702	0.5597	6.8722	3.6071
$G(s)_{p2\_reg3}$	0.3092	1.8527	0.5854	1.7791	0.7286	0.7575	3.8073	3.6738

| Plant (2) | PID Operating as Servomechanism | | | | | | ITAE | |
| | Kc | | Ti | | Td | | | |
	Hassan	MAGO	Hassan	MAGO	Hassan	MAGO	Hassan	MAGO
$G(s)_{p2\_reg1}$	N C*	0.5658	N C*	1.6705	N C*	1.0318	N C*	72.6860
$G(s)_{p2\_reg2}$	N C*	0.2731	N C*	1.0966	N C*	0.4871	N C*	69.4943
$G(s)_{p2\_reg3}$	N C*	0.9074	N C*	2.0666	N C*	0.5258	N C*	63.2413

continued on following page

Table 6. Continued

| Plant (1) | PID Operating as Servomechanism | | | | | | ITAE | |
| | Kc | | Ti | | Td | | | |
	SUNG	MAGO	SUNG	MAGO	SUNG	MAGO	SUNG	MAGO
$G_{p1\_servo1}(s)$	1.2420	1.2318	2.0550	2.1167	0.6555	0.6050	2,0986	2.0486
$G_{p1\_servo2}(s)$	9.0500	10.3237	18.009	16.8942	4.9386	5.5162	3,7911	2.8532
$G_{p1\_servo3}(s)$	16.4953	19.7929	35.689	29.7905	9.5595	10.7718	3,7937	2.7827

| Plant (1) | PID Operating as Regulator | | | | | | ITAE | |
| | Kc | | Ti | | Td | | | |
	SUNG	MAGO	SUNG	MAGO	SUNG	MAGO	SUNG	MAGO
$G_{p1\_reg1}(s)$	1.8160	1.8557	1.0120	1.7563	0.7073	0.7518	3,8100	3.6623
$G_{p1\_reg2}(s)$	12.8460	17.3252	16.7995	7.4691	-1.99e-6	2.3730	894,5522	3.6427
$G_{p1\_reg3}(s)$	21.8276	31.8262	37.7393	11.0993	-1.17e-4	3.7005	314,5554	4.4240

Figure 6. Response to step change in the input of the plant (2), as servomechanism (MAGO only)

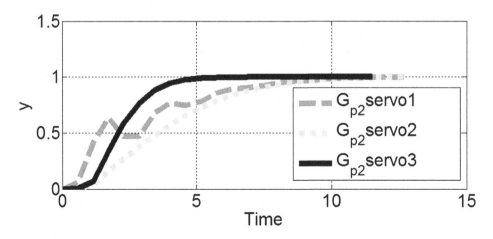

In the case of plants based on the model of equation (1), when the system operates as servomechanism, the tuning rules used are those proposed by Sung for systems operating as servomechanisms (See Table 2). Obtaining an ITAE of a value close to 3, the response behavior of the system is a smooth one, free of oscillations (See Figure 5). The rules by Sung are also used for systems operating as regulators (See Table 2). In this case, the ITAE value is considerably higher for plants *Gp1_servo3* and *Gp1_servo2*, and the system presents oscillations. From this result, it has to be concluded that the rules proposed by Sung are a good choice for the system operating as a servomechanism; while for the case where the system operates as a regulator the use of these rules should be reconsidered.

In the case of plants operating as regulators, whose model is given by the equation (2), the rules proposed by Bohl and McAvoy were used to calculate the controller parameters. The response of the closed-loop system is smooth, when using the parameters found by this method, and the value for the ITAE performance index, in all cases, is below 10. In Table 6, the results for this experiment are reported.

Due to the features that a control problem has, where the objective is to minimize a function by a suitable combination of controller parameters which can be expressed as a cost function, the solution is presented as an optimization problem. The algorithm MAGO is used to calculate the controller parameters seeking to minimize the ITAE. The results, reported in Table 5, are compared with those obtained by the traditional tuning rules. The results obtained by MAGO were very satisfactory for all cases. When the controller parameters are calculated by the MAGO, the ITAE performance index is low, whatever the plant is, represented by equation (1) or equation (2), and for the two modes of operation, servo and regulator. Additional to the above, the responses are softer and exhibit less oscillation with respect to the response where controllers are calculated with traditional methods. In the Sung case as regulator, it can be appreciated that the addressed problem has a big variability. The responses of closed loop systems where the controller parameters are obtained using the MAGO could be observed in Figure 5.

Table 6 also reports the results obtained for the plant based on equation (2). For this case, no comparative data are available, because the only tuning rule found that minimizes the performance index ITAE requiring no additional system information is proposed by Hassan (See Table 1). In the experiments with this tuning rule, the ITAE was not calculated, because it was not possible to obtain convergence to a real value of the parameters of the controller. However, with the MAGO, requiring only the minimum information of the model, it was indeed possible to find the controller parameters reaching an acceptable answer, because in a finite time less than the open-loop system settling time the reference value is achieved, see Figure 6.

LQR AND ROBUST PID TUNING

The LQR method since its introduction in the early 1960s is a control strategy that has been in the focus of research. One of the most representative properties of this control strategy is that automatically ensure closed-loop stability because it has wide margins of phase and gain (Levine, 1996), features that give robustness to the control loop.

The plant must be described in state space, equations (6) and (7), for the development of the LQR controller. From this restriction, a quadratic objective function is defined and represented as a function of the states $x(t)$ and the input $u(t)$, as in equation (15). Where $Q \in \Re^{nxn}$ and $R \in \Re^{mxm}$, semi-definite and positive-definite, respectively.

$$J = \int_{t_0}^{t_f} \left[x^T Q x + u^T R u \right] dt \tag{15}$$

When assigning weights to each of the terms of the function, a balance in output and input "energies" of the plant is performed. The control law that governs this structure of optimal states feedback control is given in equation (16).

$$u(t) = -Kx(t) \tag{16}$$

Equation (16) is the *matrix Riccati differential equation*.

$$\dot{P}(t) = P(t) BR^{-1}B^T P(t) - Q - P(t) A - A^T P(t) \tag{17}$$

When the final time (t_f) of the integral in (15) tends to infinity, solutions of the Riccati equation will remain constant at the value of the initial time; therefore equation (18) equals zero, obtaining the *algebraic equation Riccati*. When solving this equation, there is only one solution for $P(t)$. If it is replaced in equation (18), an optimal constant value K for states feedback is obtained.

$$K(t) = R^{-1}B^T P(t) \tag{18}$$

Tuning Methods for LQR

For tuning the Q and R parameters of the LQR controller, different methods are used, (Ghoreishi, 2001), some of them are:

1. **Bryson Method:** Based on the normalization of variables, seeking that the maximum acceptable value will be one. This is because the units of the states "x" (for the Q matrix) and control action "u" (for the R matrix) are very different. See equation (19). Although in many cases this method can produce very good results usually is applied as a starting point and then the tuning is refined by trial and proof.

$$Q = diag\left\{q_1, ..., q_n\right\} \quad R = diag\left\{r_1, ..., r_m\right\}$$
$$q_i = \left\{\frac{1}{x_i^2\left(\max\right)}\right\}_{i=1}^{n} \qquad r_j = \left\{\frac{1}{u_j^2\left(\max\right)}\right\}_{i=1}^{m} \tag{19}$$

2. **Trial and Proof Method:** (or heuristic method) is an iterative process that makes use of prior knowledge and behavior of the system to be controlled with the purpose of adjusting the matrices Q and R such that a desired behavior is achieved. The method requires a large amount of time to obtain a satisfactory response. An option, commonly used, is to take as starting matrices Q and R, those in equation (20a). With a positive real multiplicative factor, P, varying until obtaining the desired value and taking for R a constant value that its size will depend on the number of entries to the system *u(t)*.

$$Q = P * \left(C'C\right)$$
$$R = dig\left\{r_1, ..., r_m\right\} \tag{20a}$$

Another trial and proof way for tuning the LQR controller is the manual application of the Bryson method, equation (20b).

$$Q = dig\left\{q_1, ..., q_n\right\}$$
$$R = dig\left\{r_1, ..., r_m\right\} \tag{20b}$$

3. **Pole Allocation Method:** With this method, the poles of the closed loop system are placed in certain values defined by the analyst, thanks to prior knowledge of the process. For using this method, it is necessary to have actual measurements or otherwise apply observers to estimate the actual value of the process variables, for which there is no physical measurement.

It is evident that although there are different tuning methods for the LQR controller, all of them require at the end a tuning by trial and proof to achieve the desired results in the process. Some methods need by trial and proof a starting point for some possible values of the parameters Q and R. It can be concluded that with just this procedure is possible to obtain optimum tuning parameters for the LQR controller. This is the path taken in this chapter.

Optimal Robust PID Controller

A robust PID controller is a control strategy that meets an index of specific robustness; that is, finding a quantitative measurement of how stable is the control loop. There are different alternatives for knowing the robustness, highlighting the methods based on the internal model control (Rivera et al, 1986) and those considering the tuning from the values gain and phase margins and closed-loop gain (Lee, 2004). The latter leaded to the use of the maximum sensitivity function (named M_s) as a measure of system robustness (Aström and Hägglund, 2004; Alfaro et al, 2009).

Gain, A_m, and phase, φ_m, margins in the frequency domain are defined in equations (21) and (22), respectively. Where, ω_p and ω_g are obtained through the equations (23) and (24).

$$A_m = \frac{1}{\left| G_c(j\omega_p)G(j\omega_p) \right|} \tag{21}$$

$$\phi_m = \arg \left| G_c(j\omega_g)G_p(j\omega_g) \right| + \pi \tag{22}$$

$$\left| G_c(j\omega_p)G(j\omega_p) \right| = 1 \tag{23}$$

$$\arg \left| G_c(j\omega_g)G(j\omega_g) \right| = -\pi \tag{24}$$

The gain margin, as a measure of robustness, indicates that in the event that the system model is incorrect, the static gain may increase in a factor A_m before the system becomes unstable. Typical specification values for the gain margin are $2 \leq A_m \leq 5$.

The phase margin, as a measure of robustness, indicates that if there is an error in modeling the process, this may suffer an additional phase delay of φ_m degrees, on the frequency ω_g, before the system becomes unstable. Typical specification values for phase margin are $30° \leq \varphi_m \leq 60°$.

The sensitivity function (25) is used to determine the control loop tolerance to variations in the process to be controlled, but now is applied to establish a measure of robustness (26).

$$S(s) = \frac{1}{1 + G_c(s)G_p(s)} \tag{25}$$

$$M_S = \max_{\omega} \left| S(j\omega) \right| = \frac{1}{\min_{\omega} \left| 1 + G_c(j\omega)G_p(j\omega) \right|} \tag{26}$$

When thinking in the design of controllers, it is desirable to have small values of M_s because a high robustness is achieved. This measure of robustness can simultaneously ensure bounds for the gain and phase margins (27), (Vilanova and Alfaro, 2011).

$$A_m \geq \frac{M_S}{M_S - 1}, \phi_m \geq 2\sin^{-1}\left(\frac{1}{M_S}\right) \tag{27}$$

Typical values of M_s range in the order of 1.4 to 2; involving for the case of $M_s = 2$, an $A_m \geq 2$ and a $\varphi_m \geq 29°$. In the case of $M_s = 1.4$, values of $A_m \geq 3.5$ and $\varphi_m \geq 41°$ are guaranteed.

A robust optimal PID controller is one that meets simultaneously with an index of performance and a specified measure of robustness. This measure is established as an additional constraint in the optimization problem, minimizing just now a target function, for example an integrated performance index.

To ensure an optimal performance of the control loop and additionally its effect will be reflected in the control objective (assuring quality and efficiency in the final product) is necessary to associate the control problem to a performance index. For our case, the optimum parameters Q and R of the LQR controller are obtained when a criterion of overall performance of the control loop is minimized. These results will be compared with the response of the system using a PID (optimal and robust) tuned by the evolutionary algorithm MAGO.

Optimization Criteria

In many cases, it is easier to represent the performance of the control loop in the time domain, because it presents an overview of the whole problem without going into specifics. When thinking an optimization problem is "easier" to design a control strategy when considering as objective function an overall performance index (Levine, 1996) such as: IAE (equation (9)) and ITAE (equation (10)).

It is not often that such performance indices are used to tuning controllers in the field, but they are commonly used in the design of automatic tuning algorithms and as a reference point for the control strategies simulation (Levine, 1996).

EA have been used successfully in the tuning of the Q and R matrices from LQR controllers (Ghoreishi et al., 2011; Tijani et al, 2013) and tuning parameters of PID (Li et al, 2006, Hernandez-Riveros et al, 2014). MAGO as optimization tool has presented efficient outcomes when facing with problems in the continuous domain (Hernandez and Villada, 2012). Here, MAGO is used for tuning the LQR and PID controllers, minimizing the ITAE as performance criterion of the control loop.

The optimization problem for the LQR controller is defined in equation (28). Where Q and R are defined as in equations (29) and (30).

$$\min_{Q,R} \sum_{t_k=0}^{t_{k_f}} k \left| e(t_k) \right|$$

$s.t.$

$$eq.(6) \quad and \quad eq.(7)$$

$$u(t_k) = K_C e(t_k) + \frac{K_C}{T_i} \sum_{t_k=0}^{t_k} e(t_k) + K_C T_d \frac{\Delta e(t_k)}{\Delta k}$$

$$Q_{min} \leq Q \leq Q_{max}$$

$$R_{min} \leq R \leq R_{max}$$

(28)

$$Q = diag \begin{bmatrix} x_1 & x_2 & x_3 & x_4 & x_5 & x_6 & x_7 & x_8 \end{bmatrix}$$

(29)

$$R = x_9$$

(30)

For the analysis in state-space, it is essential to ensure that the process is controllable, therefore the models obtained from (1) and (2) in the controllable canonical form (see equations in (31)), must meet the criterion of controllability. This criterion indicates the capacity of the system to reach a final state from any initial state. For this case, the controllability matrix is computed and therefore it is verified that the rank of the matrix A and the controllability matrix are equal.

$$A = \begin{bmatrix} -0.45e^{-2} & -0.97e^{-2} & -12.7e^{-2} & -107.5e^{-2} & -579e^{-2} & -1814.4e^{-2} & -2661.1e^{-2} & -1330.7e^{-2} \\ 1 & 0 & & & \cdots & & & 0 \\ & 1 & & & & & & \\ & & 1 & & & & & \\ \vdots & & & 1 & & & & \vdots \\ & & & & 1 & & & \\ & & & & & 1 & & \\ 0 & & \cdots & & & 0 & 1 & 0 \end{bmatrix}$$

$$B = \begin{bmatrix} 1 & 0 & 0 & 0 & 0 & 0 & 0 & 0 \end{bmatrix}^T \tag{31}$$

$$C = \begin{bmatrix} 0 & 2 & -84 & 1680 & -20160 & 151200 & -665280 & 1330560 \end{bmatrix}$$

$$D = 0$$

The optimization problem for the robust optimal PID controller is defined in equation (32).

$$\min_{K_C, T_i, T_d} \sum_{t_k=0}^{t_{k_f}} k \left| e(t_k) \right|$$

s.t.

$$eq.(1) \quad or \quad eq.(2)$$

$$u(t_k) = K_C e(t_k) + \frac{K_C}{T_i} \sum_{t_k=0}^{t_k} e(t_k) + K_C T_d \frac{\Delta e(t_k)}{\Delta k} \tag{32}$$

$$1.4 \leq M_s \leq 2.0$$

$$K_{C_{min}} \leq K_C \leq K_{C_{max}}$$

$$T_{i_{min}} \leq T_i \leq T_{i_{max}}$$

$$T_{d_{min}} \leq T_d \leq T_{d_{max}}$$

RESULTS FOR LQR AND ROBUST PID TUNING ON BENCHMARK PLANTS

MAGO has been used for tuning the robust LQR and PID controllers. MAGO setting parameters are 150 generations and 100 individuals. The ITAE values obtained in simulations using MAGO as an optimization tool are presented in Table 7. Column 1 shows the models described in Table 2; column 2 shows the control loop performance index ITAE, which is divided into four columns. In the first, the values obtained in (Hernández-Riveros et al, 2016-b) for the PID controller. In the second, the PID with an additional robustness criterion. In the third, the LQR selecting optimally via MAGO the parameters Q and R, and finally, in the fourth, LQR manually tuned by trial and proof.

For plants in the mode of regulation Gp2_Reg (see Table 2), shown in Figure 7, all the responses obtained with a plain PID via MAGO present oscillation. In responses obtained with the robust PID via MAGO oscillations are also appreciated, but they are small. This is not observed in the results presented for the LQR tuned by trial and proof and with MAGO, where for all plants operating as regulator, smooth responses without oscillations were obtained. For comparison, the Robust PID-MAGO is used, but it can be seen evidently that the LQR-MAGO performs better in all cases.

Table 7. Performance Index, ITAE, for different control strategies

PLANT	ITAE			
	Optimal PID	**Robust Optimal PID**	**LQR-MAGO**	**LQR-Manual**
Gp2_Reg1	3.1052	3.1456	0.0528	0.3665
Gp2_Reg2	3.6071	5.5162	0.0633	0.3838
Gp2_Reg3	3.6738	4.7662	0.0699	0.3908
Gp1_Servo1	2.0486	2.2160	1.0371	1.5997
Gp1_Servo2	2.8532	4.1787	0.9531	1.7051
Gp1_Servo3	2.7827	2.8601	1.5140	3.1584
Gp1_Reg1	3.6623	4.8168	0.0700	1.1311
Gp1_Reg2	3.6427	4.2466	0.1904	2.3062
Gp1_Reg3	4.4240	3.4411	0.2806	1.4324
Gp2_Servo1	72.686	1.3717	0.7030	1.0120
Gp2_Servo2	69.494	1.9321	1.0128	1.7356
Gp2_Servo3	63.241	2.0490	0.9911	1.5473

Figure 7. Response of plant (2) as regulator

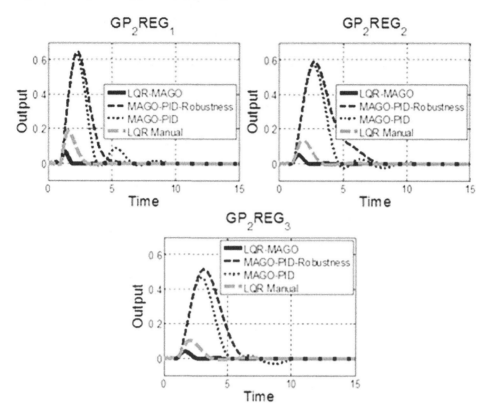

Responses tuning the Q and R parameters by MAGO are presented in Figure 8, for Gp1_Servo plants, corresponding to Table 2, equation (1). These responses are smoother than those obtained with PID-MAGO and robust-PID-MAGO. The LQR-MAGO presents a small over peak, but not affecting significantly the value of ITAE performance criteria, achieving a shorter establishment time than the other three control strategies.

Figure 9 shows the comparative results of the four controllers for each of the proposed cases, Gp1_Reg plants, corresponding to Table 2, equation (1), revealing their own robust characteristics and also, good performance in systems when operating as regulator. For this case, the evolution of dynamics of the optimization algorithm MAGO is presented in Figure 10 together with the evolution of the objective function (ITAE) throughout generations.

Regarding the evolution of the objective function, around the 100th generation the ITAE remains constant, giving to think that the algorithm has already found the solution. But when the behavior of the dynamics of MAGO are checked (Emergent,

Figure 8. Response of plant (1) as servomechanism

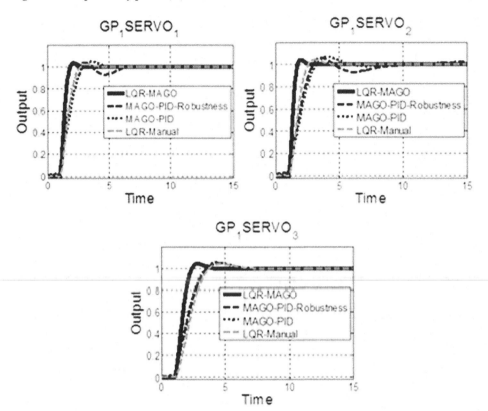

Crowd and Accidental), it can be seen that the evolution process is not yet stable, as the Emerging Dynamics dominates too quickly, but in generation 120 a better individual is found and therefore Emerging Dynamics decreases and the Crowd Dynamics grows.

In Figure 11, a predator-prey behavior type is observed for the Emerging and Crowd Dynamics, characteristic of the behavior of the species in Nature. For this case the predator, that is, the individual who benefits from the quarry to preserve its species is the Emerging Dynamics, and the Crowd Dynamics is the prey. When there is very little population in the Emerging Dynamics, i.e. very few predators, it is evident that the Crowd Dynamics increases; and when the Emergent Dynamics increases, decrease the Crowd Dynamics. When there is a point where the Emerging Dynamics dominates, that is the predator, indicates that more generations are needed. Additionally, in Figure 11, the behavior of population in different generations is shown.

The first image at left, in Figure 11, corresponds to the initial population matching to the variables X1 and X2, that is, 2 of the 10 variables used in MAGO for tuning the

Figure 9. Response of plant (1) as regulator

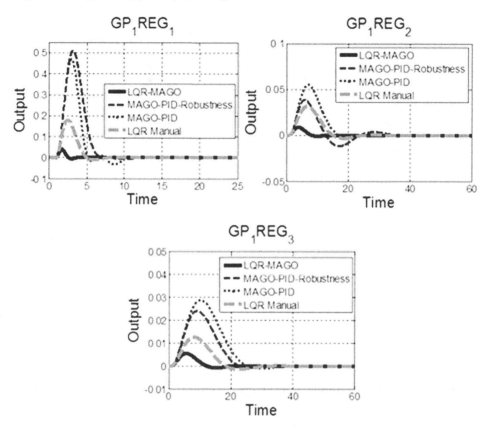

Figure 10. a) Cardinalities, b) Value of function (ITAE)

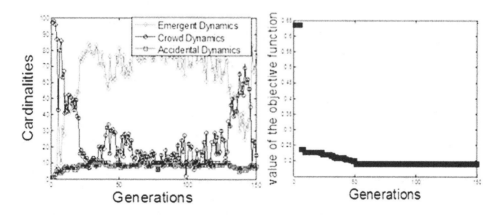

Figure 11. Population

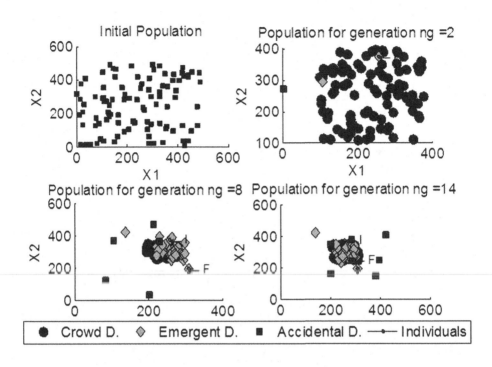

Figure 12. Dynamics Evolution (cardinalities) of MAGO

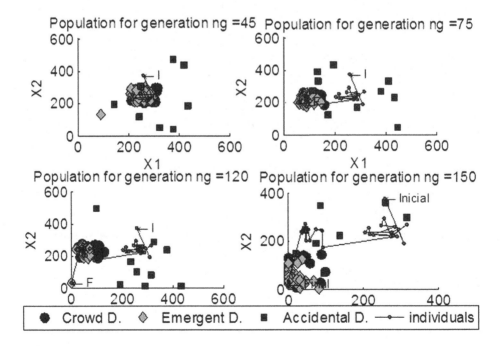

LQR. For generation 2, how the dynamics discriminates can be seen; in generation 8 the search space has been explored to find the best individual, this displacement is apparent in the following generations. See Figure 10.

In Figure 13, results obtained for the four control strategies are presented. Due to its characteristics of robustness, the LQR has very good results in processes operating as a regulator, which is evident in soft and rapid responses in the simulation of the three plants.

CONCLUSION

A method of tuning optimal robust controllers through the evolutionary algorithm MAGO has been successfully developed and implemented. The evolutionary method resolves the tuning as an optimization problem for PID and LQR controllers on several types of plants running on different modes of operation. To ensure the

Figure 13. Response of plant (2) as servomechanism

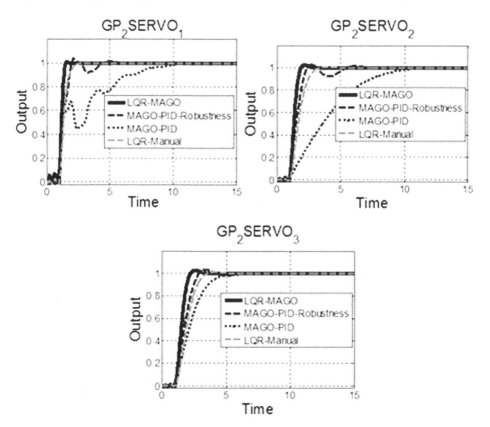

desired performance of the control loop everything is reduced to the characterization and adjusting of the value of a set of tuning parameters, generally obtained by trial and proof, whatever the chosen control strategy (PID or LQR) is. The usual tuning controller procedures involve uncertainty and time to obtain the right parameters as well as trained personal depending of the method used. This chapter showed a way to reduce these challenges. MAGO straightforwardly assesses the parameters of the controllers penalizing the error between the reference value and the output of the plant, minimizing the ITAE performance criterion.

For Second Order System Plus Time Delay models, the PID controller tuning was made by the evolutionary method without additional knowledge of the plant. Traditional methods for SOSPD systems are restricted to certain values on the behavior of the plant and are limited to an only one type of operation. Most methods for optimal tuning of SOSPD systems need experiments to be carried out directly on the plant to get additional system information required to apply those methods. These activities are not always possible to achieve because the triggering of extreme stresses and oscillations of the plant, which may create instability and damages on the system, so, that, they are not recommended. The evolutionary solution obtained with the MAGO cover all these restrictions, extends their maximum and minimum limits, does not need additional experimental information from the plants and is suitable for both, servo and regulator operating modes. The results showed that regardless of, both, the plant or controller models used, MAGO gets a better overall performance comparing to traditional methods (Bohl and McAvoy (1976), Minimum ITAE - Hassan (1993), Minimum ITAE - Sung (1996), Minimum ITAE - Sung (1996)).

For controlling complex systems holding strict performance requirements, the optimal controller LQR (Linear Quadratic Regulator) is currently used. The application of the LQR controller has been limited by the uncertainty in finding the right weighting parameters. Unlike the PID tuning methods, the LQR algorithm demands the state space model of the plant. For the proper performance of the LQR algorithm on the process, the weighting matrices Q and R should be defined by the analyst to balance the plant performance and the control effort. Common methods to find the Q and R matrices take a significant time and fail in many cases to meet the performance expected for the process. In this chapter, the algorithm MAGO was applied for calculating the Q and R matrices. The results from the evolutionary method were compared with those of the optimal and optimal-robust PID controller types and a traditional LQR. The LQR controller performs better when optimized with the MAGO algorithm.

The challenge of rely on a single method to assess the controller for different kinds of plants has been solved applying the evolutionary algorithm MAGO as a tool of optimization. The evolutionary method was applied to a set of benchmark plants, represented in, both, transfer functions and state space representation, with a control loop operating on, either, servo and regulator modes. The optimal tuning values of matrices Q and R for the LQR controller, likewise the Kc, Ti and Td parameters for the optimal-robust PID controller found by the evolutionary method achieved successful results for each of the cases studied. Noticeable results tuning with the algorithm MAGO were obtained when comparing the performance of each one of the control strategies. Uncertainty on the Q and R weight matrices and the PID parameters calculation was removed with the evolutionary adjustment.

This chapter showed that, although there are options in the traditional rules of controllers tuning, the use of heuristic algorithms it is indeed better than using the classic methods of optimal tuning. The evolutionary algorithm MAGO was used as a tool to optimize the controller parameters for the LQR and optimal-robust PID strategies working on benchmark plants. Regardless of the operating mode of the controller and the representation type of the plant used, better results are yield when optimization is made with the MAGO algorithm than with the traditional methods for optimal tuning.

ACKNOWLEDGMENT

The participation of Jorge Humberto Urrea Quintero is partially supported by COLCIENCIAS (Fondo Nacional de Financiamiento para la Ciencia, la Tecnología y la Innovación Francisco José de Caldas) under the doctoral scholarship 727-2015.

REFERENCES

Alfaro, V. M., & Vilanova, R. (2012). Optimal robust tuning for 1DoF PI/PID control unifying FOPDT/SOPDT models. *IFAC Proceedings Volumes, 45*(3), 572-577.

Alfaro, V. M., Vilanova, R., & Arrieta, O. (2009). Robust tuning of two-degree-of-freedom (2-DoF) PI/PID based cascade control systems. *Journal of Process Control, 19*(10), 1658–1670. doi:10.1016/j.jprocont.2009.08.006

Åström, K. J., & Hägglund, T. (1995). *PID controllers: Theory, design, and tuning.* Research Triangle Park, NC: ISA Publishers.

Ayala, F. J. K., & John, A. (1984). *Genética moderna* (No. 575.1 A9Y). Academic Press.

Bohl, A. H., & McAvoy, T. J. (1976). Linear feedback vs. time optima control. II. The regulator problem. *Industrial & Engineering Chemistry Process Design and Development*, *15*(1), 30–33. doi:10.1021/i260057a007

Bryson, A. J. R., & Carrier, A. (1989). A comparison of control synthesis using differential games (H-infinity) and LQR. In *Guidance, Navigation and Control Conference* (p. 3598). Academic Press.

Chang, W. D., & Yan, J. J. (2004). Optimum setting of PID controllers based on using evolutionary programming algorithm. *Zhongguo Gongcheng Xuekan*, *27*(3), 439–442. doi:10.1080/02533839.2004.9670890

Darwin, C. (1859). *The origin of species*. London: John Murray.

Fan, L., & Joo, E. M. (2009, May). Design for auto-tuning PID controller based on genetic algorithms. In *Industrial Electronics and Applications, 2009. ICIEA 2009. 4th IEEE Conference on* (pp. 1924-1928). IEEE.

Fisher, R. A. (1930). *The genetical theory of natural selection. a complete variorum edition*. Oxford University Press. doi:10.5962/bhl.title.27468

Fleming, P. J., & Purshouse, R. C. (2002). Evolutionary algorithms in control systems engineering: A survey. *Control Engineering Practice*, *10*(11), 1223–1241. doi:10.1016/S0967-0661(02)00081-3

Ghoreishi, S. A., Mohammad, A. N., & Basiri, S. O. (2011). Optimal Design of LQR Weighting Matrices based on Intelligent Optimization Methods. *International Journal of Intelligent Information Processing*, *2*(1).

Hansen, N. (2006). The CMA evolution strategy: a comparing review. *Towards a new evolutionary computation*, 75-102.

Hassan, G. A. (1993). Computer-aided tuning of analog and digital controllers. *Control and Computers*, *21*, 1–1.

Hassani, K., & Lee, W. S. (2014, May). Optimal tuning of linear quadratic regulators using quantum particle swarm optimization. In *Proceedings of the International Conference of Control, Dynamics and Robotics* (pp. 1-8). Academic Press.

Hernández-Riveros, J. A., & Carmona-Cadavid, C. V. (2016b). Evolutionary selection of optimal weighting matrices for LQR controllers and parameters of robust PID on benchmark plants. In *XVII Latin American Conference on Automatic Control CLCA* (pp. 269-378). Academic Press.

Hernández-Riveros, J. A., & Ospina, J. D. (2010). A multi dynamics algorithm for global optimization. *Mathematical and Computer Modelling*, *52*(7), 1271–1278. doi:10.1016/j.mcm.2010.03.024

Hernández-Riveros, J. A., & Urrea-Quintero, J. H. (2014). SOSPD Controllers Tuning by Means of an Evolutionary Algorithm. *International Journal of Natural Computing Research*, *4*(2), 40–58. doi:10.4018/ijncr.2014040103

Hernández-Riveros, J. A., Urrea-Quintero, J. H., & Carmona-Cadavid, C. V. (2016a). Evolutionary Tuning of Optimal PID Controllers for Second Order Systems Plus Time Delay. In *Computational Intelligence. In Studies in Computational Intelligence* (Vol. 620). Springer; doi:10.1007/978-3-642-34654-5_28

Hernández-Riveros, J. A., & Villada-Cano, D. (2012). Sensitivity Analysis of an Autonomous Evolutionary Algorithm. In Advances in Artificial Intelligence - IBERAMIA 2012 (pp. 271-280). Springer-Verlag Berlin Heidelberg.

Herreros, A., Baeyens, E., & Perán, J. R. (2002). Design of PID-type controllers using multiobjective genetic algorithms. *ISA Transactions*, *41*(4), 457–472. doi:10.1016/S0019-0578(07)60102-5 PMID:12398277

Hull, D. G. (2013). *Optimal control theory for applications*. Springer Science & Business Media.

Iruthayarajan, M. W., & Baskar, S. (2009). Evolutionary algorithms based design of multivariable PID controller. *Expert Systems with Applications*, *36*(5), 9159–9167. doi:10.1016/j.eswa.2008.12.033

Junli, L., Jianlin, M., & Guanghui, Z. (2011). Evolutionary algorithms based parameters tuning of PID controller. In *Control and Decision Conference (CCDC), May 2011 Chinese* (pp. 416-420). IEEE. doi:10.1109/CCDC.2011.5968215

Lagunas-Jiménez, R., Fernández-Anaya, G., & Martínez-García, J. C. (2006, September). Tuning of two-degrees-of-freedom PID controllers via the multiobjective genetic algorithm NSGA-II. In *Electronics, Robotics and Automotive Mechanics Conference, 2006* (*Vol. 2*, pp. 145-150). IEEE. doi:10.1109/CERMA.2006.94

Lee, C. H. (2004). A survey of PID controller design based on gain and phase margins. *International Journal of Computational Cognition*, *2*(3), 63–100.

Levine, W. S. (1996). *The Control Handbook*. CRC Press.

Lewis, F. L., & Syrmos, V. L. (1995). *Optimal control*. John Wiley & Sons.

Li, Y., Ang, K. H., & Chong, G. C. (2006). PID control system analysis and design. *IEEE Control Systems*, *26*(1), 32–41. doi:10.1109/MCS.2006.1580152

Lozano, J. A. (2006). *Towards a new evolutionary computation: advances on estimation of distribution algorithms* (Vol. 192). Springer Science & Business Media. doi:10.1007/3-540-32494-1

Montgomery, D. C. (2007). *Introduction to statistical quality control*. John Wiley & Sons.

Mora, J. (2004). *Performance and robustness of the methods based on second order models plus dead time tuning PID controllers*. Escuela de Ingeniería Eléctrica, Universidad de Costa Rica.

Nelder, J. A., & Mead, R. (1965). A simplex method for function minimization. *The Computer Journal*, *7*(4), 308–313. doi:10.1093/comjnl/7.4.308

O'Dwyer, A. (2009). *Handbook of PI and PID controller tuning rules*. World Scientific. doi:10.1142/p575

Ogunnaike, B. A., & Ray, W. H. (1994). *Process dynamics, modeling, and control*. Oxford University Press.

Roffel, B., & Betlem, B. (2007). *Process dynamics and control: modeling for control and prediction*. John Wiley & Sons.

Saad, M. S., Jamaluddin, H., & Darus, I. Z. (2012a). PID controller tuning using evolutionary algorithms. *WSEAS Transactions on Systems and Control*, *7*(4), 139–149.

Saad, M. S., Jamaluddin, H., & Darus, I. Z. M. (2012b). Implementation of PID controller tuning using differential evolution and genetic algorithms. *International Journal of Innovative Computing, Information, & Control*, *8*(11), 7761–7779.

Skolicki, Z., & De Jong, K. (2005, June). The influence of migration sizes and intervals on island models. In *Proceedings of the 7th annual conference on Genetic and evolutionary computation* (pp. 1295-1302). ACM. doi:10.1145/1068009.1068219

Solera Saborío, E. (2005). PI/PID controller tuning with IAE and ITAE criteria for double pole plants. *Escuela de Ingeniería Eléctrica, Universidad de Costa Rica, 18*.

Sung, S. W., Jungmin, O., Lee, I. B., Lee, J., & Yi, S. H. (1996). Automatic tuning of PID controller using second-order plus time delay model. *Journal of Chemical Engineering of Japan*, *29*(6), 990–999. doi:10.1252/jcej.29.990

Tavakoli, S., Griffin, I., & Fleming, P. J. (2007, September). Multi-objective optimization approach to the PI tuning problem. In *Evolutionary Computation, 2007. CEC 2007. IEEE Congress on* (pp. 3165-3171). IEEE. doi:10.1109/CEC.2007.4424876

Tijani, I. B., Akmeliawati, R., & Abdullateef, A. I. (2013, June). Control of an inverted pendulum using MODE-based optimized LQR controller. In *Industrial Electronics and Applications (ICIEA), 2013 8th IEEE Conference on* (pp. 1759-1764). IEEE. doi:10.1109/ICIEA.2013.6566653

Vilanova, R., & Alfaro, V. M. (2011). Control PID robusto: Una visión panorámica. *Revista Iberoamericana de Automática e Informática Industrial RIAI, 8*(3), 141–158. doi:10.1016/j.riai.2011.06.003

Whitley, D. (2001). An overview of evolutionary algorithms: Practical issues and common pitfalls. *Information and Software Technology, 43*(14), 817–831. doi:10.1016/S0950-5849(01)00188-4

Yu, X., & Gen, M. (2010). *Introduction to evolutionary algorithms*. Springer Science & Business Media. doi:10.1007/978-1-84996-129-5

Chapter 8
Cloud Approach for the Medical Information System:
MIS on Cloud

Ekaterine Kldiashvili
Georgia Telemedicine Union, Georgia

ABSTRACT

Healthcare informatics is an important and effective field. It is characterized by the intensive development and design of the new models and protocols. The special emphasize is done on medical information system (MIS) and cloud approaches for its implementation. It is expected that this technology can improve healthcare services, benefit healthcare research, and change the face of health information technology. This chapter discusses the application of cloud computing for the medical information system practical usage.

INTRODUCTION

There is a very clear need for the expanded application of information technology (IT) in healthcare. Clinical workflow still depends largely on manual, paper-based medical record systems, which is economically inefficient and produces significant variances in medical outcomes. Medical information system (MIS) is at the heart of IT implementation policies in healthcare systems around the world (Clamp et al, 2007; Zeng 2016). Most of these policies are based on beliefs about the positive value of MIS rather than on the available empirical evidence; as a result, policy documents comprise aspirational statements rather than detailed and realistic expectations (Banta 2003).

DOI: 10.4018/978-1-5225-5020-4.ch008

It is obvious and well known that the field of healthcare informatics is rapidly evolving. The new models and protocols of MIS are developed. They are based on implementation of profiles such as HL7 and DICOM. Despite obvious advantages and benefits (Alpert 2016), practical application of MIS in everyday practice is slow (Detmar 2001; Clamp et al., 2007; Khalifa et al., 2015) Research and development projects are ongoing in several countries around the world to develop MIS: examples include Canada, Australia, England, the United States, and Finland. MIS is used primarily for setting objectives and planning patient care, documenting the delivery of care, and assessing the outcomes of care. It includes information regarding patient needs during episodes of care provided by different healthcare professionals. The amount and quality of information available to healthcare professionals in patient care has an impact on the outcomes of patient care and the continuity of care. The information included in MIS has several different functions in the decision-making process in patient care. It also supports decision making in management and in health policy (Lane 2006; Yanamadala et al., 2016).

The term globalization involves a complex series of economic, social, technological and political changes seen as increasing interdependence and interaction between people and companies in disparate locations. The phenomenon of globalization has already reached the medical field, most importantly in the areas of knowledge, diagnosis and therapy. The access of as many people as possible to these areas should be guaranteed by a technically efficient man-machine interacting system and by an effective organization of specialists around the world. An efficiently operational and organized exchange of medical information increases the quality of diagnosis and therapy, and assures the training and continuous education of the medical personnel. The main task of a medical information system is to enable medical non-experts to gather, exchange and discuss relevant data at any time with experts at any place of the world. A wise conception of such a structured dialogue for consultations and continuing medical education is based on a user-friendly, fast, simple, efficient and sustainable system for the exchange of medical information (Detmer 2000; Detmer 2001).

Several years ago any talk related to the Internet would have to be preceded by an explanation of what it is and how it works, but at present information and communication technologies (ICT) became the essential part of our life and practical activity. eHealth can be designated as a special form of ICT; as a method of delivering of medical services by electronic means of communication, with the provider and the recipient of these services being at different places.

Efficient, effective and reliable systems for medical data registration and management are the top requirements. However, solutions have so far proved elusive and the deployment of ICT in many health sectors has required major transformational changes. One of the major problems for a full potential delivery of medical service is to provide the tools for the world-wide access. Thus, it is necessary to make radical improvements in service productivity, access to medical services, and improved quality of diagnostic with acceptable levels of patient safety. A well developed ICT could serve to breakdown many of the existing barriers to the access of healthcare in the world (Hayrinen et al, 2008).

The term "Cloud computing" was coined to denote a proposed distributed computing resources for advanced science and engineering (Fox 2011). Considerable progress has since been made on the construction of such an infrastructure. The modern technological developments revealed, that cloud computing refers to an on-demand, self-service Internet infrastructure that enables the user to access computing resources anytime from anywhere. It is a new model of delivering computing resources, not a new technology. Cloud computing provides three new advantages: massive computing resources available on demand, elimination of an up-front commitment by users, and payment for use on a short-term basis as needed. From a service point of view, cloud computing includes 3 archetypal models: software, platform, and infrastructure.

1. **Software as a Service (SaaS):** The applications (e.g. Electronic health records) are hosted by a cloud service provider and mada available to customers over a network, typically the internet.
2. **Platform as a Service (PaaS):** The development tools (eg, operation systems) are hosted in the cloud and accessed through a browser. With Paas, developers can build web applications without installing any tools on their computer, and then deploy those applications without any specialized administrative skills.
3. **Infrastructure as a Service (IaaS):** The cloud user outsources the equipment used to support operations, including storage, hardware, servers, and networking components. The provider owns the equipment and is responsible for housing, running, and maintaining it. The user typically pays on a per-use basis.

Current distributed computing technologies do not address the above concerns and requirements, and it is here precisely where MIS approach realized through cloud computing comes on the scene. Over the past five years, research and development efforts within the MIS community have produced protocols, services, and tools that address the challenges that arise when we seek to build scalable networks. Basic technologies supporting MIS include the Internet and the World Wide Web telecommunications, electronic mail, groupware, and video conferencing (Riva 2000; Riva 2002).

The present article will discuss the application of MIS for eHealth purposes. MISs vary tremendously in their purpose, scope, size, duration, structure, community, and sociology yet they all involve a broad set of common concerns and requirements, namely: the need for highly flexible sharing relationships, ranging from client-server to peer-to-peer; for sophisticated and precise levels of control over how shared resources are used, including fine-grained and multi-stakeholder access control, delegation, and application of local and global policies; for sharing of varied resources, ranging from programs, files, and data to computers, sensors, and networks; and for diverse usage modes, ranging from single user to multi-user and from performance sensitive to cost-sensitive and hence embracing issues of quality of service, scheduling, co-allocation, and accounting.

It is obvious that MIS has a great potentiality; however today there are unfortunately only a few examples of its large services. The benefits of expanding MIS use are threefold: it can improve the quality of healthcare services; it will allow a better exploitation of limited hospital resources and of expensive medical equipment; it will help to address the problem of unequal access to healthcare. MIS realized through implementation of cloud computing will offer the opportunity for improving healthcare services and for making healthcare expertise available to underserved locations.

BACKGROUND

It is well known, that eHealth is a rapidly developing application of clinical medicine where medical information is transferred via application of ICT for the purpose of consulting, remote medical procedures or examinations. It can be as simple as discussing of a case by two healthcare professionals by using of web technologies or as complex as using satellite technology and videoconferencing equipment to conduct a real-time consultation between medical specialists. eHealth encompass all applications of ICT in healthcare (telemedicine, electronic patient records, health information on the Internet, distance education, etc.).

eHealth has a longer history. The National Aeronautics and Space Administration (NASA) played an important role in the early development of this field. NASA's efforts in eHealth began in the early 1960s when humans began flying in space. Physiological parameters were telemetered from both the spacecraft and the space suits during missions (Lane 2006). These early efforts and the enhancement in communication satellites fostered the development of telemedicine and many of the medical devices in the delivery of healthcare today. At 90s of last century it became clear that ICT in general had developed much. The speed of transmission of larger amounts of information had increased and the usability of ICT for healthcare became larger. A new era for telemedicine started. The number of possible applications of the new technology developed much and continues to develop. Telemedicine is now an enabler to transcend both distance and time barriers for collaboration. As a result requests to possibilities and resources of ICT increase. Cloud computing and Medical Information System technologies have been developed (Chatman 2010).

Healthcare IT models are constantly evolving as the industry expands. MIS is a comprehensive solution that automates the clinical, administrative, and supply-chain functions. It enables healthcare providers to improve their operational effectiveness, to reduce costs and medical errors, and to enhance quality of care. The aim of MIS was and is as simple as relevant: to contribute to and ensure a high-quality, efficient patient care. The relevance of "good" MIS for high-level quality of care is obvious (Houghton 2011). Without having appropriate access to relevant data, practically no decisions on diagnostic, therapeutic, or other procedures can be made. In such a situation, consequences will be fatal for patients.

MIS users are a set of individuals and/or institutions that have direct access to computers, software, data and other resources, and to share resources in a highly controlled manner, with resource providers and consumers defining clearly and carefully just what is shared, who is allowed to share, and the conditions under which sharing occurs (Li et al, 2011; Bowman, 2013). MISs vary tremendously in their purpose, scope, size, duration, structure, community, and sociology yet they all involve a broad set of common concerns and requirements, namely: the need for highly flexible sharing relationships, ranging from client-server to peer-to-peer, for sophisticated and precise levels of control over how shared resources are used, including fine-grained and multi-stakeholder access control, delegation, and application of local and global policies; for sharing of varied resources, ranging from programs, files and data to computers, sensors, and networks; and for diverse usage modes, ranging from single user to multi-user and from performance sensitive to cost-sensitive and hence embracing issues of quality of service, scheduling, co-allocation, and accounting (Clamp et al, 2007; Chang et al, 2012). Current distributed computing technologies do not address the above concerns and requirements, and it is here precisely where MIS realized through cloud computing comes on the scene.

Healthcare is more and more complex and the fast turnover of accurate knowledge is a constant challenge. eHealth as well as application of MIS for healthcare purposes can address this. Most specialists have the resources to attend national and international scientific meetings, however most primary care team members do not have this opportunity. Developing of telemedicine networks, virtual conferences and streaming of scientific events provides an opportunity to reach front-line healthcare professionals. The medical information system can be used as a tool to facilitate the sharing of healthcare knowledge and expose the world community to outstanding achievements, resources and knowledge (Kobb et al, 2008).

MEDICAL INFORMATION SYSTEM FOR HEALTHCARE

The medical information system is successfully used for:

- **Clinical Decision Support:** Provides users with tools to acquire, manipulate, apply, and display appropriate information to aid in making accurate, timely, and evidence-based clinical decisions.
- **Electronic Medical Records (EMRs):** Contain information about patients, from personal details (such as name, age, address, and sex) to details of every aspect of care given by the clinic (ranging from routine visits to major operations).
- **Training and Research:** Patient information is available to medical personnel for training and research in eHealth and telemedicine.

By the term "EMR" we describe a computerized legal medical record created in the clinic. Usually, however, the term "electronic health record" (also electronic patient record or computerized patient record) is used. EMRs are a part of an MIS that allows storage, retrieval, and manipulation of data. This is an evolving concept defined as a longitudinal collection of electronic health information about individual patients or populations. Such records may included a whole range of data in comprehensive or summary form, including demographical data, medical history, medication and allergies, immunization status, laboratory test results, radiology images, and billing information. In accordance with our model, EMRs are generated and maintained within clinic. This is a complete record that allows managing and follows up workflow in healthcare settings and to increase patient safety through evidence-based decision support, quality management, and outcome reporting. EMRs can be continuously updated.

The medical information system has yielded significant benefits.

- Easy access to patient data. The system provides convenient access to medical records at all points of clinic. Internet-based access improves the ability to remotely access such data.
- Structured information. The data captured in clinical information system is well organized. Relevant information can be easily maintained and quickly found. The MIS reduces the likelihood of mistakes arising from illegible writing too.
- Safe and secure second opinion consultations.
- Effective quality assurance programs.

Despite of such benefits, there are still barriers that prevent the MIS from being rolled out in every healthcare organization across world.

- Initial cost of acquisition. High price of the basic infrastructure is a stumbling block for many countries and healthcare organizations.
- Privacy and security. There are still huge concerns in the healthcare industry about the privacy of patient data on computer systems and how to keep such information secure.
- Clinician resistance. Clinicians usually have 10-20 min to see their patients, and if their use of an MIS takes up more time than before, it leads to resistance.
- Integration of legacy systems. As elsewhere, this poses a stiff challenge for many organizations worldwide.

Before practical application of MIS, education and training of staff is essential. The system is a very useful and easy-for-use tool. It ensures a situation where healthcare professionals spend more time for creating knowledge from medical information than managing of medical information. Further, MIS holds the potential to reduce medical errors.

From the review and analysis of first attempts of application of MIS (Pak 2007) it has become obvious that there is a variety of problems and challenges. The healthcare systems, and the education of healthcare personnel, have to be re-organized to systems that function in a cross-border fashion. Prerequisites for this development shall be a specific emphasis on equity of access, interoperability and standardization of systems and protocols, security and legal aspects. There are technical, legal, organizational and financial problems to be solved.

Technical Problems: Although the MIS needed mostly does exist already today, there are still area-specific technical barriers that have to be overcome. The most prominent barriers are easy-to-use, intuitive, robust and smooth user interfaces and devices. The services must be offered to all users through such interfaces, and all of them have to be implemented in a uniform way. The access to the technology and systems must be smooth and transparent to the users. Otherwise they won't achieve a good acceptance.

Legal Problems: The legal barriers that have to be overcome are essentially the general ones applying to eHealth field. Responsibility, confidentiality, liability and access only to certified professionals are some of the key issues.

Organizational Problems: There are serious organizational barriers, however such as eHealth at home require smooth collaboration of different organizations. This requires a significant redesign of processes, which means a change from the enterprise-centric view to a system-wide perspective with patient at the center. Today the paradigm of service chains in healthcare built on MIS-based collaboration of service providers linked in a service provision network is still in its infancy. However, the increasing interest in recent approaches like managed care, disease management, and case management, which are strongly related to this paradigm shift, shows that the necessity of changing the way in which healthcare systems are organized is more and more recognized and continually becomes transparent. Country-specific factors, such as roles of different providers of health and social care services, insurance companies, housing providers, local authorities, and eHealth providers, need to be taken into account when introducing healthcare at home.

Financial Problems: The financial barriers largely depend on the different countries' policies. In countries with national healthcare systems these services will be a part of the overall healthcare system. In insurance based countries, where services are reimbursed on a fee-for service basis, new codes will have to be established. In countries with market-driven healthcare systems the prices need to be adapted to market prices driven by the healthcare consumers. At this time there is a little evidence on how the broad implementation of MIS based eHealth services will affect the financial situation of healthcare system in total, and its participants in particular. The challenge is to create comprehensive systems (networks of services offering the basis for patient-individual service chains) which are financially beneficial for all players.

Other Problems: The application of MIS for eHealth purposes can help to solve the huge problem of an 'elderly society'. Stakeholders, including health professionals, researchers, public officials, and the lay public must collaborate on a range of activities. These activities include initiatives to build robust health information system that provides equitable access, development of high-quality, audience-appropriate information and support services for specific health problems, and health-related decisions for all segments of the population, especially for underserved persons, training of health professionals in the science of communication and the use of communication technologies, evaluation of interventions, promotion of a critical understanding and practice of effective health communication both for end-users and for health professionals, and initiatives to gain knowledge about eHealth consumers' use of and their needs and attitudes with regards to MIS in eHealth.

In spite of the potential which application of MIS for eHealth has as mechanism too support health systems, a number of barriers, at various levels, would need to be overcome for health systems to take full advantage of these opportunities. These barriers are not unidimensional, focusing on technical knowledge as previously assumed, but rather a multidimensional construct, encompassing technical knowledge, economic viability, organizational support and behavior modification. Tree most important barriers to MIS application for eHealth adoption were identified as the problem of interoperability, acceptance of a 'new' health system, and regulatory constraints.

Interoperability is a key challenge. This is the fragmentation problem – many pieces of information, in many formats, on many platforms, in many stakeholder environments both physically (stored in different locations) and logically (not organized in the same fashion) accentuating issues of interoperability that are raised by lack of compatibility of systems and equipment. The problem of interoperability is not limited to technical standardization as typically assumed, but encompasses the complex issues of integrating cultural, financial and workflow systems. Ensuring that the 'ways of working' of health systems are interoperable is a major challenge (Latifi et al, 2006).

Acceptance of MIS in eHealth presents a particular challenge. It is important to promote the use of automated tailoring of information access and summaries to accommodate variations in culture, language, literacy, and health-related goals, as well as integrated decision-support systems that can proactively foster best practices. Unfortunately, collection and delivery of the necessary epidemiological and patient data on which such systems must be built are problematic. However, once collected, MIS can be used for timely transfer of data to central services for planning and management purposes. At the organizational level, revolutionary advances in medicine and technology as a whole during the past few decades have resulted in shifts in the boundaries between hospitals, primary healthcare, and community care. In the future, MIS in eHealth is likely to add to this by changing the way in which health services are provided, from clinical messaging (advice, results and referrals), to distributed electronic health records, increased connectivity between health services, patient appliances to assist self-management, and the use of technology to improve communication. These changes need to be sensitive to acceptance concerns related to changing established medical traditions, professional autonomy and loss of control.

Liability in connection with standards of care and medical malpractice, responsibility for security and confidentiality of patient-specific information are major legal challenges. Owing to be computerized communications involved in eHealth, determining where transactions occurred, which laws apply and which courts have jurisdiction will be problematic. At the policy level, challenges include professional standards of providing care and licensing of care givers, and regulation of medical devices and MIS and eHealth application software. Application of MIS in eHealth as well as eHealth is currently unregulated, unlike all other aspects of the health system.

MIS in eHealth raises or accentuates ethical, legal and policy issues. Confidentiality of information, protecting the privacy of patients and safeguarding the integrity of information will present significant challenges with increasing use of eHealth. There will also be gender issues to be addressed and model guidelines will be needed to resolve problems brought on by cultural differences among countries engaged in eHealth activities.

Interconnectivity comprises a lot more than merely devising and installing the technological infrastructure so as to be able to communicate and spread medical data through defined secured channels from one point on the earth to another. Interconnectivity is responsible for several aspects of MIS application for eHealth purposes when installing and running it:

- Technical aspects
- Organizational aspects
- Psychological aspects
- Social and socio-cultural aspects
- Financial aspects
- Legal aspects
- Political aspects
- Security aspects.

All these aspects are intertwined with all the sections and contributions are briefly described below. It is important to mention major features since they may serve as important criteria to be observed and integrated for the development of 'running eHealth systems".

Technical Aspects: With the availability of electronic patient record systems which try to integrate not merely both the stationary and the ambulatory medical workflow of diagnostics and therapy, but deliver real-time medical patient data in a ubiquitous fashion to hold these data available at any time and any location, the basis for a global data exchange in the field of medicine is given. The main stakes today comprise HL7 (HL7 2004) and information servers, CDA (CDA 2004), SCIPHOX (SCIPHOX 2004), and many other existing and to become documentation standards. More and more, the availability and performance of terrestrial communication lines becomes continually better: back from analogue telephone line to digital ISDN and nowadays xDSL lines. Whereas these communication line types are financially affordable usually for private and small business applications and services, such lines of even better quality (e.g. optical fiber) are today too expensive to compete adequately for a substantial market share in medicine.

Organizational Aspects: The necessary forms of organization within hospitals and the medical practices are only partially compatible with each other. As of yet, there are no general recommendations as how to organize services which have to deal with a more thought digitalization of medicine. This however, is independent of the underlying communication technology used.

Psychological Aspects: Many staff members in a medical setting – irrelevant of their hierarchical position – are still reluctant to use computer-based help in their daily routine work. It has clearly been shown that for physicians, the 'option to possess a gadget' to handle medical instructions is interesting, but the interest soon enough looses intensity after a very short period of time. For the paramedics, however, such gadgets often become integrated for good into their medical routine, and they are thought to use them much longer, much more intensely, and with a greater understanding of the gadget's practical value.

Social and Socio-Cultural Aspects: Many studies have shown that socio-cultural changes of a society towards the incorporation of electronic gadgets into daily life have great influence on the way people think and even expect how medicine should work. Technocracy has become one of the outstanding features of medicine in the opinion of most people. Irrelevant of whether this view is correct or adequate, medicine now is no longer in a condition to reluctantly defy all technological advances made. The standard of ubiquitous communicability for man has to become a feature of medicine as well. Furthermore, hierarchical structures no longer being accepted the way they used to be, a tendency can be noted which strengthens the individual's 'home right'. More and more applications and services are directly integrated into the consumers' homes, and they are expected to be both safe and trustworthy.

Financial Aspects: The ongoing everyday usage of ICT has given rise to MIS solutions associated with continually decreasing and thus affordable prices which make this technology usable for the large majority of users.

Legal Aspects: The heterogeneity of legal preconditions for carrying out eHealth applications and services, invariant of the used technology still in many countries forms a broad barrier with a national and an international component.

Political Aspects: Adjourning to the legal problems, the general attitude towards an ongoing digitalization in many countries is apparent, the way and direction, however, in which these developments are brought to flourish, are potentially different. In this situation, some coordination actions on an international level are mandatory.

Security Aspects: Security threats – not merely in the sense of a technological impact (virus attacks, worms, malicious scripts, etc.), but also concerning human behavior in carrying out national or international conflicts – are most imminent in people's minds when it comes to data security. This issue, however, has nothing to do with the underlying method of communication, but refers to the application and service layers to be applied.

The most important aspects which enable 'new' technologies to be widely accepted are:

- User-friendliness
- Reliability
- Error tolerance
- Security and privacy
- Service availability
- Quality of service
- Quality of workflow realization.

Existing solutions must be integrated into more modern software concepts. Concerning the availability MIS, ad hoc networks must be installable within short periods of time. Adequate Quality of Service shall be provided. Different technological gadgets and equipments must be interoperable so as to work together and be compatible to each other on a large scale.

Access to medical data must be authorized by the informed patient. The physician is not the proprietor of these data, whereby he may edit and manipulate them according to their 'load of truth'. Medical data must be ubiquitous for mobility's and flexibility's sake.

Clear structures of medical workflows must be elaborated and installed into both software and hardware concepts which allow for a digitalization of medical data in every respect. The acceptance that by ongoing digitalization routine aspects of work can be simplified and made more efficacious is crucial for the onset of technology apart from the postulation of user-friendliness and cognitive transparency.

The use of MIS for eHealth must go out of the hospitals and go into the homes of the health consumers. Healthcare s already being deliverable at home and the electronic documentation needs to follow. Thus, the concept of continuous socialization (with the family, with friends etc.) can be upheld better than before, and cases of hospitalization with all their aspects of microbiological contamination and psychological deprivation and depersonalization can be reduced significantly.

Establishing real world applications and services will, in the near future, definitively have the potential to help to save money, reduce redundancies, avoid a waste of resources, reduce the system-specific administrative overload and keep up and foster international bonds and treaties. Models will have to be developed which offer the same range of applications and services at the same or even better conditions (upstream and downstream velocity, data scrambling etc.) for both the health consumer and the healthcare professional based on the most suitable access technology (Lane 2006; Lareng 2002).

A unification of legal preconditions has to be proposed by each country. In the world a general legal framework will have to be imposed for developing the legal background for eHealth applications and services dealing with the transport of medical data both nationally and internationally.

Regardless of each country's healthcare policy, the general direction shall be an 'opening of data transfer through closed channels' to transmit data safely from one point to another. Therefore, on the side of the policy makers, medically expert advisors and consultants who not only know the individual healthcare situation perfectly well, but also have idea deep knowledge of the technology to be used together with a vision of where the whole development is heading to, shall be introduced to offset up the new basic laws to foster the understanding eHealth on the one hand and help the development of the needed applications and services on the other.

Data transfer has to be made safe and trustworthy. On the one side for the health consumer who wants to be assured that his medical data are not disclosed to anybody else but himself or herself. On the other side for the healthcare professional who does not want his medical workflow data exposed to unauthorized of forbidden benchmarking or other manipulation. Technologies must be developed which guarantee adequate amounts of privacy for all users of eHealth applications and services. Communication networks, thus, must exclude the possibility that their data stream is being logged and 'reverse engineered' to something human readable and something which can be associated to a real human being. Furthermore, patients can have access to the log files of their medical data viewed by 'authorized' persons thus implying a control mechanism for the accuracy and integrity of his/her own data.

The technological basis to support the communication and integration of MIS for management of medical patient data exists and can be used. However, the heterogeneity of middleware in the healthcare sector reflects the real problems for the introduction, installation, and maintenance of such technology. And this situation seems to be mostly independent of the technological nature. But apart from technological questions, the main stakes are to seamlessly integrate all of the mentioned aspects into one singular, possibly globally usable concept which enables the empowered citizen to take part in the best medical quality everywhere on the planet. Therefore, some challenges and opportunities are addressed:

- The basic technology deals with management of medical data. Thus a standardized document format is needed.
- The applications and services presently used and to be developed are independent of underlying communication carrier.

- Utilities to integrate existing middleware and to convert 'older' data sets are needed. The software used has to be transparent and user-friendly to the maximum for all users.

- Technology has to go hand in hand with the health consumers' and the healthcare professionals' needs and demands and must not be used 'role of technology push versus demand pull'.

- Socio-cultural changes need to be implicitly taken into account when it comes to developing systems which shall not only be used in a clinical context, but also be able to be integrating able into the health consumers' home.

- Legal and political aspects have to be harmonized on both a national and an international level. This is the more important on behalf of the growing mobility and flexibility of today's populations.

- The basic demand for the individual's right to be proprietor of his or her own data is that adequate data security is a mandatory step which no longer needs any arguments. The medical data are owned by the patients. External interceptions cannot be tolerated.

Therefore, interconnectivity for healthcare services has many aspects (technical, organization, psychological, social and socio-cultural, financial, legal, political, security-associated) which play a substantial intertwined role in application of MIS for eHealth. Only this application enables an efficient and efficacious performance of exchanging medical data through existing structures. With adequate definitions of both existing demand and available technology software applications and established services can be used to minimize efforts and redundancy and to maximize output and efficiency in medical data handling.

Perspectives

The possibilities of cloud computing and medical information system presented in the present article are of course not the only view that can be taken. Below are summarized and reviewed some alternative perspectives.

The Cloud is a next-generation Internet – "The Cloud" is not an alternative to "the Internet". It is rather a set of additional protocols and services that build on Internet protocols and services to support the creation and use of computation- and data-enriched environments. Any resource that is "on the Cloud" is also, by definition, "on the Net".

The Cloud is a source of free cycles – cloud computing does not imply unrestricted access to resources. Grid computing is about controlled sharing. Resource owners will typically want to enforce policies that constrain access according to group membership, ability to pay, and so forth. Hence, accounting is important, and cloud architecture must incorporate resource and collective protocols for exchanging usage and cost information, as well as for exploiting this information when deciding whether to enable sharing.

The most important and perspective application of medical information system for eHealth is education of healthcare professionals at a distance, so called distance education (eLearning). It may be defined as the application of ICT to acquire new knowledge or skills across the whole range of areas which will affect healthcare professionals, and enrich their experience in rendering the best possible care to patients throughout the process of medical care. eHealth education has the abilities to apply new concepts, and ideas in which the learner becomes an owner of that knowledge, without any respect to distance. As such, eHealth overall, and in particular eHealth education, is significant part of healthcare development, since the event f modern medicine. eHealth education process as a culture, uses for the most part, distance learning as the medium of dissemination of advanced information, and while it is an important aspect of today's education process, this medium should not be distracting, and the principles of learning and education should be unchanged. The addition of technology should not substitute for failed pedagogical process, but technology should allow that educational process, and the message to be disseminated, and tailored to individual groups and professionals, by retaining along some of the educational principles of traditional education.

The question how technology will change our world is not any more relevant. The answer to this question is obvious. The advances in eHealth education have brought significant changes in health education overall. Advanced technologies such as computers, diagnostic imaging, robotics, voice-activating machines, and remote controls have changed hospitals and operating theatres in hospitals around the western world. In parallel with these developments, the patient has become an educated and informed consumer who:

- Questions the decisions of the practitioner and demand explanations and an evidence based medicine approach
- Validates his or her expertise through web sites and other forms
- Requires that the doctor offers care, current with world standards.

Furthermore, today's patient can consult any expert in the field, in any country of the world, at any time without respect to geography and distance. At the same time, the world equilibrium has not followed the punctuation of the industrial world directed by the broad bandwidth rush, and there is a huge discrepancy between countries and continents. Subsequently, there is a great need for eHealth education to become a catalyst of equilibration among countries and nations as we move toward a perfect future and electronic globalization. The wide application of eHealth education programs, will most likely narrow significantly if not eliminate entirely, the gap between the countries delivery health systems, and between the imagination, dreams, and achievements of those who do not have the capability to apply new healthcare standards, and those who have such capabilities. For these radical changes to become a reality it will take time and investment, as well serious international collaboration, but the concept of eHealth education has the potential to offer such radical changes, and for the most part, has been accepted, adopted around the world, and has raised hopes that it will create equality and equilibrium in the education of patients and healthcare professionals.

eHealth education has potential to change the delivery of existing medical care and will create more efficient and economically sound healthcare systems, where advanced medical knowledge will prevent unnecessary transfers of patients to countries who can care for those patients, and/or prevent death and morbidity because country's medical professional will be well prepared. eHealth education will bring together a coalition of new partners with innovative boundaries and clear vision. This last element is most important, especially in countries with middle and low incomes, devastated by wars, suffering, political neglect and poverty.

The concept of eLearning, particularly in the health area, requires leadership. This leadership consists of a new generation of healthcare professional who are:

- Multi-dimensional and multi-tasked
- Have the passion to change the world
- Are not afraid to disturb the status quo, and are willing to share the knowledge among institutions and nations of the world
- View technology as the enabler of change, but not the sole answer itself.

At the same time, this concept is a direct result of demands from the public and the consumers themselves. These demands call for:

- Fundamental reshaping of healthcare education system which needs to become a priority in a global sense, and not of focused, self-limited, institutional or driven by national interests
- Execution process of electronic learning and teaching in the health area which is no different from other e-leadership challenges that include speed, leverage, adaptation, management and organization of the entire process
- Creativity and adaptation of new education processes in ever changing environment.

eHealth education is about breaking the old rules, changing the models of education, asking the toughest questions and facing the facts that break the silence, and challenges the assumptions of the status quo.

Education of health providers is a major issue in the current environment, as there is a great need for advancing the education process of all health care professionals. The report of the Institute of Medicine in 2001 states that clinical education simply has not kept pace with or has been responsive enough to shifting patient demographics and desires, changing health system expectations, evolving practice requirements and staffing arrangements, new information, focus on improving quality and new technologies. As such, healthcare providers have not been prepared adequately in either academic or continuing education venues to address these major changes in patient population. Healthcare providers are more and more asked to work on inter-disciplinary teams, often supporting patients with chronic conditions, although they may lack the training and education that is based on a team-based approach. Based on multiple reports and analysis, the twenty first century healthcare provider, and system, should ensure that all healthcare professionals be educated to deliver patient-centered care as members of an inter-disciplinary team, emphasizing evidence-based practice, quality proven approaches and informatics.

The proper techniques and methods of disseminating the existing knowledge and evidence-based medicine education programs and processes from renowned institutions and universities to countries around the world are a matter of some debate. What is not a matter of debate at all anymore is the fact that, this dissemination of knowledge and expertise should be a priority of those who possess the knowledge and skills to disseminate it. Such initiatives should come as an international concerted action and collaboration of eHealth in order to facilitate the implementation of medical information networks around the world.

The implementation of eHealth education as an expression of needs and demands from the public and healthcare providers is based on a growing concern for medical errors, advances of patient-centered healthcare systems; need to improve cost-benefit ratios and rationalizations of healthcare.

The use of well-defined education programs for healthcare providers will be the cornerstone of the new revolution of the "e-era". Current specific challenges in implementing eHealth education and other revolutionary advances for healthcare professions educations are:

- Lack of funding, lack of faculty and faculty development programs.
- Lack of coordination and integration of accreditation, licensing, and certification process at the governmental and institutional level.
- Lack of application existing evidence based medicine.

- Shortage of visionary leaders and champions.
- Crowded curricula of healthcare education for healthcare professional, often with irrelevant courses.
- Insufficient channels to share the information on the best practices, among medical professionals, governments and institutions.

eHealth in medical training could supplement greatly education of healthcare professionals in countries with middle and low incomes for example, without the expenses of moving those specialists from one country to the other for supplemental education. Eventually, eHealth education could be advanced to healthcare telementoring which could assist in the provision of medical care to underserved areas and potentially facilitate the teaching of advanced medical skills worldwide. Although there are still multiple logistical, technical and legal barriers to the widespread application of healthcare mentoring and telepresence medicine great progress has been achieved in this complex field.

eHealth education is a very important element of overall progress in the application of medical information systems. In order to be able to advance this, as an accepted culture and part of the daily practice of healthcare professionals, there are many initiatives that need to be taken, or existing one to be supported. Few issues that need resolved in order for eHealth education to prosper and be accepted are:

- 'Product' acceptance by traditional medical educators, scholars, and legislators
- Changing the old style of education to the new one and thus breaking the 'traditional' classroom healthcare teaching and learning methods
- Lack of capability and availability of technology in most of the world for disseminating the knowledge, or in other words lack of communications
- Language and cultural diversity
- Socio-economic and political status of the countries in need for eHealth education
- Legislative policies and championships for new information age.

While technological means for broadcasting and transmission of the eHealth education programs and clinical data is becoming abundant around the world, there is a great part of the planet that is not covered by Internet and will not have the ability to overcome the digital divide for decades to come. This should be our chance to advance the cause, and the issue, of infrastructure and perhaps a vision in some cases.

CONCLUSION

Perspectives and strategies for cloud computing and medical information system for eHealth are currently evolving, as emerging operative requirements would allow self-sustainable large scale exploitation while recent technological developments are available to support integrated and cost-effective solutions to such requirements. However, as far as we know few eHealth services have proceeded to large scale exploitation, even after successful technological demonstration phases. Main exploitation drawbacks, problems and deficiencies have been:

1. Partial solutions approach instead of integrated total approach to healthcare assistance needs
2. Lack of economical drive and consequently no self-sustainability for large scale exploitation
3. Insufficient H24 (24 hours/day 365 days/year) medical and social operators support
4. Insufficient networking approach for medical operators and scientific/clinical structures.

eHealth is the most important for the ensuring the safe medical care. It is well known, that the first contact with patients needing medical help is the contact with the local primary care health center. Second opinions from specialists are often required in primary care health centers. An efficient and appropriate strategy of medical care can be worked out at the initial steps of patient's contact with healthcare. Such an approach can avoid unnecessary hospitalization, and will be a substantial contribution to the reduction of health costs.

eHealth has the potential for offering the worldwide medical community the following qualitative and quantitative improvements:

1. Distance consultations, diagnosis and advice for treatment.
2. Opening up new ways for education and training. Improvement in qualification of national specialists and health technicians, by opening up international medical databases.
3. Overall improvement of service by regional centralization of resources (specialists, hardware and software packages).
4. Effectiveness and efficiency in a management of actions related to reduction of waiting times for consultations, and introduction of medical information systems.

eHealth is able to reduce healthcare costs in the following ways:

1. Reduction of operating costs through centralization and optimization of resources (expertise, laboratories, equipment and etc.).
2. Reduction in travel cost and time for specialists visiting other hospitals and centers for consulting.
3. Reduction in costs for training and updating, improvement of specialists' qualifications through distance learning and access to medical databases.

eHealth by comparison with the usual healthcare service introduces added value and a positive impact at social, economic and cultural levels. As a result, eHealth is initiating to have an important influence on many aspects of healthcare service in countries with low and middle income. By application of medical information system this process becomes easier and smoother. The medical information system significantly increases knowledge exchange and thereby ensures a better medical service.

REFERENCES

Alpert, J. S. (2016). The electronic medical record in 2016: Advantages and disadvantages. *Digital Media*, *2*(2), 48–51. doi:10.4103/2226-8561.189504

Banta, D. (2003). The development of health technology assessment. *Health Policy (Amsterdam)*, *63*(2), 121–132. doi:10.1016/S0168-8510(02)00059-3 PMID:12543525

Beitiger, J., Johnson, W., Bivens, H., Humphreys, S., & Rhea, R. (2000). Constructing the ASCI Grid. *Proc. 9th IEEE Symposium on High Performance Distributed Computing*.

Bowman, S. (2013). Impact of electronic health record systems on information integrity: Quality and safety implications. *Perspectives in Health Information Management*, *10*(Fall), 1c. PMID:24159271

Chang, C. S., Chen, S. Y., & Lan, Y. T. (2012). Motivating medical information system performance by system quality, service quality, and job satisfaction for evidence-based practice. *BMC Medical Informatics and Decision Making*, *12*(1), 135. doi:10.1186/1472-6947-12-135 PMID:23171394

Chatman, C. (2010). How cloud computing is changing the face of health care information technology. *Journal of Health Care Compliance*, *12*(3), 37–70.

Clamp, S., & Keen, J. (2007). Electronic health records: Is the evidence base any use? *Medical Informatics and the Internet in Medicine*, *32*(1), 5–10. doi:10.1080/14639230601097903 PMID:17365639

Detmer, D. (2000). Information technology for quality health care: A summary of United Kingdom and United States experiences. *Quality in Health Care*, *9*(3), 181–189. doi:10.1136/qhc.9.3.181 PMID:10980079

Detmer, D. (2001). Transforming health care in the internet era. *World Hospitals and Health Services*, *37*, 2. PMID:11696999

Dixon, R., & Stahl, J. (2008). Virtual visits in a general medicine practice: A pilot study. *Telemedicine Journal and e-Health*, *14*(6), 525–530. doi:10.1089/tmj.2007.0101 PMID:18729750

Fox, A. (2011). Computer science. Cloud computing: What's in it for me as a scientist? *Science*, *331*(6016), 406–407. doi:10.1126/science.1198981 PMID:21273473

Gabbay, J., & Walley, T. (2006). Introducing new health interventions. *British Medical Journal*, *332*(7533), 64–65. doi:10.1136/bmj.332.7533.64 PMID:16410559

Gonzalez, M., Quesada, G., Urrutia, I., & Gavidia, J. (2006). Conceptual design of an e-health strategy for the Spanish health care system. *International Journal of Health Care Quality Assurance*, *19*(2), 146–157. doi:10.1108/09526860610651681 PMID:16875096

Haughton, J. (2011). Year of the underdog: Cloud-based EHRs. *Health Management Technology*, *32*(1), 9.

Hayrinen, K., Saranto, K., & Nykanen, P. (2008). Definition, structure, content, use and impacts of electronic health records: A review of the research literature. *International Journal of Medical Informatics*, *77*(5), 291–304. doi:10.1016/j.ijmedinf.2007.09.001 PMID:17951106

Heindenreich, G., & Blobel, B. (2009). IT standards for applications in telemedicine. Towards efficient data interchange in medicine. *Bundesgesundheitsblatt, Gesundheitsforschung, Gesundheitsschutz*, *52*, 316–323. PMID:19255733

Hjelm, M. (2001). Telemedicine and in-patient. *Hospitals International*, *37*, 2.

Jannett, P., & Jackson, A., & Ho, K., & Healy, T., & Kazanjian, A., & Wollard, R., & Haydt, S., & Bates, J. (2005). The essence of telehealth readiness in rural communities: an organizational perspective. *Journal of Telemedicine and eHealth*, *11*, 137-145.

Jannett, P., Yeo, M., Pauls, M., & Graham, J. (2003). Organizational readiness for telemedicine: Implications for success and failure. *Journal of Telemedicine and Telecare, 9*(2), 27–30. doi:10.1258/135763303322596183 PMID:14728753

Kabachinski, J. (2011). What's the forecast for cloud computing in healthcare? *Biomedical Instrumentation & Technology, 45*(2), 146–150. doi:10.2345/0899-8205-45.2.146 PMID:21466336

Khalifa, M., & Alswailem, O. (2015). Hospital information system (HIS) acceptance and satisfaction: A case study of a tertiary care hospital. *Procedia Computer Science, 63*, 198–204. doi:10.1016/j.procs.2015.08.334

Kobb, R., Lane, R., & Stallings, D. (2008). E-learning and telehealth: Measuring your success. *Telemedicine Journal and e-Health, 14*(6), 576–579. doi:10.1089/tmj.2007.0103 PMID:18729757

Lam, D., & MacKenzie, C. (2005). Human and organizational factors affecting telemedicine utilization within U.S. military forces in Europe. *Telemedicine Journal and e-Health, 11*(1), 70–78. doi:10.1089/tmj.2005.11.70 PMID:15785223

Lane, K. (2006). Telemedicine news. *Telemedicine Journal and e-Health, 12*(5), 507–511. doi:10.1089/tmj.2006.12.507 PMID:16430380

Lareng, L. (2002). Telemedicine in Europe. *European Journal of Internal Medicine, 13*(1), 1–13. doi:10.1016/S0953-6205(01)00188-1 PMID:11836076

Latifi, R., Muja, S., Bekhteshi, F., & Merrell, R. (2006). The role of telemedicine and information technology in the redevelopment of medical systems: The case of Kosova. *Telemedicine Journal and e-Health, 12*(3), 332–340. doi:10.1089/tmj.2006.12.332 PMID:16796501

Li, Z. J., Chen, C., & Wang, K. (2011). Cloud computing for agent-based urban transportation systems. *IEEE Intelligent Systems, 26*(1), 73–79. doi:10.1109/MIS.2011.10

Mell, P., & Grance, T. (2010). The NIST definition of cloud computing. *Communications of the ACM, 53*(6), 50.

Merell, R., & Doarn, C. (2008). Is it time for a telemedicine breakthrough? *Telemedicine Journal and e-Health, 14*(6), 505–506. doi:10.1089/tmj.2008.8499 PMID:18729745

Moore, D. Jr, Green, J., Jay, S., Leist, J., & Maitland, F. (1994). Creating a new paradigm for CME: Seizing opportunities within the health care revolution. *The Journal of Continuing Education in the Health Professions, 14*(1), 4–31. doi:10.1002/chp.4750140102

Moura, A., & Del Giglio, A. (2000). Education via internet. *Revista da Associação Médica Brasileira, 46*(1), 47–51. PMID:10770902

Nannings, B., & Abu-Hanna, A. (2006). Decision support telemedicine systems: A conceptual model and reusable templates. *Telemedicine Journal and e-Health, 12*(6), 644–654. doi:10.1089/tmj.2006.12.644 PMID:17250486

Pak, H. (2007). Telethinking. *Telemedicine Journal and e-Health, 13*(5), 483–486. doi:10.1089/tmj.2007.9976 PMID:17999610

Riva, G. (2000). From telehealth to e-health: Internet and distributed virtual reality in health care. *Journal of CyberPsychology & Behavior, 3*(6), 989–998. doi:10.1089/109493100452255

Riva, G. (2002). The emergence of e-health: Using virtual reality and the internet for providing advanced healthcare services. *International Journal of Healthcare Technology and Management, 4*(1/2), 15–40. doi:10.1504/IJHTM.2002.001127

Rosenthal, A., Mork, P., Li, M. H., Stanford, J., Koester, D., & Reynolds, P. (2010). Cloud computing: A new business paradigm for biomedical information sharing. *Journal of Biomedical Informatics, 43*(2), 342–353. doi:10.1016/j.jbi.2009.08.014 PMID:19715773

Sloot, P., Tirado-Ramos, A., Altintas, I., Bubak, M., & Boucher, C. (2006). From molecule to man: Decision support in individualized E-Health. *Computer, 39*(11), 40–46. doi:10.1109/MC.2006.380

van Ginneken, A. M. (2002). The computerized patient record: Balancing effort and benefit. *International Journal of Medical Informatics, 65*(2), 97–119. doi:10.1016/S1386-5056(02)00007-2 PMID:12052424

Yanamadala, S., Morrison, D., Curtin, C., McDonald, K., & Hernandez-Boussard, T. (2016). Electronic health records and quality of care: An observational study modeling impact on mortality, readmissions, and complications. *Medicine, 95*(19), e3332. doi:10.1097/MD.0000000000003332 PMID:27175631

Zeng, X. (2016). The impacts of electronic health record implementation on the health care workforce. *NCMJ, 77*(2), 112–114. doi:10.18043/ncm.77.2.112 PMID:26961833

KEY TERMS AND DEFINITIONS

Computing Technology: Can be defined as the activity of using and developing computer technology, computer hardware, and software.

E-Health: An emerging field in the intersection of medical informatics, public health, and business referring to health services and information delivered or enhanced through the internet and related technologies.

E-Learning: Defined as an approach to facilitate or enhance education by electronic means such as email, computers, or the internet.

Information and Communication Technologies (ICT): An umbrella term that includes all technologies for the manipulation and communication of information.

Internet: A global system of interconnected computer networks that interchange data by packet switching using the standardized internet protocol suite (TCP/IP).

Telemedicine: Can be defined as rapid access to shared and remote medical expertise by means of telecommunications and information technologies, no matter where the patient or relevant information is located.

World Wide Web: (Commonly shortened to the web) A system of interlinked hypertext documents accessed via the internet.

Related References

To continue our tradition of advancing information science and technology research, we have compiled a list of recommended IGI Global readings. These references will provide additional information and guidance to further enrich your knowledge and assist you with your own research and future publications.

Aalmink, J., von der Dovenmühle, T., & Gómez, J. M. (2013). Enterprise tomography: Maintenance and root-cause-analysis of federated erp in enterprise clouds. In P. Ordóñez de Pablos, H. Nigro, R. Tennyson, S. Gonzalez Cisaro, & W. Karwowski (Eds.), *Advancing information management through semantic web concepts and ontologies* (pp. 133–153). Hershey, PA: IGI Global. doi:10.4018/978-1-4666-2494-8.ch007

Abu, S. T., & Tsuji, M. (2011). The development of ICT for envisioning cloud computing and innovation in South Asia. *International Journal of Innovation in the Digital Economy*, 2(1), 61–72. doi:10.4018/jide.2011010105

Abu, S. T., & Tsuji, M. (2012). The development of ICT for envisioning cloud computing and innovation in South Asia. In *Grid and cloud computing: Concepts, methodologies, tools and applications* (pp. 453–465). Hershey, PA: IGI Global. doi:10.4018/978-1-4666-0879-5.ch207

Abu, S. T., & Tsuji, M. (2013). The development of ICT for envisioning cloud computing and innovation in South Asia. In I. Oncioiu (Ed.), *Business innovation, development, and advancement in the digital economy* (pp. 35–47). Hershey, PA: IGI Global. doi:10.4018/978-1-4666-2934-9.ch003

Adams, R. (2013). The emergence of cloud storage and the need for a new digital forensic process model. In K. Ruan (Ed.), *Cybercrime and cloud forensics: Applications for investigation processes* (pp. 79–104). Hershey, PA: IGI Global. doi:10.4018/978-1-4666-2662-1.ch004

Adeyeye, M. (2013). Provisioning converged applications and services via the cloud. In D. Kanellopoulos (Ed.), *Intelligent multimedia technologies for networking applications: Techniques and tools* (pp. 248–269). Hershey, PA: IGI Global. doi:10.4018/978-1-4666-2833-5.ch010

Aggarwal, A. (2013). A systems approach to cloud computing services. In A. Bento & A. Aggarwal (Eds.), *Cloud computing service and deployment models: Layers and management* (pp. 124–136). Hershey, PA: IGI Global. doi:10.4018/978-1-4666-2187-9.ch006

Ahmed, K., Hussain, A., & Gregory, M. A. (2013). An efficient, robust, and secure SSO architecture for cloud computing implemented in a service oriented architecture. In X. Yang & L. Liu (Eds.), *Principles, methodologies, and service-oriented approaches for cloud computing* (pp. 259–282). Hershey, PA: IGI Global. doi:10.4018/978-1-4666-2854-0.ch011

Ahuja, S. P., & Mani, S. (2013). Empirical performance analysis of HPC benchmarks across variations in cloud computing. *International Journal of Cloud Applications and Computing, 3*(1), 13–26. doi:10.4018/ijcac.2013010102

Ahuja, S. P., & Rolli, A. C. (2011). Survey of the state-of-the-art of cloud computing. *International Journal of Cloud Applications and Computing, 1*(4), 34–43. doi:10.4018/ijcac.2011100103

Ahuja, S. P., & Rolli, A. C. (2013). Survey of the state-of-the-art of cloud computing. In S. Aljawarneh (Ed.), *Cloud computing advancements in design, implementation, and technologies* (pp. 252–262). Hershey, PA: IGI Global. doi:10.4018/978-1-4666-1879-4.ch018

Ahuja, S. P., & Sridharan, S. (2012). Performance evaluation of hypervisors for cloud computing. *International Journal of Cloud Applications and Computing, 2*(3), 26–67. doi:10.4018/ijcac.2012070102

Akyuz, G. A., & Rehan, M. (2013). A generic, cloud-based representation for supply chains (SC's). *International Journal of Cloud Applications and Computing, 3*(2), 12–20. doi:10.4018/ijcac.2013040102

Al-Aqrabi, H., & Liu, L. (2013). IT security and governance compliant service oriented computing in cloud computing environments. In X. Yang & L. Liu (Eds.), *Principles, methodologies, and service-oriented approaches for cloud computing* (pp. 143–163). Hershey, PA: IGI Global. doi:10.4018/978-1-4666-2854-0.ch006

Al-Zoube, M., & Wyne, M. F. (2012). Building integrated e-learning environment using cloud services and social networking sites. In Q. Jin (Ed.), *Intelligent learning systems and advancements in computer-aided instruction: Emerging studies* (pp. 214–233). Hershey, PA: IGI Global. doi:10.4018/978-1-61350-483-3.ch013

Alam, N., & Karmakar, R. (2014). Cloud computing and its application to information centre. In S. Dhamdhere (Ed.), *Cloud computing and virtualization technologies in libraries* (pp. 63–76). Hershey, PA: IGI Global. doi:10.4018/978-1-4666-4631-5. ch004

Alhaj, A., Aljawarneh, S., Masadeh, S., & Abu-Taieh, E. (2013). A secure data transmission mechanism for cloud outsourced data. *International Journal of Cloud Applications and Computing, 3*(1), 34–43. doi:10.4018/ijcac.2013010104

Alharbi, S. T. (2012). Users' acceptance of cloud computing in Saudi Arabia: An extension of technology acceptance model. *International Journal of Cloud Applications and Computing, 2*(2), 1–11. doi:10.4018/ijcac.2012040101

Ali, S. S., & Khan, M. N. (2013). ICT infrastructure framework for microfinance institutions and banks in Pakistan: An optimized approach. *International Journal of Online Marketing, 3*(2), 75–86. doi:10.4018/ijom.2013040105

Aljawarneh, S. (2011). Cloud security engineering: Avoiding security threats the right way. *International Journal of Cloud Applications and Computing, 1*(2), 64–70. doi:10.4018/ijcac.2011040105

Aljawarneh, S. (2013). Cloud security engineering: Avoiding security threats the right way. In S. Aljawarneh (Ed.), *Cloud computing advancements in design, implementation, and technologies* (pp. 147–153). Hershey, PA: IGI Global. doi:10.4018/978-1-4666-1879-4.ch010

Alshattnawi, S. (2013). Utilizing cloud computing in developing a mobile location-aware tourist guide system. *International Journal of Advanced Pervasive and Ubiquitous Computing, 5*(2), 9–18. doi:10.4018/japuc.2013040102

Alsmadi, I. (2013). Software development methodologies for cloud computing. In K. Buragga & N. Zaman (Eds.), *Software development techniques for constructive information systems design* (pp. 110–117). Hershey, PA: IGI Global. doi:10.4018/978-1-4666-3679-8.ch006

Anand, V. (2013). Survivable mapping of virtual networks onto a shared substrate network. In X. Yang & L. Liu (Eds.), *Principles, methodologies, and service-oriented approaches for cloud computing* (pp. 325–343). Hershey, PA: IGI Global. doi:10.4018/978-1-4666-2854-0.ch014

Antonova, A. (2013). Green, sustainable, or clean: What type of IT/IS technologies will we need in the future? In P. Ordóñez de Pablos (Ed.), *Green technologies and business practices: An IT approach* (pp. 151–162). Hershey, PA: IGI Global. doi:10.4018/978-1-4666-1972-2.ch008

Ardissono, L., Bosio, G., Goy, A., Petrone, G., Segnan, M., & Torretta, F. (2011). Collaboration support for activity management in a personal cloud environment. *International Journal of Distributed Systems and Technologies*, 2(4), 30–43. doi:10.4018/jdst.2011100103

Ardissono, L., Bosio, G., Goy, A., Petrone, G., Segnan, M., & Torretta, F. (2013). Collaboration support for activity management in a personal cloud environment. In N. Bessis (Ed.), *Development of distributed systems from design to application and maintenance* (pp. 199–212). Hershey, PA: IGI Global. doi:10.4018/978-1-4666-2647-8.ch012

Argiolas, M., Atzori, M., Dessì, N., & Pes, B. (2012). Dataspaces enhancing decision support systems in clouds. *International Journal of Web Portals*, 4(2), 35–55. doi:10.4018/jwp.2012040103

Arinze, B., & Anandarajan, M. (2012). Factors that determine the adoption of cloud computing: A global perspective. In M. Tavana (Ed.), *Enterprise Information Systems and Advancing Business Solutions: Emerging Models* (pp. 210–223). Hershey, PA: IGI Global. doi:10.4018/978-1-4666-1761-2.ch012

Arinze, B., & Sylla, C. (2012). Conducting research in the cloud. In L. Chao (Ed.), *Cloud computing for teaching and learning: Strategies for design and implementation* (pp. 50–63). Hershey, PA: IGI Global. doi:10.4018/978-1-4666-0957-0.ch004

Arshad, J., Townend, P., & Xu, J. (2011). An abstract model for integrated intrusion detection and severity analysis for clouds. *International Journal of Cloud Applications and Computing*, 1(1), 1–16. doi:10.4018/ijcac.2011010101

Arshad, J., Townend, P., & Xu, J. (2013). An abstract model for integrated intrusion detection and severity analysis for clouds. In S. Aljawarneh (Ed.), *Cloud computing advancements in design, implementation, and technologies* (pp. 1–17). Hershey, PA: IGI Global. doi:10.4018/978-1-4666-1879-4.ch001

Arshad, J., Townend, P., Xu, J., & Jie, W. (2012). Cloud computing security: Opportunities and pitfalls. *International Journal of Grid and High Performance Computing*, *4*(1), 52–66. doi:10.4018/jghpc.2012010104

Baars, T., & Spruit, M. (2012). Designing a secure cloud architecture: The SeCA model. *International Journal of Information Security and Privacy*, *6*(1), 14–32. doi:10.4018/jisp.2012010102

Bai, X., Gao, J. Z., & Tsai, W. (2013). Cloud scalability measurement and testing. In S. Tilley & T. Parveen (Eds.), *Software testing in the cloud: Perspectives on an emerging discipline* (pp. 356–381). Hershey, PA: IGI Global. doi:10.4018/978-1-4666-2536-5.ch017

Baldini, G., & Stirparo, P. (2014). A cognitive access framework for security and privacy protection in mobile cloud computing. In J. Rodrigues, K. Lin, & J. Lloret (Eds.), *Mobile networks and cloud computing convergence for progressive services and applications* (pp. 92–117). Hershey, PA: IGI Global. doi:10.4018/978-1-4666-4781-7.ch006

Balduf, S., Balke, T., & Eymann, T. (2012). Cultural differences in managing cloud computing service level agreements. In *Grid and cloud computing: Concepts, methodologies, tools and applications* (pp. 1237–1263). Hershey, PA: IGI Global. doi:10.4018/978-1-4666-0879-5.ch512

Banerjee, S., Sing, T. Y., Chowdhury, A. R., & Anwar, H. (2013). Motivations to adopt green ICT: A tale of two organizations. *International Journal of Green Computing*, *4*(2), 1–11. doi:10.4018/jgc.2013070101

Barreto, J., Di Sanzo, P., Palmieri, R., & Romano, P. (2013). Cloud-TM: An elastic, self-tuning transactional store for the cloud. In D. Kyriazis, A. Voulodimos, S. Gogouvitis, & T. Varvarigou (Eds.), *Data intensive storage services for cloud environments* (pp. 192–224). Hershey, PA: IGI Global. doi:10.4018/978-1-4666-3934-8.ch013

Belalem, G., & Limam, S. (2011). Fault tolerant architecture to cloud computing using adaptive checkpoint. *International Journal of Cloud Applications and Computing*, *1*(4), 60–69. doi:10.4018/ijcac.2011100105

Belalem, G., & Limam, S. (2013). Fault tolerant architecture to cloud computing using adaptive checkpoint. In S. Aljawarneh (Ed.), *Cloud computing advancements in design, implementation, and technologies* (pp. 280–289). Hershey, PA: IGI Global. doi:10.4018/978-1-4666-1879-4.ch020

Ben Belgacem, M., Abdennadher, N., & Niinimaki, M. (2012). Virtual EZ grid: A volunteer computing infrastructure for scientific medical applications. *International Journal of Handheld Computing Research, 3*(1), 74–85. doi:10.4018/jhcr.2012010105

Bhatt, S., Chaudhary, S., & Bhise, M. (2013). Migration of data between cloud and non-cloud datastores. In A. Ionita, M. Litoiu, & G. Lewis (Eds.), *Migrating legacy applications: Challenges in service oriented architecture and cloud computing environments* (pp. 206–225). Hershey, PA: IGI Global. doi:10.4018/978-1-4666-2488-7.ch009

Biancofiore, G., & Leone, S. (2014). Google apps as a cloud computing solution in Italian municipalities: Technological features and implications. In S. Leone (Ed.), *Synergic integration of formal and informal e-learning environments for adult lifelong learners* (pp. 244–274). Hershey, PA: IGI Global. doi:10.4018/978-1-4666-4655-1.ch012

Bibi, S., Katsaros, D., & Bozanis, P. (2012). How to choose the right cloud. In *Grid and cloud computing: Concepts, methodologies, tools and applications* (pp. 1530–1552). Hershey, PA: IGI Global. doi:10.4018/978-1-4666-0879-5.ch701

Bibi, S., Katsaros, D., & Bozanis, P. (2012). How to choose the right cloud. In X. Liu & Y. Li (Eds.), *Advanced design approaches to emerging software systems: Principles, methodologies and tools* (pp. 219–240). Hershey, PA: IGI Global. doi:10.4018/978-1-60960-735-7.ch010

Bitam, S., Batouche, M., & Talbi, E. (2012). A bees life algorithm for cloud computing services selection. In S. Ali, N. Abbadeni, & M. Batouche (Eds.), *Multidisciplinary computational intelligence techniques: Applications in business, engineering, and medicine* (pp. 31–46). Hershey, PA: IGI Global. doi:10.4018/978-1-4666-1830-5.ch003

Bittencourt, L. F., Madeira, E. R., & da Fonseca, N. L. (2014). Communication aspects of resource management in hybrid clouds. In H. Mouftah & B. Kantarci (Eds.), *Communication infrastructures for cloud computing* (pp. 409–433). Hershey, PA: IGI Global. doi:10.4018/978-1-4666-4522-6.ch018

Bonelli, L., Giudicianni, L., Immediata, A., & Luzzi, A. (2013). Compliance in the cloud. In D. Kyriazis, A. Voulodimos, S. Gogouvitis, & T. Varvarigou (Eds.), *Data intensive storage services for cloud environments* (pp. 109–131). Hershey, PA: IGI Global. doi:10.4018/978-1-4666-3934-8.ch008

Boniface, M., Nasser, B., Surridge, M., & Oliveros, E. (2012). Securing real-time interactive applications in federated clouds. In *Grid and cloud computing: Concepts, methodologies, tools and applications* (pp. 1822–1835). Hershey, PA: IGI Global. doi:10.4018/978-1-4666-0879-5.ch806

Boukhobza, J. (2013). Flashing in the cloud: Shedding some light on NAND flash memory storage systems. In D. Kyriazis, A. Voulodimos, S. Gogouvitis, & T. Varvarigou (Eds.), *Data intensive storage services for cloud environments* (pp. 241–266). Hershey, PA: IGI Global. doi:10.4018/978-1-4666-3934-8.ch015

Bracci, F., Corradi, A., & Foschini, L. (2014). Cloud standards: Security and interoperability issues. In H. Mouftah & B. Kantarci (Eds.), *Communication infrastructures for cloud computing* (pp. 465–495). Hershey, PA: IGI Global. doi:10.4018/978-1-4666-4522-6.ch020

Brown, A. W. (2013). Experiences with cloud technology to realize software testing factories. In S. Tilley & T. Parveen (Eds.), *Software testing in the cloud: Perspectives on an emerging discipline* (pp. 1–27). Hershey, PA: IGI Global. doi:10.4018/978-1-4666-2536-5.ch001

Calcavecchia, N. M., Celesti, A., & Di Nitto, E. (2012). Understanding decentralized and dynamic brokerage in federated cloud environments. In M. Villari, I. Brandic, & F. Tusa (Eds.), *Achieving federated and self-manageable cloud infrastructures: Theory and practice* (pp. 36–56). Hershey, PA: IGI Global. doi:10.4018/978-1-4666-1631-8.ch003

Calero, J. M., König, B., & Kirschnick, J. (2012). Cross-layer monitoring in cloud computing. In H. Rashvand & Y. Kavian (Eds.), *Using cross-layer techniques for communication systems* (pp. 328–348). Hershey, PA: IGI Global. doi:10.4018/978-1-4666-0960-0.ch014

Cardellini, V., Casalicchio, E., & Silvestri, L. (2012). Service level provisioning for cloud-based applications service level provisioning for cloud-based applications. In A. Pathan, M. Pathan, & H. Lee (Eds.), *Advancements in distributed computing and internet technologies: Trends and issues* (pp. 363–385). Hershey, PA: IGI Global. doi:10.4018/978-1-61350-110-8.ch017

Cardellini, V., Casalicchio, E., & Silvestri, L. (2012). Service level provisioning for cloud-based applications service level provisioning for cloud-based applications. In *Grid and cloud computing: Concepts, methodologies, tools and applications* (pp. 1479–1500). Hershey, PA: IGI Global. doi:10.4018/978-1-4666-0879-5.ch611

Carlin, S., & Curran, K. (2013). Cloud computing security. In K. Curran (Ed.), *Pervasive and ubiquitous technology innovations for ambient intelligence environments* (pp. 12–17). Hershey, PA: IGI Global. doi:10.4018/978-1-4666-2041-4.ch002

Carlton, G. H., & Zhou, H. (2011). A survey of cloud computing challenges from a digital forensics perspective. *International Journal of Interdisciplinary Telecommunications and Networking*, *3*(4), 1–16. doi:10.4018/jitn.2011100101

Carlton, G. H., & Zhou, H. (2012). A survey of cloud computing challenges from a digital forensics perspective. In *Grid and cloud computing: Concepts, methodologies, tools and applications* (pp. 1221–1236). Hershey, PA: IGI Global. doi:10.4018/978-1-4666-0879-5.ch511

Carlton, G. H., & Zhou, H. (2013). A survey of cloud computing challenges from a digital forensics perspective. In M. Bartolacci & S. Powell (Eds.), *Advancements and innovations in wireless communications and network technologies* (pp. 213–228). Hershey, PA: IGI Global. doi:10.4018/978-1-4666-2154-1.ch016

Carpen-Amarie, A., Costan, A., Leordeanu, C., Basescu, C., & Antoniu, G. (2012). Towards a generic security framework for cloud data management environments. *International Journal of Distributed Systems and Technologies*, *3*(1), 17–34. doi:10.4018/jdst.2012010102

Casola, V., Cuomo, A., Villano, U., & Rak, M. (2012). Access control in federated clouds: The cloudgrid case study. In M. Villari, I. Brandic, & F. Tusa (Eds.), *Achieving Federated and Self-Manageable Cloud Infrastructures: Theory and Practice* (pp. 395–417). Hershey, PA: IGI Global. doi:10.4018/978-1-4666-1631-8.ch020

Casola, V., Cuomo, A., Villano, U., & Rak, M. (2013). Access control in federated clouds: The cloudgrid case study. In *IT policy and ethics: Concepts, methodologies, tools, and applications* (pp. 148–169). Hershey, PA: IGI Global. doi:10.4018/978-1-4666-2919-6.ch008

Celesti, A., Tusa, F., & Villari, M. (2012). Toward cloud federation: Concepts and challenges. In M. Villari, I. Brandic, & F. Tusa (Eds.), *Achieving federated and self-manageable cloud infrastructures: Theory and practice* (pp. 1–17). Hershey, PA: IGI Global. doi:10.4018/978-1-4666-1631-8.ch001

Chaka, C. (2013). Virtualization and cloud computing: Business models in the virtual cloud. In A. Loo (Ed.), *Distributed computing innovations for business, engineering, and science* (pp. 176–190). Hershey, PA: IGI Global. doi:10.4018/978-1-4666-2533-4.ch009

Chang, J. (2011). A framework for analysing the impact of cloud computing on local government in the UK. *International Journal of Cloud Applications and Computing*, *1*(4), 25–33. doi:10.4018/ijcac.2011100102

Chang, J. (2013). A framework for analysing the impact of cloud computing on local government in the UK. In S. Aljawarneh (Ed.), *Cloud computing advancements in design, implementation, and technologies* (pp. 243–251). Hershey, PA: IGI Global. doi:10.4018/978-1-4666-1879-4.ch017

Chang, J., & Johnston, M. (2012). Cloud computing in local government: From the perspective of four London borough councils. *International Journal of Cloud Applications and Computing*, *2*(4), 1–15. doi:10.4018/ijcac.2012100101

Chang, K., & Wang, K. (2012). Efficient support of streaming videos through patching proxies in the cloud. *International Journal of Grid and High Performance Computing*, *4*(4), 22–36. doi:10.4018/jghpc.2012100102

Chang, R., Liao, C., & Liu, C. (2013). Choosing clouds for an enterprise: Modeling and evaluation. *International Journal of E-Entrepreneurship and Innovation*, *4*(2), 38–53. doi:10.4018/ijeei.2013040103

Chang, V., De Roure, D., Wills, G., & Walters, R. J. (2011). Case studies and organisational sustainability modelling presented by cloud computing business framework. *International Journal of Web Services Research*, *8*(3), 26–53. doi:10.4018/JWSR.2011070102

Chang, V., Li, C., De Roure, D., Wills, G., Walters, R. J., & Chee, C. (2011). The financial clouds review. *International Journal of Cloud Applications and Computing*, *1*(2), 41–63. doi:10.4018/ijcac.2011040104

Chang, V., Li, C., De Roure, D., Wills, G., Walters, R. J., & Chee, C. (2013). The financial clouds review. In S. Aljawarneh (Ed.), *Cloud computing advancements in design, implementation, and technologies* (pp. 125–146). Hershey, PA: IGI Global. doi:10.4018/978-1-4666-1879-4.ch009

Chang, V., Walters, R. J., & Wills, G. (2012). Business integration as a service. *International Journal of Cloud Applications and Computing*, *2*(1), 16–40. doi:10.4018/ijcac.2012010102

Chang, V., & Wills, G. (2013). A University of Greenwich case study of cloud computing: Education as a service. In D. Graham, I. Manikas, & D. Folinas (Eds.), *E-logistics and e-supply chain management: Applications for evolving business* (pp. 232–253). Hershey, PA: IGI Global. doi:10.4018/978-1-4666-3914-0.ch013

Chang, V., Wills, G., Walters, R. J., & Currie, W. (2012). Towards a structured cloud ROI: The University of Southampton cost-saving and user satisfaction case studies. In W. Hu & N. Kaabouch (Eds.), *Sustainable ICTs and management systems for green computing* (pp. 179–200). Hershey, PA: IGI Global. doi:10.4018/978-1-4666-1839-8.ch008

Chang, Y., Lee, Y., Juang, T., & Yen, J. (2013). Cost evaluation on building and operating cloud platform. *International Journal of Grid and High Performance Computing*, 5(2), 43–53. doi:10.4018/jghpc.2013040103

Chao, L. (2012). Cloud computing solution for internet based teaching and learning. In L. Chao (Ed.), *Cloud computing for teaching and learning: Strategies for design and implementation* (pp. 210–235). Hershey, PA: IGI Global. doi:10.4018/978-1-4666-0957-0.ch015

Chao, L. (2012). Overview of cloud computing and its application in e-learning. In L. Chao (Ed.), *Cloud computing for teaching and learning: Strategies for design and implementation* (pp. 1–16). Hershey, PA: IGI Global. doi:10.4018/978-1-4666-0957-0.ch001

Chauhan, S., Raman, A., & Singh, N. (2013). A comparative cost analysis of on premises IT infrastructure and cloud-based email services in an Indian business school. *International Journal of Cloud Applications and Computing*, 3(2), 21–34. doi:10.4018/ijcac.2013040103

Chen, C., Chao, H., Wu, T., Fan, C., Chen, J., Chen, Y., & Hsu, J. (2011). IoT-IMS communication platform for future internet. *International Journal of Adaptive, Resilient and Autonomic Systems*, 2(4), 74–94. doi:10.4018/jaras.2011100105

Chen, C., Chao, H., Wu, T., Fan, C., Chen, J., Chen, Y., & Hsu, J. (2013). IoT-IMS communication platform for future internet. In V. De Florio (Ed.), *Innovations and approaches for resilient and adaptive systems* (pp. 68–86). Hershey, PA: IGI Global. doi:10.4018/978-1-4666-2056-8.ch004

Chen, C. C. (2013). Cloud computing in case-based pedagogy: An information systems success perspective. *International Journal of Dependable and Trustworthy Information Systems*, 2(3), 1–16. doi:10.4018/jdtis.2011070101

Cheney, A. W., Riedl, R. E., Sanders, R., & Tashner, J. H. (2012). The new company water cooler: Use of 3D virtual immersive worlds to promote networking and professional learning in organizations. In Organizational learning and knowledge: Concepts, methodologies, tools and applications (pp. 2848-2861). Hershey, PA: IGI Global. doi:10.4018/978-1-60960-783-8.ch801

Chiang, C., & Yu, S. (2013). Cloud-enabled software testing based on program understanding. In S. Tilley & T. Parveen (Eds.), *Software testing in the cloud: Perspectives on an emerging discipline* (pp. 54–67). Hershey, PA: IGI Global. doi:10.4018/978-1-4666-2536-5.ch003

Chou, Y., & Oetting, J. (2011). Risk assessment for cloud-based IT systems. *International Journal of Grid and High Performance Computing, 3*(2), 1–13. doi:10.4018/jghpc.2011040101

Chou, Y., & Oetting, J. (2012). Risk assessment for cloud-based IT systems. In *Grid and cloud computing: Concepts, methodologies, tools and applications* (pp. 272–285). Hershey, PA: IGI Global. doi:10.4018/978-1-4666-0879-5.ch113

Chou, Y., & Oetting, J. (2013). Risk assessment for cloud-based IT systems. In E. Udoh (Ed.), *Applications and developments in grid, cloud, and high performance computing* (pp. 1–14). Hershey, PA: IGI Global. doi:10.4018/978-1-4666-2065-0. ch001

Cohen, F. (2013). Challenges to digital forensic evidence in the cloud. In K. Ruan (Ed.), *Cybercrime and cloud forensics: Applications for investigation processes* (pp. 59–78). Hershey, PA: IGI Global. doi:10.4018/978-1-4666-2662-1.ch003

Cossu, R., Di Giulio, C., Brito, F., & Petcu, D. (2013). Cloud computing for earth observation. In D. Kyriazis, A. Voulodimos, S. Gogouvitis, & T. Varvarigou (Eds.), *Data intensive storage services for cloud environments* (pp. 166–191). Hershey, PA: IGI Global. doi:10.4018/978-1-4666-3934-8.ch012

Costa, J. E., & Rodrigues, J. J. (2014). Mobile cloud computing: Technologies, services, and applications. In J. Rodrigues, K. Lin, & J. Lloret (Eds.), *Mobile networks and cloud computing convergence for progressive services and applications* (pp. 1–17). Hershey, PA: IGI Global. doi:10.4018/978-1-4666-4781-7.ch001

Creaner, G., & Pahl, C. (2013). Flexible coordination techniques for dynamic cloud service collaboration. In G. Ortiz & J. Cubo (Eds.), *Adaptive web services for modular and reusable software development: Tactics and solutions* (pp. 239–252). Hershey, PA: IGI Global. doi:10.4018/978-1-4666-2089-6.ch009

Crosbie, M. (2013). Hack the cloud: Ethical hacking and cloud forensics. In K. Ruan (Ed.), *Cybercrime and cloud forensics: Applications for investigation processes* (pp. 42–58). Hershey, PA: IGI Global. doi:10.4018/978-1-4666-2662-1.ch002

Curran, K., Carlin, S., & Adams, M. (2012). Security issues in cloud computing. In L. Chao (Ed.), *Cloud computing for teaching and learning: Strategies for design and implementation* (pp. 200–208). Hershey, PA: IGI Global. doi:10.4018/978-1-4666-0957-0.ch014

Dahbur, K., & Mohammad, B. (2011). Toward understanding the challenges and countermeasures in computer anti-forensics. *International Journal of Cloud Applications and Computing, 1*(3), 22–35. doi:10.4018/ijcac.2011070103

Dahbur, K., Mohammad, B., & Tarakji, A. B. (2011). Security issues in cloud computing: A survey of risks, threats and vulnerabilities. *International Journal of Cloud Applications and Computing, 1*(3), 1–11. doi:10.4018/ijcac.2011070101

Dahbur, K., Mohammad, B., & Tarakji, A. B. (2012). Security issues in cloud computing: A survey of risks, threats and vulnerabilities. In *Grid and cloud computing: Concepts, methodologies, tools and applications* (pp. 1644–1655). Hershey, PA: IGI Global. doi:10.4018/978-1-4666-0879-5.ch707

Dahbur, K., Mohammad, B., & Tarakji, A. B. (2013). Security issues in cloud computing: A survey of risks, threats and vulnerabilities. In S. Aljawarneh (Ed.), *Cloud computing advancements in design, implementation, and technologies* (pp. 154–165). Hershey, PA: IGI Global. doi:10.4018/978-1-4666-1879-4.ch011

Daim, T., Britton, M., Subramanian, G., Brenden, R., & Intarode, N. (2012). Adopting and integrating cloud computing. In E. Eyob & E. Tetteh (Eds.), *Customer-oriented global supply chains: Concepts for effective management* (pp. 175–197). Hershey, PA: IGI Global. doi:10.4018/978-1-4666-0246-5.ch011

Davis, M., & Sedsman, A. (2012). Grey areas: The legal dimensions of cloud computing. In C. Li & A. Ho (Eds.), *Crime prevention technologies and applications for advancing criminal investigation* (pp. 263–273). Hershey, PA: IGI Global. doi:10.4018/978-1-4666-1758-2.ch017

De Coster, R., & Albesher, A. (2013). The development of mobile service applications for consumers and intelligent networks. In I. Lee (Ed.), *Mobile services industries, technologies, and applications in the global economy* (pp. 273–289). Hershey, PA: IGI Global. doi:10.4018/978-1-4666-1981-4.ch017

De Filippi, P. (2014). Ubiquitous computing in the cloud: User empowerment vs. user obsequity. In J. Pelet & P. Papadopoulou (Eds.), *User behavior in ubiquitous online environments* (pp. 44–63). Hershey, PA: IGI Global. doi:10.4018/978-1-4666-4566-0.ch003

De Silva, S. (2013). Key legal issues with cloud computing: A UK law perspective. In A. Bento & A. Aggarwal (Eds.), *Cloud computing service and deployment models: Layers and management* (pp. 242–256). Hershey, PA: IGI Global. doi:10.4018/978-1-4666-2187-9.ch013

Deed, C., & Cragg, P. (2013). Business impacts of cloud computing. In A. Bento & A. Aggarwal (Eds.), *Cloud computing service and deployment models: Layers and management* (pp. 274–288). Hershey, PA: IGI Global. doi:10.4018/978-1-4666-2187-9.ch015

Deng, M., Petkovic, M., Nalin, M., & Baroni, I. (2013). Home healthcare in cloud computing. In M. Cruz-Cunha, I. Miranda, & P. Gonçalves (Eds.), *Handbook of research on ICTs and management systems for improving efficiency in healthcare and social care* (pp. 614–634). Hershey, PA: IGI Global. doi:10.4018/978-1-4666-3990-4.ch032

Desai, A. M., & Mock, K. (2013). Security in cloud computing. In A. Bento & A. Aggarwal (Eds.), *Cloud computing service and deployment models: Layers and management* (pp. 208–221). Hershey, PA: IGI Global. doi:10.4018/978-1-4666-2187-9.ch011

Deshpande, R. M., Patle, B. V., & Bhoskar, R. D. (2014). Planning and implementation of cloud computing in NIT's in India: Special reference to VNIT. In S. Dhamdhere (Ed.), *Cloud computing and virtualization technologies in libraries* (pp. 90–106). Hershey, PA: IGI Global. doi:10.4018/978-1-4666-4631-5.ch006

Dhamdhere, S. N., & Lihitkar, R. (2014). The university cloud library model and the role of the cloud librarian. In S. Dhamdhere (Ed.), *Cloud computing and virtualization technologies in libraries* (pp. 150–161). Hershey, PA: IGI Global. doi:10.4018/978-1-4666-4631-5.ch009

Di Martino, S., Ferrucci, F., Maggio, V., & Sarro, F. (2013). Towards migrating genetic algorithms for test data generation to the cloud. In S. Tilley & T. Parveen (Eds.), *Software testing in the cloud: Perspectives on an emerging discipline* (pp. 113–135). Hershey, PA: IGI Global. doi:10.4018/978-1-4666-2536-5.ch006

Di Sano, M., Di Stefano, A., Morana, G., & Zito, D. (2013). FSaaS: Configuring policies for managing shared files among cooperating, distributed applications. *International Journal of Web Portals*, 5(1), 1–14. doi:10.4018/jwp.2013010101

Dippl, S., Jaeger, M. C., Luhn, A., Shulman-Peleg, A., & Vernik, G. (2013). Towards federation and interoperability of cloud storage systems. In D. Kyriazis, A. Voulodimos, S. Gogouvitis, & T. Varvarigou (Eds.), *Data intensive storage services for cloud environments* (pp. 60–71). Hershey, PA: IGI Global. doi:10.4018/978-1-4666-3934-8.ch005

Distefano, S., & Puliafito, A. (2012). The cloud@home volunteer and interoperable cloud through the future internet. In M. Villari, I. Brandic, & F. Tusa (Eds.), *Achieving federated and self-manageable cloud infrastructures: Theory and practice* (pp. 79–96). Hershey, PA: IGI Global. doi:10.4018/978-1-4666-1631-8.ch005

Djoleto, W. (2013). Cloud computing and ecommerce or ebusiness: "The now it way" – An overview. In *Electronic commerce and organizational leadership: perspectives and methodologies* (pp. 239–254). Hershey, PA: IGI Global. doi:10.4018/978-1-4666-2982-0.ch010

Dollmann, T. J., Loos, P., Fellmann, M., Thomas, O., Hoheisel, A., Katranuschkov, P., & Scherer, R. (2011). Design and usage of a process-centric collaboration methodology for virtual organizations in hybrid environments. *International Journal of Intelligent Information Technologies*, *7*(1), 45–64. doi:10.4018/jiit.2011010104

Dollmann, T. J., Loos, P., Fellmann, M., Thomas, O., Hoheisel, A., Katranuschkov, P., & Scherer, R. (2013). Design and usage of a process-centric collaboration methodology for virtual organizations in hybrid environments. In V. Sugumaran (Ed.), *Organizational efficiency through intelligent information technologies* (pp. 45–64). Hershey, PA: IGI Global. doi:10.4018/978-1-4666-2047-6.ch004

Dreher, P., & Vouk, M. (2012). Utilizing open source cloud computing environments to provide cost effective support for university education and research. In L. Chao (Ed.), *Cloud computing for teaching and learning: Strategies for design and implementation* (pp. 32–49). Hershey, PA: IGI Global. doi:10.4018/978-1-4666-0957-0.ch003

Drum, D., Becker, D., & Fish, M. (2013). Technology adoption in troubled times: A cloud computing case study. *Journal of Cases on Information Technology*, *15*(2), 57–71. doi:10.4018/jcit.2013040104

Dunaway, D. M. (2013). Creating virtual collaborative learning experiences for aspiring teachers. In R. Hartshorne, T. Heafner, & T. Petty (Eds.), *Teacher education programs and online learning tools: Innovations in teacher preparation* (pp. 167–180). Hershey, PA: IGI Global. doi:10.4018/978-1-4666-1906-7.ch009

Dykstra, J. (2013). Seizing electronic evidence from cloud computing environments. In K. Ruan (Ed.), *Cybercrime and cloud forensics: Applications for investigation processes* (pp. 156–185). Hershey, PA: IGI Global. doi:10.4018/978-1-4666-2662-1.ch007

El-Refaey, M., & Rimal, B. P. (2012). Grid, SOA and cloud computing: On-demand computing models. In *Grid and cloud computing: Concepts, methodologies, tools and applications* (pp. 12–51). Hershey, PA: IGI Global. doi:10.4018/978-1-4666-0879-5.ch102

El-Refaey, M., & Rimal, B. P. (2012). Grid, SOA and cloud computing: On-demand computing models. In N. Preve (Ed.), *Computational and data grids: Principles, applications and design* (pp. 45–85). Hershey, PA: IGI Global. doi:10.4018/978-1-61350-113-9.ch003

Elnaffar, S., Maamar, Z., & Sheng, Q. Z. (2013). When clouds start socializing: The sky model. *International Journal of E-Business Research*, 9(2), 1–7. doi:10.4018/jebr.2013040101

Elwood, S., & Keengwe, J. (2012). Microbursts: A design format for mobile cloud computing. *International Journal of Information and Communication Technology Education*, 8(2), 102–110. doi:10.4018/jicte.2012040109

Emeakaroha, V. C., Netto, M. A., Calheiros, R. N., & De Rose, C. A. (2012). Achieving flexible SLA and resource management in clouds. In M. Villari, I. Brandic, & F. Tusa (Eds.), *Achieving federated and self-manageable cloud infrastructures: Theory and practice* (pp. 266–287). Hershey, PA: IGI Global. doi:10.4018/978-1-4666-1631-8.ch014

Etro, F. (2013). The economics of cloud computing. In A. Bento & A. Aggarwal (Eds.), *Cloud computing service and deployment models: Layers and management* (pp. 296–309). Hershey, PA: IGI Global. doi:10.4018/978-1-4666-2187-9.ch017

Ezugwu, A. E., Buhari, S. M., & Junaidu, S. B. (2013). Virtual machine allocation in cloud computing environment. *International Journal of Cloud Applications and Computing*, 3(2), 47–60. doi:10.4018/ijcac.2013040105

Fauzi, A. H., & Taylor, H. (2013). Secure community trust stores for peer-to-peer e-commerce applications using cloud services. *International Journal of E-Entrepreneurship and Innovation*, 4(1), 1–15. doi:10.4018/jeei.2013010101

Ferguson-Boucher, K., & Endicott-Popovsky, B. (2013). Forensic readiness in the cloud (FRC): Integrating records management and digital forensics. In K. Ruan (Ed.), *Cybercrime and cloud forensics: Applications for investigation processes* (pp. 105–128). Hershey, PA: IGI Global. doi:10.4018/978-1-4666-2662-1.ch005

Ferraro de Souza, R., Westphall, C. B., dos Santos, D. R., & Westphall, C. M. (2013). A review of PACS on cloud for archiving secure medical images. *International Journal of Privacy and Health Information Management*, *1*(1), 53–62. doi:10.4018/ijphim.2013010104

Firdhous, M., Hassan, S., & Ghazali, O. (2013). Statistically enhanced multi-dimensional trust computing mechanism for cloud computing. *International Journal of Mobile Computing and Multimedia Communications*, *5*(2), 1–17. doi:10.4018/jmcmc.2013040101

Formisano, C., Bonelli, L., Balraj, K. R., & Shulman-Peleg, A. (2013). Cloud access control mechanisms. In D. Kyriazis, A. Voulodimos, S. Gogouvitis, & T. Varvarigou (Eds.), *Data intensive storage services for cloud environments* (pp. 94–108). Hershey, PA: IGI Global. doi:10.4018/978-1-4666-3934-8.ch007

Frank, H., & Mesentean, S. (2012). Efficient communication interfaces for distributed energy resources. In E. Udoh (Ed.), *Evolving developments in grid and cloud computing: Advancing research* (pp. 185–196). Hershey, PA: IGI Global. doi:10.4018/978-1-4666-0056-0.ch013

Gallina, B., & Guelfi, N. (2012). Reusing transaction models for dependable cloud computing. In H. Yang & X. Liu (Eds.), *Software reuse in the emerging cloud computing era* (pp. 248–277). Hershey, PA: IGI Global. doi:10.4018/978-1-4666-0897-9.ch011

Garofalo, D. A. (2013). Empires of the future: Libraries, technology, and the academic environment. In E. Iglesias (Ed.), *Robots in academic libraries: Advancements in library automation* (pp. 180–206). Hershey, PA: IGI Global. doi:10.4018/978-1-4666-3938-6.ch010

Gebremeskel, G. B., He, Z., & Jing, X. (2013). Semantic integrating for intelligent cloud data mining platform and cloud based business intelligence for optimization of mobile social networks. In V. Bhatnagar (Ed.), *Data mining in dynamic social networks and fuzzy systems* (pp. 173–211). Hershey, PA: IGI Global. doi:10.4018/978-1-4666-4213-3.ch009

Gentleman, W. M. (2013). Using the cloud for testing NOT adjunct to development. In S. Tilley & T. Parveen (Eds.), *Software testing in the cloud: Perspectives on an emerging discipline* (pp. 216–230). Hershey, PA: IGI Global. doi:10.4018/978-1-4666-2536-5.ch010

Ghafoor, K. Z., Mohammed, M. A., Abu Bakar, K., Sadiq, A. S., & Lloret, J. (2014). Vehicular cloud computing: Trends and challenges. In J. Rodrigues, K. Lin, & J. Lloret (Eds.), *Mobile networks and cloud computing convergence for progressive services and applications* (pp. 262–274). Hershey, PA: IGI Global. doi:10.4018/978-1-4666-4781-7.ch014

Giannakaki, M. (2012). The "right to be forgotten" in the era of social media and cloud computing. In C. Akrivopoulou & N. Garipidis (Eds.), *Human rights and risks in the digital era: Globalization and the effects of information technologies* (pp. 10–24). Hershey, PA: IGI Global. doi:10.4018/978-1-4666-0891-7.ch002

Gillam, L., Li, B., & O'Loughlin, J. (2012). Teaching clouds: Lessons taught and lessons learnt. In L. Chao (Ed.), *Cloud computing for teaching and learning: Strategies for design and implementation* (pp. 82–94). Hershey, PA: IGI Global. doi:10.4018/978-1-4666-0957-0.ch006

Gonsowski, D. (2013). Compliance in the cloud and the implications on electronic discovery. In K. Ruan (Ed.), *Cybercrime and cloud forensics: Applications for investigation processes* (pp. 230–250). Hershey, PA: IGI Global. doi:10.4018/978-1-4666-2662-1.ch009

Gonzalez-Sanchez, J., Conley, Q., Chavez-Echeagaray, M., & Atkinson, R. K. (2012). Supporting the assembly process by leveraging augmented reality, cloud computing, and mobile devices. *International Journal of Cyber Behavior, Psychology and Learning*, 2(3), 86–102. doi:10.4018/ijcbpl.2012070107

Gopinath, R., & Geetha, B. (2013). An e-learning system based on secure data storage services in cloud computing. *International Journal of Information Technology and Web Engineering*, 8(2), 1–17. doi:10.4018/jitwe.2013040101

Gossin, P. C., & LaBrie, R. C. (2013). Data center waste management. In P. Ordóñez de Pablos (Ed.), *Green technologies and business practices: An IT approach* (pp. 226–235). Hershey, PA: IGI Global. doi:10.4018/978-1-4666-1972-2.ch014

Goswami, V., Patra, S. S., & Mund, G. B. (2012). Performance analysis of cloud computing centers for bulk services. *International Journal of Cloud Applications and Computing*, 2(4), 53–65. doi:10.4018/ijcac.2012100104

Goswami, V., & Sahoo, C. N. (2013). Optimal resource usage in multi-cloud computing environment. *International Journal of Cloud Applications and Computing*, *3*(1), 44–57. doi:10.4018/ijcac.2013010105

Gräuler, M., Teuteberg, F., Mahmoud, T., & Gómez, J. M. (2013). Requirements prioritization and design considerations for the next generation of corporate environmental management information systems: A foundation for innovation. *International Journal of Information Technologies and Systems Approach*, *6*(1), 98–116. doi:10.4018/jitsa.2013010106

Grieve, G. P., & Heston, K. (2012). Finding liquid salvation: Using the cardean ethnographic method to document second life residents and religious cloud communities. In N. Zagalo, L. Morgado, & A. Boa-Ventura (Eds.), *Virtual worlds and metaverse platforms: New communication and identity paradigms* (pp. 288–305). Hershey, PA: IGI Global. doi:10.4018/978-1-60960-854-5.ch019

Grispos, G., Storer, T., & Glisson, W. B. (2012). Calm before the storm: The challenges of cloud computing in digital forensics. *International Journal of Digital Crime and Forensics*, *4*(2), 28–48. doi:10.4018/jdcf.2012040103

Grispos, G., Storer, T., & Glisson, W. B. (2013). Calm before the storm: The challenges of cloud computing in digital forensics. In C. Li (Ed.), *Emerging digital forensics applications for crime detection, prevention, and security* (pp. 211–233). Hershey, PA: IGI Global. doi:10.4018/978-1-4666-4006-1.ch015

Guster, D., & Lee, O. F. (2011). Enhancing the disaster recovery plan through virtualization. *Journal of Information Technology Research*, *4*(4), 18–40. doi:10.4018/jitr.2011100102

Hanawa, T., & Sato, M. (2013). D-Cloud: Software testing environment for dependable distributed systems using cloud computing technology. In S. Tilley & T. Parveen (Eds.), *Software testing in the cloud: Perspectives on an emerging discipline* (pp. 340–355). Hershey, PA: IGI Global. doi:10.4018/978-1-4666-2536-5.ch016

Hardy, J., Liu, L., Lei, C., & Li, J. (2013). Internet-based virtual computing infrastructure for cloud computing. In X. Yang & L. Liu (Eds.), *Principles, methodologies, and service-oriented approaches for cloud computing* (pp. 371–389). Hershey, PA: IGI Global. doi:10.4018/978-1-4666-2854-0.ch016

Hashizume, K., Yoshioka, N., & Fernandez, E. B. (2013). Three misuse patterns for cloud computing. In D. Rosado, D. Mellado, E. Fernandez-Medina, & M. Piattini (Eds.), *Security engineering for cloud computing: Approaches and tools* (pp. 36–53). Hershey, PA: IGI Global. doi:10.4018/978-1-4666-2125-1.ch003

Hassan, Q. F., Riad, A. M., & Hassan, A. E. (2012). Understanding cloud computing. In H. Yang & X. Liu (Eds.), *Software reuse in the emerging cloud computing era* (pp. 204–227). Hershey, PA: IGI Global. doi:10.4018/978-1-4666-0897-9.ch009

Hasselmeyer, P., Katsaros, G., Koller, B., & Wieder, P. (2012). Cloud monitoring. In M. Villari, I. Brandic, & F. Tusa (Eds.), *Achieving federated and self-manageable cloud infrastructures: Theory and practice* (pp. 97–116). Hershey, PA: IGI Global. doi:10.4018/978-1-4666-1631-8.ch006

Hertzler, B. T., Frost, E., Bressler, G. H., & Goehring, C. (2011). Experience report: Using a cloud computing environment during Haiti and Exercise24. *International Journal of Information Systems for Crisis Response and Management, 3*(1), 50–64. doi:10.4018/jiscrm.2011010104

Hertzler, B. T., Frost, E., Bressler, G. H., & Goehring, C. (2013). Experience report: Using a cloud computing environment during Haiti and Exercise24. In M. Jennex (Ed.), *Using social and information technologies for disaster and crisis management* (pp. 52–66). Hershey, PA: IGI Global. doi:10.4018/978-1-4666-2788-8.ch004

Ho, R. (2013). Cloud computing and enterprise migration strategies. In A. Loo (Ed.), *Distributed computing innovations for business, engineering, and science* (pp. 156–175). Hershey, PA: IGI Global. doi:10.4018/978-1-4666-2533-4.ch008

Hobona, G., Jackson, M., & Anand, S. (2012). Implementing geospatial web services for cloud computing. In *Grid and cloud computing: Concepts, methodologies, tools and applications* (pp. 615–636). Hershey, PA: IGI Global. doi:10.4018/978-1-4666-0879-5.ch305

Hochstein, L., Schott, B., & Graybill, R. B. (2011). Computational engineering in the cloud: Benefits and challenges. *Journal of Organizational and End User Computing, 23*(4), 31–50. doi:10.4018/joeuc.2011100103

Hochstein, L., Schott, B., & Graybill, R. B. (2013). Computational engineering in the cloud: Benefits and challenges. In A. Dwivedi & S. Clarke (Eds.), *Innovative strategies and approaches for end-user computing advancements* (pp. 314–332). Hershey, PA: IGI Global. doi:10.4018/978-1-4666-2059-9.ch017

Honarvar, A. R. (2013). Developing an elastic cloud computing application through multi-agent systems. *International Journal of Cloud Applications and Computing, 3*(1), 58–64. doi:10.4018/ijcac.2013010106

Hossain, S. (2013). Cloud computing terms, definitions, and taxonomy. In A. Bento & A. Aggarwal (Eds.), *Cloud computing service and deployment models: Layers and management* (pp. 1–25). Hershey, PA: IGI Global. doi:10.4018/978-1-4666-2187-9.ch001

Hudzia, B., Sinclair, J., & Lindner, M. (2013). Deploying and running enterprise grade applications in a federated cloud. In *Supply chain management: Concepts, methodologies, tools, and applications* (pp. 1350–1370). Hershey, PA: IGI Global. doi:10.4018/978-1-4666-2625-6.ch080

Hung, S., Shieh, J., & Lee, C. (2011). Migrating android applications to the cloud. *International Journal of Grid and High Performance Computing, 3*(2), 14–28. doi:10.4018/jghpc.2011040102

Hung, S., Shieh, J., & Lee, C. (2013). Migrating android applications to the cloud. In E. Udoh (Ed.), *Applications and developments in grid, cloud, and high performance computing* (pp. 307–322). Hershey, PA: IGI Global. doi:10.4018/978-1-4666-2065-0.ch020

Islam, S., Mouratidis, H., & Weippl, E. R. (2013). A goal-driven risk management approach to support security and privacy analysis of cloud-based system. In D. Rosado, D. Mellado, E. Fernandez-Medina, & M. Piattini (Eds.), *Security engineering for cloud computing: Approaches and tools* (pp. 97–122). Hershey, PA: IGI Global. doi:10.4018/978-1-4666-2125-1.ch006

Itani, W., Kayssi, A., & Chehab, A. (2013). Hardware-based security for ensuring data privacy in the cloud. In D. Rosado, D. Mellado, E. Fernandez-Medina, & M. Piattini (Eds.), *Security engineering for cloud computing: Approaches and tools* (pp. 147–170). Hershey, PA: IGI Global. doi:10.4018/978-1-4666-2125-1.ch008

Jackson, A., & Weiland, M. (2013). Cloud computing for scientific simulation and high performance computing. In X. Yang & L. Liu (Eds.), *Principles, methodologies, and service-oriented approaches for cloud computing* (pp. 51–70). Hershey, PA: IGI Global. doi:10.4018/978-1-4666-2854-0.ch003

Jaeger, M. C., & Hohenstein, U. (2013). Content centric storage and current storage systems. In D. Kyriazis, A. Voulodimos, S. Gogouvitis, & T. Varvarigou (Eds.), *Data intensive storage services for cloud environments* (pp. 27–46). Hershey, PA: IGI Global. doi:10.4018/978-1-4666-3934-8.ch003

James, J. I., Shosha, A. F., & Gladyshev, P. (2013). Digital forensic investigation and cloud computing. In K. Ruan (Ed.), *Cybercrime and cloud forensics: Applications for investigation processes* (pp. 1–41). Hershey, PA: IGI Global. doi:10.4018/978-1-4666-2662-1.ch001

Jena, R. K. (2013). Green computing to green business. In P. Ordóñez de Pablos (Ed.), *Green technologies and business practices: An IT approach* (pp. 138–150). Hershey, PA: IGI Global. doi:10.4018/978-1-4666-1972-2.ch007

Jeyarani, R., & Nagaveni, N. (2012). A heuristic meta scheduler for optimal resource utilization and improved QoS in cloud computing environment. *International Journal of Cloud Applications and Computing, 2*(1), 41–52. doi:10.4018/ijcac.2012010103

Jeyarani, R., Nagaveni, N., & Ram, R. V. (2011). Self adaptive particle swarm optimization for efficient virtual machine provisioning in cloud. *International Journal of Intelligent Information Technologies, 7*(2), 25–44. doi:10.4018/jiit.2011040102

Jeyarani, R., Nagaveni, N., & Ram, R. V. (2013). Self adaptive particle swarm optimization for efficient virtual machine provisioning in cloud. In V. Sugumaran (Ed.), *Organizational efficiency through intelligent information technologies* (pp. 88–107). Hershey, PA: IGI Global. doi:10.4018/978-1-4666-2047-6.ch006

Jeyarani, R., Nagaveni, N., Sadasivam, S. K., & Rajarathinam, V. R. (2011). Power aware meta scheduler for adaptive VM provisioning in IaaS cloud. *International Journal of Cloud Applications and Computing, 1*(3), 36–51. doi:10.4018/ijcac.2011070104

Jeyarani, R., Nagaveni, N., Sadasivam, S. K., & Rajarathinam, V. R. (2013). Power aware meta scheduler for adaptive VM provisioning in IaaS cloud. In S. Aljawarneh (Ed.), *Cloud computing advancements in design, implementation, and technologies* (pp. 190–204). Hershey, PA: IGI Global. doi:10.4018/978-1-4666-1879-4.ch014

Jiang, J., Huang, X., Wu, Y., & Yang, G. (2013). Campus cloud storage and preservation: From distributed file system to data sharing service. In X. Yang & L. Liu (Eds.), *Principles, methodologies, and service-oriented approaches for cloud computing* (pp. 284–301). Hershey, PA: IGI Global. doi:10.4018/978-1-4666-2854-0.ch012

Jing, S. (2012). The application exploration of cloud computing in information technology teaching. *International Journal of Advanced Pervasive and Ubiquitous Computing, 4*(4), 23–27. doi:10.4018/japuc.2012100104

Johansson, D., & Wiberg, M. (2012). Conceptually advancing "application mobility" towards design: Applying a concept-driven approach to the design of mobile IT for home care service groups. *International Journal of Ambient Computing and Intelligence, 4*(3), 20–32. doi:10.4018/jaci.2012070102

Jorda, J., & M'zoughi, A. (2013). Securing cloud storage. In D. Rosado, D. Mellado, E. Fernandez-Medina, & M. Piattini (Eds.), *Security engineering for cloud computing: Approaches and tools* (pp. 171–190). Hershey, PA: IGI Global. doi:10.4018/978-1-4666-2125-1.ch009

Juiz, C., & Alexander de Pous, V. (2014). Cloud computing: IT governance, legal, and public policy aspects. In I. Portela & F. Almeida (Eds.), *Organizational, legal, and technological dimensions of information system administration* (pp. 139–166). Hershey, PA: IGI Global. doi:10.4018/978-1-4666-4526-4.ch009

Kaisler, S. H., Money, W., & Cohen, S. J. (2013). Cloud computing: A decision framework for small businesses. In A. Bento & A. Aggarwal (Eds.), *Cloud computing service and deployment models: Layers and management* (pp. 151–172). Hershey, PA: IGI Global. doi:10.4018/978-1-4666-2187-9.ch008

Kanamori, Y., & Yen, M. Y. (2013). Cloud computing security and risk management. In A. Bento & A. Aggarwal (Eds.), *Cloud computing service and deployment models: Layers and management* (pp. 222–240). Hershey, PA: IGI Global. doi:10.4018/978-1-4666-2187-9.ch012

Karadsheh, L., & Alhawari, S. (2011). Applying security policies in small business utilizing cloud computing technologies. *International Journal of Cloud Applications and Computing*, *1*(2), 29–40. doi:10.4018/ijcac.2011040103

Karadsheh, L., & Alhawari, S. (2013). Applying security policies in small business utilizing cloud computing technologies. In S. Aljawarneh (Ed.), *Cloud computing advancements in design, implementation, and technologies* (pp. 112–124). Hershey, PA: IGI Global. doi:10.4018/978-1-4666-1879-4.ch008

Kaupins, G. (2012). Laws associated with mobile computing in the cloud. *International Journal of Wireless Networks and Broadband Technologies*, *2*(3), 1–9. doi:10.4018/ijwnbt.2012070101

Kemp, M. L., Robb, S., & Deans, P. C. (2013). The legal implications of cloud computing. In A. Bento & A. Aggarwal (Eds.), *Cloud computing service and deployment models: Layers and management* (pp. 257–272). Hershey, PA: IGI Global. doi:10.4018/978-1-4666-2187-9.ch014

Khan, N., Ahmad, N., Herawan, T., & Inayat, Z. (2012). Cloud computing: Locally sub-clouds instead of globally one cloud. *International Journal of Cloud Applications and Computing*, *2*(3), 68–85. doi:10.4018/ijcac.2012070103

Khan, N., Noraziah, A., Ismail, E. I., Deris, M. M., & Herawan, T. (2012). Cloud computing: Analysis of various platforms. *International Journal of E-Entrepreneurship and Innovation*, *3*(2), 51–59. doi:10.4018/jeei.2012040104

Khansa, L., Forcade, J., Nambari, G., Parasuraman, S., & Cox, P. (2012). Proposing an intelligent cloud-based electronic health record system. *International Journal of Business Data Communications and Networking*, *8*(3), 57–71. doi:10.4018/jbdcn.2012070104

Kierkegaard, S. (2012). Not every cloud brings rain: Legal risks on the horizon. In M. Gupta, J. Walp, & R. Sharman (Eds.), *Strategic and practical approaches for information security governance: Technologies and applied solutions* (pp. 181–194). Hershey, PA: IGI Global. doi:10.4018/978-1-4666-0197-0.ch011

Kifayat, K., Shamsa, T. B., Mackay, M., Merabti, M., & Shi, Q. (2013). Real time risk management in cloud computation. In D. Rosado, D. Mellado, E. Fernandez-Medina, & M. Piattini (Eds.), *Security engineering for cloud computing: Approaches and tools* (pp. 123–145). Hershey, PA: IGI Global. doi:10.4018/978-1-4666-2125-1.ch007

King, T. M., Ganti, A. S., & Froslie, D. (2013). Towards improving the testability of cloud application services. In S. Tilley & T. Parveen (Eds.), *Software testing in the cloud: Perspectives on an emerging discipline* (pp. 322–339). Hershey, PA: IGI Global. doi:10.4018/978-1-4666-2536-5.ch015

Kipp, A., Schneider, R., & Schubert, L. (2013). Encapsulation of complex HPC services. In C. Rückemann (Ed.), *Integrated information and computing systems for natural, spatial, and social sciences* (pp. 153–176). Hershey, PA: IGI Global. doi:10.4018/978-1-4666-2190-9.ch008

Kldiashvili, E. (2012). The cloud computing as the tool for implementation of virtual organization technology for ehealth. *Journal of Information Technology Research*, *5*(1), 18–34. doi:10.4018/jitr.2012010102

Kldiashvili, E. (2013). Implementation of telecytology in georgia for quality assurance programs. *Journal of Information Technology Research*, *6*(2), 24–45. doi:10.4018/jitr.2013040102

Kosmatov, N. (2013). Concolic test generation and the cloud: deployment and verification perspectives. In S. Tilley & T. Parveen (Eds.), *Software testing in the cloud: Perspectives on an emerging discipline* (pp. 231–251). Hershey, PA: IGI Global. doi:10.4018/978-1-4666-2536-5.ch011

Kotamarti, R. M., Thornton, M. A., & Dunham, M. H. (2012). Quantum computing approach for alignment-free sequence search and classification. In S. Ali, N. Abbadeni, & M. Batouche (Eds.), *Multidisciplinary computational intelligence techniques: Applications in business, engineering, and medicine* (pp. 279–300). Hershey, PA: IGI Global. doi:10.4018/978-1-4666-1830-5.ch017

Kremmydas, D., Petsakos, A., & Rozakis, S. (2012). Parametric optimization of linear and non-linear models via parallel computing to enhance web-spatial DSS interactivity. *International Journal of Decision Support System Technology*, *4*(1), 14–29. doi:10.4018/jdsst.2012010102

Krishnadas, N., & Pillai, R. R. (2013). Cloud computing diagnosis: A comprehensive study. In X. Yang & L. Liu (Eds.), *Principles, methodologies, and service-oriented approaches for cloud computing* (pp. 1–18). Hershey, PA: IGI Global. doi:10.4018/978-1-4666-2854-0.ch001

Kübert, R., & Katsaros, G. (2011). Using free software for elastic web hosting on a private cloud. *International Journal of Cloud Applications and Computing*, *1*(2), 14–28. doi:10.4018/ijcac.2011040102

Kübert, R., & Katsaros, G. (2013). Using free software for elastic web hosting on a private cloud. In S. Aljawarneh (Ed.), *Cloud computing advancements in design, implementation, and technologies* (pp. 97–111). Hershey, PA: IGI Global. doi:10.4018/978-1-4666-1879-4.ch007

Kumar, P. S., Ashok, M. S., & Subramanian, R. (2012). A publicly verifiable dynamic secret sharing protocol for secure and dependable data storage in cloud computing. *International Journal of Cloud Applications and Computing*, *2*(3), 1–25. doi:10.4018/ijcac.2012070101

Lasluisa, S., Rodero, I., & Parashar, M. (2013). Software design for passing sarbanes-oxley in cloud computing. In C. Rückemann (Ed.), *Integrated information and computing systems for natural, spatial, and social sciences* (pp. 27–42). Hershey, PA: IGI Global. doi:10.4018/978-1-4666-2190-9.ch002

Lasluisa, S., Rodero, I., & Parashar, M. (2014). Software design for passing sarbanes-oxley in cloud computing. In *Software design and development: Concepts, methodologies, tools, and applications* (pp. 1659–1674). Hershey, PA: IGI Global. doi:10.4018/978-1-4666-4301-7.ch080

Lee, W. N. (2013). An economic analysis of cloud: "Software as a service" (saas) computing and "virtual desktop infrastructure" (VDI) models. In A. Bento & A. Aggarwal (Eds.), *Cloud computing service and deployment models: Layers and management* (pp. 289–295). Hershey, PA: IGI Global. doi:10.4018/978-1-4666-2187-9.ch016

Levine, K., & White, B. A. (2011). A crisis at hafford furniture: Cloud computing case study. *Journal of Cases on Information Technology, 13*(1), 57–71. doi:10.4018/jcit.2011010104

Levine, K., & White, B. A. (2013). A crisis at Hafford furniture: Cloud computing case study. In M. Khosrow-Pour (Ed.), *Cases on emerging information technology research and applications* (pp. 70–87). Hershey, PA: IGI Global. doi:10.4018/978-1-4666-3619-4.ch004

Li, J., Meng, L., Zhu, Z., Li, X., Huai, J., & Liu, L. (2013). CloudRank: A cloud service ranking method based on both user feedback and service testing. In X. Yang & T. Liu (Eds.), *Principles, methodologies, and service-oriented approaches for cloud computing* (pp. 230–258). Hershey, PA: IGI Global. doi:10.4018/978-1-4666-2854-0.ch010

Liang, T., Lu, F., & Chiu, J. (2012). A hybrid resource reservation method for workflows in clouds. *International Journal of Grid and High Performance Computing, 4*(4), 1–21. doi:10.4018/jghpc.2012100101

Lorenz, M., Rath-Wiggins, L., Runde, W., Messina, A., Sunna, P., Dimino, G., ... Borgotallo, R. (2013). Media convergence and cloud technologies: Smart storage, better workflows. In D. Kyriazis, A. Voulodimos, S. Gogouvitis, & T. Varvarigou (Eds.), *Data intensive storage services for cloud environments* (pp. 132–144). Hershey, PA: IGI Global. doi:10.4018/978-1-4666-3934-8.ch009

M., S. G., & G., S. K. (2012). An enterprise mashup integration service framework for clouds. *International Journal of Cloud Applications and Computing, 2*(2), 31-40. doi:10.4018/ijcac.2012040103

Maharana, S. K., Mali, P. B., Prabhakar, G. J. S., & Kumar, V. (2011). Cloud computing applied for numerical study of thermal characteristics of SIP. *International Journal of Cloud Applications and Computing, 1*(3), 12–21. doi:10.4018/ijcac.2011070102

Maharana, S. K., Mali, P. B., Prabhakar, G. J. S., & Kumar, V. (2013). Cloud computing applied for numerical study of thermal characteristics of SIP. In S. Aljawarneh (Ed.), *Cloud computing advancements in design, implementation, and technologies* (pp. 166–175). Hershey, PA: IGI Global. doi:10.4018/978-1-4666-1879-4.ch012

Maharana, S. K., P, G. P., & Bhati, A. (2012). A study of cloud computing for retinal image processing through MATLAB. *International Journal of Cloud Applications and Computing*, 2(2), 59–69. doi:10.4018/ijcac.2012040106

Maharana, S. K., Prabhakar, P. G., & Bhati, A. (2013). A study of cloud computing for retinal image processing through MATLAB. In *Image processing: Concepts, methodologies, tools, and applications* (pp. 101–111). Hershey, PA: IGI Global. doi:10.4018/978-1-4666-3994-2.ch006

Mahesh, S., Landry, B. J., Sridhar, T., & Walsh, K. R. (2011). A decision table for the cloud computing decision in small business. *Information Resources Management Journal*, 24(3), 9–25. doi:10.4018/irmj.2011070102

Mahesh, S., Landry, B. J., Sridhar, T., & Walsh, K. R. (2013). A decision table for the cloud computing decision in small business. In M. Khosrow-Pour (Ed.), *Managing information resources and technology: Emerging Applications and theories* (pp. 159–176). Hershey, PA: IGI Global. doi:10.4018/978-1-4666-3616-3.ch012

Marquezan, C. C., Metzger, A., Pohl, K., Engen, V., Boniface, M., Phillips, S. C., & Zlatev, Z. (2013). Adaptive future internet applications: Opportunities and challenges for adaptive web services technology. In G. Ortiz & J. Cubo (Eds.), *Adaptive web services for modular and reusable software development: Tactics and solutions* (pp. 333–353). Hershey, PA: IGI Global. doi:10.4018/978-1-4666-2089-6.ch014

Marshall, P. J. (2012). Cloud computing: Next generation education. In L. Chao (Ed.), *Cloud computing for teaching and learning: Strategies for design and implementation* (pp. 180–185). Hershey, PA: IGI Global. doi:10.4018/978-1-4666-0957-0.ch012

Martinez-Ortiz, A. (2012). Open cloud technologies. In L. Vaquero, J. Cáceres, & J. Hierro (Eds.), *Open source cloud computing systems: Practices and paradigms* (pp. 1–17). Hershey, PA: IGI Global. doi:10.4018/978-1-4666-0098-0.ch001

Massonet, P., Michot, A., Naqvi, S., Villari, M., & Latanicki, J. (2013). Securing the external interfaces of a federated infrastructure cloud. In *IT policy and ethics: Concepts, methodologies, tools, and applications* (pp. 1876–1903). Hershey, PA: IGI Global. doi:10.4018/978-1-4666-2919-6.ch082

Mavrogeorgi, N., Gogouvitis, S. V., Voulodimos, A., & Alexandrou, V. (2013). SLA management in storage clouds. In D. Kyriazis, A. Voulodimos, S. Gogouvitis, & T. Varvarigou (Eds.), *Data intensive storage services for cloud environments* (pp. 72–93). Hershey, PA: IGI Global. doi:10.4018/978-1-4666-3934-8.ch006

Mehta, H. K. (2013). Cloud selection for e-business a parameter based solution. In K. Tarnay, S. Imre, & L. Xu (Eds.), *Research and development in e-business through service-oriented solutions* (pp. 199–207). Hershey, PA: IGI Global. doi:10.4018/978-1-4666-4181-5.ch009

Mehta, H. K., & Gupta, E. (2013). Economy based resource allocation in IaaS cloud. *International Journal of Cloud Applications and Computing, 3*(2), 1–11. doi:10.4018/ijcac.2013040101

Miah, S. J. (2012). Cloud-based intelligent DSS design for emergency professionals. In S. Ali, N. Abbadeni, & M. Batouche (Eds.), *Multidisciplinary computational intelligence techniques: Applications in business, engineering, and medicine* (pp. 47–60). Hershey, PA: IGI Global. doi:10.4018/978-1-4666-1830-5.ch004

Miah, S. J. (2013). Cloud-based intelligent DSS design for emergency professionals. In *Data mining: Concepts, methodologies, tools, and applications* (pp. 991–1003). Hershey, PA: IGI Global. doi:10.4018/978-1-4666-2455-9.ch050

Mikkilineni, R. (2012). Architectural resiliency in distributed computing. *International Journal of Grid and High Performance Computing, 4*(4), 37–51. doi:10.4018/jghpc.2012100103

Millham, R. (2012). Software asset re-use: Migration of data-intensive legacy system to the cloud computing paradigm. In H. Yang & X. Liu (Eds.), *Software reuse in the emerging cloud computing era* (pp. 1–27). Hershey, PA: IGI Global. doi:10.4018/978-1-4666-0897-9.ch001

Mircea, M. (2011). Building the agile enterprise with service-oriented architecture, business process management and decision management. *International Journal of E-Entrepreneurship and Innovation, 2*(4), 32–48. doi:10.4018/jeei.2011100103

Modares, H., Lloret, J., Moravejosharieh, A., & Salleh, R. (2014). Security in mobile cloud computing. In J. Rodrigues, K. Lin, & J. Lloret (Eds.), *Mobile networks and cloud computing convergence for progressive services and applications* (pp. 79–91). Hershey, PA: IGI Global. doi:10.4018/978-1-4666-4781-7.ch005

Moedjiono, S., & Mas'at, A. (2012). Cloud computing implementation strategy for information dissemination on meteorology, climatology, air quality, and geophysics (MKKuG). *Journal of Information Technology Research, 5*(3), 71–84. doi:10.4018/jitr.2012070104

Moiny, J. (2012). Cloud based social network sites: Under whose control? In A. Dudley, J. Braman, & G. Vincenti (Eds.), *Investigating cyber law and cyber ethics: Issues, impacts and practices* (pp. 147–219). Hershey, PA: IGI Global. doi:10.4018/978-1-61350-132-0.ch009

Moreno, I. S., & Xu, J. (2011). Energy-efficiency in cloud computing environments: Towards energy savings without performance degradation. *International Journal of Cloud Applications and Computing*, *1*(1), 17–33. doi:10.4018/ijcac.2011010102

Moreno, I. S., & Xu, J. (2013). Energy-efficiency in cloud computing environments: Towards energy savings without performance degradation. In S. Aljawarneh (Ed.), *Cloud computing advancements in design, implementation, and technologies* (pp. 18–36). Hershey, PA: IGI Global. doi:10.4018/978-1-4666-1879-4.ch002

Muñoz, A., Maña, A., & González, J. (2013). Dynamic security properties monitoring architecture for cloud computing. In D. Rosado, D. Mellado, E. Fernandez-Medina, & M. Piattini (Eds.), *Security engineering for cloud computing: Approaches and tools* (pp. 1–18). Hershey, PA: IGI Global. doi:10.4018/978-1-4666-2125-1.ch001

Mvelase, P., Dlodlo, N., Williams, Q., & Adigun, M. O. (2011). Custom-made cloud enterprise architecture for small medium and micro enterprises. *International Journal of Cloud Applications and Computing*, *1*(3), 52–63. doi:10.4018/ijcac.2011070105

Mvelase, P., Dlodlo, N., Williams, Q., & Adigun, M. O. (2012). Custom-made cloud enterprise architecture for small medium and micro enterprises. In *Grid and cloud computing: Concepts, methodologies, tools and applications* (pp. 589–601). Hershey, PA: IGI Global. doi:10.4018/978-1-4666-0879-5.ch303

Mvelase, P., Dlodlo, N., Williams, Q., & Adigun, M. O. (2013). Custom-made cloud enterprise architecture for small medium and micro enterprises. In S. Aljawarneh (Ed.), *Cloud computing advancements in design, implementation, and technologies* (pp. 205–217). Hershey, PA: IGI Global. doi:10.4018/978-1-4666-1879-4.ch015

Naeem, M. A., Dobbie, G., & Weber, G. (2014). Big data management in the context of real-time data warehousing. In W. Hu & N. Kaabouch (Eds.), *Big data management, technologies, and applications* (pp. 150–176). Hershey, PA: IGI Global. doi:10.4018/978-1-4666-4699-5.ch007

Ofosu, W. K., & Saliah-Hassane, H. (2013). Cloud computing in the education environment for developing nations. *International Journal of Interdisciplinary Telecommunications and Networking*, *5*(3), 54–62. doi:10.4018/jitn.2013070106

Oliveros, E., Cucinotta, T., Phillips, S. C., Yang, X., Middleton, S., & Voith, T. (2012). Monitoring and metering in the cloud. In D. Kyriazis, T. Varvarigou, & K. Konstanteli (Eds.), *Achieving real-time in distributed computing: From grids to clouds* (pp. 94–114). Hershey, PA: IGI Global. doi:10.4018/978-1-60960-827-9.ch006

Orton, I., Alva, A., & Endicott-Popovsky, B. (2013). Legal process and requirements for cloud forensic investigations. In K. Ruan (Ed.), *Cybercrime and cloud forensics: Applications for investigation processes* (pp. 186–229). Hershey, PA: IGI Global. doi:10.4018/978-1-4666-2662-1.ch008

Pakhira, A., & Andras, P. (2013). Leveraging the cloud for large-scale software testing – A case study: Google Chrome on Amazon. In S. Tilley & T. Parveen (Eds.), *Software testing in the cloud: Perspectives on an emerging discipline* (pp. 252–279). Hershey, PA: IGI Global. doi:10.4018/978-1-4666-2536-5.ch012

Pal, K., & Karakostas, B. (2013). The use of cloud computing in shipping logistics. In D. Graham, I. Manikas, & D. Folinas (Eds.), *E-logistics and e-supply chain management: Applications for evolving business* (pp. 104–124). Hershey, PA: IGI Global. doi:10.4018/978-1-4666-3914-0.ch006

Pal, S. (2013). Cloud computing: Security concerns and issues. In A. Bento & A. Aggarwal (Eds.), *Cloud computing service and deployment models: Layers and management* (pp. 191–207). Hershey, PA: IGI Global. doi:10.4018/978-1-4666-2187-9.ch010

Pal, S. (2013). Storage security and technical challenges of cloud computing. In D. Kyriazis, A. Voulodimos, S. Gogouvitis, & T. Varvarigou (Eds.), *Data intensive storage services for cloud environments* (pp. 225–240). Hershey, PA: IGI Global. doi:10.4018/978-1-4666-3934-8.ch014

Palanivel, K., & Kuppuswami, S. (2014). A cloud-oriented reference architecture to digital library systems. In S. Dhamdhere (Ed.), *Cloud computing and virtualization technologies in libraries* (pp. 230–254). Hershey, PA: IGI Global. doi:10.4018/978-1-4666-4631-5.ch014

Paletta, M. (2012). Intelligent clouds: By means of using multi-agent systems environments. In L. Chao (Ed.), *Cloud computing for teaching and learning: Strategies for design and implementation* (pp. 254–279). Hershey, PA: IGI Global. doi:10.4018/978-1-4666-0957-0.ch017

Pallot, M., Le Marc, C., Richir, S., Schmidt, C., & Mathieu, J. (2012). Innovation gaming: An immersive experience environment enabling co-creation. In M. Cruz-Cunha (Ed.), *Handbook of research on serious games as educational, business and research tools* (pp. 1–24). Hershey, PA: IGI Global. doi:10.4018/978-1-4666-0149-9.ch001

Pankowska, M. (2011). Information technology resources virtualization for sustainable development. *International Journal of Applied Logistics*, 2(2), 35–48. doi:10.4018/jal.2011040103

Pankowska, M. (2013). Information technology resources virtualization for sustainable development. In Z. Luo (Ed.), *Technological solutions for modern logistics and supply chain management* (pp. 248–262). Hershey, PA: IGI Global. doi:10.4018/978-1-4666-2773-4.ch016

Parappallil, J. J., Zarvic, N., & Thomas, O. (2012). A context and content reflection on business-IT alignment research. *International Journal of IT/Business Alignment and Governance*, 3(2), 21–37. doi:10.4018/jitbag.2012070102

Parashar, V., Vishwakarma, M. L., & Parashar, R. (2014). A new framework for building academic library through cloud computing. In S. Dhamdhere (Ed.), *Cloud computing and virtualization technologies in libraries* (pp. 107–123). Hershey, PA: IGI Global. doi:10.4018/978-1-4666-4631-5.ch007

Pendyala, V. S., & Holliday, J. (2012). Cloud as a computer. In X. Liu & Y. Li (Eds.), *Advanced design approaches to emerging software systems: Principles, methodologies and tools* (pp. 241–249). Hershey, PA: IGI Global. doi:10.4018/978-1-60960-735-7.ch011

Petruch, K., Tamm, G., & Stantchev, V. (2012). Deriving in-depth knowledge from IT-performance data simulations. *International Journal of Knowledge Society Research*, 3(2), 13–29. doi:10.4018/jksr.2012040102

Philipson, G. (2011). A framework for green computing. *International Journal of Green Computing*, 2(1), 12–26. doi:10.4018/jgc.2011010102

Philipson, G. (2013). A framework for green computing. In K. Ganesh & S. Anbuudayasankar (Eds.), *International and interdisciplinary studies in green computing* (pp. 12–26). Hershey, PA: IGI Global. doi:10.4018/978-1-4666-2646-1.ch002

Phythian, M. (2013). The 'cloud' of unknowing – What a government cloud may and may not offer: A practitioner perspective. *International Journal of Technoethics*, 4(1), 1–10. doi:10.4018/jte.2013010101

Pym, D., & Sadler, M. (2012). Information stewardship in cloud computing. In *Grid and cloud computing: Concepts, methodologies, tools and applications* (pp. 185–202). Hershey, PA: IGI Global. doi:10.4018/978-1-4666-0879-5.ch109

Pym, D., & Sadler, M. (2012). Information stewardship in cloud computing. In S. Galup (Ed.), *Technological applications and advancements in service science, management, and engineering* (pp. 52–69). Hershey, PA: IGI Global. doi:10.4018/978-1-4666-1583-0.ch004

Qiu, J., Ekanayake, J., Gunarathne, T., Choi, J. Y., Bae, S., & Ruan, Y. … Tang, H. (2013). Data intensive computing for bioinformatics. In Bioinformatics: Concepts, methodologies, tools, and applications (pp. 287-321). Hershey, PA: IGI Global. doi:10.4018/978-1-4666-3604-0.ch016

Rabaey, M. (2012). A public economics approach to enabling enterprise architecture with the government cloud in Belgium. In P. Saha (Ed.), *Enterprise architecture for connected e-government: Practices and innovations* (pp. 467–493). Hershey, PA: IGI Global. doi:10.4018/978-1-4666-1824-4.ch020

Rabaey, M. (2013). A complex adaptive system thinking approach of government e-procurement in a cloud computing environment. In P. Ordóñez de Pablos, J. Lovelle, J. Gayo, & R. Tennyson (Eds.), *E-procurement management for successful electronic government systems* (pp. 193–219). Hershey, PA: IGI Global. doi:10.4018/978-1-4666-2119-0.ch013

Rabaey, M. (2013). Holistic investment framework for cloud computing: A management-philosophical approach based on complex adaptive systems. In A. Bento & A. Aggarwal (Eds.), *Cloud computing service and deployment models: Layers and management* (pp. 94–122). Hershey, PA: IGI Global. doi:10.4018/978-1-4666-2187-9.ch005

Rak, M., Ficco, M., Luna, J., Ghani, H., Suri, N., Panica, S., & Petcu, D. (2012). Security issues in cloud federations. In M. Villari, I. Brandic, & F. Tusa (Eds.), *Achieving federated and self-manageable cloud infrastructures: Theory and practice* (pp. 176–194). Hershey, PA: IGI Global. doi:10.4018/978-1-4666-1631-8.ch010

Ramanathan, R. (2013). Extending service-driven architectural approaches to the cloud. In R. Ramanathan & K. Raja (Eds.), *Service-driven approaches to architecture and enterprise integration* (pp. 334–359). Hershey, PA: IGI Global. doi:10.4018/978-1-4666-4193-8.ch013

Ramírez, M., Gutiérrez, A., Monguet, J. M., & Muñoz, C. (2012). An internet cost model, assignment of costs based on actual network use. *International Journal of Web Portals*, *4*(4), 19–34. doi:10.4018/jwp.2012100102

Rashid, A., Wang, W. Y., & Tan, F. B. (2013). Value co-creation in cloud services. In A. Lin, J. Foster, & P. Scifleet (Eds.), *Consumer information systems and relationship management: Design, implementation, and use* (pp. 74–91). Hershey, PA: IGI Global. doi:10.4018/978-1-4666-4082-5.ch005

Ratten, V. (2012). Cloud computing services: Theoretical foundations of ethical and entrepreneurial adoption behaviour. *International Journal of Cloud Applications and Computing, 2*(2), 48–58. doi:10.4018/ijcac.2012040105

Ratten, V. (2013). Exploring behaviors and perceptions affecting the adoption of cloud computing. *International Journal of Innovation in the Digital Economy, 4*(3), 51–68. doi:10.4018/jide.2013070104

Ravi, V. (2012). Cloud computing paradigm for indian education sector. *International Journal of Cloud Applications and Computing, 2*(2), 41–47. doi:10.4018/ijcac.2012040104

Rawat, A., Kapoor, P., & Sushil, R. (2014) Application of cloud computing in library information service sector. In S. Dhamdhere (Ed.), *Cloud computing and virtualization technologies in libraries* (pp. 77–89). Hershey, PA: IGI Global. doi:10.4018/978-1-4666-4631-5.ch005

Reich, C., Hübner, S., & Kuijs, H. (2012). Cloud computing for on-demand virtual desktops and labs. In L. Chao (Ed.), *Cloud computing for teaching and learning: strategies for design and implementation* (pp. 111–125). Hershey, PA: IGI Global. doi:10.4018/978-1-4666-0957-0.ch008

Rice, R. W. (2013). Testing in the cloud: Balancing the value and risks of cloud computing. In S. Tilley & T. Parveen (Eds.), *Software testing in the cloud: Perspectives on an emerging discipline* (pp. 404–416). Hershey, PA: IGI Global. doi:10.4018/978-1-4666-2536-5.ch019

Ruan, K. (2013). Designing a forensic-enabling cloud ecosystem. In K. Ruan (Ed.), *Cybercrime and cloud forensics: Applications for investigation processes* (pp. 331–344). Hershey, PA: IGI Global. doi:10.4018/978-1-4666-2662-1.ch014

Sabetzadeh, F., & Tsui, E. (2011). Delivering knowledge services in the cloud. *International Journal of Knowledge and Systems Science, 2*(4), 14–20. doi:10.4018/jkss.2011100102

Sabetzadeh, F., & Tsui, E. (2013). Delivering knowledge services in the cloud. In G. Yang (Ed.), *Multidisciplinary studies in knowledge and systems science* (pp. 247–254). Hershey, PA: IGI Global. doi:10.4018/978-1-4666-3998-0.ch017

Saedi, A., & Iahad, N. A. (2013). Future research on cloud computing adoption by small and medium-sized enterprises: A critical analysis of relevant theories. *International Journal of Actor-Network Theory and Technological Innovation, 5*(2), 1–16. doi:10.4018/jantti.2013040101

Saha, D., & Sridhar, V. (2011). Emerging areas of research in business data communications. *International Journal of Business Data Communications and Networking, 7*(4), 52–59. doi:10.4018/IJBDCN.2011100104

Saha, D., & Sridhar, V. (2013). Platform on platform (PoP) model for meta-networking: A new paradigm for networks of the future. *International Journal of Business Data Communications and Networking, 9*(1), 1–10. doi:10.4018/jbdcn.2013010101

Sahlin, J. P. (2013). Cloud computing: Past, present, and future. In X. Yang & L. Liu (Eds.), *Principles, methodologies, and service-oriented approaches for cloud computing* (pp. 19–50). Hershey, PA: IGI Global. doi:10.4018/978-1-4666-2854-0.ch002

Salama, M., & Shawish, A. (2012). Libraries: From the classical to cloud-based era. *International Journal of Digital Library Systems, 3*(3), 14–32. doi:10.4018/jdls.2012070102

Sánchez, C. M., Molina, D., Vozmediano, R. M., Montero, R. S., & Llorente, I. M. (2012). On the use of the hybrid cloud computing paradigm. In M. Villari, I. Brandic, & F. Tusa (Eds.), *Achieving federated and self-manageable cloud infrastructures: Theory and practice* (pp. 196–218). Hershey, PA: IGI Global. doi:10.4018/978-1-4666-1631-8.ch011

Sasikala, P. (2011). Architectural strategies for green cloud computing: Environments, infrastructure and resources. *International Journal of Cloud Applications and Computing, 1*(4), 1–24. doi:10.4018/ijcac.2011100101

Sasikala, P. (2011). Cloud computing in higher education: Opportunities and issues. *International Journal of Cloud Applications and Computing, 1*(2), 1–13. doi:10.4018/ijcac.2011040101

Sasikala, P. (2011). Cloud computing towards technological convergence. *International Journal of Cloud Applications and Computing, 1*(4), 44–59. doi:10.4018/ijcac.2011100104

Sasikala, P. (2012). Cloud computing and e-governance: Advances, opportunities and challenges. *International Journal of Cloud Applications and Computing, 2*(4), 32–52. doi:10.4018/ijcac.2012100103

Sasikala, P. (2012). Cloud computing in higher education: Opportunities and issues. In *Grid and cloud computing: Concepts, methodologies, tools and applications* (pp. 1672–1685). Hershey, PA: IGI Global. doi:10.4018/978-1-4666-0879-5.ch709

Sasikala, P. (2012). Cloud computing towards technological convergence. In *Grid and cloud computing: Concepts, methodologies, tools and applications* (pp. 1576–1592). Hershey, PA: IGI Global. doi:10.4018/978-1-4666-0879-5.ch703

Sasikala, P. (2013). Architectural strategies for green cloud computing: Environments, infrastructure and resources. In S. Aljawarneh (Ed.), *Cloud computing advancements in design, implementation, and technologies* (pp. 218–242). Hershey, PA: IGI Global. doi:10.4018/978-1-4666-1879-4.ch016

Sasikala, P. (2013). Cloud computing in higher education: Opportunities and issues. In S. Aljawarneh (Ed.), *Cloud computing advancements in design, implementation, and technologies* (pp. 83–96). Hershey, PA: IGI Global. doi:10.4018/978-1-4666-1879-4.ch006

Sasikala, P. (2013). Cloud computing towards technological convergence. In S. Aljawarneh (Ed.), *Cloud computing advancements in design, implementation, and technologies* (pp. 263–279). Hershey, PA: IGI Global. doi:10.4018/978-1-4666-1879-4.ch019

Sasikala, P. (2013). New media cloud computing: Opportunities and challenges. *International Journal of Cloud Applications and Computing*, *3*(2), 61–72. doi:10.4018/ijcac.2013040106

Schrödl, H., & Wind, S. (2013). Requirements engineering for cloud application development. In A. Bento & A. Aggarwal (Eds.), *Cloud computing service and deployment models: Layers and management* (pp. 137–150). Hershey, PA: IGI Global. doi:10.4018/978-1-4666-2187-9.ch007

Sclater, N. (2012). Legal and contractual issues of cloud computing for educational institutions. In L. Chao (Ed.), *Cloud computing for teaching and learning: Strategies for design and implementation* (pp. 186–199). Hershey, PA: IGI Global. doi:10.4018/978-1-4666-0957-0.ch013

Sen, J. (2014). Security and privacy issues in cloud computing. In A. Ruiz-Martinez, R. Marin-Lopez, & F. Pereniguez-Garcia (Eds.), *Architectures and protocols for secure information technology infrastructures* (pp. 1–45). Hershey, PA: IGI Global. doi:10.4018/978-1-4666-4514-1.ch001

Shah, B. (2013). Cloud environment controls assessment framework. In *IT policy and ethics: Concepts, methodologies, tools, and applications* (pp. 1822–1847). Hershey, PA: IGI Global. doi:10.4018/978-1-4666-2919-6.ch080

Shah, B. (2013). Cloud environment controls assessment framework. In S. Tilley & T. Parveen (Eds.), *Software testing in the cloud: Perspectives on an emerging discipline* (pp. 28–53). Hershey, PA: IGI Global. doi:10.4018/978-1-4666-2536-5. ch002

Shang, X., Zhang, R., & Chen, Y. (2012). Internet of things (IoT) service architecture and its application in e-commerce. *Journal of Electronic Commerce in Organizations*, *10*(3), 44–55. doi:10.4018/jeco.2012070104

Shankararaman, V., & Kit, L. E. (2013). Integrating the cloud scenarios and solutions. In A. Bento & A. Aggarwal (Eds.), *Cloud computing service and deployment models: Layers and management* (pp. 173–189). Hershey, PA: IGI Global. doi:10.4018/978-1-4666-2187-9.ch009

Sharma, A., & Maurer, F. (2013). A roadmap for software engineering for the cloud: Results of a systematic review. In X. Wang, N. Ali, I. Ramos, & R. Vidgen (Eds.), *Agile and lean service-oriented development: Foundations, theory, and practice* (pp. 48–63). Hershey, PA: IGI Global. doi:10.4018/978-1-4666-2503-7.ch003

Sharma, A., & Maurer, F. (2014). A roadmap for software engineering for the cloud: Results of a systematic review. In *Software design and development: Concepts, methodologies, tools, and applications* (pp. 1–16). Hershey, PA: IGI Global. doi:10.4018/978-1-4666-4301-7.ch001

Sharma, S. C., & Bagoria, H. (2014). Libraries and cloud computing models: A changing paradigm. In S. Dhamdhere (Ed.), *Cloud computing and virtualization technologies in libraries* (pp. 124–149). Hershey, PA: IGI Global. doi:10.4018/978-1-4666-4631-5.ch008

Shawish, A., & Salama, M. (2013). Cloud computing in academia, governments, and industry. In X. Yang & L. Liu (Eds.), *Principles, methodologies, and service-oriented approaches for cloud computing* (pp. 71–114). Hershey, PA: IGI Global. doi:10.4018/978-1-4666-2854-0.ch004

Shebanow, A., Perez, R., & Howard, C. (2012). The effect of firewall testing types on cloud security policies. *International Journal of Strategic Information Technology and Applications*, *3*(3), 60–68. doi:10.4018/jsita.2012070105

Sheikhalishahi, M., Devare, M., Grandinetti, L., & Incutti, M. C. (2012). A complementary approach to grid and cloud distributed computing paradigms. In *Grid and cloud computing: Concepts, methodologies, tools and applications* (pp. 1929–1942). Hershey, PA: IGI Global. doi:10.4018/978-1-4666-0879-5.ch811

Sheikhalishahi, M., Devare, M., Grandinetti, L., & Incutti, M. C. (2012). A complementary approach to grid and cloud distributed computing paradigms. In N. Preve (Ed.), *Computational and data grids: Principles, applications and design* (pp. 31–44). Hershey, PA: IGI Global. doi:10.4018/978-1-61350-113-9.ch002

Shen, Y., Li, Y., Wu, L., Liu, S., & Wen, Q. (2014). Cloud computing overview. In Y. Shen, Y. Li, L. Wu, S. Liu, & Q. Wen (Eds.), *Enabling the new era of cloud computing: Data security, transfer, and management* (pp. 1–24). Hershey, PA: IGI Global. doi:10.4018/978-1-4666-4801-2.ch001

Shen, Y., Li, Y., Wu, L., Liu, S., & Wen, Q. (2014). Main components of cloud computing. In Y. Shen, Y. Li, L. Wu, S. Liu, & Q. Wen (Eds.), *Enabling the new era of cloud computing: Data security, transfer, and management* (pp. 25–50). Hershey, PA: IGI Global. doi:10.4018/978-1-4666-4801-2.ch002

Shen, Y., Yang, J., & Keskin, T. (2014). Impact of cultural differences on the cloud computing ecosystems in the USA and China. In Y. Shen, Y. Li, L. Wu, S. Liu, & Q. Wen (Eds.), *Enabling the new era of cloud computing: Data security, transfer, and management* (pp. 269–283). Hershey, PA: IGI Global. doi:10.4018/978-1-4666-4801-2.ch014

Shetty, S., & Rawat, D. B. (2013). Cloud computing based cognitive radio networking. In N. Meghanathan & Y. Reddy (Eds.), *Cognitive radio technology applications for wireless and mobile ad hoc networks* (pp. 153–164). Hershey, PA: IGI Global. doi:10.4018/978-1-4666-4221-8.ch008

Shi, Z., & Beard, C. (2014). QoS in the mobile cloud computing environment. In J. Rodrigues, K. Lin, & J. Lloret (Eds.), *Mobile networks and cloud computing convergence for progressive services and applications* (pp. 200–217). Hershey, PA: IGI Global. doi:10.4018/978-1-4666-4781-7.ch011

Shuster, L. (2013). Enterprise integration: Challenges and solution architecture. In R. Ramanathan & K. Raja (Eds.), *Service-driven approaches to architecture and enterprise integration* (pp. 43–66). Hershey, PA: IGI Global. doi:10.4018/978-1-4666-4193-8.ch002

Siahos, Y., Papanagiotou, I., Georgopoulos, A., Tsamis, F., & Papaioannou, I. (2012). An architecture paradigm for providing cloud services in school labs based on open source software to enhance ICT in education. *International Journal of Cyber Ethics in Education*, 2(1), 44–57. doi:10.4018/ijcee.2012010105

Simon, E., & Estublier, J. (2013). Model driven integration of heterogeneous software artifacts in service oriented computing. In A. Ionita, M. Litoiu, & G. Lewis (Eds.), *Migrating legacy applications: Challenges in service oriented architecture and cloud computing environments* (pp. 332–360). Hershey, PA: IGI Global. doi:10.4018/978-1-4666-2488-7.ch014

Singh, J., & Kumar, V. (2013). Compliance and regulatory standards for cloud computing. In R. Khurana & R. Aggarwal (Eds.), *Interdisciplinary perspectives on business convergence, computing, and legality* (pp. 54–64). Hershey, PA: IGI Global. doi:10.4018/978-1-4666-4209-6.ch006

Singh, V. V. (2012). Software development using service syndication based on API handshake approach between cloud-based and SOA-based reusable services. In H. Yang & X. Liu (Eds.), *Software reuse in the emerging cloud computing era* (pp. 136–157). Hershey, PA: IGI Global. doi:10.4018/978-1-4666-0897-9.ch006

Smeitink, M., & Spruit, M. (2013). Maturity for sustainability in IT: Introducing the MITS. *International Journal of Information Technologies and Systems Approach*, 6(1), 39–56. doi:10.4018/jitsa.2013010103

Smith, P. A., & Cockburn, T. (2013). Socio-digital technologies. In *Dynamic leadership models for global business: Enhancing digitally connected environments* (pp. 142–168). Hershey, PA: IGI Global. doi:10.4018/978-1-4666-2836-6.ch006

Sneed, H. M. (2013). Testing web services in the cloud. In S. Tilley & T. Parveen (Eds.), *Software testing in the cloud: Perspectives on an emerging discipline* (pp. 136–173). Hershey, PA: IGI Global. doi:10.4018/978-1-4666-2536-5.ch007

Solomon, B., Ionescu, D., Gadea, C., & Litoiu, M. (2013). Geographically distributed cloud-based collaborative application. In A. Ionita, M. Litoiu, & G. Lewis (Eds.), *Migrating legacy applications: Challenges in service oriented architecture and cloud computing environments* (pp. 248–274). Hershey, PA: IGI Global. doi:10.4018/978-1-4666-2488-7.ch011

Song, W., & Xiao, Z. (2013). An infrastructure-as-a-service cloud: On-demand resource provisioning. In X. Yang & L. Liu (Eds.), *Principles, methodologies, and service-oriented approaches for cloud computing* (pp. 302–324). Hershey, PA: IGI Global. doi:10.4018/978-1-4666-2854-0.ch013

Sood, S. K. (2013). A value based dynamic resource provisioning model in cloud. *International Journal of Cloud Applications and Computing, 3*(1), 1–12. doi:10.4018/ijcac.2013010101

Sotiriadis, S., Bessis, N., & Antonopoulos, N. (2012). Exploring inter-cloud load balancing by utilizing historical service submission records. *International Journal of Distributed Systems and Technologies, 3*(3), 72–81. doi:10.4018/jdst.2012070106

Soyata, T., Ba, H., Heinzelman, W., Kwon, M., & Shi, J. (2014). Accelerating mobile-cloud computing: A survey. In H. Mouftah & B. Kantarci (Eds.), *Communication infrastructures for cloud computing* (pp. 175–197). Hershey, PA: IGI Global. doi:10.4018/978-1-4666-4522-6.ch008

Spyridopoulos, T., & Katos, V. (2011). Requirements for a forensically ready cloud storage service. *International Journal of Digital Crime and Forensics, 3*(3), 19–36. doi:10.4018/jdcf.2011070102

Spyridopoulos, T., & Katos, V. (2013). Data recovery strategies for cloud environments. In K. Ruan (Ed.), *Cybercrime and cloud forensics: Applications for investigation processes* (pp. 251–265). Hershey, PA: IGI Global. doi:10.4018/978-1-4666-2662-1.ch010

Srinivasa, K. G, S, H. R. C., H, M. K. S., & Venkatesh, N. (2012). MeghaOS: A framework for scalable, interoperable cloud based operating system. *International Journal of Cloud Applications and Computing, 2*(1), 53–70. doi:10.4018/ijcac.2012010104

Stantchev, V., & Stantcheva, L. (2012). Extending traditional IT-governance knowledge towards SOA and cloud governance. *International Journal of Knowledge Society Research, 3*(2), 30–43. doi:10.4018/jksr.2012040103

Stantchev, V., & Tamm, G. (2012). Reducing information asymmetry in cloud marketplaces. *International Journal of Human Capital and Information Technology Professionals, 3*(4), 1–10. doi:10.4018/jhcitp.2012100101

Steinbuß, S., & Weißenberg, N. (2013). Service design and process design for the logistics mall cloud. In X. Yang & L. Liu (Eds.), *Principles, methodologies, and service-oriented approaches for cloud computing* (pp. 186–206). Hershey, PA: IGI Global. doi:10.4018/978-1-4666-2854-0.ch008

Stender, J., Berlin, M., & Reinefeld, A. (2013). XtreemFS: A file system for the cloud. In D. Kyriazis, A. Voulodimos, S. Gogouvitis, & T. Varvarigou (Eds.), *Data intensive storage services for cloud environments* (pp. 267–285). Hershey, PA: IGI Global. doi:10.4018/978-1-4666-3934-8.ch016

Sticklen, D. J., & Issa, T. (2011). An initial examination of free and proprietary software-selection in organizations. *International Journal of Web Portals*, *3*(4), 27–43. doi:10.4018/jwp.2011100103

Sun, Y., White, J., Gray, J., & Gokhale, A. (2012). Model-driven automated error recovery in cloud computing. In *Grid and cloud computing: Concepts, methodologies, tools and applications* (pp. 680–700). Hershey, PA: IGI Global. doi:10.4018/978-1-4666-0879-5.ch308

Sun, Z., Yang, Y., Zhou, Y., & Cruickshank, H. (2014). Agent-based resource management for mobile cloud. In J. Rodrigues, K. Lin, & J. Lloret (Eds.), *Mobile networks and cloud computing convergence for progressive services and applications* (pp. 118–134). Hershey, PA: IGI Global. doi:10.4018/978-1-4666-4781-7.ch007

Sutherland, S. (2013). Convergence of interoperability of cloud computing, service oriented architecture and enterprise architecture. *International Journal of E-Entrepreneurship and Innovation*, *4*(1), 43–51. doi:10.4018/jeei.2013010104

Takabi, H., & Joshi, J. B. (2013). Policy management in cloud: Challenges and approaches. In D. Rosado, D. Mellado, E. Fernandez-Medina, & M. Piattini (Eds.), *Security engineering for cloud computing: Approaches and tools* (pp. 191–211). Hershey, PA: IGI Global. doi:10.4018/978-1-4666-2125-1.ch010

Takabi, H., & Joshi, J. B. (2013). Policy management in cloud: Challenges and approaches. In *IT policy and ethics: Concepts, methodologies, tools, and applications* (pp. 814–834). Hershey, PA: IGI Global. doi:10.4018/978-1-4666-2919-6.ch037

Takabi, H., Joshi, J. B., & Ahn, G. (2013). Security and privacy in cloud computing: Towards a comprehensive framework. In X. Yang & L. Liu (Eds.), *Principles, methodologies, and service-oriented approaches for cloud computing* (pp. 164–184). Hershey, PA: IGI Global. doi:10.4018/978-1-4666-2854-0.ch007

Takabi, H., Zargar, S. T., & Joshi, J. B. (2014). Mobile cloud computing and its security and privacy challenges. In D. Rawat, B. Bista, & G. Yan (Eds.), *Security, privacy, trust, and resource management in mobile and wireless communications* (pp. 384–407). Hershey, PA: IGI Global. doi:10.4018/978-1-4666-4691-9.ch016

Teixeira, C., Pinto, J. S., Ferreira, F., Oliveira, A., Teixeira, A., & Pereira, C. (2013). Cloud computing enhanced service development architecture for the living usability lab. In R. Martinho, R. Rijo, M. Cruz-Cunha, & J. Varajão (Eds.), *Information systems and technologies for enhancing health and social care* (pp. 33–53). Hershey, PA: IGI Global. doi:10.4018/978-1-4666-3667-5.ch003

Thimm, H. (2012). Cloud-based collaborative decision making: Design considerations and architecture of the GRUPO-MOD system. *International Journal of Decision Support System Technology*, *4*(4), 39–59. doi:10.4018/jdsst.2012100103

Thomas, P. (2012). Harnessing the potential of cloud computing to transform higher education. In L. Chao (Ed.), *Cloud computing for teaching and learning: Strategies for design and implementation* (pp. 147–158). Hershey, PA: IGI Global. doi:10.4018/978-1-4666-0957-0.ch010

Toka, A., Aivazidou, E., Antoniou, A., & Arvanitopoulos-Darginis, K. (2013). Cloud computing in supply chain management: An overview. In D. Graham, I. Manikas, & D. Folinas (Eds.), *E-logistics and e-supply chain management: Applications for evolving business* (pp. 218–231). Hershey, PA: IGI Global. doi:10.4018/978-1-4666-3914-0.ch012

Torrealba, S. M., Morales, P. M., Campos, J. M., & Meza, S. M. (2013). A software tool to support risks analysis about what should or should not go to the cloud. In D. Rosado, D. Mellado, E. Fernandez-Medina, & M. Piattini (Eds.), *Security engineering for cloud computing: Approaches and tools* (pp. 72–96). Hershey, PA: IGI Global. doi:10.4018/978-1-4666-2125-1.ch005

Trivedi, M., & Suthar, V. (2013). Cloud computing: A feasible platform for ICT enabled health science libraries in India. *International Journal of User-Driven Healthcare*, *3*(2), 69–77. doi:10.4018/ijudh.2013040108

Truong, H., Pham, T., Thoai, N., & Dustdar, S. (2012). Cloud computing for education and research in developing countries. In L. Chao (Ed.), *Cloud computing for teaching and learning: Strategies for design and implementation* (pp. 64–80). Hershey, PA: IGI Global. doi:10.4018/978-1-4666-0957-0.ch005

Tsirmpas, C., Giokas, K., Iliopoulou, D., & Koutsouris, D. (2012). Magnetic resonance imaging and magnetic resonance spectroscopy cloud computing framework. *International Journal of Reliable and Quality E-Healthcare*, *1*(4), 1–12. doi:10.4018/ijrqeh.2012100101

Turner, H., White, J., Reed, J., Galindo, J., Porter, A., Marathe, M., ... Gokhale, A. (2013). Building a cloud-based mobile application testbed. In *IT policy and ethics: Concepts, methodologies, tools, and applications* (pp. 879–899). Hershey, PA: IGI Global. doi:10.4018/978-1-4666-2919-6.ch040

Turner, H., White, J., Reed, J., Galindo, J., Porter, A., Marathe, M., ... Gokhale, A. (2013). Building a cloud-based mobile application testbed. In S. Tilley & T. Parveen (Eds.), *Software testing in the cloud: Perspectives on an emerging discipline* (pp. 382–403). Hershey, PA: IGI Global. doi:10.4018/978-1-4666-2536-5.ch018

Tusa, F., Paone, M., & Villari, M. (2012). CLEVER: A cloud middleware beyond the federation. In M. Villari, I. Brandic, & F. Tusa (Eds.), *Achieving federated and self-manageable cloud infrastructures: Theory and practice* (pp. 219–241). Hershey, PA: IGI Global. doi:10.4018/978-1-4666-1631-8.ch012

Udoh, E. (2012). Technology acceptance model applied to the adoption of grid and cloud technology. *International Journal of Grid and High Performance Computing*, *4*(1), 1–20. doi:10.4018/jghpc.2012010101

Vannoy, S. A. (2011). A structured content analytic assessment of business services advertisements in the cloud-based web services marketplace. *International Journal of Dependable and Trustworthy Information Systems*, *2*(1), 18–49. doi:10.4018/jdtis.2011010102

Vaquero, L. M., Cáceres, J., & Morán, D. (2011). The challenge of service level scalability for the cloud. *International Journal of Cloud Applications and Computing*, *1*(1), 34–44. doi:10.4018/ijcac.2011010103

Vaquero, L. M., Cáceres, J., & Moran, D. (2013). The challenge of service level scalability for the cloud. In S. Aljawarneh (Ed.), *Cloud computing advancements in design, implementation, and technologies* (pp. 37–48). Hershey, PA: IGI Global. doi:10.4018/978-1-4666-1879-4.ch003

Venkatraman, R., Venkatraman, S., & Asaithambi, S. P. (2013). A practical cloud services implementation framework for e-businesses. In K. Tarnay, S. Imre, & L. Xu (Eds.), *Research and development in e-business through service-oriented solutions* (pp. 167–198). Hershey, PA: IGI Global. doi:10.4018/978-1-4666-4181-5.ch008

Venkatraman, S. (2013). Software engineering research gaps in the cloud. *Journal of Information Technology Research*, *6*(1), 1–19. doi:10.4018/jitr.2013010101

Vijaykumar, S., Rajkarthick, K. S., & Priya, J. (2012). Innovative business opportunities and smart business management techniques from green cloud TPS. *International Journal of Asian Business and Information Management*, *3*(4), 62–72. doi:10.4018/jabim.2012100107

Wang, C., Lam, K. T., & Ma, K. R. K. (2012). A computation migration approach to elasticity of cloud computing. In J. Abawajy, M. Pathan, M. Rahman, A. Pathan, & M. Deris (Eds.) Network and traffic engineering in emerging distributed computing applications (pp. 145-178). Hershey, PA: IGI Global. doi:10.4018/978-1-4666-1888-6.ch007

Related References

Wang, D., & Wu, J. (2014). Carrier-grade distributed cloud computing: Demands, challenges, designs, and future perspectives. In H. Mouftah & B. Kantarci (Eds.), *Communication infrastructures for cloud computing* (pp. 264–281). Hershey, PA: IGI Global. doi:10.4018/978-1-4666-4522-6.ch012

Wang, H., & Philips, D. (2012). Implement virtual programming lab with cloud computing for web-based distance education. In L. Chao (Ed.), *Cloud computing for teaching and learning: Strategies for design and implementation* (pp. 95–110). Hershey, PA: IGI Global. doi:10.4018/978-1-4666-0957-0.ch007

Warneke, D. (2013). Ad-hoc parallel data processing on pay-as-you-go clouds with nephele. In A. Loo (Ed.), *Distributed computing innovations for business, engineering, and science* (pp. 191–218). Hershey, PA: IGI Global. doi:10.4018/978-1-4666-2533-4.ch010

Wei, Y., & Blake, M. B. (2013). Adaptive web services monitoring in cloud environments. *International Journal of Web Portals*, *5*(1), 15–27. doi:10.4018/jwp.2013010102

White, S. C., Sedigh, S., & Hurson, A. R. (2013). Security concepts for cloud computing. In X. Yang & L. Liu (Eds.), *Principles, methodologies, and service-oriented approaches for cloud computing* (pp. 116–142). Hershey, PA: IGI Global. doi:10.4018/978-1-4666-2854-0.ch005

Williams, A. J. (2013). The role of emerging technologies in developing and sustaining diverse suppliers in competitive markets. In *Enterprise resource planning: Concepts, methodologies, tools, and applications* (pp. 1550–1560). Hershey, PA: IGI Global. doi:10.4018/978-1-4666-4153-2.ch082

Williams, A. J. (2013). The role of emerging technologies in developing and sustaining diverse suppliers in competitive markets. In J. Lewis, A. Green, & D. Surry (Eds.), *Technology as a tool for diversity leadership: Implementation and future implications* (pp. 95–105). Hershey, PA: IGI Global. doi:10.4018/978-1-4666-2668-3.ch007

Wilson, L., Goh, T. T., & Wang, W. Y. (2012). Big data management challenges in a meteorological organisation. *International Journal of E-Adoption*, *4*(2), 1–14. doi:10.4018/jea.2012040101

Wu, R., Ahn, G., & Hu, H. (2012). Towards HIPAA-compliant healthcare systems in cloud computing. *International Journal of Computational Models and Algorithms in Medicine*, *3*(2), 1–22. doi:10.4018/jcmam.2012040101

Xiao, J., Wang, M., Wang, L., & Zhu, X. (2013). Design and implementation of C-iLearning: A cloud-based intelligent learning system. *International Journal of Distance Education Technologies, 11*(3), 79–97. doi:10.4018/jdet.2013070106

Xing, R., Wang, Z., & Peterson, R. L. (2011). Redefining the information technology in the 21st century. *International Journal of Strategic Information Technology and Applications, 2*(1), 1–10. doi:10.4018/jsita.2011010101

Xu, L., Huang, D., Tsai, W., & Atkinson, R. K. (2012). V-lab: A mobile, cloud-based virtual laboratory platform for hands-on networking courses. *International Journal of Cyber Behavior, Psychology and Learning, 2*(3), 73–85. doi:10.4018/ijcbpl.2012070106

Xu, Y., & Mao, S. (2014). Mobile cloud media: State of the art and outlook. In J. Rodrigues, K. Lin, & J. Lloret (Eds.), *Mobile networks and cloud computing convergence for progressive services and applications* (pp. 18–38). Hershey, PA: IGI Global. doi:10.4018/978-1-4666-4781-7.ch002

Xu, Z., Yan, B., & Zou, Y. (2013). Beyond hadoop: Recent directions in data computing for internet services. In S. Aljawarneh (Ed.), *Cloud computing advancements in design, implementation, and technologies* (pp. 49–66). Hershey, PA: IGI Global. doi:10.4018/978-1-4666-1879-4.ch004

Yan, Z. (2014). Trust management in mobile cloud computing. In *Trust management in mobile environments: Autonomic and usable models* (pp. 54–93). Hershey, PA: IGI Global. doi:10.4018/978-1-4666-4765-7.ch004

Yang, D. X. (2012). QoS-oriented service computing: Bringing SOA into cloud environment. In X. Liu & Y. Li (Eds.), *Advanced design approaches to emerging software systems: Principles, methodologies and tools* (pp. 274–296). Hershey, PA: IGI Global. doi:10.4018/978-1-60960-735-7.ch013

Yang, H., Huff, S. L., & Tate, M. (2013). Managing the cloud for information systems agility. In A. Bento & A. Aggarwal (Eds.), *Cloud computing service and deployment models: Layers and management* (pp. 70–93). Hershey, PA: IGI Global. doi:10.4018/978-1-4666-2187-9.ch004

Yang, M., Kuo, C., & Yeh, Y. (2011). Dynamic rightsizing with quality-controlled algorithms in virtualization environments. *International Journal of Grid and High Performance Computing, 3*(2), 29–43. doi:10.4018/jghpc.2011040103

Yang, X. (2012). QoS-oriented service computing: Bringing SOA into cloud environment. In *Grid and cloud computing: Concepts, methodologies, tools and applications* (pp. 1621–1643). Hershey, PA: IGI Global. doi:10.4018/978-1-4666-0879-5.ch706

Yang, Y., Chen, J., & Hu, H. (2012). The convergence between cloud computing and cable TV. *International Journal of Technology Diffusion*, *3*(2), 1–11. doi:10.4018/jtd.2012040101

Yassein, M. O., Khamayseh, Y. M., & Hatamleh, A. M. (2013). Intelligent randomize round robin for cloud computing. *International Journal of Cloud Applications and Computing*, *3*(1), 27–33. doi:10.4018/ijcac.2013010103

Yau, S. S., An, H. G., & Buduru, A. B. (2012). An approach to data confidentiality protection in cloud environments. *International Journal of Web Services Research*, *9*(3), 67–83. doi:10.4018/jwsr.2012070104

Yu, W. D., Adiga, A. S., Rao, S., & Panakkel, M. J. (2012). A SOA based system development methodology for cloud computing environment: Using uhealthcare as practice. *International Journal of E-Health and Medical Communications*, *3*(4), 42–63. doi:10.4018/jehmc.2012100104

Yu, W. D., & Bhagwat, R. (2011). Modeling emergency and telemedicine heath support system: A service oriented architecture approach using cloud computing. *International Journal of E-Health and Medical Communications*, *2*(3), 63–88. doi:10.4018/jehmc.2011070104

Yu, W. D., & Bhagwat, R. (2013). Modeling emergency and telemedicine health support system: A service oriented architecture approach using cloud computing. In J. Rodrigues (Ed.), *Digital advances in medicine, e-health, and communication technologies* (pp. 187–213). Hershey, PA: IGI Global. doi:10.4018/978-1-4666-2794-9.ch011

Yuan, D., Lewandowski, C., & Zhong, J. (2012). Developing a private cloud based IP telephony laboratory and curriculum. In L. Chao (Ed.), *Cloud computing for teaching and learning: Strategies for design and implementation* (pp. 126–145). Hershey, PA: IGI Global. doi:10.4018/978-1-4666-0957-0.ch009

Yuvaraj, M. (2014). Cloud libraries: Issues and challenges. In S. Dhamdhere (Ed.), *Cloud computing and virtualization technologies in libraries* (pp. 316–338). Hershey, PA: IGI Global. doi:10.4018/978-1-4666-4631-5.ch018

Zaman, M., Simmers, C. A., & Anandarajan, M. (2013). Using an ethical framework to examine linkages between "going green" in research practices and information and communication technologies. In B. Medlin (Ed.), *Integrations of technology utilization and social dynamics in organizations* (pp. 243–262). Hershey, PA: IGI Global. doi:10.4018/978-1-4666-1948-7.ch015

Zapata, B. C., & Alemán, J. L. (2013). Security risks in cloud computing: An analysis of the main vulnerabilities. In D. Rosado, D. Mellado, E. Fernandez-Medina, & M. Piattini (Eds.), *Security engineering for cloud computing: Approaches and tools* (pp. 55–71). Hershey, PA: IGI Global. doi:10.4018/978-1-4666-2125-1.ch004

Zapata, B. C., & Alemán, J. L. (2014). Security risks in cloud computing: An analysis of the main vulnerabilities. In *Software design and development: Concepts, methodologies, tools, and applications* (pp. 936–952). Hershey, PA: IGI Global. doi:10.4018/978-1-4666-4301-7.ch045

Zardari, S., Faniyi, F., & Bahsoon, R. (2013). Using obstacles for systematically modeling, analysing, and mitigating risks in cloud adoption. In I. Mistrik, A. Tang, R. Bahsoon, & J. Stafford (Eds.), *Aligning enterprise, system, and software architectures* (pp. 275–296). Hershey, PA: IGI Global. doi:10.4018/978-1-4666-2199-2.ch014

Zech, P., Kalb, P., Felderer, M., & Breu, R. (2013). Threatening the cloud: Securing services and data by continuous, model-driven negative security testing. In S. Tilley & T. Parveen (Eds.), *Software testing in the cloud: Perspectives on an emerging discipline* (pp. 280–304). Hershey, PA: IGI Global. doi:10.4018/978-1-4666-2536-5.ch013

Zhang, F., Cao, J., Cai, H., & Wu, C. (2011). Provisioning virtual resources adaptively in elastic compute cloud platforms. *International Journal of Web Services Research*, *8*(3), 54–69. doi:10.4018/jwsr.2011070103

Zhang, G., Li, C., Xue, S., Liu, Y., Zhang, Y., & Xing, C. (2012). A new electronic commerce architecture in the cloud. *Journal of Electronic Commerce in Organizations*, *10*(4), 42–56. doi:10.4018/jeco.2012100104

Zhang, J., Yao, J., Chen, S., & Levy, D. (2011). Facilitating biodefense research with mobile-cloud computing. *International Journal of Systems and Service-Oriented Engineering*, *2*(3), 18–31. doi:10.4018/jssoe.2011070102

Related References

Zhang, J., Yao, J., Chen, S., & Levy, D. (2013). Facilitating biodefense research with mobile-cloud computing. In D. Chiu (Ed.), *Mobile and web innovations in systems and service-oriented engineering* (pp. 318–332). Hershey, PA: IGI Global. doi:10.4018/978-1-4666-2470-2.ch017

Zheng, S., Chen, F., Yang, H., & Li, J. (2013). An approach to evolving legacy software system into cloud computing environment. In X. Yang & L. Liu (Eds.), *Principles, methodologies, and service-oriented approaches for cloud computing* (pp. 207–229). Hershey, PA: IGI Global. doi:10.4018/978-1-4666-2854-0.ch009

Zhou, J., Athukorala, K., Gilman, E., Riekki, J., & Ylianttila, M. (2012). Cloud architecture for dynamic service composition. *International Journal of Grid and High Performance Computing, 4*(2), 17–31. doi:10.4018/jghpc.2012040102

Compilation of References

Aalmink, J., von der Dovenmühle, T., & Gómez, J. M. (2013). Enterprise tomography: Maintenance and root-cause-analysis of federated erp in enterprise clouds. In P. Ordóñez de Pablos, H. Nigro, R. Tennyson, S. Gonzalez Cisaro, & W. Karwowski (Eds.), *Advancing information management through semantic web concepts and ontologies* (pp. 133–153). Hershey, PA: IGI Global. doi:10.4018/978-1-4666-2494-8.ch007

Abbasimehr, H., Tarokh, M. J., & Setak, M. (2011). Determination of Algorithms Making Balance Between Accuracy and Comprehensibility in Churn Prediction Setting. *International Journal of Information Retrieval Research, 1*(2), 39–54. doi:10.4018/IJIRR.2011040103

Abdullah-Al-Wadud, M., Kabir, M. H., Dewan, M. A. A., & Chae, O. (2007). A dynamic histogram equalization for image contrast enhancement. *IEEE Transactions on Consumer Electronics, 53*(2), 593–600. doi:10.1109/TCE.2007.381734

Abu, S. T., & Tsuji, M. (2011). The development of ICT for envisioning cloud computing and innovation in South Asia. *International Journal of Innovation in the Digital Economy, 2*(1), 61–72. doi:10.4018/jide.2011010105

Abu, S. T., & Tsuji, M. (2012). The development of ICT for envisioning cloud computing and innovation in South Asia. In *Grid and cloud computing: Concepts, methodologies, tools and applications* (pp. 453–465). Hershey, PA: IGI Global. doi:10.4018/978-1-4666-0879-5.ch207

Abu, S. T., & Tsuji, M. (2013). The development of ICT for envisioning cloud computing and innovation in South Asia. In I. Oncioiu (Ed.), *Business innovation, development, and advancement in the digital economy* (pp. 35–47). Hershey, PA: IGI Global. doi:10.4018/978-1-4666-2934-9.ch003

Acharjya, D. P., & Kauser, A. P. (2015). Swarm Intelligence in Solving Bio-Inspired Computing Problems: Reviews, Perspectives, and Challenges. In S. Bhattacharyya & P. Dutta (Eds.), *Handbook of Research on Swarm Intelligence in Engineering* (pp. 74–98). Hershey, PA: Engineering Science Reference; doi:10.4018/978-1-4666-8291-7.ch003

Adams, R. (2013). The emergence of cloud storage and the need for a new digital forensic process model. In K. Ruan (Ed.), *Cybercrime and cloud forensics: Applications for investigation processes* (pp. 79–104). Hershey, PA: IGI Global. doi:10.4018/978-1-4666-2662-1.ch004

Adeyeye, M. (2013). Provisioning converged applications and services via the cloud. In D. Kanellopoulos (Ed.), *Intelligent multimedia technologies for networking applications: Techniques and tools* (pp. 248–269). Hershey, PA: IGI Global. doi:10.4018/978-1-4666-2833-5.ch010

Adhikari, R., & Agrawal, R. K. (2013). Hybridization of Artificial Neural Network and Particle Swarm Optimization Methods for Time Series Forecasting. *International Journal of Applied Evolutionary Computation, 4*(3), 75–90. doi:10.4018/jaec.2013070107

Afify, A. (2013). Intelligent Computation for Manufacturing. In Z. Li & A. Al-Ahmari (Eds.), *Formal Methods in Manufacturing Systems: Recent Advances* (pp. 211–246). Hershey, PA: Engineering Science Reference; doi:10.4018/978-1-4666-4034-4.ch009

Afzal, W., Torkar, R., & Feldt, R. (2009). A systematic review of search-based testing for non-functional system properties. *Information and Software Technology, 51*(6), 957–976. doi:10.1016/j.infsof.2008.12.005

Aggarwal, A. (2013). A systems approach to cloud computing services. In A. Bento & A. Aggarwal (Eds.), *Cloud computing service and deployment models: Layers and management* (pp. 124–136). Hershey, PA: IGI Global. doi:10.4018/978-1-4666-2187-9.ch006

Agosta, L. (2000). *The Essential Guide to Data Warehousing*. Upper Saddle River, NJ: Prentice Hall.

Ahmed, K., Hussain, A., & Gregory, M. A. (2013). An efficient, robust, and secure SSO architecture for cloud computing implemented in a service oriented architecture. In X. Yang & L. Liu (Eds.), *Principles, methodologies, and service-oriented approaches for cloud computing* (pp. 259–282). Hershey, PA: IGI Global. doi:10.4018/978-1-4666-2854-0.ch011

Ahuja, S. P., & Mani, S. (2013). Empirical performance analysis of HPC benchmarks across variations in cloud computing. *International Journal of Cloud Applications and Computing, 3*(1), 13–26. doi:10.4018/ijcac.2013010102

Ahuja, S. P., & Rolli, A. C. (2011). Survey of the state-of-the-art of cloud computing. *International Journal of Cloud Applications and Computing, 1*(4), 34–43. doi:10.4018/ijcac.2011100103

Ahuja, S. P., & Rolli, A. C. (2013). Survey of the state-of-the-art of cloud computing. In S. Aljawarneh (Ed.), *Cloud computing advancements in design, implementation, and technologies* (pp. 252–262). Hershey, PA: IGI Global. doi:10.4018/978-1-4666-1879-4.ch018

Ahuja, S. P., & Sridharan, S. (2012). Performance evaluation of hypervisors for cloud computing. *International Journal of Cloud Applications and Computing, 2*(3), 26–67. doi:10.4018/ijcac.2012070102

Akyuz, G. A., & Rehan, M. (2013). A generic, cloud-based representation for supply chains (SC's). *International Journal of Cloud Applications and Computing, 3*(2), 12–20. doi:10.4018/ijcac.2013040102

Alam, S., Dobbie, G., Koh, Y. S., & Rehman, S. U. (2014). Biologically Inspired Techniques for Data Mining: A Brief Overview of Particle Swarm Optimization for KDD. In S. Alam, G. Dobbie, Y. Koh, & S. ur Rehman (Eds.), Biologically-Inspired Techniques for Knowledge Discovery and Data Mining (pp. 1-10). Hershey, PA: Information Science Reference. doi:10.4018/978-1-4666-6078-6.ch001

Alam, N., & Karmakar, R. (2014). Cloud computing and its application to information centre. In S. Dhamdhere (Ed.), *Cloud computing and virtualization technologies in libraries* (pp. 63–76). Hershey, PA: IGI Global. doi:10.4018/978-1-4666-4631-5.ch004

Al-Aqrabi, H., & Liu, L. (2013). IT security and governance compliant service oriented computing in cloud computing environments. In X. Yang & L. Liu (Eds.), *Principles, methodologies, and service-oriented approaches for cloud computing* (pp. 143–163). Hershey, PA: IGI Global. doi:10.4018/978-1-4666-2854-0.ch006

Aleksander, I., & Morton, H. (1995). *An introduction to neural computing.* International Thompson Computer Press.

Alfaro, V. M., & Vilanova, R. (2012). Optimal robust tuning for 1DoF PI/PID control unifying FOPDT/SOPDT models. *IFAC Proceedings Volumes, 45*(3), 572-577.

Alfaro, V. M., Vilanova, R., & Arrieta, O. (2009). Robust tuning of two-degree-of-freedom (2-DoF) PI/PID based cascade control systems. *Journal of Process Control, 19*(10), 1658–1670. doi:10.1016/j.jprocont.2009.08.006

Alhaj, A., Aljawarneh, S., Masadeh, S., & Abu-Taieh, E. (2013). A secure data transmission mechanism for cloud outsourced data. *International Journal of Cloud Applications and Computing, 3*(1), 34–43. doi:10.4018/ijcac.2013010104

Alharbi, S. T. (2012). Users' acceptance of cloud computing in Saudi Arabia: An extension of technology acceptance model. *International Journal of Cloud Applications and Computing, 2*(2), 1–11. doi:10.4018/ijcac.2012040101

Ali, H., & Khan, F. A. (2013). Attributed multi-objective comprehensive learning particle swarm optimization for optimal security of networks. *Applied Soft Computing, 13*(9), 3903–3921. doi:10.1016/j.asoc.2013.04.015

Alippi, C. (2003). A Perturbation Size-Independent Analysis of Robustness in Neural Networks by Randomized Algorithms. In M. Mohammadian, R. Sarker, & X. Yao (Eds.), *Computational Intelligence in Control* (pp. 22–40). Hershey, PA: Idea Group Publishing; doi:10.4018/978-1-59140-037-0.ch002

Ali, S. S., & Khan, M. N. (2013). ICT infrastructure framework for microfinance institutions and banks in Pakistan: An optimized approach. *International Journal of Online Marketing, 3*(2), 75–86. doi:10.4018/ijom.2013040105

Ali, S., Briand, L. C., Hemmati, H., & Panesar-Walawege, R. K. (2009). A systematic review of the application and empirical investigation of search-based test-case generation. *IEEE Transactions on Software Engineering*, *99*(1).

Aljawarneh, S. (2011). Cloud security engineering: Avoiding security threats the right way. *International Journal of Cloud Applications and Computing*, *1*(2), 64–70. doi:10.4018/ijcac.2011040105

Aljawarneh, S. (2013). Cloud security engineering: Avoiding security threats the right way. In S. Aljawarneh (Ed.), *Cloud computing advancements in design, implementation, and technologies* (pp. 147–153). Hershey, PA: IGI Global. doi:10.4018/978-1-4666-1879-4.ch010

Almeida, F., & Santos, M. (2014). A Conceptual Framework for Big Data Analysis. In I. Portela & F. Almeida (Eds.), *Organizational, Legal, and Technological Dimensions of Information System Administration* (pp. 199–223). Hershey, PA: Information Science Reference; doi:10.4018/978-1-4666-4526-4.ch011

Alpert, J. S. (2016). The electronic medical record in 2016: Advantages and disadvantages. *Digital Media*, *2*(2), 48–51. doi:10.4103/2226-8561.189504

Alshattnawi, S. (2013). Utilizing cloud computing in developing a mobile location-aware tourist guide system. *International Journal of Advanced Pervasive and Ubiquitous Computing*, *5*(2), 9–18. doi:10.4018/japuc.2013040102

Alsmadi, I. (2013). Software development methodologies for cloud computing. In K. Buragga & N. Zaman (Eds.), *Software development techniques for constructive information systems design* (pp. 110–117). Hershey, PA: IGI Global. doi:10.4018/978-1-4666-3679-8.ch006

Al-Zoube, M., & Wyne, M. F. (2012). Building integrated e-learning environment using cloud services and social networking sites. In Q. Jin (Ed.), *Intelligent learning systems and advancements in computer-aided instruction: Emerging studies* (pp. 214–233). Hershey, PA: IGI Global. doi:10.4018/978-1-61350-483-3.ch013

Anagnostopoulos, C., & Hadjiefthymiades, S. (2012). Swarm Intelligence in Autonomic Computing: The Particle Swarm Optimization Case. In P. Cong-Vinh (Ed.), *Formal and Practical Aspects of Autonomic Computing and Networking: Specification, Development, and Verification* (pp. 97–117). Hershey, PA: Information Science Reference; doi:10.4018/978-1-60960-845-3.ch004

Anand, S., Burke, E. K., Chen, T. Y., Clark, J., Cohen, M. B., Grieskamp, W., ... Mcminn, P. (2013). An orchestrated survey of methodologies for automated software test case generation. *Journal of Systems and Software*, *86*(8), 1978–2001. doi:10.1016/j.jss.2013.02.061

Anand, V. (2013). Survivable mapping of virtual networks onto a shared substrate network. In X. Yang & L. Liu (Eds.), *Principles, methodologies, and service-oriented approaches for cloud computing* (pp. 325–343). Hershey, PA: IGI Global. doi:10.4018/978-1-4666-2854-0.ch014

Antonova, A. (2013). Green, sustainable, or clean: What type of IT/IS technologies will we need in the future? In P. Ordóñez de Pablos (Ed.), *Green technologies and business practices: An IT approach* (pp. 151–162). Hershey, PA: IGI Global. doi:10.4018/978-1-4666-1972-2.ch008

Aoki, M. (1987). *State Space Modeling of Time Series*. Springer-Verlag. doi:10.1007/978-3-642-96985-0

Arcuri, A. (2008). On the automation of fixing software bugs. In *ICSE companion '08: Companion of the 30th international conference on software engineering* (pp. 1003–1006). New York, NY: ACM. doi:10.1145/1370175.1370223

Arcuri, A. (2009). *Automatic software generation and improvement through search based techniques* (Doctoral dissertation). University of Birmingham.

Arcuri, A., & Fraser, G. (2014). On the Effectiveness of Whole Test Suite Generation. In Lecture Notes in Computer Science (pp. 1–15). Academic Press. doi:10.1007/978-3-319-09940-8_1

Arcuri, A., & Yao, X. (2007a). Coevolving programs and unit tests from their specification. In *ASE '07: Proceedings of the twenty-second IEEE/ACM international conference on automated software engineering* (pp. 397–400). New York, NY: ACM. doi:10.1145/1321631.1321693

Arcuri, A., & Yao, X. (2007c). On test data generation of object-oriented software. In *Taicpart-mutation '07: Proceedings of the testing: Academic and industrial conference practice and research techniques - mutation* (pp. 72–76). Washington, DC: IEEE Computer Society. doi:10.1109/TAIC.PART.2007.11

Arcuri, A., & Yao, X. (2007d). *Search based testing of containers for object-oriented software* (Tech. Rep. No. CSR-07-3). University of Birmingham, School of Computer Science.

Arcuri, A., & Yao, X. (2008a). A novel co-evolutionary approach to automatic software bug fixing. In *Proceedings of the IEEE congress on evolutionary computation (CEC '08)* (p. 162-168). IEEE Computer Society. doi:10.1109/CEC.2008.4630793

Arcuri, A., White, D. R., Clark, J., & Yao, X. (2008). Multi-objective improvement of software using co-evolution and smart seeding. In *Proceedings of the 7th international conference on simulated evolution and learning (seal '08)* (p. 61-70). Springer. doi:10.1007/978-3-540-89694-4_7

Arcuri, A., & Yao, X. (2007b). A memetic algorithm for test data generation of object-oriented software. In *Proceedings of the 2007 ieee congress on evolutionary computation (CEC)* (p. 2048-2055). IEEE. doi:10.1109/CEC.2007.4424725

Arcuri, A., & Yao, X. (2008b). Search based software testing of object-oriented containers. *Information Sciences*, *178*(15), 3075–3095. doi:10.1016/j.ins.2007.11.024

Ardissono, L., Bosio, G., Goy, A., Petrone, G., Segnan, M., & Torretta, F. (2011). Collaboration support for activity management in a personal cloud environment. *International Journal of Distributed Systems and Technologies*, *2*(4), 30–43. doi:10.4018/jdst.2011100103

Ardissono, L., Bosio, G., Goy, A., Petrone, G., Segnan, M., & Torretta, F. (2013). Collaboration support for activity management in a personal cloud environment. In N. Bessis (Ed.), *Development of distributed systems from design to application and maintenance* (pp. 199–212). Hershey, PA: IGI Global. doi:10.4018/978-1-4666-2647-8.ch012

Argiolas, M., Atzori, M., Dessì, N., & Pes, B. (2012). Dataspaces enhancing decision support systems in clouds. *International Journal of Web Portals*, *4*(2), 35–55. doi:10.4018/jwp.2012040103

Arinze, B., & Anandarajan, M. (2012). Factors that determine the adoption of cloud computing: A global perspective. In M. Tavana (Ed.), *Enterprise Information Systems and Advancing Business Solutions: Emerging Models* (pp. 210–223). Hershey, PA: IGI Global. doi:10.4018/978-1-4666-1761-2.ch012

Arinze, B., & Sylla, C. (2012). Conducting research in the cloud. In L. Chao (Ed.), *Cloud computing for teaching and learning: Strategies for design and implementation* (pp. 50–63). Hershey, PA: IGI Global. doi:10.4018/978-1-4666-0957-0.ch004

Arora, V., & Ravi, V. (2013). Data Mining using Advanced Ant Colony Optimization Algorithm and Application to Bankruptcy Prediction. *International Journal of Information Systems and Social Change*, *4*(3), 33–56. doi:10.4018/jissc.2013070103

Arshad, J., Townend, P., & Xu, J. (2011). An abstract model for integrated intrusion detection and severity analysis for clouds. *International Journal of Cloud Applications and Computing*, *1*(1), 1–16. doi:10.4018/ijcac.2011010101

Arshad, J., Townend, P., & Xu, J. (2013). An abstract model for integrated intrusion detection and severity analysis for clouds. In S. Aljawarneh (Ed.), *Cloud computing advancements in design, implementation, and technologies* (pp. 1–17). Hershey, PA: IGI Global. doi:10.4018/978-1-4666-1879-4.ch001

Arshad, J., Townend, P., Xu, J., & Jie, W. (2012). Cloud computing security: Opportunities and pitfalls. *International Journal of Grid and High Performance Computing*, *4*(1), 52–66. doi:10.4018/jghpc.2012010104

Åström, K. J., & Hägglund, T. (1995). *PID controllers: Theory, design, and tuning*. Research Triangle Park, NC: ISA Publishers.

Ayala, F. J. K., & John, A. (1984). *Genética moderna* (No. 575.1 A9Y). Academic Press.

Baars, T., & Spruit, M. (2012). Designing a secure cloud architecture: The SeCA model. *International Journal of Information Security and Privacy*, *6*(1), 14–32. doi:10.4018/jisp.2012010102

Babahajyani, P., Habibi, F., & Bevrani, H. (2014). An On-Line PSO-Based Fuzzy Logic Tuning Approach: Microgrid Frequency Control Case Study. In P. Vasant (Ed.), *Handbook of Research on Novel Soft Computing Intelligent Algorithms: Theory and Practical Applications* (pp. 589–616). Hershey, PA: Information Science Reference; doi:10.4018/978-1-4666-4450-2.ch020

Bai, X., Gao, J. Z., & Tsai, W. (2013). Cloud scalability measurement and testing. In S. Tilley & T. Parveen (Eds.), *Software testing in the cloud: Perspectives on an emerging discipline* (pp. 356–381). Hershey, PA: IGI Global. doi:10.4018/978-1-4666-2536-5.ch017

Bakshi, K. (2014). Technologies for Big Data. In W. Hu & N. Kaabouch (Eds.), *Big Data Management, Technologies, and Applications* (pp. 1–22). Hershey, PA: Information Science Reference; doi:10.4018/978-1-4666-4699-5.ch001

Baldini, G., & Stirparo, P. (2014). A cognitive access framework for security and privacy protection in mobile cloud computing. In J. Rodrigues, K. Lin, & J. Lloret (Eds.), *Mobile networks and cloud computing convergence for progressive services and applications* (pp. 92–117). Hershey, PA: IGI Global. doi:10.4018/978-1-4666-4781-7.ch006

Balduf, S., Balke, T., & Eymann, T. (2012). Cultural differences in managing cloud computing service level agreements. In *Grid and cloud computing: Concepts, methodologies, tools and applications* (pp. 1237–1263). Hershey, PA: IGI Global. doi:10.4018/978-1-4666-0879-5.ch512

Banerjee, S., Sing, T. Y., Chowdhury, A. R., & Anwar, H. (2013). Motivations to adopt green ICT: A tale of two organizations. *International Journal of Green Computing, 4*(2), 1–11. doi:10.4018/jgc.2013070101

Bang, J., Dholakia, N., Hamel, L., & Shin, S. (2009). Customer Relationship Management and Knowledge Discovery in Database. In J. Erickson (Ed.), *Database Technologies: Concepts, Methodologies, Tools, and Applications* (pp. 1778–1786). Hershey, PA: Information Science Reference; doi:10.4018/978-1-60566-058-5.ch107

Banks, A., Vincent, J., & Anyakoha, C. (2008). A review of particle swarm optimization. Part II: Hybridisation, combinatorial, multicriteria and constrained optimization, and indicative applications. *Natural Computing, 7*(1), 109–124. doi:10.1007/s11047-007-9050-z

Banta, D. (2003). The development of health technology assessment. *Health Policy (Amsterdam), 63*(2), 121–132. doi:10.1016/S0168-8510(02)00059-3 PMID:12543525

Barbey, S., & Strohmeier, A. (1994). The problematics of testing object-oriented software. In M. Ross, C. A. Brebbia, G. Staples, & J. Stapleton (Eds.), *SQM'94 second conference on software quality management* (Vol. 2, pp. 411–426). Academic Press.

Baresi, L., & Miraz, M. (2010). Testful: automatic unit-test generation for java classes. In *Proceedings of the 32nd ACM/IEEE international conference on software engineering - volume 2* (pp. 281–284). New York, NY: ACM. doi:10.1145/1810295.1810353

Baresi, L., Lanzi, P. L., & Miraz, M. (2010). Testful: An evolutionary test approach for java. In *Proceedings of the 2010 third international conference on software testing, verification and validation* (pp. 185–194). Washington, DC: IEEE Computer Society. doi:10.1109/ICST.2010.54

Barreto, G. (2002). *Modelagem computacional distribuída e paralela de sistemas e de séries temporais multivariáveis no espaço de estado* (PhD thesis). Universidade Estadual de Campinas.

Barreto, J., Di Sanzo, P., Palmieri, R., & Romano, P. (2013). Cloud-TM: An elastic, self-tuning transactional store for the cloud. In D. Kyriazis, A. Voulodimos, S. Gogouvitis, & T. Varvarigou (Eds.), *Data intensive storage services for cloud environments* (pp. 192–224). Hershey, PA: IGI Global. doi:10.4018/978-1-4666-3934-8.ch013

Beitiger, J., Johnson, W., Bivens, H., Humphreys, S., & Rhea, R. (2000). Constructing the ASCI Grid. *Proc. 9th IEEE Symposium on High Performance Distributed Computing.*

Beizer, B. (1990). *Software testing techniques.* New York: John Wiley & Sons, Inc.

Belalem, G., & Limam, S. (2011). Fault tolerant architecture to cloud computing using adaptive checkpoint. *International Journal of Cloud Applications and Computing, 1*(4), 60–69. doi:10.4018/ijcac.2011100105

Belalem, G., & Limam, S. (2013). Fault tolerant architecture to cloud computing using adaptive checkpoint. In S. Aljawarneh (Ed.), *Cloud computing advancements in design, implementation, and technologies* (pp. 280–289). Hershey, PA: IGI Global. doi:10.4018/978-1-4666-1879-4.ch020

Ben Belgacem, M., Abdennadher, N., & Niinimaki, M. (2012). Virtual EZ grid: A volunteer computing infrastructure for scientific medical applications. *International Journal of Handheld Computing Research, 3*(1), 74–85. doi:10.4018/jhcr.2012010105

Berry, J. A. M. Linoff Gordon, (2000). Mastering data mining. John Wiley &Sons Inc.

Berry, J. A. M., & Linoff, G. (1997). *Data mining techniques for marketing sales and customer support.* John Wiley &Sons Inc.

Berryman, A. (2002). *Population Cycles: The Case for Trophic Interactions.* Oxford, UK: Oxford University Press.

Bertolino, A. (2007). Software testing research: Achievements, challenges, dreams. In *Fose '07: 2007 future of software engineering* (pp. 85–103). Washington, DC: IEEE Computer Society.

Betti, M., Facchini, L., & Biagini, P. (2015). Damage detection on a three-storey steel frame using artificial neural networks and genetic algorithms. *Meccanica, 50*(3), 875–886. doi:10.1007/s11012-014-0085-9

Bhatt, S., Chaudhary, S., & Bhise, M. (2013). Migration of data between cloud and non-cloud datastores. In A. Ionita, M. Litoiu, & G. Lewis (Eds.), *Migrating legacy applications: Challenges in service oriented architecture and cloud computing environments* (pp. 206–225). Hershey, PA: IGI Global. doi:10.4018/978-1-4666-2488-7.ch009

Biancofiore, G., & Leone, S. (2014). Google apps as a cloud computing solution in Italian municipalities: Technological features and implications. In S. Leone (Ed.), *Synergic integration of formal and informal e-learning environments for adult lifelong learners* (pp. 244–274). Hershey, PA: IGI Global. doi:10.4018/978-1-4666-4655-1.ch012

Bibi, S., Katsaros, D., & Bozanis, P. (2012). How to choose the right cloud. In *Grid and cloud computing: Concepts, methodologies, tools and applications* (pp. 1530–1552). Hershey, PA: IGI Global. doi:10.4018/978-1-4666-0879-5.ch701

Bibi, S., Katsaros, D., & Bozanis, P. (2012). How to choose the right cloud. In X. Liu & Y. Li (Eds.), *Advanced design approaches to emerging software systems: Principles, methodologies and tools* (pp. 219–240). Hershey, PA: IGI Global. doi:10.4018/978-1-60960-735-7.ch010

Bitam, S., Batouche, M., & Talbi, E. (2012). A bees life algorithm for cloud computing services selection. In S. Ali, N. Abbadeni, & M. Batouche (Eds.), *Multidisciplinary computational intelligence techniques: Applications in business, engineering, and medicine* (pp. 31–46). Hershey, PA: IGI Global. doi:10.4018/978-1-4666-1830-5.ch003

Bittencourt, L. F., Madeira, E. R., & da Fonseca, N. L. (2014). Communication aspects of resource management in hybrid clouds. In H. Mouftah & B. Kantarci (Eds.), *Communication infrastructures for cloud computing* (pp. 409–433). Hershey, PA: IGI Global. doi:10.4018/978-1-4666-4522-6.ch018

Bodaly, R. A., Clayton, J. W., Lindsey, C. C., & Vuorinen, J. (1992). Evolution of Lake Whitefish (Coregonus clupeaformis) in North America during the Pleistocene: Genetic Differentiation between Sympatric Populations. *Canadian Journal of Fisheries and Aquatic Sciences, 49*(4), 769–779. doi:10.1139/f92-086

Boeringer, D. W., & Werner, D. H. (2003). A comparison of particle swarm optimization and genetic algorithms for a phased array synthesis problem. *IEEE International Symposium on Antennas and Propagation*, 181-184. doi:10.1109/APS.2003.1217430

Bohl, A. H., & McAvoy, T. J. (1976). Linear feedback vs. time optima control. II. The regulator problem. *Industrial & Engineering Chemistry Process Design and Development, 15*(1), 30–33. doi:10.1021/i260057a007

Bonelli, L., Giudicianni, L., Immediata, A., & Luzzi, A. (2013). Compliance in the cloud. In D. Kyriazis, A. Voulodimos, S. Gogouvitis, & T. Varvarigou (Eds.), *Data intensive storage services for cloud environments* (pp. 109–131). Hershey, PA: IGI Global. doi:10.4018/978-1-4666-3934-8.ch008

Boniface, M., Nasser, B., Surridge, M., & Oliveros, E. (2012). Securing real-time interactive applications in federated clouds. In *Grid and cloud computing: Concepts, methodologies, tools and applications* (pp. 1822–1835). Hershey, PA: IGI Global. doi:10.4018/978-1-4666-0879-5.ch806

Bonyadi, M. R., Michalewicz, Z., & Li, X. (2014). An analysis of the velocity updating rule of the particle swarm optimization algorithm. *Journal of Heuristics, 20*(4), 417–452. doi:10.1007/s10732-014-9245-2

Booch, G., Maksimchuk, R. A., Engel, M. W., Young, B. J., Conallen, J., & Houston, K. A. (2007). *Object-oriented analysis and design with applications* (3rd ed.). Addison-Wesley Professional.

Boukhobza, J. (2013). Flashing in the cloud: Shedding some light on NAND flash memory storage systems. In D. Kyriazis, A. Voulodimos, S. Gogouvitis, & T. Varvarigou (Eds.), *Data intensive storage services for cloud environments* (pp. 241–266). Hershey, PA: IGI Global. doi:10.4018/978-1-4666-3934-8.ch015

Boussaa, M., Barais, O., Sunye, G., & Baudry, B. (2015). A Novelty Search Approach for Automatic Test Data Generation. *2015 IEEE/ACM 8th International Workshop on Search-Based Software Testing*. doi:10.1109/SBST.2015.17

Bowman, S. (2013). Impact of electronic health record systems on information integrity: Quality and safety implications. *Perspectives in Health Information Management*, *10*(Fall), 1c. PMID:24159271

Bracci, F., Corradi, A., & Foschini, L. (2014). Cloud standards: Security and interoperability issues. In H. Mouftah & B. Kantarci (Eds.), *Communication infrastructures for cloud computing* (pp. 465–495). Hershey, PA: IGI Global. doi:10.4018/978-1-4666-4522-6.ch020

BrankeJ. (2007). *KIT*. Retrieved from http://www.aifb.uni-karlsruhe.de/ ~jbr/MovPeaks/

Brent, R., & Bruck, J. (2006). Can computers help to explain biology? *Nature*, *440*(7083), 416–417. doi:10.1038/440416a PMID:16554784

Brown, A. W. (2013). Experiences with cloud technology to realize software testing factories. In S. Tilley & T. Parveen (Eds.), *Software testing in the cloud: Perspectives on an emerging discipline* (pp. 1–27). Hershey, PA: IGI Global. doi:10.4018/978-1-4666-2536-5.ch001

Brown, J. H., & Lomolino, M. V. (2006). *Biogeography*. Sinauer Associates.

Bryson, A. J. R., & Carrier, A. (1989). A comparison of control synthesis using differential games (H-infinity) and LQR. In *Guidance, Navigation and Control Conference* (p. 3598). Academic Press.

Buezas, F. S., Rosales, M. B., & Filipich, C. P. (2011). Damage detection with genetic algorithms taking into account a crack contact model. *Engineering Fracture Mechanics*, *78*(4), 695–712. doi:10.1016/j.engfracmech.2010.11.008

Bürger, R., & Lande, R. (1994). On the distribution of the mean and variance of a quantitative trait under mutation-selection-drift balance. *Genetics*, *138*, 901–912. PMID:7851784

Calcavecchia, N. M., Celesti, A., & Di Nitto, E. (2012). Understanding decentralized and dynamic brokerage in federated cloud environments. In M. Villari, I. Brandic, & F. Tusa (Eds.), *Achieving federated and self-manageable cloud infrastructures: Theory and practice* (pp. 36–56). Hershey, PA: IGI Global. doi:10.4018/978-1-4666-1631-8.ch003

Calero, J. M., König, B., & Kirschnick, J. (2012). Cross-layer monitoring in cloud computing. In H. Rashvand & Y. Kavian (Eds.), *Using cross-layer techniques for communication systems* (pp. 328–348). Hershey, PA: IGI Global. doi:10.4018/978-1-4666-0960-0.ch014

Caponetto, R., Fortuna, L., Fazzino, S., & Xibilia, M. G. (2003). Chaotic Sequences to Improve the Performance of Evolutionary Algorithms. *IEEE Transactions on Evolutionary Computation*, 7(3), 289–304. doi:10.1109/TEVC.2003.810069

Cardellini, V., Casalicchio, E., & Silvestri, L. (2012). Service level provisioning for cloud-based applications service level provisioning for cloud-based applications. In *Grid and cloud computing: Concepts, methodologies, tools and applications* (pp. 1479–1500). Hershey, PA: IGI Global. doi:10.4018/978-1-4666-0879-5.ch611

Cardellini, V., Casalicchio, E., & Silvestri, L. (2012). Service level provisioning for cloud-based applications service level provisioning for cloud-based applications. In A. Pathan, M. Pathan, & H. Lee (Eds.), *Advancements in distributed computing and internet technologies: Trends and issues* (pp. 363–385). Hershey, PA: IGI Global. doi:10.4018/978-1-61350-110-8.ch017

Carlin, S., & Curran, K. (2013). Cloud computing security. In K. Curran (Ed.), *Pervasive and ubiquitous technology innovations for ambient intelligence environments* (pp. 12–17). Hershey, PA: IGI Global. doi:10.4018/978-1-4666-2041-4.ch002

Carlton, G. H., & Zhou, H. (2011). A survey of cloud computing challenges from a digital forensics perspective. *International Journal of Interdisciplinary Telecommunications and Networking*, 3(4), 1–16. doi:10.4018/jitn.2011100101

Carlton, G. H., & Zhou, H. (2012). A survey of cloud computing challenges from a digital forensics perspective. In *Grid and cloud computing: Concepts, methodologies, tools and applications* (pp. 1221–1236). Hershey, PA: IGI Global. doi:10.4018/978-1-4666-0879-5.ch511

Carlton, G. H., & Zhou, H. (2013). A survey of cloud computing challenges from a digital forensics perspective. In M. Bartolacci & S. Powell (Eds.), *Advancements and innovations in wireless communications and network technologies* (pp. 213–228). Hershey, PA: IGI Global. doi:10.4018/978-1-4666-2154-1.ch016

Carpen-Amarie, A., Costan, A., Leordeanu, C., Basescu, C., & Antoniu, G. (2012). Towards a generic security framework for cloud data management environments. *International Journal of Distributed Systems and Technologies*, 3(1), 17–34. doi:10.4018/jdst.2012010102

Casola, V., Cuomo, A., Villano, U., & Rak, M. (2012). Access control in federated clouds: The cloudgrid case study. In M. Villari, I. Brandic, & F. Tusa (Eds.), *Achieving Federated and Self-Manageable Cloud Infrastructures: Theory and Practice* (pp. 395–417). Hershey, PA: IGI Global. doi:10.4018/978-1-4666-1631-8.ch020

Casola, V., Cuomo, A., Villano, U., & Rak, M. (2013). Access control in federated clouds: The cloudgrid case study. In *IT policy and ethics: Concepts, methodologies, tools, and applications* (pp. 148–169). Hershey, PA: IGI Global. doi:10.4018/978-1-4666-2919-6.ch008

Castro, L. N. D. (2007). Fundamentals of natural computing: An overview. *Physics of Life Reviews*, 4(1), 1–36. doi:10.1016/j.plrev.2006.10.002

Celesti, A., Tusa, F., & Villari, M. (2012). Toward cloud federation: Concepts and challenges. In M. Villari, I. Brandic, & F. Tusa (Eds.), *Achieving federated and self-manageable cloud infrastructures: Theory and practice* (pp. 1–17). Hershey, PA: IGI Global. doi:10.4018/978-1-4666-1631-8.ch001

Chaka, C. (2013). Virtualization and cloud computing: Business models in the virtual cloud. In A. Loo (Ed.), *Distributed computing innovations for business, engineering, and science* (pp. 176–190). Hershey, PA: IGI Global. doi:10.4018/978-1-4666-2533-4.ch009

Chang, C. S., Chen, S. Y., & Lan, Y. T. (2012). Motivating medical information system performance by system quality, service quality, and job satisfaction for evidence-based practice. *BMC Medical Informatics and Decision Making*, *12*(1), 135. doi:10.1186/1472-6947-12-135 PMID:23171394

Chang, J. (2011). A framework for analysing the impact of cloud computing on local government in the UK. *International Journal of Cloud Applications and Computing*, *1*(4), 25–33. doi:10.4018/ijcac.2011100102

Chang, J. (2013). A framework for analysing the impact of cloud computing on local government in the UK. In S. Aljawarneh (Ed.), *Cloud computing advancements in design, implementation, and technologies* (pp. 243–251). Hershey, PA: IGI Global. doi:10.4018/978-1-4666-1879-4.ch017

Chang, J., & Johnston, M. (2012). Cloud computing in local government: From the perspective of four London borough councils. *International Journal of Cloud Applications and Computing*, *2*(4), 1–15. doi:10.4018/ijcac.2012100101

Chang, K., & Wang, K. (2012). Efficient support of streaming videos through patching proxies in the cloud. *International Journal of Grid and High Performance Computing*, *4*(4), 22–36. doi:10.4018/jghpc.2012100102

Chang, R., Liao, C., & Liu, C. (2013). Choosing clouds for an enterprise: Modeling and evaluation. *International Journal of E-Entrepreneurship and Innovation*, *4*(2), 38–53. doi:10.4018/ijeei.2013040103

Chang, V., De Roure, D., Wills, G., & Walters, R. J. (2011). Case studies and organisational sustainability modelling presented by cloud computing business framework. *International Journal of Web Services Research*, *8*(3), 26–53. doi:10.4018/JWSR.2011070102

Chang, V., Li, C., De Roure, D., Wills, G., Walters, R. J., & Chee, C. (2011). The financial clouds review. *International Journal of Cloud Applications and Computing*, *1*(2), 41–63. doi:10.4018/ijcac.2011040104

Chang, V., Li, C., De Roure, D., Wills, G., Walters, R. J., & Chee, C. (2013). The financial clouds review. In S. Aljawarneh (Ed.), *Cloud computing advancements in design, implementation, and technologies* (pp. 125–146). Hershey, PA: IGI Global. doi:10.4018/978-1-4666-1879-4.ch009

Chang, V., Walters, R. J., & Wills, G. (2012). Business integration as a service. *International Journal of Cloud Applications and Computing*, *2*(1), 16–40. doi:10.4018/ijcac.2012010102

Chang, V., & Wills, G. (2013). A University of Greenwich case study of cloud computing: Education as a service. In D. Graham, I. Manikas, & D. Folinas (Eds.), *E-logistics and e-supply chain management: Applications for evolving business* (pp. 232–253). Hershey, PA: IGI Global. doi:10.4018/978-1-4666-3914-0.ch013

Chang, V., Wills, G., Walters, R. J., & Currie, W. (2012). Towards a structured cloud ROI: The University of Southampton cost-saving and user satisfaction case studies. In W. Hu & N. Kaabouch (Eds.), *Sustainable ICTs and management systems for green computing* (pp. 179–200). Hershey, PA: IGI Global. doi:10.4018/978-1-4666-1839-8.ch008

Chang, W. D., & Yan, J. J. (2004). Optimum setting of PID controllers based on using evolutionary programming algorithm. *Zhongguo Gongcheng Xuekan*, *27*(3), 439–442. doi:10.1080/025338 39.2004.9670890

Chang, Y., Lee, Y., Juang, T., & Yen, J. (2013). Cost evaluation on building and operating cloud platform. *International Journal of Grid and High Performance Computing*, *5*(2), 43–53. doi:10.4018/jghpc.2013040103

Chao, L. (2012). Cloud computing solution for internet based teaching and learning. In L. Chao (Ed.), *Cloud computing for teaching and learning: Strategies for design and implementation* (pp. 210–235). Hershey, PA: IGI Global. doi:10.4018/978-1-4666-0957-0.ch015

Chao, L. (2012). Overview of cloud computing and its application in e-learning. In L. Chao (Ed.), *Cloud computing for teaching and learning: Strategies for design and implementation* (pp. 1–16). Hershey, PA: IGI Global. doi:10.4018/978-1-4666-0957-0.ch001

Chatman, C. (2010). How cloud computing is changing the face of health care information technology. *Journal of Health Care Compliance*, *12*(3), 37–70.

Chauhan, S., Raman, A., & Singh, N. (2013). A comparative cost analysis of on premises IT infrastructure and cloud-based email services in an Indian business school. *International Journal of Cloud Applications and Computing*, *3*(2), 21–34. doi:10.4018/ijcac.2013040103

Chawla, P., Chana, I., & Rana, A. (2015). A novel strategy for automatic test data generation using soft computing technique. *Frontiers of Computer Science*, *9*(3), 346–363. doi:10.1007/s11704-014-3496-9

Chen, S. D., & Ramli, A. R. (2003). *Contrast Enhancement using Recursive Mean Separated Histogram Equalization for Scalable Brightness Preservation*. Academic Press.

Chen, C. C. (2013). Cloud computing in case-based pedagogy: An information systems success perspective. *International Journal of Dependable and Trustworthy Information Systems*, *2*(3), 1–16. doi:10.4018/jdtis.2011070101

Chen, C., Chao, H., Wu, T., Fan, C., Chen, J., Chen, Y., & Hsu, J. (2011). IoT-IMS communication platform for future internet. *International Journal of Adaptive, Resilient and Autonomic Systems*, *2*(4), 74–94. doi:10.4018/jaras.2011100105

Chen, C., Chao, H., Wu, T., Fan, C., Chen, J., Chen, Y., & Hsu, J. (2013). IoT-IMS communication platform for future internet. In V. De Florio (Ed.), *Innovations and approaches for resilient and adaptive systems* (pp. 68–86). Hershey, PA: IGI Global. doi:10.4018/978-1-4666-2056-8.ch004

Cheney, A. W., Riedl, R. E., Sanders, R., & Tashner, J. H. (2012). The new company water cooler: Use of 3D virtual immersive worlds to promote networking and professional learning in organizations. In Organizational learning and knowledge: Concepts, methodologies, tools and applications (pp. 2848-2861). Hershey, PA: IGI Global. doi:10.4018/978-1-60960-783-8.ch801

Cheng, H. D., & Shi, J. (2004). A simple and effective histogram equalization approach to image enhancement. *Digital Signal Processing*, *14*(2), 158–170. doi:10.1016/j.dsp.2003.07.002

Cheng, S., Shi, Y., & Qin, Q. (2013). A Study of Normalized Population Diversity in Particle Swarm Optimization. *International Journal of Swarm Intelligence Research*, *4*(1), 1–34. doi:10.4018/jsir.2013010101

Chen, S. D., & Ramli, A. R. (2003). Minimum Mean Brightness Error Bi-Histogram Equalization in Contrast Enhancement. *IEEE Transactions on Consumer Electronics*, *49*(4), 1310–1319. doi:10.1109/TCE.2003.1261234

Chen, S. D., & Ramli, A. R. (2004). Preserving Brightness in histogram equalization based contrast enhancement techniques. *Digital Signal Processing*, *14*(5), 413–428. doi:10.1016/j.dsp.2004.04.001

Cheon, Y., & Kim, M. (2006). A specification-based fitness function for evolutionary testing of object-oriented programs. In *Gecco '06: Proceedings of the 8th annual conference on genetic and evolutionary computation* (pp. 1953–1954). New York: ACM. doi:10.1145/1143997.1144322

Cheon, Y., Kim, M., & Perumandla, A. (2005). A complete automation of unit testing for java programs. In H. R. Arabnia & H. Reza (Eds.), *Proceedings of the international conference on software engineering research and practice, SERP 2005* (vol. 1, pp. 290–295). CSREA Press.

Chiang, C., & Yu, S. (2013). Cloud-enabled software testing based on program understanding. In S. Tilley & T. Parveen (Eds.), *Software testing in the cloud: Perspectives on an emerging discipline* (pp. 54–67). Hershey, PA: IGI Global. doi:10.4018/978-1-4666-2536-5.ch003

Chisari, C., Bedon, C., & Amadio, C. (2015). Dynamic and static identification of base-isolated bridges using genetic algorithms. *Engineering Structures*, *102*(11), 80–92. doi:10.1016/j.engstruct.2015.07.043

Chou, J., & Ghaboussi, J. (2001). Genetic algorithm in structural damage detection. *Computers & Structures*, *79*(14), 1335–1353. doi:10.1016/S0045-7949(01)00027-X

Chou, Y., & Oetting, J. (2011). Risk assessment for cloud-based IT systems. *International Journal of Grid and High Performance Computing*, *3*(2), 1–13. doi:10.4018/jghpc.2011040101

Chou, Y., & Oetting, J. (2012). Risk assessment for cloud-based IT systems. In *Grid and cloud computing: Concepts, methodologies, tools and applications* (pp. 272–285). Hershey, PA: IGI Global. doi:10.4018/978-1-4666-0879-5.ch113

Chou, Y., & Oetting, J. (2013). Risk assessment for cloud-based IT systems. In E. Udoh (Ed.), *Applications and developments in grid, cloud, and high performance computing* (pp. 1–14). Hershey, PA: IGI Global. doi:10.4018/978-1-4666-2065-0.ch001

Civicioglu, P., & Besdok, E. (2013). A conceptual comparison of the cuckoo-search, particle swarm optimization, differential evolution and artificial bee colony algorithms. *Artificial Intelligence Review, 39*(4), 315–346. doi:10.1007/s10462-011-9276-0

Clamp, S., & Keen, J. (2007). Electronic health records: Is the evidence base any use? *Medical Informatics and the Internet in Medicine, 32*(1), 5–10. doi:10.1080/14639230601097903 PMID:17365639

Clerc, M. (1999). The swarm and the queen: towards a deterministic and adaptive particle swarm optimization. *Evolutionary Computation, 1999. CEC 99. Proceedings of the 1999 Congress on.* doi:10.1109/CEC.1999.785513

Clerck, M. (2013). *Particle Swarm Optimization*. London: Iste.

Clerc, M., & Kennedy, J. (2002). The particle swarm - explosion, stability, and convergence in a multidimensional complex space. *Trans. Evol. Comp, 6*(1), 58–73. doi:10.1109/4235.985692

Cody-Kenny, B., Galván-López, E., & Barrett, S. (2015). locoGP: Improving Performance by Genetic Programming Java Source Code. In *Proceedings of the Companion Publication of the 2015 on Genetic and Evolutionary Computation Conference - GECCO Companion '15* (pp. 811–818). New York: ACM Press.

Coelho, L. D. S., Sauer, J. G., & Rudek, M. (2009). Differential evolution optimization combined with chaotic sequences for image contrast enhancement. *Chaos, Solitons, and Fractals, 42*(1), 522–529. doi:10.1016/j.chaos.2009.01.012

Coelho, L. S., & Mariani, V. C. (2008). Use of chaotic sequences in a biologically inspired algorithm for engineering design optimization. *Expert Systems with Applications, 34*(3), 1905–1913. doi:10.1016/j.eswa.2007.02.002

Cohen, F. (2013). Challenges to digital forensic evidence in the cloud. In K. Ruan (Ed.), *Cybercrime and cloud forensics: Applications for investigation processes* (pp. 59–78). Hershey, PA: IGI Global. doi:10.4018/978-1-4666-2662-1.ch003

Cohen, I. R. (2000). *Tending Adam's garden: evolving the cognitive immune self*. London, UK: Academic Press.

Cohen, I. R. (2009). Real and artificial immune systems: computing the state of the body, Nature Reviews: Immunology. *Nature Reviews. Immunology, 7*(07), 569–574. doi:10.1038/nri2102 PMID:17558422

Cohen, I. R., & Harel, D. (2007). Explaining a complex living system: Dynamics, multi-scaling and emergence. *Journal of the Royal Society, Interface, 4*(13), 175–182. doi:10.1098/rsif.2006.0173 PMID:17251153

Cossu, R., Di Giulio, C., Brito, F., & Petcu, D. (2013). Cloud computing for earth observation. In D. Kyriazis, A. Voulodimos, S. Gogouvitis, & T. Varvarigou (Eds.), *Data intensive storage services for cloud environments* (pp. 166–191). Hershey, PA: IGI Global. doi:10.4018/978-1-4666-3934-8.ch012

Costa, J. E., & Rodrigues, J. J. (2014). Mobile cloud computing: Technologies, services, and applications. In J. Rodrigues, K. Lin, & J. Lloret (Eds.), *Mobile networks and cloud computing convergence for progressive services and applications* (pp. 1–17). Hershey, PA: IGI Global. doi:10.4018/978-1-4666-4781-7.ch001

Cox, C. B., & Moore, P. D. (2010). *Biogeography - An Ecological and Evolutionary Approach.* Wiley.

Coyne, J. A., & Orr, H. A. (1999). The evolutionary genetics of speciation. In A. E. Magurran & R. M. May (Eds.), *Evolution of Biological Diversity.* Oxford University Press.

Creaner, G., & Pahl, C. (2013). Flexible coordination techniques for dynamic cloud service collaboration. In G. Ortiz & J. Cubo (Eds.), *Adaptive web services for modular and reusable software development: Tactics and solutions* (pp. 239–252). Hershey, PA: IGI Global. doi:10.4018/978-1-4666-2089-6.ch009

Crosbie, M. (2013). Hack the cloud: Ethical hacking and cloud forensics. In K. Ruan (Ed.), *Cybercrime and cloud forensics: Applications for investigation processes* (pp. 42–58). Hershey, PA: IGI Global. doi:10.4018/978-1-4666-2662-1.ch002

Cunha, J., Cogan, S., & Berthod, C. (1999). Application of genetic algorithms for the identification of elastic constants of composite materials from dynamic tests. *International Journal for Numerical Methods in Engineering*, *45*(7), 891–900. doi:10.1002/(SICI)1097-0207(19990710)45:7<891::AID-NME610>3.0.CO;2-1

Curran, K., Carlin, S., & Adams, M. (2012). Security issues in cloud computing. In L. Chao (Ed.), *Cloud computing for teaching and learning: Strategies for design and implementation* (pp. 200–208). Hershey, PA: IGI Global. doi:10.4018/978-1-4666-0957-0.ch014

Cutello, V., & Nicosia, G. (2002). An immunological approach to combinatorial optimization problems. In Advances in Artificial Intelligence IBERAMIA, (pp. 361-370). Academic Press.

Cutello, V., Narizi, G., Nicosia, G., & Pavone, M. (2005). Clonal selection algorithms: A comparative case study usign effective mutation potentials. In *4th Intl. Conference on Artificial Immune Systems*, (pp. 13-28). Academic Press. doi:10.1007/11536444_2

Cutello, V., Narizi, G., Nicosia, G., & Pavone, M. (2006). Real coded clonal selection algorithm for global numerical optimization using a new inversely proportional hypermutation operator. In *21st Annual ACM Symposium on Applied Computing*, (pp. 950–954). Academic Press.

Dahbur, K., & Mohammad, B. (2011). Toward understanding the challenges and countermeasures in computer anti-forensics. *International Journal of Cloud Applications and Computing*, *1*(3), 22–35. doi:10.4018/ijcac.2011070103

Dahbur, K., Mohammad, B., & Tarakji, A. B. (2011). Security issues in cloud computing: A survey of risks, threats and vulnerabilities. *International Journal of Cloud Applications and Computing*, *1*(3), 1–11. doi:10.4018/ijcac.2011070101

Dahbur, K., Mohammad, B., & Tarakji, A. B. (2012). Security issues in cloud computing: A survey of risks, threats and vulnerabilities. In *Grid and cloud computing: Concepts, methodologies, tools and applications* (pp. 1644–1655). Hershey, PA: IGI Global. doi:10.4018/978-1-4666-0879-5. ch707

Dahbur, K., Mohammad, B., & Tarakji, A. B. (2013). Security issues in cloud computing: A survey of risks, threats and vulnerabilities. In S. Aljawarneh (Ed.), *Cloud computing advancements in design, implementation, and technologies* (pp. 154–165). Hershey, PA: IGI Global. doi:10.4018/978-1-4666-1879-4.ch011

Daim, T., Britton, M., Subramanian, G., Brenden, R., & Intarode, N. (2012). Adopting and integrating cloud computing. In E. Eyob & E. Tetteh (Eds.), *Customer-oriented global supply chains: Concepts for effective management* (pp. 175–197). Hershey, PA: IGI Global. doi:10.4018/978-1-4666-0246-5.ch011

Darwin, C. (1859). *The origin of species*. London. John Murray.

Davis, M. D., & Weyuker, E. J. (1981). Pseudo-oracles for non-testable programs. In *ACM 81: Proceedings of the Acm '81 conference* (pp. 254–257). New York: ACM. doi:10.1145/800175.809889

Davis, M., & Sedsman, A. (2012). Grey areas: The legal dimensions of cloud computing. In C. Li & A. Ho (Eds.), *Crime prevention technologies and applications for advancing criminal investigation* (pp. 263–273). Hershey, PA: IGI Global. doi:10.4018/978-1-4666-1758-2.ch017

de Aguiar, M., Barange, M., Baptestin, M., Kaufman, L., & Bar-Yam, Y. (2009). Global patterns of speciation and diversity. *Nature*, *460*(16), 384–387. doi:10.1038/nature08168 PMID:19606148

de Castro, L. N., & Von Zuben, F. J. (2000). The clonal selection algorithm with engineering applications. In *Workshop proceedings of the GECCO 2000*, (pp. 36-37). Academic Press.

de Castro, L. N., & Timmis, J. (2002). *Artificial Immune Systems - A new computational intelligence approach*. Springer Verlag.

de Castro, L. N., & Timmis, J. (2002). *Artificial Immune Systems: A New Computational Intelligence Approach*. Springer-Verlag.

de Castro, L. N., & Von Zuben, F. J. (2002). Learning and optimization using the clonal selection principle. *IEEE Transactions on Evolutionary Computation*, *6*(3), 239–251. doi:10.1109/TEVC.2002.1011539

De Coster, R., & Albesher, A. (2013). The development of mobile service applications for consumers and intelligent networks. In I. Lee (Ed.), *Mobile services industries, technologies, and applications in the global economy* (pp. 273–289). Hershey, PA: IGI Global. doi:10.4018/978-1-4666-1981-4.ch017

De Filippi, P. (2014). Ubiquitous computing in the cloud: User empowerment vs. user obsequity. In J. Pelet & P. Papadopoulou (Eds.), *User behavior in ubiquitous online environments* (pp. 44–63). Hershey, PA: IGI Global. doi:10.4018/978-1-4666-4566-0.ch003

de França, F. O., Coelho, G. P., Castro, P. A., & Von Zuben, F. J. (2010). Conceptual and Practical Aspects of the aiNet Family of Algorithms. *International Journal of Natural Computing Research*, 35.

De Nicola, R., & Hennessy, M. C. B. (1984). Testing equivalences for processes. *Theoretical Computer Science*, *34*(1-2), 83–133. doi:10.1016/0304-3975(84)90113-0

De Silva, S. (2013). Key legal issues with cloud computing: A UK law perspective. In A. Bento & A. Aggarwal (Eds.), *Cloud computing service and deployment models: Layers and management* (pp. 242–256). Hershey, PA: IGI Global. doi:10.4018/978-1-4666-2187-9.ch013

Deed, C., & Cragg, P. (2013). Business impacts of cloud computing. In A. Bento & A. Aggarwal (Eds.), *Cloud computing service and deployment models: Layers and management* (pp. 274–288). Hershey, PA: IGI Global. doi:10.4018/978-1-4666-2187-9.ch015

Deng, M., Petkovic, M., Nalin, M., & Baroni, I. (2013). Home healthcare in cloud computing. In M. Cruz-Cunha, I. Miranda, & P. Gonçalves (Eds.), *Handbook of research on ICTs and management systems for improving efficiency in healthcare and social care* (pp. 614–634). Hershey, PA: IGI Global. doi:10.4018/978-1-4666-3990-4.ch032

Denning, P. (2008). The computing field: Structure. In *Encyclopedia of Computer Science and Engineering* (pp. 615–623). Wiley Interscience.

Denning, P. J. (2001). *The Invisible Future: The Seamless Integration of Thecnology in Everyday Life*. McGraw-Hill.

Denning, P. J. (2007). Computing is a natural science. *Communications of the ACM*, *50*(7), 13–18. doi:10.1145/1272516.1272529

Der Valle, Y., Venayagamoorthy, G. K., Mohagheghi, S., Hernandez, J. C., & Harley, R. G. (2008). Particle swarm optimization: Basic concepts, variants and applications in power systems. *IEEE Transactions on Evolutionary Computation*, *12*(2), 171–195. doi:10.1109/TEVC.2007.896686

Desai, A. M., & Mock, K. (2013). Security in cloud computing. In A. Bento & A. Aggarwal (Eds.), *Cloud computing service and deployment models: Layers and management* (pp. 208–221). Hershey, PA: IGI Global. doi:10.4018/978-1-4666-2187-9.ch011

Deshpande, R. M., Patle, B. V., & Bhoskar, R. D. (2014). Planning and implementation of cloud computing in NIT's in India: Special reference to VNIT. In S. Dhamdhere (Ed.), *Cloud computing and virtualization technologies in libraries* (pp. 90–106). Hershey, PA: IGI Global. doi:10.4018/978-1-4666-4631-5.ch006

Detmer, D. (2000). Information technology for quality health care: A summary of United Kingdom and United States experiences. *Quality in Health Care*, *9*(3), 181–189. doi:10.1136/qhc.9.3.181 PMID:10980079

Detmer, D. (2001). Transforming health care in the internet era. *World Hospitals and Health Services, 37*, 2. PMID:11696999

Devi, V. S. (2014). Learning Using Soft Computing Techniques. In B. Tripathy & D. Acharjya (Eds.), *Global Trends in Intelligent Computing Research and Development* (pp. 51–67). Hershey, PA: Information Science Reference. doi:10.4018/978-1-4666-4936-1.ch003

Dhal, K. G., & Das, S. (2017). Combination of histogram segmentation and modification to preserve the original brightness of the image. *Pattern Recognition and Image Analysis, 27*(2), 200-212.

Dhal, K. G., & Das, S. (2017). Cuckoo search with search strategies and proper objective function for brightness preserving image enhancement. *Pattern Recognition and Image Analysis.*

Dhal, K. G., & Das, S. (2017):Colour Retinal images enhancement using Modified Histogram Equalization methods and Firefly Algorithm, Int. Jr. of Biomedical Engineering and Technology (InderScience Publication), (in publication house).

Dhal, K. G., Namtirtha, A., Quraishi, I. M., & Das, S. (2016). Grey level image enhancement using Particle Swarm Optimization with Levy Flight: An Eagle Strategy Approach. *Int. Conf. on Emerging Trends in Computer Sc, And Information* (ETCSIT-2015).

Dhal, K. G., Quraishi, I. M., & Das, S. (2015). Development of firefly algorithm via chaotic sequence and population diversity to enhance the image contrast. In Natural Computing (Vol. 14, pp. 1–12). Academic Press.

Dhal, K., G., & Das, S (2015). Diversity Conserved Chaotic Artificial Bee Colony Algorithm based Brightness Preserved Histogram Equalization and Contrast Stretching Method. *International Journal of Natural Computing Research, 5*, 45-73.

Dhal, K.G, Quraishi, I. M., & Das, S. (2015). Performance Enhancement of Differential Evolution by Incorporating Lévy Flight and Chaotic Sequence for the Cases of Satellite Images. *Int. J. of Applied Metaheuristic Computing, 6*, 69-81.

Dhal, K.G, Quraishi, I. M., & Das, S. (2015):Performance Analysis of Chaotic Lévy Bat Algorithm and Chaotic Cuckoo Search Algorithm for Gray Level Image Enhancement. *Information Systems Design and Intelligent Applications*, 233-244.

Dhal, K.G, Quraishi, I. M., & Das, S. (2017). An improved cuckoo search based optimal ranged brightness preserved histogram equalization and contrast stretching method. *Int. Jr. of Swarm intelligence Research, 8*, 1-29.

Dhal, K. G., Quraishi, I. M., & Das, S. (2015). *A Chaotic Lévy flight Approach in Bat and Firefly Algorithm for Gray level image Enhancement. I.J. Image, Graphics and Signal Processing*, 7, 69–76.

Dhal, K. G., Sen, M., & Das, S. (2017). Cuckoo search based modified Bi-Histogram Equalization method to enhance the cancerous tissues in Mammography images. *International Journal of Medical Engineering and Informatics.*

Dhal, K. G., Sen, S., Sarkar, K., & Das, S. (2016). *Entropy based range optimized brightness preserved histogram equalization for image contrast enhancement* (Vol. 6). Int. Jr. of Computer Vision and Image Processing.

Dhamdhere, S. N., & Lihitkar, R. (2014). The university cloud library model and the role of the cloud librarian. In S. Dhamdhere (Ed.), *Cloud computing and virtualization technologies in libraries* (pp. 150–161). Hershey, PA: IGI Global. doi:10.4018/978-1-4666-4631-5.ch009

Dharsana, C. S. S., Jennifer, D. N., Askarunisha, A., & Ramaraj, N. (2007). Java based test case generation and optimization using evolutionary testing. In *ICCIMA '07: Proceedings of the international conference on computational intelligence and multimedia applications (ICCIMA 2007)* (pp. 44–49). Washington, DC: IEEE Computer Society. doi:10.1109/ICCIMA.2007.445

Di Martino, S., Ferrucci, F., Maggio, V., & Sarro, F. (2013). Towards migrating genetic algorithms for test data generation to the cloud. In S. Tilley & T. Parveen (Eds.), *Software testing in the cloud: Perspectives on an emerging discipline* (pp. 113–135). Hershey, PA: IGI Global. doi:10.4018/978-1-4666-2536-5.ch006

Di Sano, M., Di Stefano, A., Morana, G., & Zito, D. (2013). FSaaS: Configuring policies for managing shared files among cooperating, distributed applications. *International Journal of Web Portals*, 5(1), 1–14. doi:10.4018/jwp.2013010101

Dippl, S., Jaeger, M. C., Luhn, A., Shulman-Peleg, A., & Vernik, G. (2013). Towards federation and interoperability of cloud storage systems. In D. Kyriazis, A. Voulodimos, S. Gogouvitis, & T. Varvarigou (Eds.), *Data intensive storage services for cloud environments* (pp. 60–71). Hershey, PA: IGI Global. doi:10.4018/978-1-4666-3934-8.ch005

Distefano, S., & Puliafito, A. (2012). The cloud@home volunteer and interoperable cloud through the future internet. In M. Villari, I. Brandic, & F. Tusa (Eds.), *Achieving federated and self-manageable cloud infrastructures: Theory and practice* (pp. 79–96). Hershey, PA: IGI Global. doi:10.4018/978-1-4666-1631-8.ch005

Dixon, R., & Stahl, J. (2008). Virtual visits in a general medicine practice: A pilot study. *Telemedicine Journal and e-Health*, 14(6), 525–530. doi:10.1089/tmj.2007.0101 PMID:18729750

Djoleto, W. (2013). Cloud computing and ecommerce or ebusiness: "The now it way" – An overview. In *Electronic commerce and organizational leadership: perspectives and methodologies* (pp. 239–254). Hershey, PA: IGI Global. doi:10.4018/978-1-4666-2982-0.ch010

Dollmann, T. J., Loos, P., Fellmann, M., Thomas, O., Hoheisel, A., Katranuschkov, P., & Scherer, R. (2011). Design and usage of a process-centric collaboration methodology for virtual organizations in hybrid environments. *International Journal of Intelligent Information Technologies*, 7(1), 45–64. doi:10.4018/jiit.2011010104

Dollmann, T. J., Loos, P., Fellmann, M., Thomas, O., Hoheisel, A., Katranuschkov, P., & Scherer, R. (2013). Design and usage of a process-centric collaboration methodology for virtual organizations in hybrid environments. In V. Sugumaran (Ed.), *Organizational efficiency through intelligent information technologies* (pp. 45–64). Hershey, PA: IGI Global. doi:10.4018/978-1-4666-2047-6.ch004

Dorigo, M., & Blum, C. (2005). Ant colony optimization theory: A survey. *Theoretical Computer Science, 344*(2–3), 243–278. doi:10.1016/j.tcs.2005.05.020

Dorigo, M., Maniezzo, V., & Colorni, A. (1996). The Ant System: Optimization by a Colony of Cooperating Agents. *IEEE Transactions on Systems, Man, and Cybernetics, 26*(1), 29–41. doi:10.1109/3477.484436 PMID:18263004

Dowek, G. (2012). The physical Church Thesis as an explanation of the Galileo Thesis. *Natural Computing, 11*, 247-251.

Dreher, P., & Vouk, M. (2012). Utilizing open source cloud computing environments to provide cost effective support for university education and research. In L. Chao (Ed.), *Cloud computing for teaching and learning: Strategies for design and implementation* (pp. 32–49). Hershey, PA: IGI Global. doi:10.4018/978-1-4666-0957-0.ch003

Dresner, H. (2008). *Performance management revolution.* John Wiley &Sons Inc.

Drum, D., Becker, D., & Fish, M. (2013). Technology adoption in troubled times: A cloud computing case study. *Journal of Cases on Information Technology, 15*(2), 57–71. doi:10.4018/jcit.2013040104

Dunaway, D. M. (2013). Creating virtual collaborative learning experiences for aspiring teachers. In R. Hartshorne, T. Heafner, & T. Petty (Eds.), *Teacher education programs and online learning tools: Innovations in teacher preparation* (pp. 167–180). Hershey, PA: IGI Global. doi:10.4018/978-1-4666-1906-7.ch009

Dyer, B. D. (2003). *A Field Guide to Bacteria.* Comstock Publishing.

Dykstra, J. (2013). Seizing electronic evidence from cloud computing environments. In K. Ruan (Ed.), *Cybercrime and cloud forensics: Applications for investigation processes* (pp. 156–185). Hershey, PA: IGI Global. doi:10.4018/978-1-4666-2662-1.ch007

Echelle, A., & Kornfield, I. (1984). *Evolution of Fish Species Flocks.* University of Maine Press.

Eckel, B. (2002). *Thinking in java.* Prentice Hall Professional Technical Reference.

Elamvazuthi, I., Vasant, P., & Ganesan, T. (2012). Integration of Fuzzy Logic Techniques into DSS for Profitability Quantification in a Manufacturing Environment. In M. Khan & A. Ansari (Eds.), *Handbook of Research on Industrial Informatics and Manufacturing Intelligence: Innovations and Solutions* (pp. 171–192). Hershey, PA: Information Science Reference; doi:10.4018/978-1-4666-0294-6.ch007

Elnaffar, S., Maamar, Z., & Sheng, Q. Z. (2013). When clouds start socializing: The sky model. *International Journal of E-Business Research*, *9*(2), 1–7. doi:10.4018/jebr.2013040101

El-Refaey, M., & Rimal, B. P. (2012). Grid, SOA and cloud computing: On-demand computing models. In *Grid and cloud computing: Concepts, methodologies, tools and applications* (pp. 12–51). Hershey, PA: IGI Global. doi:10.4018/978-1-4666-0879-5.ch102

El-Refaey, M., & Rimal, B. P. (2012). Grid, SOA and cloud computing: On-demand computing models. In N. Preve (Ed.), *Computational and data grids: Principles, applications and design* (pp. 45–85). Hershey, PA: IGI Global. doi:10.4018/978-1-61350-113-9.ch003

El-Shorbagy. (2013). *Numerical Optimization & Swarm Intelligence for optimization: Trust Region Algorithm & Particle Swarm Optimization.* LAP LAMBERT Academic Publishing.

Elwood, S., & Keengwe, J. (2012). Microbursts: A design format for mobile cloud computing. *International Journal of Information and Communication Technology Education*, *8*(2), 102–110. doi:10.4018/jicte.2012040109

Emeakaroha, V. C., Netto, M. A., Calheiros, R. N., & De Rose, C. A. (2012). Achieving flexible SLA and resource management in clouds. In M. Villari, I. Brandic, & F. Tusa (Eds.), *Achieving federated and self-manageable cloud infrastructures: Theory and practice* (pp. 266–287). Hershey, PA: IGI Global. doi:10.4018/978-1-4666-1631-8.ch014

Etro, F. (2013). The economics of cloud computing. In A. Bento & A. Aggarwal (Eds.), *Cloud computing service and deployment models: Layers and management* (pp. 296–309). Hershey, PA: IGI Global. doi:10.4018/978-1-4666-2187-9.ch017

Ezugwu, A. E., Buhari, S. M., & Junaidu, S. B. (2013). Virtual machine allocation in cloud computing environment. *International Journal of Cloud Applications and Computing*, *3*(2), 47–60. doi:10.4018/ijcac.2013040105

Fan, L., & Joo, E. M. (2009, May). Design for auto-tuning PID controller based on genetic algorithms. In *Industrial Electronics and Applications, 2009. ICIEA 2009. 4th IEEE Conference on* (pp. 1924-1928). IEEE.

Fauzi, A. H., & Taylor, H. (2013). Secure community trust stores for peer-to-peer e-commerce applications using cloud services. *International Journal of E-Entrepreneurship and Innovation*, *4*(1), 1–15. doi:10.4018/jeei.2013010101

Fear, K., & Price, T. (1998). The adaptive surface in ecology. *Oikos*, *82*(3), 440–448. doi:10.2307/3546365

Feng, J., Xu, L., & Ramamurthy, B. (2009). Overlay Construction in Mobile Peer-to-Peer Networks. In B. Seet (Ed.), *Mobile Peer-to-Peer Computing for Next Generation Distributed Environments: Advancing Conceptual and Algorithmic Applications* (pp. 51–67). Hershey, PA: Information Science Reference. doi:10.4018/978-1-60566-715-7.ch003

Ferguson-Boucher, K., & Endicott-Popovsky, B. (2013). Forensic readiness in the cloud (FRC): Integrating records management and digital forensics. In K. Ruan (Ed.), *Cybercrime and cloud forensics: Applications for investigation processes* (pp. 105–128). Hershey, PA: IGI Global. doi:10.4018/978-1-4666-2662-1.ch005

Ferraro de Souza, R., Westphall, C. B., dos Santos, D. R., & Westphall, C. M. (2013). A review of PACS on cloud for archiving secure medical images. *International Journal of Privacy and Health Information Management*, *1*(1), 53–62. doi:10.4018/ijphim.2013010104

Ferrer, J., Chicano, F., & Alba, E. (2009). Dealing with inheritance in oo evolutionary testing. In *Gecco '09: Proceedings of the 11th annual conference on genetic and evolutionary computation* (pp. 1665–1672). New York: ACM. doi:10.1145/1569901.1570124

Firdhous, M., Hassan, S., & Ghazali, O. (2013). Statistically enhanced multi-dimensional trust computing mechanism for cloud computing. *International Journal of Mobile Computing and Multimedia Communications*, *5*(2), 1–17. doi:10.4018/jmcmc.2013040101

Fisher, R. A. (1930). *The genetical theory of natural selection: a complete variorum edition.* Oxford University Press. doi:10.5962/bhl.title.27468

Fleming, P. J., & Purshouse, R. C. (2002). Evolutionary algorithms in control systems engineering: A survey. *Control Engineering Practice*, *10*(11), 1223–1241. doi:10.1016/S0967-0661(02)00081-3

Formisano, C., Bonelli, L., Balraj, K. R., & Shulman-Peleg, A. (2013). Cloud access control mechanisms. In D. Kyriazis, A. Voulodimos, S. Gogouvitis, & T. Varvarigou (Eds.), *Data intensive storage services for cloud environments* (pp. 94–108). Hershey, PA: IGI Global. doi:10.4018/978-1-4666-3934-8.ch007

Fox, A. (2011). Computer science. Cloud computing: What's in it for me as a scientist? *Science*, *331*(6016), 406–407. doi:10.1126/science.1198981 PMID:21273473

Franco, G., Betti, R., & Lus, H. (2004). Identification of structural systems using an evolutionary strategy. *Journal of Engineering Mechanics*, *130*(10), 1125–1139. doi:10.1061/(ASCE)0733-9399(2004)130:10(1125)

Frank, H., & Mesentean, S. (2012). Efficient communication interfaces for distributed energy resources. In E. Udoh (Ed.), *Evolving developments in grid and cloud computing: Advancing research* (pp. 185–196). Hershey, PA: IGI Global. doi:10.4018/978-1-4666-0056-0.ch013

Fraser, G., & Arcuri, A. (2011b). *Evosuite – automatic test suite generation for java.* Available from http://www.evosuite.org/

Fraser, G., & Arcuri, A. (2012). Sound empirical evidence in software testing. In *34th international conference on software engineering, ICSE 2012* (pp. 178–188). IEEE. doi:10.1109/ICSE.2012.6227195

Fraser, G., & Arcuri, A. (2011a). Evosuite: automatic test suite generation for object-oriented software. In *Proceedings of the 19th ACM SIGSOFT symposium and the 13th European conference on foundations of software engineering* (pp. 416–419). New York: ACM. doi:10.1145/2025113.2025179

Fraser, G., & Arcuri, A. (2011c). Evolutionary generation of whole test suites. In *Proceedings of the 2011 11th international conference on quality software* (pp. 31–40). Washington, DC: IEEE Computer Society. doi:10.1109/QSIC.2011.19

Fraser, G., & Arcuri, A. (2013). Whole test suite generation. *IEEE Transactions on Software Engineering, 39*(2), 276–291. doi:10.1109/TSE.2012.14

Fraser, G., & Arcuri, A. (2014). A Large-Scale Evaluation of Automated Unit Test Generation Using EvoSuite. *ACM Transactions on Software Engineering and Methodology, 24*(2), 1–42. doi:10.1145/2685612

Fraser, G., Arcuri, A., & McMinn, P. (2013). Test suite generation with memetic algorithms. In *Proceeding of the fifteenth annual conference on genetic and evolutionary computation conference* (pp. 1437–1444). New York: ACM. doi:10.1145/2463372.2463548

Fraser, G., & Zeller, A. (2011). Exploiting common object usage in test case generation. In *Proceedings of the 2011 fourth ieee international conference on software testing, verification and validation* (pp. 80–89). Washington, DC: IEEE Computer Society. doi:10.1109/ICST.2011.53

Gabbay, J., & Walley, T. (2006). Introducing new health interventions. *British Medical Journal, 332*(7533), 64–65. doi:10.1136/bmj.332.7533.64 PMID:16410559

Gallina, B., & Guelfi, N. (2012). Reusing transaction models for dependable cloud computing. In H. Yang & X. Liu (Eds.), *Software reuse in the emerging cloud computing era* (pp. 248–277). Hershey, PA: IGI Global. doi:10.4018/978-1-4666-0897-9.ch011

Gao, L., & Hailu, A. (2010). Comprehensive learning particle swarm optimizer for constrained mixed-variable optimization problems. *International Journal of Computational Intelligence Systems, 3*(6), 832–842. doi:10.1080/18756891.2010.9727745

Garofalo, D. A. (2013). Empires of the future: Libraries, technology, and the academic environment. In E. Iglesias (Ed.), *Robots in academic libraries: Advancements in library automation* (pp. 180–206). Hershey, PA: IGI Global. doi:10.4018/978-1-4666-3938-6.ch010

Garrido, P., & Lemahieu, W. (2008). Collective Intelligence. In G. Putnik & M. Cruz-Cunha (Eds.), *Encyclopedia of Networked and Virtual Organizations* (pp. 280–287). Hershey, PA: Information Science Reference. doi:10.4018/978-1-59904-885-5.ch037

Gavrilets, S., & Vose, A. (2005). Dynamic patterns of adaptive radiation. *PNAS, 12*(50), 18040-18045.

Gavrilets, S., & Losos, J. (2009). Adaptive Radiation: Contrasting Theory with Data. *Science, 323.* PMID:19197052

Gebremeskel, G. B., He, Z., & Jing, X. (2013). Semantic integrating for intelligent cloud data mining platform and cloud based business intelligence for optimization of mobile social networks. In V. Bhatnagar (Ed.), *Data mining in dynamic social networks and fuzzy systems* (pp. 173–211). Hershey, PA: IGI Global. doi:10.4018/978-1-4666-4213-3.ch009

Gentleman, W. M. (2013). Using the cloud for testing NOT adjunct to development. In S. Tilley & T. Parveen (Eds.), *Software testing in the cloud: Perspectives on an emerging discipline* (pp. 216–230). Hershey, PA: IGI Global. doi:10.4018/978-1-4666-2536-5.ch010

Ghafoor, K. Z., Mohammed, M. A., Abu Bakar, K., Sadiq, A. S., & Lloret, J. (2014). Vehicular cloud computing: Trends and challenges. In J. Rodrigues, K. Lin, & J. Lloret (Eds.), *Mobile networks and cloud computing convergence for progressive services and applications* (pp. 262–274). Hershey, PA: IGI Global. doi:10.4018/978-1-4666-4781-7.ch014

Gholizadeh, S. (2013). Layout optimization of truss structures by hybridizing cellular automata and particle swarm optimization. *Computers & Structures*, *125*(1), 86–99. doi:10.1016/j.compstruc.2013.04.024

Ghoreishi, S. A., Mohammad, A. N., & Basiri, S. O. (2011). Optimal Design of LQR Weighting Matrices based on Intelligent Optimization Methods. *International Journal of Intelligent Information Processing*, *2*(1).

Giannakaki, M. (2012). The "right to be forgotten" in the era of social media and cloud computing. In C. Akrivopoulou & N. Garipidis (Eds.), *Human rights and risks in the digital era: Globalization and the effects of information technologies* (pp. 10–24). Hershey, PA: IGI Global. doi:10.4018/978-1-4666-0891-7.ch002

Giesbrecht, M., & Bottura, C. P. (2011). Immuno inspired approaches to model discrete time series at state space. In *Proceedings of the Fourth International Workshop on Advanced Computational Intelligence* (pp. 750-756). Wuhan: IEEE. doi:10.1109/IWACI.2011.6160107

Giesbrecht, M., & Bottura, C. P. (2015). Recursive Immuno-Inspired Algorithm for Time Variant Discrete Multivariable Dynamic System State Space Identification. *International Journal of Natural Computing Research*, 32.

Giesbrecht, M., & Bottura, C. P. (2016). An immuno inspired proposal to solve the time series realization problem. In *2016 IEEE Congress on Evolutionary Computation (CEC)* (pp. 1786-1792). Vancouver: IEEE.

Gillam, L., Li, B., & O'Loughlin, J. (2012). Teaching clouds: Lessons taught and lessons learnt. In L. Chao (Ed.), *Cloud computing for teaching and learning: Strategies for design and implementation* (pp. 82–94). Hershey, PA: IGI Global. doi:10.4018/978-1-4666-0957-0.ch006

Ginzburg, L. R., & Colyvan, M. (2004). *Ecological Orbits: How Planets Move and Populations Grow*. New York: Oxford University Press.

Giudici, P. (2003). *Applied Data Mining: Statistical Methods for Business and Industry*. John Wiley &Sons Inc.

Giudici, P., & Figini, S. (2009). *Applied Data Mining for Business and Industry (Statistics in Practice)*. Wiley. doi:10.1002/9780470745830

Goffi, A., Gorla, A., Mattavelli, A., Pezzè, M., & Tonella, P. (2014). Search-based synthesis of equivalent method sequences. *Proceedings of the 22nd ACM SIGSOFT International Symposium on Foundations of Software Engineering - FSE 2014*. doi:10.1145/2635868.2635888

Gonsalves, T. (2015). Hybrid Swarm Intelligence. In M. Khosrow-Pour (Ed.), *Encyclopedia of Information Science and Technology* (3rd ed.; pp. 175–186). Hershey, PA: Information Science Reference. doi:10.4018/978-1-4666-5888-2.ch018

Gonsowski, D. (2013). Compliance in the cloud and the implications on electronic discovery. In K. Ruan (Ed.), *Cybercrime and cloud forensics: Applications for investigation processes* (pp. 230–250). Hershey, PA: IGI Global. doi:10.4018/978-1-4666-2662-1.ch009

Gonzalez, M., Quesada, G., Urrutia, I., & Gavidia, J. (2006). Conceptual design of an e-health strategy for the Spanish health care system. *International Journal of Health Care Quality Assurance*, *19*(2), 146–157. doi:10.1108/09526860610651681 PMID:16875096

Gonzalez, R. C., & Woods, R. E. (2002). *Digital Image Processing* (2nd ed.). New York: Prentice Hall.

Gonzalez-Sanchez, J., Conley, Q., Chavez-Echeagaray, M., & Atkinson, R. K. (2012). Supporting the assembly process by leveraging augmented reality, cloud computing, and mobile devices. *International Journal of Cyber Behavior, Psychology and Learning*, *2*(3), 86–102. doi:10.4018/ijcbpl.2012070107

Google. (2004). *Google scholar*. Available from http://scholar.google.com/

Gopinath, R., & Geetha, B. (2013). An e-learning system based on secure data storage services in cloud computing. *International Journal of Information Technology and Web Engineering*, *8*(2), 1–17. doi:10.4018/jitwe.2013040101

Gorai, A., & Ghosh, A. (2009). Gray-level Image Enhancement By Particle Swarm Optimization. *Proceedings of World Congress on Nature & Biologically Inspired Computing*. doi:10.1109/NABIC.2009.5393603

Gossin, P. C., & LaBrie, R. C. (2013). Data center waste management. In P. Ordóñez de Pablos (Ed.), *Green technologies and business practices: An IT approach* (pp. 226–235). Hershey, PA: IGI Global. doi:10.4018/978-1-4666-1972-2.ch014

Goswami, V., Patra, S. S., & Mund, G. B. (2012). Performance analysis of cloud computing centers for bulk services. *International Journal of Cloud Applications and Computing*, *2*(4), 53–65. doi:10.4018/ijcac.2012100104

Goswami, V., & Sahoo, C. N. (2013). Optimal resource usage in multi-cloud computing environment. *International Journal of Cloud Applications and Computing*, *3*(1), 44–57. doi:10.4018/ijcac.2013010105

Gräuler, M., Teuteberg, F., Mahmoud, T., & Gómez, J. M. (2013). Requirements prioritization and design considerations for the next generation of corporate environmental management information systems: A foundation for innovation. *International Journal of Information Technologies and Systems Approach*, 6(1), 98–116. doi:10.4018/jitsa.2013010106

Grieve, G. P., & Heston, K. (2012). Finding liquid salvation: Using the cardean ethnographic method to document second life residents and religious cloud communities. In N. Zagalo, L. Morgado, & A. Boa-Ventura (Eds.), *Virtual worlds and metaverse platforms: New communication and identity paradigms* (pp. 288–305). Hershey, PA: IGI Global. doi:10.4018/978-1-60960-854-5.ch019

Grispos, G., Storer, T., & Glisson, W. B. (2012). Calm before the storm: The challenges of cloud computing in digital forensics. *International Journal of Digital Crime and Forensics*, 4(2), 28–48. doi:10.4018/jdcf.2012040103

Grispos, G., Storer, T., & Glisson, W. B. (2013). Calm before the storm: The challenges of cloud computing in digital forensics. In C. Li (Ed.), *Emerging digital forensics applications for crime detection, prevention, and security* (pp. 211–233). Hershey, PA: IGI Global. doi:10.4018/978-1-4666-4006-1.ch015

Gross, F., Fraser, G., & Zeller, A. (2012). Search-based system testing: high coverage, no false alarms. *Proceedings of the 2012 International Symposium on Software Testing and Analysis - ISSTA 2012*. doi:10.1145/2338965.2336762

Gupta, N. K., & Rohil, M. K. (2008). Using genetic algorithm for unit testing of object oriented software. In *ICETET '08: Proceedings of the 2008 first international conference on emerging trends in engineering and technology* (pp. 308–313). Washington, DC: IEEE Computer Society. doi:10.1109/ICETET.2008.137

Guster, D., & Lee, O. F. (2011). Enhancing the disaster recovery plan through virtualization. *Journal of Information Technology Research*, 4(4), 18–40. doi:10.4018/jitr.2011100102

Hanawa, T., & Sato, M. (2013). D-Cloud: Software testing environment for dependable distributed systems using cloud computing technology. In S. Tilley & T. Parveen (Eds.), *Software testing in the cloud: Perspectives on an emerging discipline* (pp. 340–355). Hershey, PA: IGI Global. doi:10.4018/978-1-4666-2536-5.ch016

Han, J., & Kamber, M. (2006). *Data Mining: Concepts and Techniques*. Morgan Kaufmann.

Hansen, N. (2006). The CMA evolution strategy: a comparing review. *Towards a new evolutionary computation*, 75-102.

Hardy, J., Liu, L., Lei, C., & Li, J. (2013). Internet-based virtual computing infrastructure for cloud computing. In X. Yang & L. Liu (Eds.), *Principles, methodologies, and service-oriented approaches for cloud computing* (pp. 371–389). Hershey, PA: IGI Global. doi:10.4018/978-1-4666-2854-0.ch016

Harel, D. (2003). A grand challenge for computing: Full reactive modeling of a multi-cellular anima. *Bull. EATCS*, 81, 226–235.

Harman, M., Hassoun, Y., Lakhotia, K., McMinn, P., & Wegener, J. (2007). The impact of input domain reduction on search-based test data generation. In *Esec-fse '07: Proceedings of the 6th joint meeting of the European software engineering conference and the ACM SIGSOFT symposium on the foundations of software engineering* (pp. 155–164). New York: ACM Press. doi:10.1145/1287624.1287647

Harman, M., Mansouri, S. A., & Zhang, Y. (2009). *Search based software engineering: A comprehensive analysis and review of trends techniques and applications* (Tech. Rep. No. TR-09-03). Academic Press.

Harman, M., Mansouri, S. A., & Zhang, Y. (2012). Search-based software engineering: Trends, techniques and applications. *ACM Comput. Surv., 45*(1), 11:1–11:61.

Harman, M. (2007). The current state and future of search based software engineering. In *FOSE '07: 2007 future of software engineering* (pp. 342–357). Washington, DC: IEEE Computer Society. doi:10.1109/FOSE.2007.29

Harman, M., & McMinn, P. (2010). A theoretical and empirical study of search-based testing: Local, global, and hybrid search. *Software Engineering. IEEE Transactions on, 36*(2), 226–247.

Hart, E., Bersini, H., & Santos, F. C. (2007). How affinity influences tolerance in an idiotypic network. *Journal of Theoretical Biology, 249*(3), 422–436. doi:10.1016/j.jtbi.2007.07.019 PMID:17904580

Harte, J. (2011). *Maximum Entropy and Ecology: A Theory of Abundance, Distribution, and Energetics*. Oxford University Press. doi:10.1093/acprof:oso/9780199593415.001.0001

Hashemi, S., Kiani, S., Noroozi, N., & Moghaddam, M. E. (2010). An image contrast enhancement method based on genetic algorithm. *Pattern Recognition Letters, 31*(13), 1816–1824. doi:10.1016/j.patrec.2009.12.006

Hashizume, K., Yoshioka, N., & Fernandez, E. B. (2013). Three misuse patterns for cloud computing. In D. Rosado, D. Mellado, E. Fernandez-Medina, & M. Piattini (Eds.), *Security engineering for cloud computing: Approaches and tools* (pp. 36–53). Hershey, PA: IGI Global. doi:10.4018/978-1-4666-2125-1.ch003

Hassan, F. R., Koh, S. P., Tiong, S. K., Chong, K. H., & Abdalla, A. N. (2011). Investigation of induction motor parameter identification using particle swarm optimization-based RBF neural network (PSO-RBFNN). *International Journal of Physical Sciences, 6*(9), 4564–4570.

Hassan, G. A. (1993). Computer-aided tuning of analog and digital controllers. *Control and Computers, 21*, 1–1.

Hassani, K., & Lee, W. S. (2014, May). Optimal tuning of linear quadratic regulators using quantum particle swarm optimization. In *Proceedings of the International Conference of Control, Dynamics and Robotics* (pp. 1-8). Academic Press.

Hassan, Q. F., Riad, A. M., & Hassan, A. E. (2012). Understanding cloud computing. In H. Yang & X. Liu (Eds.), *Software reuse in the emerging cloud computing era* (pp. 204–227). Hershey, PA: IGI Global. doi:10.4018/978-1-4666-0897-9.ch009

Hasselmeyer, P., Katsaros, G., Koller, B., & Wieder, P. (2012). Cloud monitoring. In M. Villari, I. Brandic, & F. Tusa (Eds.), *Achieving federated and self-manageable cloud infrastructures: Theory and practice* (pp. 97–116). Hershey, PA: IGI Global. doi:10.4018/978-1-4666-1631-8.ch006

Haughton, J. (2011). Year of the underdog: Cloud-based EHRs. *Health Management Technology*, *32*(1), 9.

Haynes, T. D., Schoenefeld, D. A., & Wainwright, R. L. (1996). Type inheritance in strongly typed genetic programming. In P. J. Angeline & K. E. Kinnear Jr., (Eds.), *Advances in genetic programming 2* (pp. 359–376). Cambridge, MA: MIT Press.

Hayrinen, K., Saranto, K., & Nykanen, P. (2008). Definition, structure, content, use and impacts of electronic health records: A review of the research literature. *International Journal of Medical Informatics*, *77*(5), 291–304. doi:10.1016/j.ijmedinf.2007.09.001 PMID:17951106

Heindenreich, G., & Blobel, B. (2009). IT standards for applications in telemedicine. Towards efficient data interchange in medicine. *Bundesgesundheitsblatt, Gesundheitsforschung, Gesundheitsschutz*, *52*, 316–323. PMID:19255733

Hemalatha, M. (2012). A Predictive Modeling of Retail Satisfaction: A Data Mining Approach to Retail Service Industry. In P. Ordóñez de Pablos & M. Lytras (Eds.), *Knowledge Management and Drivers of Innovation in Services Industries* (pp. 175–189). Hershey, PA: Information Science Reference. doi:10.4018/978-1-4666-0948-8.ch014

Hengeveld, R. (1990). *Dynamic Biogeography*. Cambridge University Press.

He, Q., & Wang, L. (2007). An effective co-evolutionary particle swarm optimization for constrained engineering design problems. *Engineering Applications of Artificial Intelligence*, *20*(1), 89–99. doi:10.1016/j.engappai.2006.03.003

Hernández-Riveros, J. A., & Carmona-Cadavid, C. V. (2016b). Evolutionary selection of optimal weighting matrices for LQR controllers and parameters of robust PID on benchmark plants. In *XVII Latin American Conference on Automatic Control CLCA* (pp. 269-378). Academic Press.

Hernández-Riveros, J. A., & Villada-Cano, D. (2012). Sensitivity Analysis of an Autonomous Evolutionary Algorithm. In Advances in Artificial Intelligence - IBERAMIA 2012 (pp. 271-280). Springer-Verlag Berlin Heidelberg.

Hernández-Riveros, J. A., & Ospina, J. D. (2010). A multi dynamics algorithm for global optimization. *Mathematical and Computer Modelling*, *52*(7), 1271–1278. doi:10.1016/j.mcm.2010.03.024

Hernández-Riveros, J. A., & Urrea-Quintero, J. H. (2014). SOSPD Controllers Tuning by Means of an Evolutionary Algorithm. *International Journal of Natural Computing Research*, *4*(2), 40–58. doi:10.4018/ijncr.2014040103

Hernández-Riveros, J. A., Urrea-Quintero, J. H., & Carmona-Cadavid, C. V. (2016a). Evolutionary Tuning of Optimal PID Controllers for Second Order Systems Plus Time Delay. In *Computational Intelligence. In Studies in Computational Intelligence* (Vol. 620). Springer; doi:10.1007/978-3-642-34654-5_28

Herreros, A., Baeyens, E., & Perán, J. R. (2002). Design of PID-type controllers using multiobjective genetic algorithms. *ISA Transactions*, *41*(4), 457–472. doi:10.1016/S0019-0578(07)60102-5 PMID:12398277

Hertzler, B. T., Frost, E., Bressler, G. H., & Goehring, C. (2011). Experience report: Using a cloud computing environment during Haiti and Exercise24. *International Journal of Information Systems for Crisis Response and Management*, *3*(1), 50–64. doi:10.4018/jiscrm.2011010104

Hertzler, B. T., Frost, E., Bressler, G. H., & Goehring, C. (2013). Experience report: Using a cloud computing environment during Haiti and Exercise24. In M. Jennex (Ed.), *Using social and information technologies for disaster and crisis management* (pp. 52–66). Hershey, PA: IGI Global. doi:10.4018/978-1-4666-2788-8.ch004

He, W., Zhao, R., & Zhu, Q. (2015). Integrating Evolutionary Testing with Reinforcement Learning for Automated Test Generation of Object-Oriented Software. *Liangzi Dianzi Xuebao. Liangzi Dianzi Xuebao*, *24*(1), 38–45.

Hillis, W. D. (1990). Co-evolving parasites improve simulated evolution as an optimization procedure. *Physica D. Nonlinear Phenomena*, *42*(1-3), 228–234. doi:10.1016/0167-2789(90)90076-2

Hjelm, M. (2001). Telemedicine and in-patient. *Hospitals International*, *37*, 2.

Ho, B. L., & Kalman, R. E. (1966). Effective construction of linear state variable models from input-output functions. *Regelungstechnik -zeitschrift für steuern, regeln und automatisieren*, 545–548.

Hobona, G., Jackson, M., & Anand, S. (2012). Implementing geospatial web services for cloud computing. In *Grid and cloud computing: Concepts, methodologies, tools and applications* (pp. 615–636). Hershey, PA: IGI Global. doi:10.4018/978-1-4666-0879-5.ch305

Hochstein, L., Schott, B., & Graybill, R. B. (2011). Computational engineering in the cloud: Benefits and challenges. *Journal of Organizational and End User Computing*, *23*(4), 31–50. doi:10.4018/joeuc.2011100103

Hochstein, L., Schott, B., & Graybill, R. B. (2013). Computational engineering in the cloud: Benefits and challenges. In A. Dwivedi & S. Clarke (Eds.), *Innovative strategies and approaches for end-user computing advancements* (pp. 314–332). Hershey, PA: IGI Global. doi:10.4018/978-1-4666-2059-9.ch017

Holland. (2000). Building blocks, cohort genetic algorithms, and hyperplane-defined functions. *Evolutionary Computation*, 373-391.

Holland, J. H. (1962). Outline for a logical theory of adaptive systems. *Journal of the Association for Computing Machinery*, *9*(3), 297–314. doi:10.1145/321127.321128

Honarvar, A. R. (2013). Developing an elastic cloud computing application through multi-agent systems. *International Journal of Cloud Applications and Computing, 3*(1), 58–64. doi:10.4018/ijcac.2013010106

Ho, R. (2013). Cloud computing and enterprise migration strategies. In A. Loo (Ed.), *Distributed computing innovations for business, engineering, and science* (pp. 156–175). Hershey, PA: IGI Global. doi:10.4018/978-1-4666-2533-4.ch008

Hossain, S. (2013). Cloud computing terms, definitions, and taxonomy. In A. Bento & A. Aggarwal (Eds.), *Cloud computing service and deployment models: Layers and management* (pp. 1–25). Hershey, PA: IGI Global. doi:10.4018/978-1-4666-2187-9.ch001

Huang, H., Qin, H., Hao, Z., & Lim, A. (2012). Example-based learning particle swarm optimization for continuous optimization. *Information Sciences, 182*(1), 125–138. doi:10.1016/j.ins.2010.10.018

Huang, V. L., Suganthan, P. N., & Liang, J. J. (2006). Comprehensive learning particle swarm optimizer for solving multiobjective optimization problems. *International Journal of Intelligent Systems, 21*(2), 209–226. doi:10.1002/int.20128

Hudzia, B., Sinclair, J., & Lindner, M. (2013). Deploying and running enterprise grade applications in a federated cloud. In *Supply chain management: Concepts, methodologies, tools, and applications* (pp. 1350–1370). Hershey, PA: IGI Global. doi:10.4018/978-1-4666-2625-6.ch080

Hull, D. G. (2013). *Optimal control theory for applications*. Springer Science & Business Media.

Hung, S., Shieh, J., & Lee, C. (2011). Migrating android applications to the cloud. *International Journal of Grid and High Performance Computing, 3*(2), 14–28. doi:10.4018/jghpc.2011040102

Hung, S., Shieh, J., & Lee, C. (2013). Migrating android applications to the cloud. In E. Udoh (Ed.), *Applications and developments in grid, cloud, and high performance computing* (pp. 307–322). Hershey, PA: IGI Global. doi:10.4018/978-1-4666-2065-0.ch020

Hussain, A., & Liatsis, P. (2009). A Novel Recurrent Polynomial Neural Network for Financial Time Series Prediction. In M. Zhang (Ed.), *Artificial Higher Order Neural Networks for Economics and Business* (pp. 190–211). Hershey, PA: Information Science Reference. doi:10.4018/978-1-59904-897-0.ch009

Ibrahim, H., & Kong, N.S.P. (2007). Brightness Preserving Dynamic Histogram Equalization for Image Contrast Enhancement. *IEEE Transactions on Consumer Electronics, 53*(4), 1752-1758.

Inkumsah, K., & Xie, T. (2007). Evacon: A framework for integrating evolutionary and concolic testing for object-oriented programs. In *Proc. 22nd IEEE/ACM international conference on automated software engineering (ase 2007)* (pp. 425–428). IEEE. doi:10.1145/1321631.1321700

Inkumsah, K., & Xie, T. (2008). Improving structural testing of object-oriented programs via integrating evolutionary testing and symbolic execution. *Proc. 23rd ieee/acm international conference on automated software engineering (ASE 2008).* doi:10.1109/ASE.2008.40

Iruthayarajan, M. W., & Baskar, S. (2009). Evolutionary algorithms based design of multivariable PID controller. *Expert Systems with Applications*, *36*(5), 9159–9167. doi:10.1016/j.eswa.2008.12.033

Islam, S., Mouratidis, H., & Weippl, E. R. (2013). A goal-driven risk management approach to support security and privacy analysis of cloud-based system. In D. Rosado, D. Mellado, E. Fernandez-Medina, & M. Piattini (Eds.), *Security engineering for cloud computing: Approaches and tools* (pp. 97–122). Hershey, PA: IGI Global. doi:10.4018/978-1-4666-2125-1.ch006

Itani, W., Kayssi, A., & Chehab, A. (2013). Hardware-based security for ensuring data privacy in the cloud. In D. Rosado, D. Mellado, E. Fernandez-Medina, & M. Piattini (Eds.), *Security engineering for cloud computing: Approaches and tools* (pp. 147–170). Hershey, PA: IGI Global. doi:10.4018/978-1-4666-2125-1.ch008

Iwasaki, M., Miwa, M., & Matsui, N. (2005). GA-based evolutionary identification algorithm for unknown structured mechatronic systems. *IEEE Transactions on Industrial Electronics*, *52*(1), 300–305. doi:10.1109/TIE.2004.841075

Jackson, A., & Weiland, M. (2013). Cloud computing for scientific simulation and high performance computing. In X. Yang & L. Liu (Eds.), *Principles, methodologies, and service-oriented approaches for cloud computing* (pp. 51–70). Hershey, PA: IGI Global. doi:10.4018/978-1-4666-2854-0.ch003

Jaeger, M. C., & Hohenstein, U. (2013). Content centric storage and current storage systems. In D. Kyriazis, A. Voulodimos, S. Gogouvitis, & T. Varvarigou (Eds.), *Data intensive storage services for cloud environments* (pp. 27–46). Hershey, PA: IGI Global. doi:10.4018/978-1-4666-3934-8.ch003

James, J. I., Shosha, A. F., & Gladyshev, P. (2013). Digital forensic investigation and cloud computing. In K. Ruan (Ed.), *Cybercrime and cloud forensics: Applications for investigation processes* (pp. 1–41). Hershey, PA: IGI Global. doi:10.4018/978-1-4666-2662-1.ch001

Janecek, A., & Tan, Y. (2011). Swarm Intelligence for Non-Negative Matrix Factorization. *International Journal of Swarm Intelligence Research*, *2*(4), 12–34. doi:10.4018/jsir.2011100102

Janecek, A., & Tan, Y. (2015). Swarm Intelligence for Dimensionality Reduction: How to Improve the Non-Negative Matrix Factorization with Nature-Inspired Optimization Methods. In Y. Shi (Ed.), *Emerging Research on Swarm Intelligence and Algorithm Optimization* (pp. 285–309). Hershey, PA: Information Science Reference. doi:10.4018/978-1-4666-6328-2.ch013

Jannett, P., & Jackson, A., & Ho, K., & Healy, T., & Kazanjian, A., & Wollard, R., & Haydt, S., & Bates, J. (2005). The essence of telehealth readiness in rural communities: an organizational perspective. *Journal of Telemedicine and eHealth*, *11*, 137-145.

Jannett, P., Yeo, M., Pauls, M., & Graham, J. (2003). Organizational readiness for telemedicine: Implications for success and failure. *Journal of Telemedicine and Telecare*, *9*(2), 27–30. doi:10.1258/135763303322596183 PMID:14728753

Jena, R. K. (2013). Green computing to green business. In P. Ordóñez de Pablos (Ed.), *Green technologies and business practices: An IT approach* (pp. 138–150). Hershey, PA: IGI Global. doi:10.4018/978-1-4666-1972-2.ch007

Jensen, F. (2001). *Bayesian networks and decision graphs*. Springer. doi:10.1007/978-1-4757-3502-4

Jeyarani, R., & Nagaveni, N. (2012). A heuristic meta scheduler for optimal resource utilization and improved QoS in cloud computing environment. *International Journal of Cloud Applications and Computing, 2*(1), 41–52. doi:10.4018/ijcac.2012010103

Jeyarani, R., Nagaveni, N., & Ram, R. V. (2011). Self adaptive particle swarm optimization for efficient virtual machine provisioning in cloud. *International Journal of Intelligent Information Technologies, 7*(2), 25–44. doi:10.4018/jiit.2011040102

Jeyarani, R., Nagaveni, N., & Ram, R. V. (2013). Self adaptive particle swarm optimization for efficient virtual machine provisioning in cloud. In V. Sugumaran (Ed.), *Organizational efficiency through intelligent information technologies* (pp. 88–107). Hershey, PA: IGI Global. doi:10.4018/978-1-4666-2047-6.ch006

Jeyarani, R., Nagaveni, N., Sadasivam, S. K., & Rajarathinam, V. R. (2011). Power aware meta scheduler for adaptive VM provisioning in IaaS cloud. *International Journal of Cloud Applications and Computing, 1*(3), 36–51. doi:10.4018/ijcac.2011070104

Jeyarani, R., Nagaveni, N., Sadasivam, S. K., & Rajarathinam, V. R. (2013). Power aware meta scheduler for adaptive VM provisioning in IaaS cloud. In S. Aljawarneh (Ed.), *Cloud computing advancements in design, implementation, and technologies* (pp. 190–204). Hershey, PA: IGI Global. doi:10.4018/978-1-4666-1879-4.ch014

Jiang, J., Huang, X., Wu, Y., & Yang, G. (2013). Campus cloud storage and preservation: From distributed file system to data sharing service. In X. Yang & L. Liu (Eds.), *Principles, methodologies, and service-oriented approaches for cloud computing* (pp. 284–301). Hershey, PA: IGI Global. doi:10.4018/978-1-4666-2854-0.ch012

Jing, S. (2012). The application exploration of cloud computing in information technology teaching. *International Journal of Advanced Pervasive and Ubiquitous Computing, 4*(4), 23–27. doi:10.4018/japuc.2012100104

Johansson, D., & Wiberg, M. (2012). Conceptually advancing "application mobility" towards design: Applying a concept-driven approach to the design of mobile IT for home care service groups. *International Journal of Ambient Computing and Intelligence, 4*(3), 20–32. doi:10.4018/jaci.2012070102

Jorda, J., & M'zoughi, A. (2013). Securing cloud storage. In D. Rosado, D. Mellado, E. Fernandez-Medina, & M. Piattini (Eds.), *Security engineering for cloud computing: Approaches and tools* (pp. 171–190). Hershey, PA: IGI Global. doi:10.4018/978-1-4666-2125-1.ch009

Jorgensen, S. E., Patten, B. C., & Stragkraba, M. (1992). Ecosystems emerging: Toward an ecology of complex systems in a complex future. *Ecological Modelling, 62*(1-3), 1–27. doi:10.1016/0304-3800(92)90080-X

Juiz, C., & Alexander de Pous, V. (2014). Cloud computing: IT governance, legal, and public policy aspects. In I. Portela & F. Almeida (Eds.), *Organizational, legal, and technological dimensions of information system administration* (pp. 139–166). Hershey, PA: IGI Global. doi:10.4018/978-1-4666-4526-4.ch009

Junli, L., Jianlin, M., & Guanghui, Z. (2011). Evolutionary algorithms based parameters tuning of PID controller. In *Control and Decision Conference (CCDC), May 2011 Chinese* (pp. 416-420). IEEE. doi:10.1109/CCDC.2011.5968215

Kabachinski, J. (2011). What's the forecast for cloud computing in healthcare? *Biomedical Instrumentation & Technology, 45*(2), 146–150. doi:10.2345/0899-8205-45.2.146 PMID:21466336

Kaisler, S. H., Money, W., & Cohen, S. J. (2013). Cloud computing: A decision framework for small businesses. In A. Bento & A. Aggarwal (Eds.), *Cloud computing service and deployment models: Layers and management* (pp. 151–172). Hershey, PA: IGI Global. doi:10.4018/978-1-4666-2187-9.ch008

Kanamori, Y., & Yen, M. Y. (2013). Cloud computing security and risk management. In A. Bento & A. Aggarwal (Eds.), *Cloud computing service and deployment models: Layers and management* (pp. 222–240). Hershey, PA: IGI Global. doi:10.4018/978-1-4666-2187-9.ch012

Karadsheh, L., & Alhawari, S. (2011). Applying security policies in small business utilizing cloud computing technologies. *International Journal of Cloud Applications and Computing, 1*(2), 29–40. doi:10.4018/ijcac.2011040103

Karadsheh, L., & Alhawari, S. (2013). Applying security policies in small business utilizing cloud computing technologies. In S. Aljawarneh (Ed.), *Cloud computing advancements in design, implementation, and technologies* (pp. 112–124). Hershey, PA: IGI Global. doi:10.4018/978-1-4666-1879-4.ch008

Kauffman, S. (1996). *The Origins of Order: Self-Organization and Selection in Evolution.* Oxford University Press.

Kaufman, L., & Ochumba, P. (1993). Evolutinary and conservation biology of cichlid fishes as revealed by faunal remnants in northern Lake Victoria. *Conservation Biology, 7*(3), 719–730. doi:10.1046/j.1523-1739.1993.07030719.x

Kaupins, G. (2012). Laws associated with mobile computing in the cloud. *International Journal of Wireless Networks and Broadband Technologies, 2*(3), 1–9. doi:10.4018/ijwnbt.2012070101

Kaur, H., Chauhan, R., & Wasan, S. K. (2015). A Bayesian Network Model for Probability Estimation. In M. Khosrow-Pour (Ed.), *Encyclopedia of Information Science and Technology* (3rd ed.; pp. 1551–1558). Hershey, PA: Information Science Reference. doi:10.4018/978-1-4666-5888-2.ch148

Kawamura, H., & Suzuki, K. (2011). Pheromone-style Communication for Swarm Intelligence. In S. Chen, Y. Kambayashi, & H. Sato (Eds.), *Multi-Agent Applications with Evolutionary Computation and Biologically Inspired Technologies: Intelligent Techniques for Ubiquity and Optimization* (pp. 294–307). Hershey, PA: Medical Information Science Reference. doi:10.4018/978-1-60566-898-7.ch016

Kemp, M. L., Robb, S., & Deans, P. C. (2013). The legal implications of cloud computing. In A. Bento & A. Aggarwal (Eds.), *Cloud computing service and deployment models: Layers and management* (pp. 257–272). Hershey, PA: IGI Global. doi:10.4018/978-1-4666-2187-9.ch014

Kennedy, J., & Eberhart, R. (1995). Particle swarm optimization. *Proceedings of IEEE international conference on neural networks*. doi:10.1109/ICNN.1995.488968

Kennedy, J., Eberhart, R. C., & Shi, Y. (2001). *Swarm Intelligence*. San Francisco, CA: Morgan Kaufmann.

Khalifa, M., & Alswailem, O. (2015). Hospital information system (HIS) acceptance and satisfaction: A case study of a tertiary care hospital. *Procedia Computer Science*, *63*, 198–204. doi:10.1016/j.procs.2015.08.334

Khan, N., Ahmad, N., Herawan, T., & Inayat, Z. (2012). Cloud computing: Locally sub-clouds instead of globally one cloud. *International Journal of Cloud Applications and Computing*, *2*(3), 68–85. doi:10.4018/ijcac.2012070103

Khan, N., Noraziah, A., Ismail, E. I., Deris, M. M., & Herawan, T. (2012). Cloud computing: Analysis of various platforms. *International Journal of E-Entrepreneurship and Innovation*, *3*(2), 51–59. doi:10.4018/jeei.2012040104

Khansa, L., Forcade, J., Nambari, G., Parasuraman, S., & Cox, P. (2012). Proposing an intelligent cloud-based electronic health record system. *International Journal of Business Data Communications and Networking*, *8*(3), 57–71. doi:10.4018/jbdcn.2012070104

Kierkegaard, S. (2012). Not every cloud brings rain: Legal risks on the horizon. In M. Gupta, J. Walp, & R. Sharman (Eds.), *Strategic and practical approaches for information security governance: Technologies and applied solutions* (pp. 181–194). Hershey, PA: IGI Global. doi:10.4018/978-1-4666-0197-0.ch011

Kifayat, K., Shamsa, T. B., Mackay, M., Merabti, M., & Shi, Q. (2013). Real time risk management in cloud computation. In D. Rosado, D. Mellado, E. Fernandez-Medina, & M. Piattini (Eds.), *Security engineering for cloud computing: Approaches and tools* (pp. 123–145). Hershey, PA: IGI Global. doi:10.4018/978-1-4666-2125-1.ch007

Kim, Y.T. (1997). Contrast enhancement using brightness preserving bi-histogram equalization. *IEEE Trans. Consum. Electron, 43*(1), 1–8.

Kim, M., Park, M., & Park, J. (2009). When Customer Satisfaction Isn't Good Enough: The Role of Switching Incentives and Barriers Affecting Customer Behavior in Korean Mobile Communications Services. In I. Lee (Ed.), *Handbook of Research on Telecommunications Planning and Management for Business* (pp. 351–363). Hershey, PA: Information Science Reference. doi:10.4018/978-1-60566-194-0.ch022

King, T. M., Ganti, A. S., & Froslie, D. (2013). Towards improving the testability of cloud application services. In S. Tilley & T. Parveen (Eds.), *Software testing in the cloud: Perspectives on an emerging discipline* (pp. 322–339). Hershey, PA: IGI Global. doi:10.4018/978-1-4666-2536-5.ch015

Kipp, A., Schneider, R., & Schubert, L. (2013). Encapsulation of complex HPC services. In C. Rückemann (Ed.), *Integrated information and computing systems for natural, spatial, and social sciences* (pp. 153–176). Hershey, PA: IGI Global. doi:10.4018/978-1-4666-2190-9.ch008

Kldiashvili, E. (2012). The cloud computing as the tool for implementation of virtual organization technology for ehealth. *Journal of Information Technology Research*, *5*(1), 18–34. doi:10.4018/jitr.2012010102

Kldiashvili, E. (2013). Implementation of telecytology in georgia for quality assurance programs. *Journal of Information Technology Research*, *6*(2), 24–45. doi:10.4018/jitr.2013040102

Klepac, G. (2010). Preparing for New Competition in the Retail Industry. In A. Syvajarvi & J. Stenvall (Eds.), *Data Mining in Public and Private Sectors: Organizational and Government Applications* (pp. 245–266). Hershey, PA: Information Science Reference. doi:10.4018/978-1-60566-906-9.ch013

Klepac, G. (2014). Data Mining Models as a Tool for Churn Reduction and Custom Product Development in Telecommunication Industries. In P. Vasant (Ed.), *Handbook of Research on Novel Soft Computing Intelligent Algorithms: Theory and Practical Applications* (pp. 511–537). Hershey, PA: Information Science Reference. doi:10.4018/978-1-4666-4450-2.ch017

Klepac, G., & Berg, K. L. (2015a). Proposal of Analytical Model for Business Problems Solving in Big Data Environment. In J. Girard, D. Klein, & K. Berg (Eds.), *Strategic Data-Based Wisdom in the Big Data Era* (pp. 209–228). Hershey, PA: Information Science Reference. doi:10.4018/978-1-4666-8122-4.ch012

Klepac, G., Kopal, R., & Mršić, L. (2015). *Developing Churn Models Using Data Mining Techniques and Social Network Analysis* (pp. 1–361). Hershey, PA: IGI Global. doi:10.4018/978-1-4666-6288-9

Klepac, G., Mrsic, L., & Kopal, R. (2016). Efficient Risk Profiling Using Bayesian Networks and Particle Swarm Optimization Algorithm. In D. Jakóbczak (Ed.), *Analyzing Risk through Probabilistic Modeling in Operations Research* (pp. 91–124). Hershey, PA: Business Science Reference. doi:10.4018/978-1-4666-9458-3.ch004

Kobb, R., Lane, R., & Stallings, D. (2008). E-learning and telehealth: Measuring your success. *Telemedicine Journal and e-Health*, *14*(6), 576–579. doi:10.1089/tmj.2007.0103 PMID:18729757

Koh, C. G., Chen, Y. F., & Liaw, C. Y. (2003). A hybrid computational strategy for identification of structural parameters. *Computers & Structures, 81*(2), 107–117. doi:10.1016/S0045-7949(02)00344-9

Konstantinos, E. P., & Michael, N. V. (2010). Applications in Machine Learning. In K. Parsopoulos & M. Vrahatis (Eds.), *Particle Swarm Optimization and Intelligence: Advances and Applications* (pp. 149–167). Hershey, PA: Information Science Reference. doi:10.4018/978-1-61520-666-7.ch006

Konstantinos, E. P., & Michael, N. V. (2010). Established and Recently Proposed Variants of Particle Swarm Optimization. In K. Parsopoulos & M. Vrahatis (Eds.), *Particle Swarm Optimization and Intelligence: Advances and Applications* (pp. 88–132). Hershey, PA: Information Science Reference. doi:10.4018/978-1-61520-666-7.ch004

Koshiyama, A. S., Escovedo, T., Dias, M. D., Vellasco, M. M., & Pacheco, M. A. (2012). Combining Forecasts: A Genetic Programming Approach. *International Journal of Natural Computing Research*, 18.

Koomutov, N. (2013). Concolic test generation and the cloud: deployment and verification perspectives. In S. Tilley & T. Parveen (Eds.), *Software testing in the cloud: Perspectives on an emerging discipline* (pp. 231–251). Hershey, PA: IGI Global. doi:10.4018/978-1-4666-2536-5.ch011

Kotamarti, R. M., Thornton, M. A., & Dunham, M. H. (2012). Quantum computing approach for alignment-free sequence search and classification. In S. Ali, N. Abbadeni, & M. Batouche (Eds.), *Multidisciplinary computational intelligence techniques: Applications in business, engineering, and medicine* (pp. 279–300). Hershey, PA: IGI Global. doi:10.4018/978-1-4666-1830-5.ch017

Koza, J. R. (1992). *Genetic programming: On the programming of computers by means of natural selection (complex adaptive systems)*. The MIT Press.

Koza, J. R. (1994). *Genetic programming II: Automatic discovery of reusable programs*. Cambridge, MA: The MIT Press.

Kremmydas, D., Petsakos, A., & Rozakis, S. (2012). Parametric optimization of linear and non-linear models via parallel computing to enhance web-spatial DSS interactivity. *International Journal of Decision Support System Technology, 4*(1), 14–29. doi:10.4018/jdsst.2012010102

Kress, M., Mostaghim, S., & Seese, D. (2010). Intelligent Business Process Execution using Particle Swarm Optimization. In Information Resources Management: Concepts, Methodologies, Tools and Applications (pp. 797-815). Hershey, PA: Information Science Reference. doi:10.4018/978-1-61520-965-1.ch319

Krishnadas, N., & Pillai, R. R. (2013). Cloud computing diagnosis: A comprehensive study. In X. Yang & L. Liu (Eds.), *Principles, methodologies, and service-oriented approaches for cloud computing* (pp. 1–18). Hershey, PA: IGI Global. doi:10.4018/978-1-4666-2854-0.ch001

Kübert, R., & Katsaros, G. (2011). Using free software for elastic web hosting on a private cloud. *International Journal of Cloud Applications and Computing*, *1*(2), 14–28. doi:10.4018/ijcac.2011040102

Kübert, R., & Katsaros, G. (2013). Using free software for elastic web hosting on a private cloud. In S. Aljawarneh (Ed.), *Cloud computing advancements in design, implementation, and technologies* (pp. 97–111). Hershey, PA: IGI Global. doi:10.4018/978-1-4666-1879-4.ch007

Kumar, P. S., Ashok, M. S., & Subramanian, R. (2012). A publicly verifiable dynamic secret sharing protocol for secure and dependable data storage in cloud computing. *International Journal of Cloud Applications and Computing*, *2*(3), 1–25. doi:10.4018/ijcac.2012070101

Kurbatsky, V., Sidorov, D., Tomin, N., & Spiryaev, V. (2014). Optimal Training of Artificial Neural Networks to Forecast Power System State Variables. *International Journal of Energy Optimization and Engineering*, *3*(1), 65–82. doi:10.4018/ijeoe.2014010104

Lagunas-Jiménez, R., Fernández-Anaya, G., & Martínez-García, J. C. (2006, September). Tuning of two-degrees-of-freedom PID controllers via the multiobjective genetic algorithm NSGA-II. In *Electronics, Robotics and Automotive Mechanics Conference, 2006* (Vol. 2, pp. 145-150). IEEE. doi:10.1109/CERMA.2006.94

Lam, D., & MacKenzie, C. (2005). Human and organizational factors affecting telemedicine utilization within U.S. military forces in Europe. *Telemedicine Journal and e-Health*, *11*(1), 70–78. doi:10.1089/tmj.2005.11.70 PMID:15785223

Lande, R. (1985). Genetic variation and phenotypic evolution during allopatric speciation. *American Naturalist*, *116*(4), 463–479. doi:10.1086/283642

Lane, K. (2006). Telemedicine news. *Telemedicine Journal and e-Health*, *12*(5), 507–511. doi:10.1089/tmj.2006.12.507 PMID:16430380

Lareng, L. (2002). Telemedicine in Europe. *European Journal of Internal Medicine*, *13*(1), 1–13. doi:10.1016/S0953-6205(01)00188-1 PMID:11836076

Larose, D. T. (2005). *Discovering Knowledge in Data: An Introduction to Data Mining*. John Wiley &Sons Inc.

Lasluisa, S., Rodero, I., & Parashar, M. (2013). Software design for passing sarbanes-oxley in cloud computing. In C. Rückemann (Ed.), *Integrated information and computing systems for natural, spatial, and social sciences* (pp. 27–42). Hershey, PA: IGI Global. doi:10.4018/978-1-4666-2190-9.ch002

Lasluisa, S., Rodero, I., & Parashar, M. (2014). Software design for passing sarbanes-oxley in cloud computing. In *Software design and development: Concepts, methodologies, tools, and applications* (pp. 1659–1674). Hershey, PA: IGI Global. doi:10.4018/978-1-4666-4301-7.ch080

Latifi, R., Muja, S., Bekhteshi, F., & Merrell, R. (2006). The role of telemedicine and information technology in the redevelopment of medical systems: The case of Kosova. *Telemedicine Journal and e-Health*, *12*(3), 332–340. doi:10.1089/tmj.2006.12.332 PMID:16796501

Leandro, C. (2009). A novel particle swarm optimization approach using Henon map and implicit filtering local search for economic load dispatch. *Chaos, Solitons, and Fractals*, *39*(2), 510–518. doi:10.1016/j.chaos.2007.01.093

Lee, C. H. (2004). A survey of PID controller design based on gain and phase margins. *International Journal of Computational Cognition*, *2*(3), 63–100.

Lee, K., & Paik, T. (2006). A Neural Network Approach to Cost Minimizatin in a Production Scheduling Setting. In J. Rabuñal & J. Dorado (Eds.), *Artificial Neural Networks in Real-Life Applications* (pp. 297–313). Hershey, PA: Idea Group Publishing. doi:10.4018/978-1-59140-902-1.ch014

Lee, W. N. (2013). An economic analysis of cloud: "Software as a service" (saas) computing and "virtual desktop infrastructure" (VDI) models. In A. Bento & A. Aggarwal (Eds.), *Cloud computing service and deployment models: Layers and management* (pp. 289–295). Hershey, PA: IGI Global. doi:10.4018/978-1-4666-2187-9.ch016

Lehman, J., & Stanley, K. O. (2010). Efficiently evolving programs through the search for novelty. *Proceedings of the 12th annual conference on Genetic and evolutionary computation - GECCO '10*. doi:10.1145/1830483.1830638

Levine, K., & White, B. A. (2011). A crisis at hafford furniture: Cloud computing case study. *Journal of Cases on Information Technology*, *13*(1), 57–71. doi:10.4018/jcit.2011010104

Levine, K., & White, B. A. (2013). A crisis at Hafford furniture: Cloud computing case study. In M. Khosrow-Pour (Ed.), *Cases on emerging information technology research and applications* (pp. 70–87). Hershey, PA: IGI Global. doi:10.4018/978-1-4666-3619-4.ch004

Levine, W. S. (1996). *The Control Handbook*. CRC Press.

Levin, R. I., & Lieven, N. A. J. (1998). Dynamic finite element model updating using simulated annealing and genetic algorithms. *Mechanical Systems and Signal Processing*, *12*(1), 91–120. doi:10.1006/mssp.1996.0136

Lewis, F. L., & Syrmos, V. L. (1995). *Optimal control*. John Wiley & Sons.

Liang, J. J., Qin, A. K., Suganthan, P. N., & Baskar, S. (2006). Comprehensive learning particle swarm optimizer for global optimization of multimodal functions. *Evolutionary Computation. IEEE Transactions on*, *10*(3), 281–295.

Liang, J. J., Qin, A. K., Suganthan, P., & Baskar, S. (2004). Evaluation of Comprehensive Learning Particle Swarm Optimizer. In N. Pal, N. Kasabov, R. Mudi, S. Pal, & S. Parui (Eds.), *Neural Information Processing* (Vol. 3316, pp. 230–235). Springer Berlin Heidelberg. doi:10.1007/978-3-540-30499-9_34

Liang, T., Lu, F., & Chiu, J. (2012). A hybrid resource reservation method for workflows in clouds. *International Journal of Grid and High Performance Computing*, *4*(4), 1–21. doi:10.4018/jghpc.2012100101

Liaskos, K., & Roper, M. (2007, September). *Automatic test-data generation: An immunological approach.* IEEE Computer Society.

Liaskos, K., & Roper, M. (2008). Hybridizing evolutionary testing with artificial immune systems and local search. In *ICSTW '08: Proceedings of the 2008 IEEE international conference on software testing verification and validation workshop* (pp. 211–220). Washington, DC: IEEE Computer Society. doi:10.1109/ICSTW.2008.21

Liaskos, K., Roper, M., & Wood, M. (2007). Investigating data-flow coverage of classes using evolutionary algorithms. In *GECCO '07: Proceedings of the 9th annual conference on genetic and evolutionary computation* (pp. 1140–1140). New York: ACM. doi:10.1145/1276958.1277183

Li, H., & Li, S. (2012). Quantum particle swarm evolutionary algorithm with application to system identification. In *Proceedings of 2012 International Conference on Measurement, Information and Control* (pp. 1032-1036). Harbin: IEEE. doi:10.1109/MIC.2012.6273477

Lihoreau, M., Chittka, L., & Raine, N. (2010). Travel Optimization by Foraging Bumblebees through Readjustments of Traplines after Discovery of New Feeding Locations. *American Naturalist, 176*(6), 744–757. doi:10.1086/657042 PMID:20973670

Li, J., Meng, L., Zhu, Z., Li, X., Huai, J., & Liu, L. (2013). CloudRank: A cloud service ranking method based on both user feedback and service testing. In X. Yang & L. Liu (Eds.), *Principles, methodologies, and service-oriented approaches for cloud computing* (pp. 230–258). Hershey, PA: IGI Global. doi:10.4018/978-1-4666-2854-0.ch010

Lillegraven, J. A. (1972). Ordinal and familial diversity in Cenozoic mammals. *Taxon, 21*(2/3), 261–274. doi:10.2307/1218194

Limpert, E., Stahel, W., & Abbt, M. (2001). Log-normal distributions across the sciences: Keys and clues. *Bioscience, 51*(5), 342–352. doi:10.1641/0006-3568(2001)051[0341:LNDATS]2.0.CO;2

Liu, X., Wang, B., & Liu, H. (2005). Evolutionary search in the context of object-oriented programs. *Mic'05: Proceedings of the sixth metaheuristics international conference.*

Li, Y., Ang, K. H., & Chong, G. C. (2006). PID control system analysis and design. *IEEE Control Systems, 26*(1), 32–41. doi:10.1109/MCS.2006.1580152

Li, Z. J., Chen, C., & Wang, K. (2011). Cloud computing for agent-based urban transportation systems. *IEEE Intelligent Systems, 26*(1), 73–79. doi:10.1109/MIS.2011.10

Lloyd. (2006). *Programming the Universe: A Quantum Computer Scientist Takes On the Cosmos.* Knopf.

LloydS. (2002). Retrieved from http://edge.org/conversation/the-computational-universe

Lorenz, M., Rath-Wiggins, L., Runde, W., Messina, A., Sunna, P., Dimino, G., ... Borgotallo, R. (2013). Media convergence and cloud technologies: Smart storage, better workflows. In D. Kyriazis, A. Voulodimos, S. Gogouvitis, & T. Varvarigou (Eds.), *Data intensive storage services for cloud environments* (pp. 132–144). Hershey, PA: IGI Global. doi:10.4018/978-1-4666-3934-8.ch009

Lozano, J. A. (2006). *Towards a new evolutionary computation: advances on estimation of distribution algorithms* (Vol. 192). Springer Science & Business Media. doi:10.1007/3-540-32494-1

Lu, X. L., Li, P. Z., & Chen, Y. Q. (2003). *Benchmark Test of a 12-Story Reinforced Concrete Frame Model on Shaking Table.* Study Report of State Key Laboratory for Disaster Reduction in Civil Engineering, Tongji University (A20030609-405).

M., S. G., & G., S. K. (2012). An enterprise mashup integration service framework for clouds. *International Journal of Cloud Applications and Computing, 2*(2), 31-40. doi:10.4018/ijcac.2012040103

Magurran, A. (1999). Population differentiation without speciation. In A. Magurran & R. M. May (Eds.), *Evolution of Biological Diversity.* Oxford, UK: Oxford University Press.

Maharana, S. K., Mali, P. B., Prabhakar, G. J. S., & Kumar, V. (2011). Cloud computing applied for numerical study of thermal characteristics of SIP. *International Journal of Cloud Applications and Computing, 1*(3), 12–21. doi:10.4018/ijcac.2011070102

Maharana, S. K., Mali, P. B., Prabhakar, G. J. S., & Kumar, V. (2013). Cloud computing applied for numerical study of thermal characteristics of SIP. In S. Aljawarneh (Ed.), *Cloud computing advancements in design, implementation, and technologies* (pp. 166–175). Hershey, PA: IGI Global. doi:10.4018/978-1-4666-1879-4.ch012

Maharana, S. K., P, G. P., & Bhati, A. (2012). A study of cloud computing for retinal image processing through MATLAB. *International Journal of Cloud Applications and Computing, 2*(2), 59–69. doi:10.4018/ijcac.2012040106

Maharana, S. K., Prabhakar, P. G., & Bhati, A. (2013). A study of cloud computing for retinal image processing through MATLAB. In *Image processing: Concepts, methodologies, tools, and applications* (pp. 101–111). Hershey, PA: IGI Global. doi:10.4018/978-1-4666-3994-2.ch006

Mahesh, S., Landry, B. J., Sridhar, T., & Walsh, K. R. (2011). A decision table for the cloud computing decision in small business. *Information Resources Management Journal, 24*(3), 9–25. doi:10.4018/irmj.2011070102

Mahesh, S., Landry, B. J., Sridhar, T., & Walsh, K. R. (2013). A decision table for the cloud computing decision in small business. In M. Khosrow-Pour (Ed.), *Managing information resources and technology: Emerging Applications and theories* (pp. 159–176). Hershey, PA: IGI Global. doi:10.4018/978-1-4666-3616-3.ch012

Maia, R., & de Castro, L. N. (2012). Bee Colonies as Model for Multimodal Continuous Optimization: The OptBees Algorithm. *Proceedings of the IEEE Congress on Evolutionary Computation,* (pp. 1-8). doi:10.1109/CEC.2012.6252975

Majhi, B., & Panda, G. (2009). Identification of IIR systems using comprehensive learning particle swarm optimisation. *International Journal of Power and Energy Conversion, 1*(1), 105–124. doi:10.1504/IJPEC.2009.023478

Malhotra, R. (2014). SIDE: A Decision Support System Using a Combination of Swarm Intelligence and Data Envelopment Analysis. *International Journal of Strategic Decision Sciences*, *5*(1), 39–58. doi:10.4018/ijsds.2014010103

Mantere, T., & Alander, J. T. (2005). Evolutionary software engineering, a review. *Applied Soft Computing*, *5*(3), 315–331. doi:10.1016/j.asoc.2004.08.004

Maragathavalli, P. (2011). *Search-based software test data generation using evolutionary computation.* CoRR, abs/1103.0125

J. J. Marciniak (Ed.). (1994). *Encyclopedia of software engineering.* New York: Wiley-Interscience.

Marquezan, C. C., Metzger, A., Pohl, K., Engen, V., Boniface, M., Phillips, S. C., & Zlatev, Z. (2013). Adaptive future internet applications: Opportunities and challenges for adaptive web services technology. In G. Ortiz & J. Cubo (Eds.), *Adaptive web services for modular and reusable software development: Tactics and solutions* (pp. 333–353). Hershey, PA: IGI Global. doi:10.4018/978-1-4666-2089-6.ch014

Marshall, P. J. (2012). Cloud computing: Next generation education. In L. Chao (Ed.), *Cloud computing for teaching and learning: Strategies for design and implementation* (pp. 180–185). Hershey, PA: IGI Global. doi:10.4018/978-1-4666-0957-0.ch012

Martinez-Ortiz, A. (2012). Open cloud technologies. In L. Vaquero, J. Cáceres, & J. Hierro (Eds.), *Open source cloud computing systems: Practices and paradigms* (pp. 1–17). Hershey, PA: IGI Global. doi:10.4018/978-1-4666-0098-0.ch001

Massonet, P., Michot, A., Naqvi, S., Villari, M., & Latanicki, J. (2013). Securing the external interfaces of a federated infrastructure cloud. In *IT policy and ethics: Concepts, methodologies, tools, and applications* (pp. 1876–1903). Hershey, PA: IGI Global. doi:10.4018/978-1-4666-2919-6.ch082

Mattavelli, A., Goffi, A., & Gorla, A. (2015). Synthesis of Equivalent Method Calls in Guava. In Lecture Notes in Computer Science (pp. 248–254). Academic Press. doi:10.1007/978-3-319-22183-0_19

Mavrogeorgi, N., Gogouvitis, S. V., Voulodimos, A., & Alexandrou, V. (2013). SLA management in storage clouds. In D. Kyriazis, A. Voulodimos, S. Gogouvitis, & T. Varvarigou (Eds.), *Data intensive storage services for cloud environments* (pp. 72–93). Hershey, PA: IGI Global. doi:10.4018/978-1-4666-3934-8.ch006

Mayer, D. G. (2002). *Evolutionary algorithms and agricultural systems.* Springer. doi:10.1007/978-1-4615-1717-7

McMinn, P. (2009). Search-based failure discovery using testability transformations to generate pseudo-oracles. In *GECCO '09: Proceedings of the 11th annual conference on genetic and evolutionary computation* (pp. 1689–1696). New York: ACM. doi:10.1145/1569901.1570127

McMinn, P. (2011). Search-based software testing: Past, present and future. In *Software testing, verification and validation workshops (ICSTW), 2011 IEEE fourth international conference on* (p. 153-163). IEEE.

McMinn, P., & Holcombe, M. (2003). *The state problem for evolutionary testing.* Available from citeseer.ist.psu.edu/mcminn03state.html

McMinn, P. (2004). Search-based software test data generation: A survey. *Software Testing, Verification & Reliability, 14*(2), 105–156. doi:10.1002/stvr.294

Mehta, P., Goyal, S., & Long, T. (2009). Information processing and signal integration in bacterial quorum sensing. Molecular Systems Biology, 5.

Mehta, H. K. (2013). Cloud selection for e-business a parameter based solution. In K. Tarnay, S. Imre, & L. Xu (Eds.), *Research and development in e-business through service-oriented solutions* (pp. 199–207). Hershey, PA: IGI Global. doi:10.4018/978-1-4666-4181-5.ch009

Mehta, H. K., & Gupta, E. (2013). Economy based resource allocation in IaaS cloud. *International Journal of Cloud Applications and Computing, 3*(2), 1–11. doi:10.4018/ijcac.2013040101

Mell, P., & Grance, T. (2010). The NIST definition of cloud computing. *Communications of the ACM, 53*(6), 50.

Merell, R., & Doarn, C. (2008). Is it time for a telemedicine breakthrough? *Telemedicine Journal and e-Health, 14*(6), 505–506. doi:10.1089/tmj.2008.8499 PMID:18729745

Miah, S. J. (2012). Cloud-based intelligent DSS design for emergency professionals. In S. Ali, N. Abbadeni, & M. Batouche (Eds.), *Multidisciplinary computational intelligence techniques: Applications in business, engineering, and medicine* (pp. 47–60). Hershey, PA: IGI Global. doi:10.4018/978-1-4666-1830-5.ch004

Miah, S. J. (2013). Cloud-based intelligent DSS design for emergency professionals. In *Data mining: Concepts, methodologies, tools, and applications* (pp. 991–1003). Hershey, PA: IGI Global. doi:10.4018/978-1-4666-2455-9.ch050

Michalewicz, Z. (1994). Genetic algorithms + data structures = evolution programs (2nd ed.). New York: Springer-Verlag New York, Inc.

Mikkilineni, R. (2012). Architectural resiliency in distributed computing. *International Journal of Grid and High Performance Computing, 4*(4), 37–51. doi:10.4018/jghpc.2012100103

Millham, R. (2012). Software asset re-use: Migration of data-intensive legacy system to the cloud computing paradigm. In H. Yang & X. Liu (Eds.), *Software reuse in the emerging cloud computing era* (pp. 1–27). Hershey, PA: IGI Global. doi:10.4018/978-1-4666-0897-9.ch001

Milne, B. T. (1998). Motivation and Benefits of Complex Systems Approaches in Ecology. *Ecosystems (New York, N.Y.), 1*(5), 449–456. doi:10.1007/s100219900040

Miraz, M., Lanzi, P. L., & Baresi, L. (2011). *Testful – an evolutionary testing framework for java.* Available from https://code.google.com/p/testful/

Miraz, M., Lanzi, P. L., & Baresi, L. (2009). Testful: using a hybrid evolutionary algorithm for testing stateful systems. In *Proceedings of the 11th annual conference on genetic and evolutionary computation* (pp. 1947–1948). New York: ACM. doi:10.1145/1569901.1570252

Mircea, M. (2011). Building the agile enterprise with service-oriented architecture, business process management and decision management. *International Journal of E-Entrepreneurship and Innovation*, *2*(4), 32–48. doi:10.4018/jeei.2011100103

Modares, H., Lloret, J., Moravejosharieh, A., & Salleh, R. (2014). Security in mobile cloud computing. In J. Rodrigues, K. Lin, & J. Lloret (Eds.), *Mobile networks and cloud computing convergence for progressive services and applications* (pp. 79–91). Hershey, PA: IGI Global. doi:10.4018/978-1-4666-4781-7.ch005

Moedjiono, S., & Mas'at, A. (2012). Cloud computing implementation strategy for information dissemination on meteorology, climatology, air quality, and geophysics (MKKuG). *Journal of Information Technology Research*, *5*(3), 71–84. doi:10.4018/jitr.2012070104

Moiny, J. (2012). Cloud based social network sites: Under whose control? In A. Dudley, J. Braman, & G. Vincenti (Eds.), *Investigating cyber law and cyber ethics: Issues, impacts and practices* (pp. 147–219). Hershey, PA: IGI Global. doi:10.4018/978-1-61350-132-0.ch009

Montana, D. J. (1993). Strongly typed genetic programming (Tech. Rep. No. #7866). Academic Press.

Montana, D. J. (1995). Strongly typed genetic programming. *Evolutionary Computation*, *3*(2), 199–230. doi:10.1162/evco.1995.3.2.199

Montgomery, D. C. (2007). *Introduction to statistical quality control.* John Wiley & Sons.

Moore, D. Jr, Green, J., Jay, S., Leist, J., & Maitland, F. (1994). Creating a new paradigm for CME: Seizing opportunities within the health care revolution. *The Journal of Continuing Education in the Health Professions*, *14*(1), 4–31. doi:10.1002/chp.4750140102

Mora, J. (2004). *Performance and robustness of the methods based on second order models plus dead time tuning PID controllers.* Escuela de Ingeniería Eléctrica, Universidad de Costa Rica.

Moreno, I. S., & Xu, J. (2011). Energy-efficiency in cloud computing environments: Towards energy savings without performance degradation. *International Journal of Cloud Applications and Computing*, *1*(1), 17–33. doi:10.4018/ijcac.2011010102

Moreno, I. S., & Xu, J. (2013). Energy-efficiency in cloud computing environments: Towards energy savings without performance degradation. In S. Aljawarneh (Ed.), *Cloud computing advancements in design, implementation, and technologies* (pp. 18–36). Hershey, PA: IGI Global. doi:10.4018/978-1-4666-1879-4.ch002

Moura, A., & Del Giglio, A. (2000). Education via internet. *Revista da Associação Médica Brasileira, 46*(1), 47–51. PMID:10770902

Mouser, C. R., & Dunn, S. A. (2005). Comparing genetic algorithms and particle swarm optimisation for an inverse problem exercise. *The ANZIAM Journal, 46*, C89–C101. doi:10.21914/anziamj.v46i0.949

Muñoz, A., Maña, A., & González, J. (2013). Dynamic security properties monitoring architecture for cloud computing. In D. Rosado, D. Mellado, E. Fernandez-Medina, & M. Piattini (Eds.), *Security engineering for cloud computing: Approaches and tools* (pp. 1–18). Hershey, PA: IGI Global. doi:10.4018/978-1-4666-2125-1.ch001

Mvelase, P., Dlodlo, N., Williams, Q., & Adigun, M. O. (2011). Custom-made cloud enterprise architecture for small medium and micro enterprises. *International Journal of Cloud Applications and Computing, 1*(3), 52–63. doi:10.4018/ijcac.2011070105

Mvelase, P., Dlodlo, N., Williams, Q., & Adigun, M. O. (2012). Custom-made cloud enterprise architecture for small medium and micro enterprises. In *Grid and cloud computing: Concepts, methodologies, tools and applications* (pp. 589–601). Hershey, PA: IGI Global. doi:10.4018/978-1-4666-0879-5.ch303

Mvelase, P., Dlodlo, N., Williams, Q., & Adigun, M. O. (2013). Custom-made cloud enterprise architecture for small medium and micro enterprises. In S. Aljawarneh (Ed.), *Cloud computing advancements in design, implementation, and technologies* (pp. 205–217). Hershey, PA: IGI Global. doi:10.4018/978-1-4666-1879-4.ch015

Myers, A. A., & Giller, P. S. (1991). *Analytical Biogeography*. Chapman & Hall.

Myers, G. J., & Sandler, C. (2004). *The art of software testing*. John Wiley & Sons.

Naeem, M. A., Dobbie, G., & Weber, G. (2014). Big data management in the context of real-time data warehousing. In W. Hu & N. Kaabouch (Eds.), *Big data management, technologies, and applications* (pp. 150–176). Hershey, PA: IGI Global. doi:10.4018/978-1-4666-4699-5.ch007

Nannings, B., & Abu-Hanna, A. (2006). Decision support telemedicine systems: A conceptual model and reusable templates. *Telemedicine Journal and e-Health, 12*(6), 644–654. doi:10.1089/tmj.2006.12.644 PMID:17250486

Nelder, J. A., & Mead, R. (1965). A simplex method for function minimization. *The Computer Journal, 7*(4), 308–313. doi:10.1093/comjnl/7.4.308

Nguyen, S., & Kachitvichyanukul, V. (2010). Movement Strategies for Multi-Objective Particle Swarm Optimization. *International Journal of Applied Metaheuristic Computing, 1*(3), 59–79. doi:10.4018/jamc.2010070105

Nogueira, A. F., Ribeiro, J. C. B., de Vega, F. F., & Zenha-Rela, M. A. (2013). ecrash: An empirical study on the apache ant project. In *Proceedings of the 5th international symposium on search based software engineering (SSBSE '13)* (Vol. 8084). St. Petersburg, Russia: Springer. doi:10.1007/978-3-642-39742-4_25

Nogueira, A. F., Ribeiro, J. C. B., Fernández de Vega, F., & Zenha-Rela, M. A. (2014). Object-Oriented Evolutionary Testing: A Review of Evolutionary Approaches to the Generation of Test Data for Object-Oriented Software. *International Journal of Natural Computing Research*, *4*(4), 15–35. doi:10.4018/ijncr.2014100102

O'Dwyer, A. (2009). *Handbook of PI and PID controller tuning rules*. World Scientific. doi:10.1142/p575

Ofosu, W. K., & Saliah-Hassane, H. (2013). Cloud computing in the education environment for developing nations. *International Journal of Interdisciplinary Telecommunications and Networking*, *5*(3), 54–62. doi:10.4018/jitn.2013070106

Ogunnaike, B. A., & Ray, W. H. (1994). *Process dynamics, modeling, and control*. Oxford University Press.

Okun, O. (2014). Bayesian Variable Selection. In J. Wang (Ed.), *Encyclopedia of Business Analytics and Optimization* (pp. 241–250). Hershey, PA: Business Science Reference. doi:10.4018/978-1-4666-5202-6.ch023

Oliveros, E., Cucinotta, T., Phillips, S. C., Yang, X., Middleton, S., & Voith, T. (2012). Monitoring and metering in the cloud. In D. Kyriazis, T. Varvarigou, & K. Konstanteli (Eds.), *Achieving real-time in distributed computing: From grids to clouds* (pp. 94–114). Hershey, PA: IGI Global. doi:10.4018/978-1-60960-827-9.ch006

Olson, E. A. (2011). *Particle Swarm Optimization: Theory, Techniques and Applications (Engineering Tools, Techniques and Tables)*. Nova Science Pub Inc.

Olsson, J. R. (1994). *Inductive functional programming using incremental program transformation and execution of logic programs by iterative-deepening a* sld-tree search* (research report No. 189). University of Oslo.

Orton, I., Alva, A., & Endicott-Popovsky, B. (2013). Legal process and requirements for cloud forensic investigations. In K. Ruan (Ed.), *Cybercrime and cloud forensics: Applications for investigation processes* (pp. 186–229). Hershey, PA: IGI Global. doi:10.4018/978-1-4666-2662-1.ch008

Pacheco, C., & Ernst, M. D. (2007). Randoop: feedback-directed random testing for java. In *Oopsla '07: Companion to the 22nd ACM SIGPLAN conference on object-oriented programming systems and applications companion* (pp. 815–816). New York: ACM. doi:10.1145/1297846.1297902

Pacini, E., Mateos, C., & Garino, C. G. (2013). Schedulers Based on Ant Colony Optimization for Parameter Sweep Experiments in Distributed Environments. In S. Bhattacharyya & P. Dutta (Eds.), *Handbook of Research on Computational Intelligence for Engineering, Science, and Business* (pp. 410–448). Hershey, PA: Information Science Reference. doi:10.4018/978-1-4666-2518-1.ch016

Pak, H. (2007). Telethinking. *Telemedicine Journal and e-Health*, *13*(5), 483–486. doi:10.1089/tmj.2007.9976 PMID:17999610

Pakhira, A., & Andras, P. (2013). Leveraging the cloud for large-scale software testing – A case study: Google Chrome on Amazon. In S. Tilley & T. Parveen (Eds.), *Software testing in the cloud: Perspectives on an emerging discipline* (pp. 252–279). Hershey, PA: IGI Global. doi:10.4018/978-1-4666-2536-5.ch012

Palanivel, K., & Kuppuswami, S. (2014). A cloud-oriented reference architecture to digital library systems. In S. Dhamdhere (Ed.), *Cloud computing and virtualization technologies in libraries* (pp. 230–254). Hershey, PA: IGI Global. doi:10.4018/978-1-4666-4631-5.ch014

Paletta, M. (2012). Intelligent clouds: By means of using multi-agent systems environments. In L. Chao (Ed.), *Cloud computing for teaching and learning: Strategies for design and implementation* (pp. 254–279). Hershey, PA: IGI Global. doi:10.4018/978-1-4666-0957-0.ch017

Pal, K., & Karakostas, B. (2013). The use of cloud computing in shipping logistics. In D. Graham, I. Manikas, & D. Folinas (Eds.), *E-logistics and e-supply chain management: Applications for evolving business* (pp. 104–124). Hershey, PA: IGI Global. doi:10.4018/978-1-4666-3914-0.ch006

Pallot, M., Le Marc, C., Richir, S., Schmidt, C., & Mathieu, J. (2012). Innovation gaming: An immersive experience environment enabling co-creation. In M. Cruz-Cunha (Ed.), *Handbook of research on serious games as educational, business and research tools* (pp. 1–24). Hershey, PA: IGI Global. doi:10.4018/978-1-4666-0149-9.ch001

Pal, S. (2013). Cloud computing: Security concerns and issues. In A. Bento & A. Aggarwal (Eds.), *Cloud computing service and deployment models: Layers and management* (pp. 191–207). Hershey, PA: IGI Global. doi:10.4018/978-1-4666-2187-9.ch010

Pal, S. (2013). Storage security and technical challenges of cloud computing. In D. Kyriazis, A. Voulodimos, S. Gogouvitis, & T. Varvarigou (Eds.), *Data intensive storage services for cloud environments* (pp. 225–240). Hershey, PA: IGI Global. doi:10.4018/978-1-4666-3934-8.ch014

Panichella, A., Kifetew, F. M., & Tonella, P. (2015a). Reformulating Branch Coverage as a Many-Objective Optimization Problem. In *2015 IEEE 8th International Conference on Software Testing, Verification and Validation (ICST)*. IEEE. doi:10.1109/ICST.2015.7102604

Panichella, A., Kifetew, F. M., & Tonella, P. (2015b). Results for EvoSuite -- MOSA at the Third Unit Testing Tool Competition. In *2015 IEEE/ACM 8th International Workshop on Search-Based Software Testing*. IEEE. doi:10.1109/sbst.2015.14

Pankowska, M. (2011). Information technology resources virtualization for sustainable development. *International Journal of Applied Logistics*, 2(2), 35–48. doi:10.4018/jal.2011040103

Pankowska, M. (2013). Information technology resources virtualization for sustainable development. In Z. Luo (Ed.), *Technological solutions for modern logistics and supply chain management* (pp. 248–262). Hershey, PA: IGI Global. doi:10.4018/978-1-4666-2773-4.ch016

Parappallil, J. J., Zarvic, N., & Thomas, O. (2012). A context and content reflection on business-IT alignment research. *International Journal of IT/Business Alignment and Governance*, 3(2), 21–37. doi:10.4018/jitbag.2012070102

Parashar, V., Vishwakarma, M. L., & Parashar, R. (2014). A new framework for building academic library through cloud computing. In S. Dhamdhere (Ed.), *Cloud computing and virtualization technologies in libraries* (pp. 107–123). Hershey, PA: IGI Global. doi:10.4018/978-1-4666-4631-5.ch007

Pasti, R., de Castro, L. N., & Von Zuben, F. J. (2011). Ecosystems Computing. *International Journal of Natural Computing Research*, *2*(4), 47–67. doi:10.4018/jncr.2011100104

Pavlov, Y., & Fraser, G. (2012). Semi-automatic search-based test generation. In *Proceedings of the 2012 ieee fifth international conference on software testing, verification and validation* (pp. 777–784). Washington, DC: IEEE Computer Society. doi:10.1109/ICST.2012.176

Pendyala, V. S., & Holliday, J. (2012). Cloud as a computer. In X. Liu & Y. Li (Eds.), *Advanced design approaches to emerging software systems: Principles, methodologies and tools* (pp. 241–249). Hershey, PA: IGI Global. doi:10.4018/978-1-60960-735-7.ch011

Perera, R., Fang, S. E., & Ruiz, A. (2010). Application of particle swarm optimization and genetic algorithms to multiobjective damage identification inverse problems with modelling errors. *Meccanica*, *45*(5), 723–734. doi:10.1007/s11012-009-9264-5

Perry, M. J., Koh, C. G., & Choo, Y. S. (2006). Modified genetic algorithm strategy for structural identification. *Computers & Structures*, *84*(8), 529–540. doi:10.1016/j.compstruc.2005.11.008

Petruch, K., Tamm, G., & Stantchev, V. (2012). Deriving in-depth knowledge from IT-performance data simulations. *International Journal of Knowledge Society Research*, *3*(2), 13–29. doi:10.4018/jksr.2012040102

Philipson, G. (2011). A framework for green computing. *International Journal of Green Computing*, *2*(1), 12–26. doi:10.4018/jgc.2011010102

Philipson, G. (2013). A framework for green computing. In K. Ganesh & S. Anbuudayasankar (Eds.), *International and interdisciplinary studies in green computing* (pp. 12–26). Hershey, PA: IGI Global. doi:10.4018/978-1-4666-2646-1.ch002

Phythian, M. (2013). The 'cloud' of unknowing – What a government cloud may and may not offer: A practitioner perspective. *International Journal of Technoethics*, *4*(1), 1–10. doi:10.4018/jte.2013010101

Piotrowski, A. P., Napiorkowski, M. J., Napiorkowski, J. J., & Rowinski, P. M. (2017). Swarm intelligence and evolutionary algorithms: Performance versus speed. *Information Sciences*, *384*, 34–85. doi:10.1016/j.ins.2016.12.028

Poli, R., Kennedy, J., & Blackwell, T. (2007). Particle swarm optimization: An overview. *Swarm Intelligence*, *1*(1), 33–57. doi:10.1007/s11721-007-0002-0

Poli, R., Langdon, W. B., & Mcphee, N. F. (2008). *A field guide to genetic programming. Lulu Enterprises*. UK Ltd.

Pratt, S. C., Mallon, E. B., Sumpter, D. J., & Franks, N. (2002). Quorum sensing, recruitment, and collective decision-making during colony emigration by the ant Leptothorax albipennis. *Behavioral Ecology and Sociobiology*, *52*(2), 117–12. doi:10.1007/s00265-002-0487-x

Provata, A., Sokolov, I. M., & Spagnolo, B. (2008). Ecological Complex Systems. *European Physical Journal. B, Condensed Matter and Complex Systems*, *65*(3), 304–314. doi:10.1140/epjb/e2008-00380-9

Pym, D., & Sadler, M. (2012). Information stewardship in cloud computing. In S. Galup (Ed.), *Technological applications and advancements in service science, management, and engineering* (pp. 52–69). Hershey, PA: IGI Global. doi:10.4018/978-1-4666-1583-0.ch004

Pym, D., & Sadler, M. (2012). Information stewardship in cloud computing. In *Grid and cloud computing: Concepts, methodologies, tools and applications* (pp. 185–202). Hershey, PA: IGI Global. doi:10.4018/978-1-4666-0879-5.ch109

Qi, J., Li, Y., Li, C., & Zhang, Y. (2009). Telecommunication Customer Detainment Management. In I. Lee (Ed.), *Handbook of Research on Telecommunications Planning and Management for Business* (pp. 379–399). Hershey, PA: Information Science Reference. doi:10.4018/978-1-60566-194-0.ch024

Qiu, J., Ekanayake, J., Gunarathne, T., Choi, J. Y., Bae, S., & Ruan, Y. … Tang, H. (2013). Data intensive computing for bioinformatics. In Bioinformatics: Concepts, methodologies, tools, and applications (pp. 287-321). Hershey, PA: IGI Global. doi:10.4018/978-1-4666-3604-0.ch016

Quraishi, I. M., De, M., Dhal, K.G, Mondal, S., & Das, G. (2013). *Novel hybrid approach to restore historical degraded documents*. IEEE. DOI: 10.1109/ISSP.2013.6526899

Quraishi, I. M., Dhal, K.G, Paul Chowdhury, J., Pattanayak, K., & De, M., (2012). *A novel hybrid approach to enhance low resolution images using particle swarm optimization*. IEEE. DOI: 10.1109/PDGC.2012.6449941

Rabaey, M. (2012). A public economics approach to enabling enterprise architecture with the government cloud in Belgium. In P. Saha (Ed.), *Enterprise architecture for connected e-government: Practices and innovations* (pp. 467–493). Hershey, PA: IGI Global. doi:10.4018/978-1-4666-1824-4.ch020

Rabaey, M. (2013). A complex adaptive system thinking approach of government e-procurement in a cloud computing environment. In P. Ordóñez de Pablos, J. Lovelle, J. Gayo, & R. Tennyson (Eds.), *E-procurement management for successful electronic government systems* (pp. 193–219). Hershey, PA: IGI Global. doi:10.4018/978-1-4666-2119-0.ch013

Rabaey, M. (2013). Holistic investment framework for cloud computing: A management-philosophical approach based on complex adaptive systems. In A. Bento & A. Aggarwal (Eds.), *Cloud computing service and deployment models: Layers and management* (pp. 94–122). Hershey, PA: IGI Global. doi:10.4018/978-1-4666-2187-9.ch005

Rajesh, R., Pugazhendhi, S., & Ganesh, K. (2013). Genetic Algorithm and Particle Swarm Optimization for Solving Balanced Allocation Problem of Third Party Logistics Providers. In J. Wang (Ed.), *Management Innovations for Intelligent Supply Chains* (pp. 184–203). Hershey, PA: Business Science Reference. doi:10.4018/978-1-4666-2461-0.ch010

Rak, M., Ficco, M., Luna, J., Ghani, H., Suri, N., Panica, S., & Petcu, D. (2012). Security issues in cloud federations. In M. Villari, I. Brandic, & F. Tusa (Eds.), *Achieving federated and self-manageable cloud infrastructures: Theory and practice* (pp. 176–194). Hershey, PA: IGI Global. doi:10.4018/978-1-4666-1631-8.ch010

Ramanathan, R. (2013). Extending service-driven architectural approaches to the cloud. In R. Ramanathan & K. Raja (Eds.), *Service-driven approaches to architecture and enterprise integration* (pp. 334–359). Hershey, PA: IGI Global. doi:10.4018/978-1-4666-4193-8.ch013

Ramírez, M., Gutiérrez, A., Monguet, J. M., & Muñoz, C. (2012). An internet cost model, assignment of costs based on actual network use. *International Journal of Web Portals*, *4*(4), 19–34. doi:10.4018/jwp.2012100102

Rashid, A., Wang, W. Y., & Tan, F. B. (2013). Value co-creation in cloud services. In A. Lin, J. Foster, & P. Scifleet (Eds.), *Consumer information systems and relationship management: Design, implementation, and use* (pp. 74–91). Hershey, PA: IGI Global. doi:10.4018/978-1-4666-4082-5.ch005

Ratten, V. (2012). Cloud computing services: Theoretical foundations of ethical and entrepreneurial adoption behaviour. *International Journal of Cloud Applications and Computing*, *2*(2), 48–58. doi:10.4018/ijcac.2012040105

Ratten, V. (2013). Exploring behaviors and perceptions affecting the adoption of cloud computing. *International Journal of Innovation in the Digital Economy*, *4*(3), 51–68. doi:10.4018/jide.2013070104

Ravi, V. (2012). Cloud computing paradigm for indian education sector. *International Journal of Cloud Applications and Computing*, *2*(2), 41–47. doi:10.4018/ijcac.2012040104

Rawat, A., Kapoor, P., & Sushil, R. (2014). Application of cloud computing in library information service sector. In S. Dhamdhere (Ed.), *Cloud computing and virtualization technologies in libraries* (pp. 77–89). Hershey, PA: IGI Global. doi:10.4018/978-1-4666-4631-5.ch005

Reich, C., Hübner, S., & Kuijs, H. (2012). Cloud computing for on-demand virtual desktops and labs. In L. Chao (Ed.), *Cloud computing for teaching and learning: strategies for design and implementation* (pp. 111–125). Hershey, PA: IGI Global. doi:10.4018/978-1-4666-0957-0.ch008

Ribeiro, J. C. B. (2008). Search-based test case generation for object-oriented java software using strongly-typed genetic programming. In *GECCO '08: Proceedings of the 2008 gecco conference companion on genetic and evolutionary computation* (pp. 1819–1822). New York: ACM. doi:10.1145/1388969.1388979

Ribeiro, J. C. B. (2010). *Contributions for improving genetic programming-based approaches to the evolutionary testing of object-oriented software* (Doctoral dissertation). Universidad de Extremadura, España.

Ribeiro, J. C. B., de Vega, F. F., & Zenha-Rela, M. (2007). Using dynamic analysis of java bytecode for evolutionary object-oriented unit testing. In *Sbrc wtf 2007: Proceedings of the 8th workshop on testing and fault tolerance at the 25th Brazilian symposium on computer networks and distributed systems* (pp. 143–156). Brazilian Computer Society (SBC).

Ribeiro, J. C. B., Nogueira, A. F., de Vega, F. F., & Zenha-Rela, M. A. (2013). *eCrash – evolutionary testing for object-oriented software.* Available from http://sourceforge.net/projects/ecrashtesting/

Ribeiro, J. C. B., Zenha-Rela, M. A., & de Vega, F. F. (2008). Strongly-typed genetic programming and purity analysis: input domain reduction for evolutionary testing problems. In *Gecco '08: Proceedings of the 10th annual conference on genetic and evolutionary computation* (pp. 1783–1784). New York: ACM. doi:10.1145/1389095.1389439

Ribeiro, J. C. B., Zenha-Rela, M. A., & de Vega, F. F. (2010a). Adaptive evolutionary testing: an adaptive approach to search-based test case generation for object-oriented software. In Nicso 2010 - international workshop on nature inspired cooperative strategies for optimization. Springer. doi:10.1007/978-3-642-12538-6_16

Ribeiro, J. C. B., Zenha-Rela, M. A., & de Vega, F. F. (2010b). Enabling object reuse on genetic programming-based approaches to object-oriented evolutionary testing. In *Eurogp 2010 - 13th european conference on genetic programming.* Springer. doi:10.1007/978-3-642-12148-7_19

Ribeiro, J. C. B., Zenha-Rela, M., & de Vega, F. F. (2007). ecrash: a framework for performing evolutionary testing on third-party java components. In *Cedi jaem'07: Proceedings of the i jornadas sobre algoritmos evolutivos y metaheuristicas at the ii congreso español de informática* (pp. 137–144). Academic Press.

Ribeiro, J. C. B., Zenha-Rela, M. A., & Vega, F. (2009). Test case evaluation and input domain reduction strategies for the evolutionary testing of object-oriented software. *Information and Software Technology, 51*(11), 1534–1548. doi:10.1016/j.infsof.2009.06.009

Rice, R. W. (2013). Testing in the cloud: Balancing the value and risks of cloud computing. In S. Tilley & T. Parveen (Eds.), *Software testing in the cloud: Perspectives on an emerging discipline* (pp. 404–416). Hershey, PA: IGI Global. doi:10.4018/978-1-4666-2536-5.ch019

Ridley, M. (2004). *Evolution* (3rd ed.). Wiley-Blackwell.

Riva, G. (2000). From telehealth to e-health: Internet and distributed virtual reality in health care. *Journal of CyberPsychology & Behavior, 3*(6), 989–998. doi:10.1089/109493100452255

Riva, G. (2002). The emergence of e-health: Using virtual reality and the internet for providing advanced healthcare services. *International Journal of Healthcare Technology and Management, 4*(1/2), 15–40. doi:10.1504/IJHTM.2002.001127

Rodriguez-Vazquez, K., Fonseca, C., & Fleming, P. (2004). Identifying the structure of nonlinear dynamic systems using multiobjective genetic programming. *IEEE Transactions on Systems, Man, and Cybernetics. Part A, Systems and Humans, 34*(4), 531–545. doi:10.1109/TSMCA.2004.826299

Roffel, B., & Betlem, B. (2007). *Process dynamics and control: modeling for control and prediction.* John Wiley & Sons.

Rojas, J. M., Vivanti, M., Arcuri, A., & Fraser, G. (2016). A detailed investigation of the effectiveness of whole test suite generation. *Empirical Software Engineering, 22*(2), 852–893. doi:10.1007/s10664-015-9424-2

Rosenthal, A., Mork, P., Li, M. H., Stanford, J., Koester, D., & Reynolds, P. (2010). Cloud computing: A new business paradigm for biomedical information sharing. *Journal of Biomedical Informatics, 43*(2), 342–353. doi:10.1016/j.jbi.2009.08.014 PMID:19715773

Rosenzweig, M. (1995). *Species Diversity in Space and Time.* Cambridge University Press. doi:10.1017/CBO9780511623387

Ruan, K. (2013). Designing a forensic-enabling cloud ecosystem. In K. Ruan (Ed.), *Cybercrime and cloud forensics: Applications for investigation processes* (pp. 331–344). Hershey, PA: IGI Global. doi:10.4018/978-1-4666-2662-1.ch014

Saad, M. S., Jamaluddin, H., & Darus, I. Z. (2012a). PID controller tuning using evolutionary algorithms. *WSEAS Transactions on Systems and Control, 7*(4), 139–149.

Saad, M. S., Jamaluddin, H., & Darus, I. Z. M. (2012b). Implementation of PID controller tuning using differential evolution and genetic algorithms. *International Journal of Innovative Computing, Information, & Control, 8*(11), 7761–7779.

Sabetzadeh, F., & Tsui, E. (2011). Delivering knowledge services in the cloud. *International Journal of Knowledge and Systems Science, 2*(4), 14–20. doi:10.4018/jkss.2011100102

Sabetzadeh, F., & Tsui, E. (2013). Delivering knowledge services in the cloud. In G. Yang (Ed.), *Multidisciplinary studies in knowledge and systems science* (pp. 247–254). Hershey, PA: IGI Global. doi:10.4018/978-1-4666-3998-0.ch017

Saedi, A., & Iahad, N. A. (2013). Future research on cloud computing adoption by small and medium-sized enterprises: A critical analysis of relevant theories. *International Journal of Actor-Network Theory and Technological Innovation, 5*(2), 1–16. doi:10.4018/jantti.2013040101

Sagarna, R., Arcuri, A., & Yao, X. (2007). Estimation of distribution algorithms for testing object oriented software. In D. Srinivasan & L. Wang (Eds.), 2007 IEEE congress on evolutionary computation. Singapore: IEEE Press. doi:10.1109/CEC.2007.4424504

Saha, D., & Sridhar, V. (2011). Emerging areas of research in business data communications. *International Journal of Business Data Communications and Networking, 7*(4), 52–59. doi:10.4018/IJBDCN.2011100104

Saha, D., & Sridhar, V. (2013). Platform on platform (PoP) model for meta-networking: A new paradigm for networks of the future. *International Journal of Business Data Communications and Networking*, 9(1), 1–10. doi:10.4018/jbdcn.2013010101

Sahlin, J. P. (2013). Cloud computing: Past, present, and future. In X. Yang & L. Liu (Eds.), *Principles, methodologies, and service-oriented approaches for cloud computing* (pp. 19–50). Hershey, PA: IGI Global. doi:10.4018/978-1-4666-2854-0.ch002

Salama, M., & Shawish, A. (2012). Libraries: From the classical to cloud-based era. *International Journal of Digital Library Systems*, 3(3), 14–32. doi:10.4018/jdls.2012070102

Sánchez, C. M., Molina, D., Vozmediano, R. M., Montero, R. S., & Llorente, I. M. (2012). On the use of the hybrid cloud computing paradigm. In M. Villari, I. Brandic, & F. Tusa (Eds.), *Achieving federated and self-manageable cloud infrastructures: Theory and practice* (pp. 196–218). Hershey, PA: IGI Global. doi:10.4018/978-1-4666-1631-8.ch011

Sarkar, S., Paul, S., Burman, R., Das, S., & Chaudhuri, S. S. (2015). A Fuzzy Entropy Based Multi-Level Image Thresholding Using Differential Evolution. *SEMCCO*, *2014*, 386–395.

Sasikala, P. (2011). Architectural strategies for green cloud computing: Environments, infrastructure and resources. *International Journal of Cloud Applications and Computing*, 1(4), 1–24. doi:10.4018/ijcac.2011100101

Sasikala, P. (2011). Cloud computing in higher education: Opportunities and issues. *International Journal of Cloud Applications and Computing*, 1(2), 1–13. doi:10.4018/ijcac.2011040101

Sasikala, P. (2011). Cloud computing towards technological convergence. *International Journal of Cloud Applications and Computing*, 1(4), 44–59. doi:10.4018/ijcac.2011100104

Sasikala, P. (2012). Cloud computing and e-governance: Advances, opportunities and challenges. *International Journal of Cloud Applications and Computing*, 2(4), 32–52. doi:10.4018/ijcac.2012100103

Sasikala, P. (2012). Cloud computing in higher education: Opportunities and issues. In *Grid and cloud computing: Concepts, methodologies, tools and applications* (pp. 1672–1685). Hershey, PA: IGI Global. doi:10.4018/978-1-4666-0879-5.ch709

Sasikala, P. (2012). Cloud computing towards technological convergence. In *Grid and cloud computing: Concepts, methodologies, tools and applications* (pp. 1576–1592). Hershey, PA: IGI Global. doi:10.4018/978-1-4666-0879-5.ch703

Sasikala, P. (2013). Architectural strategies for green cloud computing: Environments, infrastructure and resources. In S. Aljawarneh (Ed.), *Cloud computing advancements in design, implementation, and technologies* (pp. 218–242). Hershey, PA: IGI Global. doi:10.4018/978-1-4666-1879-4.ch016

Sasikala, P. (2013). Cloud computing in higher education: Opportunities and issues. In S. Aljawarneh (Ed.), *Cloud computing advancements in design, implementation, and technologies* (pp. 83–96). Hershey, PA: IGI Global. doi:10.4018/978-1-4666-1879-4.ch006

Sasikala, P. (2013). Cloud computing towards technological convergence. In S. Aljawarneh (Ed.), *Cloud computing advancements in design, implementation, and technologies* (pp. 263–279). Hershey, PA: IGI Global. doi:10.4018/978-1-4666-1879-4.ch019

Sasikala, P. (2013). New media cloud computing: Opportunities and challenges. *International Journal of Cloud Applications and Computing, 3*(2), 61–72. doi:10.4018/ijcac.2013040106

Schoener, T. W. (1991). Ecological interactions. In A. A. Myers & P. S. Giller (Eds.), Analytical Biogeography (pp. 255-295). Chapman & Hall.

Schrödl, H., & Wind, S. (2013). Requirements engineering for cloud application development. In A. Bento & A. Aggarwal (Eds.), *Cloud computing service and deployment models: Layers and management* (pp. 137–150). Hershey, PA: IGI Global. doi:10.4018/978-1-4666-2187-9.ch007

Schwenk, G., Padilla, D. G., Bakken, G. S., & Full, R. J. (2009). Grand challenges in organismal biology. *Integrative and Comparative Biology, 49*(1), 7–14. doi:10.1093/icb/icp034 PMID:21669841

Sclater, N. (2012). Legal and contractual issues of cloud computing for educational institutions. In L. Chao (Ed.), *Cloud computing for teaching and learning: Strategies for design and implementation* (pp. 186–199). Hershey, PA: IGI Global. doi:10.4018/978-1-4666-0957-0.ch013

Seesing, A. (2006). *Evotest: Test case generation using genetic programming and software analysis* (Master's thesis). Delft University of Technology.

Seesing, A., & Gross, H.-G. (2006). A genetic programming approach to automated test generation for object-oriented software. *International Transactions on System Science and Applications, 1*(2), 127–134.

Sen, J. (2014). Security and privacy issues in cloud computing. In A. Ruiz-Martinez, R. Marin-Lopez, & F. Pereniguez-Garcia (Eds.), *Architectures and protocols for secure information technology infrastructures* (pp. 1–45). Hershey, PA: IGI Global. doi:10.4018/978-1-4666-4514-1.ch001

Shah, B. (2013). Cloud environment controls assessment framework. In *IT policy and ethics: Concepts, methodologies, tools, and applications* (pp. 1822–1847). Hershey, PA: IGI Global. doi:10.4018/978-1-4666-2919-6.ch080

Shah, B. (2013). Cloud environment controls assessment framework. In S. Tilley & T. Parveen (Eds.), *Software testing in the cloud: Perspectives on an emerging discipline* (pp. 28–53). Hershey, PA: IGI Global. doi:10.4018/978-1-4666-2536-5.ch002

Shamshiri, S., Just, R., Rojas, J. M., Fraser, G., McMinn, P., & Arcuri, A. (2015). Do Automatically Generated Unit Tests Find Real Faults? An Empirical Study of Effectiveness and Challenges (T). In *2015 30th IEEE/ACM International Conference on Automated Software Engineering (ASE)*. IEEE. doi:10.1109/ase.2015.86

Shamshiri, S., Rojas, J. M., Fraser, G., & McMinn, P. (2015). Random or Genetic Algorithm Search for Object-Oriented Test Suite Generation? *Proceedings of the 2015 on Genetic and Evolutionary Computation Conference - GECCO '15*. doi:10.1145/2739480.2754696

Shang, X., Zhang, R., & Chen, Y. (2012). Internet of things (IoT) service architecture and its application in e-commerce. *Journal of Electronic Commerce in Organizations*, *10*(3), 44–55. doi:10.4018/jeco.2012070104

Shankararaman, V., & Kit, L. E. (2013). Integrating the cloud scenarios and solutions. In A. Bento & A. Aggarwal (Eds.), *Cloud computing service and deployment models: Layers and management* (pp. 173–189). Hershey, PA: IGI Global. doi:10.4018/978-1-4666-2187-9.ch009

Shanmugavadivu, P., Balasubramanian, K., & Muruganandam, A. (2014). Particle swarm optimized bi-histogram equalization for contrast enhancement and brightness preservation of images. *The Visual Computer*, *30*(4), 387–399. doi:10.1007/s00371-013-0863-8

Shannon, C. E. (2001, January). A mathematical theory of communication. ACM SIGMOBILE Mobile Computing and Communications Review, 3-55.

Sharkey, A. J., & Sharkey, N. (2006). The Application of Swarm Intelligence to Collective Robots. In J. Fulcher (Ed.), *Advances in Applied Artificial Intelligence* (pp. 157–185). Hershey, PA: Idea Group Publishing. doi:10.4018/978-1-59140-827-7.ch006

Sharma, A., & Maurer, F. (2013). A roadmap for software engineering for the cloud: Results of a systematic review. In X. Wang, N. Ali, I. Ramos, & R. Vidgen (Eds.), *Agile and lean service-oriented development: Foundations, theory, and practice* (pp. 48–63). Hershey, PA: IGI Global. doi:10.4018/978-1-4666-2503-7.ch003

Sharma, A., & Maurer, F. (2014). A roadmap for software engineering for the cloud: Results of a systematic review. In *Software design and development: Concepts, methodologies, tools, and applications* (pp. 1–16). Hershey, PA: IGI Global. doi:10.4018/978-1-4666-4301-7.ch001

Sharma, S. C., & Bagoria, H. (2014). Libraries and cloud computing models: A changing paradigm. In S. Dhamdhere (Ed.), *Cloud computing and virtualization technologies in libraries* (pp. 124–149). Hershey, PA: IGI Global. doi:10.4018/978-1-4666-4631-5.ch008

Shawish, A., & Salama, M. (2013). Cloud computing in academia, governments, and industry. In X. Yang & L. Liu (Eds.), *Principles, methodologies, and service-oriented approaches for cloud computing* (pp. 71–114). Hershey, PA: IGI Global. doi:10.4018/978-1-4666-2854-0.ch004

Shebanow, A., Perez, R., & Howard, C. (2012). The effect of firewall testing types on cloud security policies. *International Journal of Strategic Information Technology and Applications*, *3*(3), 60–68. doi:10.4018/jsita.2012070105

Sheikhalishahi, M., Devare, M., Grandinetti, L., & Incutti, M. C. (2012). A complementary approach to grid and cloud distributed computing paradigms. In *Grid and cloud computing: Concepts, methodologies, tools and applications* (pp. 1929–1942). Hershey, PA: IGI Global. doi:10.4018/978-1-4666-0879-5.ch811

Sheikhalishahi, M., Devare, M., Grandinetti, L., & Incutti, M. C. (2012). A complementary approach to grid and cloud distributed computing paradigms. In N. Preve (Ed.), *Computational and data grids: Principles, applications and design* (pp. 31–44). Hershey, PA: IGI Global. doi:10.4018/978-1-61350-113-9.ch002

Sheikholeslami, R., & Kaveh, A. (2013). A Survey of Chaos Embedded Meta-Heuristic Algorithms. Int. J. Optim. Civil. *Eng.*, *3*(4), 617–633.

Shen, Y., Li, Y., Wu, L., Liu, S., & Wen, Q. (2014). Cloud computing overview. In Y. Shen, Y. Li, L. Wu, S. Liu, & Q. Wen (Eds.), *Enabling the new era of cloud computing: Data security, transfer, and management* (pp. 1–24). Hershey, PA: IGI Global. doi:10.4018/978-1-4666-4801-2.ch001

Shen, Y., Li, Y., Wu, L., Liu, S., & Wen, Q. (2014). Main components of cloud computing. In Y. Shen, Y. Li, L. Wu, S. Liu, & Q. Wen (Eds.), *Enabling the new era of cloud computing: Data security, transfer, and management* (pp. 25–50). Hershey, PA: IGI Global. doi:10.4018/978-1-4666-4801-2.ch002

Shen, Y., Yang, J., & Keskin, T. (2014). Impact of cultural differences on the cloud computing ecosystems in the USA and China. In Y. Shen, Y. Li, L. Wu, S. Liu, & Q. Wen (Eds.), *Enabling the new era of cloud computing: Data security, transfer, and management* (pp. 269–283). Hershey, PA: IGI Global. doi:10.4018/978-1-4666-4801-2.ch014

Shetty, S., & Rawat, D. B. (2013). Cloud computing based cognitive radio networking. In N. Meghanathan & Y. Reddy (Eds.), *Cognitive radio technology applications for wireless and mobile ad hoc networks* (pp. 153–164). Hershey, PA: IGI Global. doi:10.4018/978-1-4666-4221-8.ch008

Shi, Y. (2001). Particle swarm optimization: developments, applications and resources. *Proceedings of the Congress on Evolutionary Computation*, 81-86.

Shi, Y. (2012). *Innovations and Developments of Swarm Intelligence Applications*. Hershey, PA: IGI Global. doi:10.4018/978-1-4666-1592-2

Shi, Y., & Eberhart, R. (1998). A modified particle swarm optimizer. *Proceedings of IEEE International Conference on Evolutionary Computation*, 69-73.

Shi, Z., & Beard, C. (2014). QoS in the mobile cloud computing environment. In J. Rodrigues, K. Lin, & J. Lloret (Eds.), *Mobile networks and cloud computing convergence for progressive services and applications* (pp. 200–217). Hershey, PA: IGI Global. doi:10.4018/978-1-4666-4781-7.ch011

Shuster, L. (2013). Enterprise integration: Challenges and solution architecture. In R. Ramanathan & K. Raja (Eds.), *Service-driven approaches to architecture and enterprise integration* (pp. 43–66). Hershey, PA: IGI Global. doi:10.4018/978-1-4666-4193-8.ch002

Siahos, Y., Papanagiotou, I., Georgopoulos, A., Tsamis, F., & Papaioannou, I. (2012). An architecture paradigm for providing cloud services in school labs based on open source software to enhance ICT in education. *International Journal of Cyber Ethics in Education*, *2*(1), 44–57. doi:10.4018/ijcee.2012010105

Sim, K. S., Tso, C. P., & Tan, Y. Y. (2007). Recursive sub-image histogram equalization applied to gray scale image. *Pattern Recognition Letter, 28*, 1209-1221.

Simmons, I. (1982). *Biogeographical Processes.* Allen & Unwin.

Simon, E., & Estublier, J. (2013). Model driven integration of heterogeneous software artifacts in service oriented computing. In A. Ionita, M. Litoiu, & G. Lewis (Eds.), *Migrating legacy applications: Challenges in service oriented architecture and cloud computing environments* (pp. 332–360). Hershey, PA: IGI Global. doi:10.4018/978-1-4666-2488-7.ch014

Simpson, G. G. (1955). *The Major Features of Evolution.* New York: Columbia University.

Singh, J., & Kumar, V. (2013). Compliance and regulatory standards for cloud computing. In R. Khurana & R. Aggarwal (Eds.), *Interdisciplinary perspectives on business convergence, computing, and legality* (pp. 54–64). Hershey, PA: IGI Global. doi:10.4018/978-1-4666-4209-6.ch006

Singh, S., & Singh, J. N. (2012). *Application of Particle Swarm Optimization: In the field of Image Processing.* LAP LAMBERT Academic Publishing.

Singh, V. V. (2012). Software development using service syndication based on API handshake approach between cloud-based and SOA-based reusable services. In H. Yang & X. Liu (Eds.), *Software reuse in the emerging cloud computing era* (pp. 136–157). Hershey, PA: IGI Global. doi:10.4018/978-1-4666-0897-9.ch006

Skolicki, Z., & De Jong, K. (2005, June). The influence of migration sizes and intervals on island models. In *Proceedings of the 7th annual conference on Genetic and evolutionary computation* (pp. 1295-1302). ACM. doi:10.1145/1068009.1068219

Sloot, P., Tirado-Ramos, A., Altintas, I., Bubak, M., & Boucher, C. (2006). From molecule to man: Decision support in individualized E-Health. *Computer, 39*(11), 40–46. doi:10.1109/MC.2006.380

Smeitink, M., & Spruit, M. (2013). Maturity for sustainability in IT: Introducing the MITS. *International Journal of Information Technologies and Systems Approach, 6*(1), 39–56. doi:10.4018/jitsa.2013010103

Smith, P. A., & Cockburn, T. (2013). Socio-digital technologies. In *Dynamic leadership models for global business: Enhancing digitally connected environments* (pp. 142–168). Hershey, PA: IGI Global. doi:10.4018/978-1-4666-2836-6.ch006

Sneed, H. M. (2013). Testing web services in the cloud. In S. Tilley & T. Parveen (Eds.), *Software testing in the cloud: Perspectives on an emerging discipline* (pp. 136–173). Hershey, PA: IGI Global. doi:10.4018/978-1-4666-2536-5.ch007

Solera Saborío, E. (2005). PI/PID controller tuning with IAE and ITAE criteria for double pole plants. *Escuela de Ingeniería Eléctrica, Universidad de Costa Rica, 18.*

Solomon, B., Ionescu, D., Gadea, C., & Litoiu, M. (2013). Geographically distributed cloud-based collaborative application. In A. Ionita, M. Litoiu, & G. Lewis (Eds.), *Migrating legacy applications: Challenges in service oriented architecture and cloud computing environments* (pp. 248–274). Hershey, PA: IGI Global. doi:10.4018/978-1-4666-2488-7.ch011

Song, W., & Xiao, Z. (2013). An infrastructure-as-a-service cloud: On-demand resource provisioning. In X. Yang & L. Liu (Eds.), *Principles, methodologies, and service-oriented approaches for cloud computing* (pp. 302–324). Hershey, PA: IGI Global. doi:10.4018/978-1-4666-2854-0.ch013

Sood, S. K. (2013). A value based dynamic resource provisioning model in cloud. *International Journal of Cloud Applications and Computing, 3*(1), 1–12. doi:10.4018/ijcac.2013010101

Sotiriadis, S., Bessis, N., & Antonopoulos, N. (2012). Exploring inter-cloud load balancing by utilizing historical service submission records. *International Journal of Distributed Systems and Technologies, 3*(3), 72–81. doi:10.4018/jdst.2012070106

Soyata, T., Ba, H., Heinzelman, W., Kwon, M., & Shi, J. (2014). Accelerating mobile-cloud computing: A survey. In H. Mouftah & B. Kantarci (Eds.), *Communication infrastructures for cloud computing* (pp. 175–197). Hershey, PA: IGI Global. doi:10.4018/978-1-4666-4522-6.ch008

Spyridopoulos, T., & Katos, V. (2011). Requirements for a forensically ready cloud storage service. *International Journal of Digital Crime and Forensics, 3*(3), 19–36. doi:10.4018/jdcf.2011070102

Spyridopoulos, T., & Katos, V. (2013). Data recovery strategies for cloud environments. In K. Ruan (Ed.), *Cybercrime and cloud forensics: Applications for investigation processes* (pp. 251–265). Hershey, PA: IGI Global. doi:10.4018/978-1-4666-2662-1.ch010

Srinivasa, K. G., S, H. R. C., H, M. K. S., & Venkatesh, N. (2012). MeghaOS: A framework for scalable, interoperable cloud based operating system. *International Journal of Cloud Applications and Computing, 2*(1), 53–70. doi:10.4018/ijcac.2012010104

Stantchev, V., & Stantcheva, L. (2012). Extending traditional IT-governance knowledge towards SOA and cloud governance. *International Journal of Knowledge Society Research, 3*(2), 30–43. doi:10.4018/jksr.2012040103

Stantchev, V., & Tamm, G. (2012). Reducing information asymmetry in cloud marketplaces. *International Journal of Human Capital and Information Technology Professionals, 3*(4), 1–10. doi:10.4018/jhcitp.2012100101

Steinbuß, S., & Weißenberg, N. (2013). Service design and process design for the logistics mall cloud. In X. Yang & L. Liu (Eds.), *Principles, methodologies, and service-oriented approaches for cloud computing* (pp. 186–206). Hershey, PA: IGI Global. doi:10.4018/978-1-4666-2854-0.ch008

Stender, J., Berlin, M., & Reinefeld, A. (2013). XtreemFS: A file system for the cloud. In D. Kyriazis, A. Voulodimos, S. Gogouvitis, & T. Varvarigou (Eds.), *Data intensive storage services for cloud environments* (pp. 267–285). Hershey, PA: IGI Global. doi:10.4018/978-1-4666-3934-8.ch016

Sticklen, D. J., & Issa, T. (2011). An initial examination of free and proprietary software-selection in organizations. *International Journal of Web Portals, 3*(4), 27–43. doi:10.4018/jwp.2011100103

Strecker, U. (2002). Cyprinodon esconditus, a new pupfish from Laguna Chichancanab, Yucatan, Mexico (Cyprinodontidae). *Cybium, 26*, 301–307.

Sung, S. W., Jungmin, O., Lee, I. B., Lee, J., & Yi, S. H. (1996). Automatic tuning of PID controller using second-order plus time delay model. *Journal of Chemical Engineering of Japan, 29*(6), 990–999. doi:10.1252/jcej.29.990

Sun, Y., White, J., Gray, J., & Gokhale, A. (2012). Model-driven automated error recovery in cloud computing. In *Grid and cloud computing: Concepts, methodologies, tools and applications* (pp. 680–700). Hershey, PA: IGI Global. doi:10.4018/978-1-4666-0879-5.ch308

Sun, Z., Yang, Y., Zhou, Y., & Cruickshank, H. (2014). Agent-based resource management for mobile cloud. In J. Rodrigues, K. Lin, & J. Lloret (Eds.), *Mobile networks and cloud computing convergence for progressive services and applications* (pp. 118–134). Hershey, PA: IGI Global. doi:10.4018/978-1-4666-4781-7.ch007

Sutherland, S. (2013). Convergence of interoperability of cloud computing, service oriented architecture and enterprise architecture. *International Journal of E-Entrepreneurship and Innovation, 4*(1), 43–51. doi:10.4018/jeei.2013010104

Swings, J., & De Ley, J. (1977). The biology of Zymomonas. *Bacteriological Reviews, 41*, 1–46. PMID:16585

Takabi, H., & Joshi, J. B. (2013). Policy management in cloud: Challenges and approaches. In *IT policy and ethics: Concepts, methodologies, tools, and applications* (pp. 814–834). Hershey, PA: IGI Global. doi:10.4018/978-1-4666-2919-6.ch037

Takabi, H., & Joshi, J. B. (2013). Policy management in cloud: Challenges and approaches. In D. Rosado, D. Mellado, E. Fernandez-Medina, & M. Piattini (Eds.), *Security engineering for cloud computing: Approaches and tools* (pp. 191–211). Hershey, PA: IGI Global. doi:10.4018/978-1-4666-2125-1.ch010

Takabi, H., Joshi, J. B., & Ahn, G. (2013). Security and privacy in cloud computing: Towards a comprehensive framework. In X. Yang & L. Liu (Eds.), *Principles, methodologies, and service-oriented approaches for cloud computing* (pp. 164–184). Hershey, PA: IGI Global. doi:10.4018/978-1-4666-2854-0.ch007

Takabi, H., Zargar, S. T., & Joshi, J. B. (2014). Mobile cloud computing and its security and privacy challenges. In D. Rawat, B. Bista, & G. Yan (Eds.), *Security, privacy, trust, and resource management in mobile and wireless communications* (pp. 384–407). Hershey, PA: IGI Global. doi:10.4018/978-1-4666-4691-9.ch016

Taleizadeh, A. A., & Cárdenas-Barrón, L. E. (2013). Metaheuristic Algorithms for Supply Chain Management Problems. In Supply Chain Management: Concepts, Methodologies, Tools, and Applications (pp. 1814-1837). Hershey, PA: Business Science Reference. doi:10.4018/978-1-4666-2625-6.ch106

Tamariz, A. D. (2005). *Modelagem computacional de dados e controle inteligente no espaço de estado* (PhD thesis). Universidade Estadual de Campinas.

Tamariz, A. D., Bottura, C. P., & Barreto, G. (2005). Iterative MOESP type algorithm for discrete time variant system identification. *Proceedings of the 13th Mediterranean Conference on Control and Automation (MED 2005)*. doi:10.1109/.2005.1467048

Tang, H., Xie, L., & Xue, S. (2015). Usage of Comprehensive Learning Particle Swarm Optimization for Parameter Identification of Structural System. *International Journal of Natural Computing Research*, 15.

Tang, H., Xue, S., & Fan, C. (2008). Differential evolution strategy for structural system identification. *Computers & Structures*, *86*(21), 2004–2012. doi:10.1016/j.compstruc.2008.05.001

Tang, H., Zhang, W., Xie, L., & Xue, S. (2013). Multi stage approach for structural damage identification using particle swarm optimization. *Bulletin of Mathematical Biology*, *11*(1), 2289–2303.

Tassey, G. (2002). *The economic impacts of inadequate infrastructure for software testing (Tech. Rep.)*. National Institute of Standards and Technology.

Tavakoli, S., Griffin, I., & Fleming, P. J. (2007, September). Multi-objective optimization approach to the PI tuning problem. In *Evolutionary Computation, 2007. CEC 2007. IEEE Congress on* (pp. 3165-3171). IEEE. doi:10.1109/CEC.2007.4424876

Teixeira, C., Pinto, J. S., Ferreira, F., Oliveira, A., Teixeira, A., & Pereira, C. (2013). Cloud computing enhanced service development architecture for the living usability lab. In R. Martinho, R. Rijo, M. Cruz-Cunha, & J. Varajão (Eds.), *Information systems and technologies for enhancing health and social care* (pp. 33–53). Hershey, PA: IGI Global. doi:10.4018/978-1-4666-3667-5.ch003

The Apache Software Foundation. (2012). *The apache ant project, release 1.8.4.* Available from http://ant.apache.org/

Thimm, H. (2012). Cloud-based collaborative decision making: Design considerations and architecture of the GRUPO-MOD system. *International Journal of Decision Support System Technology*, *4*(4), 39–59. doi:10.4018/jdsst.2012100103

Thomas, P. (2012). Harnessing the potential of cloud computing to transform higher education. In L. Chao (Ed.), *Cloud computing for teaching and learning: Strategies for design and implementation* (pp. 147–158). Hershey, PA: IGI Global. doi:10.4018/978-1-4666-0957-0.ch010

Tijani, I. B., Akmeliawati, R., & Abdullateef, A. I. (2013, June). Control of an inverted pendulum using MODE-based optimized LQR controller. In *Industrial Electronics and Applications (ICIEA), 2013 8th IEEE Conference on* (pp. 1759-1764). IEEE. doi:10.1109/ICIEA.2013.6566653

Toka, A., Aivazidou, E., Antoniou, A., & Arvanitopoulos-Darginis, K. (2013). Cloud computing in supply chain management: An overview. In D. Graham, I. Manikas, & D. Folinas (Eds.), *E-logistics and e-supply chain management: Applications for evolving business* (pp. 218–231). Hershey, PA: IGI Global. doi:10.4018/978-1-4666-3914-0.ch012

Tonella, P. (2004a). *eToc – evolutionary testing of classes*. Available from http://star.fbk.eu/etoc/

Tonella, P. (2004b). Evolutionary testing of classes. In *Issta '04: Proceedings of the 2004 acm sigsoft international symposium on software testing and analysis* (pp. 119–128). New York: ACM Press. doi:10.1145/1007512.1007528

Torrealba, S. M., Morales, P. M., Campos, J. M., & Meza, S. M. (2013). A software tool to support risks analysis about what should or should not go to the cloud. In D. Rosado, D. Mellado, E. Fernandez-Medina, & M. Piattini (Eds.), *Security engineering for cloud computing: Approaches and tools* (pp. 72–96). Hershey, PA: IGI Global. doi:10.4018/978-1-4666-2125-1.ch005

Tosun, Ö. (2014). Artificial Bee Colony Algorithm. In J. Wang (Ed.), *Encyclopedia of Business Analytics and Optimization* (pp. 179–192). Hershey, PA: Business Science Reference. doi:10.4018/978-1-4666-5202-6.ch018

Trivedi, M., & Suthar, V. (2013). Cloud computing: A feasible platform for ICT enabled health science libraries in India. *International Journal of User-Driven Healthcare*, *3*(2), 69–77. doi:10.4018/ijudh.2013040108

Truong, H., Pham, T., Thoai, N., & Dustdar, S. (2012). Cloud computing for education and research in developing countries. In L. Chao (Ed.), *Cloud computing for teaching and learning: Strategies for design and implementation* (pp. 64–80). Hershey, PA: IGI Global. doi:10.4018/978-1-4666-0957-0.ch005

Tsirmpas, C., Giokas, K., Iliopoulou, D., & Koutsouris, D. (2012). Magnetic resonance imaging and magnetic resonance spectroscopy cloud computing framework. *International Journal of Reliable and Quality E-Healthcare*, *1*(4), 1–12. doi:10.4018/ijrqeh.2012100101

Turner, H., White, J., Reed, J., Galindo, J., Porter, A., Marathe, M., ... Gokhale, A. (2013). Building a cloud-based mobile application testbed. In *IT policy and ethics: Concepts, methodologies, tools, and applications* (pp. 879–899). Hershey, PA: IGI Global. doi:10.4018/978-1-4666-2919-6.ch040

Turner, H., White, J., Reed, J., Galindo, J., Porter, A., Marathe, M., ... Gokhale, A. (2013). Building a cloud-based mobile application testbed. In S. Tilley & T. Parveen (Eds.), *Software testing in the cloud: Perspectives on an emerging discipline* (pp. 382–403). Hershey, PA: IGI Global. doi:10.4018/978-1-4666-2536-5.ch018

Tusa, F., Paone, M., & Villari, M. (2012). CLEVER: A cloud middleware beyond the federation. In M. Villari, I. Brandic, & F. Tusa (Eds.), *Achieving federated and self-manageable cloud infrastructures: Theory and practice* (pp. 219–241). Hershey, PA: IGI Global. doi:10.4018/978-1-4666-1631-8.ch012

Udoh, E. (2012). Technology acceptance model applied to the adoption of grid and cloud technology. *International Journal of Grid and High Performance Computing, 4*(1), 1–20. doi:10.4018/jghpc.2012010101

Van den Bergh, F., & Engelbrecht, A. P. (2006). A study of particle swarm optimization particle trajectories. *Information Sciences, 176*(8), 937–971. doi:10.1016/j.ins.2005.02.003

van Ginneken, A. M. (2002). The computerized patient record: Balancing effort and benefit. *International Journal of Medical Informatics, 65*(2), 97–119. doi:10.1016/S1386-5056(02)00007-2 PMID:12052424

Vannoy, S. A. (2011). A structured content analytic assessment of business services advertisements in the cloud-based web services marketplace. *International Journal of Dependable and Trustworthy Information Systems, 2*(1), 18–49. doi:10.4018/jdtis.2011010102

Vaquero, L. M., Cáceres, J., & Morán, D. (2011). The challenge of service level scalability for the cloud. *International Journal of Cloud Applications and Computing, 1*(1), 34–44. doi:10.4018/ijcac.2011010103

Vaquero, L. M., Cáceres, J., & Morán, D. (2013). The challenge of service level scalability for the cloud. In S. Aljawarneh (Ed.), *Cloud computing advancements in design, implementation, and technologies* (pp. 37–48). Hershey, PA: IGI Global. doi:10.4018/978-1-4666-1879-4.ch003

Varshney, S., & Mehrotra, M. (2013). Search based software test data generation for structural testing: A perspective. *SIGSOFT Softw. Eng. Notes, 38*(4), 1–6. doi:10.1145/2492248.2492277

Venkatraman, R., Venkatraman, S., & Asaithambi, S. P. (2013). A practical cloud services implementation framework for e-businesses. In K. Tarnay, S. Imre, & L. Xu (Eds.), *Research and development in e-business through service-oriented solutions* (pp. 167–198). Hershey, PA: IGI Global. doi:10.4018/978-1-4666-4181-5.ch008

Venkatraman, S. (2013). Software engineering research gaps in the cloud. *Journal of Information Technology Research, 6*(1), 1–19. doi:10.4018/jitr.2013010101

Verhaegen, M., & Dewilde, P. (1992). Subspace model identification - part I: The output-error state-space model identification class of algorithms. *International Journal of Control, 56*(5), 1187–1210. doi:10.1080/00207179208934363

Verhaegen, M., & Verdult, V. (2007). *Filtering and System Identification – A Least Squares Approach*. Cambridge University Press. doi:10.1017/CBO9780511618888

Vijaykumar, S., Rajkarthick, K. S., & Priya, J. (2012). Innovative business opportunities and smart business management techniques from green cloud TPS. *International Journal of Asian Business and Information Management, 3*(4), 62–72. doi:10.4018/jabim.2012100107

Vilanova, R., & Alfaro, V. M. (2011). Control PID robusto: Una visión panorámica. *Revista Iberoamericana de Automática e Informática Industrial RIAI, 8*(3), 141–158. doi:10.1016/j.riai.2011.06.003

Vittori, G., Talbot, G., Gautrais, J., Fourcassié, V., Araújo, A. F. R., & Theraulaz, G. (2006). Path Efficiency of Ant Foraging Trails in an Artificial Network. *Journal of Theoretical Biology*, *239*(4), 507–515. doi:10.1016/j.jtbi.2005.08.017 PMID:16199059

Wakizono, M., Hatanaka, T., & Uosaki, K. (2006). Time Varying System Identification with Immune Based Evolutionary Computation. In *2006 SICE-ICASE International Joint Conference* (pp. 5608-5613). Busan: IEEE. doi:10.1109/SICE.2006.315098

Walker, S. I., & Davies, P. C. (2013). The algorithmic origins of life. *Journal of the Royal Society, Interface*, 10. PMID:23235265

Wang, C., Lam, K. T., & Ma, K. R. K. (2012). A computation migration approach to elasticity of cloud computing. In J. Abawajy, M. Pathan, M. Rahman, A. Pathan, & M. Deris (Eds.) Network and traffic engineering in emerging distributed computing applications (pp. 145-178). Hershey, PA: IGI Global. doi:10.4018/978-1-4666-1888-6.ch007

Wang, D., & Wu, J. (2014). Carrier-grade distributed cloud computing: Demands, challenges, designs, and future perspectives. In H. Mouftah & B. Kantarci (Eds.), *Communication infrastructures for cloud computing* (pp. 264–281). Hershey, PA: IGI Global. doi:10.4018/978-1-4666-4522-6.ch012

Wang, H., & Philips, D. (2012). Implement virtual programming lab with cloud computing for web-based distance education. In L. Chao (Ed.), *Cloud computing for teaching and learning: Strategies for design and implementation* (pp. 95–110). Hershey, PA: IGI Global. doi:10.4018/978-1-4666-0957-0.ch007

Wappler, S. (2007). *Automatic generation of object-oriented unit tests using genetic programming* (Doctoral dissertation). Technischen Universitat Berlin.

Wappler, S., & Lammermann, F. (2005). Using evolutionary algorithms for the unit testing of object-oriented software. In *Gecco '05: Proceedings of the 2005 conference on genetic and evolutionary computation* (pp. 1053–1060). New York: ACM Press. doi:10.1145/1068009.1068187

Wappler, S., & Schieferdecker, I. (2007). Improving evolutionary class testing in the presence of non-public methods. In *Ase '07: Proceedings of the twenty-second ieee/acm international conference on automated software engineering* (pp. 381–384). New York: ACM. doi:10.1145/1321631.1321689

Wappler, S., & Wegener, J. (2006b). Evolutionary unit testing of object-oriented software using strongly-typed genetic programming. In *Gecco '06: Proceedings of the 8th annual conference on genetic and evolutionary computation* (pp. 1925–1932). New York: ACM Press. doi:10.1145/1143997.1144317

Wappler, S., & Wegener, J. (2006a). Evolutionary unit testing of object-oriented software using a hybrid evolutionary algorithm. In *Cec '06: Proceedings of the 2006 ieee congress on evolutionary computation* (pp. 851–858). IEEE. doi:10.1109/CEC.2006.1688400

Warneke, D. (2013). Ad-hoc parallel data processing on pay-as-you-go clouds with nephele. In A. Loo (Ed.), *Distributed computing innovations for business, engineering, and science* (pp. 191–218). Hershey, PA: IGI Global. doi:10.4018/978-1-4666-2533-4.ch010

Wegener, J., Baresel, A., & Sthamer, H. (2001). Evolutionary test environment for automatic structural testing. *Information and Software Technology, 43*(14), 841-854.

Wei, Y., & Blake, M. B. (2013). Adaptive web services monitoring in cloud environments. *International Journal of Web Portals, 5*(1), 15–27. doi:10.4018/jwp.2013010102

Welch, J. J., & Waxman, D. (2002). Nonequivalent Loci and the Distribution of Mutant Effects. *Genetics, 161,* 897–904. PMID:12072483

White, S. C., Sedigh, S., & Hurson, A. R. (2013). Security concepts for cloud computing. In X. Yang & L. Liu (Eds.), *Principles, methodologies, and service-oriented approaches for cloud computing* (pp. 116–142). Hershey, PA: IGI Global. doi:10.4018/978-1-4666-2854-0.ch005

Whitley, D. (2001). An overview of evolutionary algorithms: Practical issues and common pitfalls. *Information and Software Technology, 43*(14), 817–831. doi:10.1016/S0950-5849(01)00188-4

Wilke, D. N., Kok, S., & Groenwold, A. A. (2010). Comparison of linear and classical velocity update rules in particle swarm optimization: Notes on diversity. *International Journal for Numerical Methods in Engineering, 70*(8), 985–1008. doi:10.1002/nme.1914

Williams, A. J. (2013). The role of emerging technologies in developing and sustaining diverse suppliers in competitive markets. In *Enterprise resource planning: Concepts, methodologies, tools, and applications* (pp. 1550–1560). Hershey, PA: IGI Global. doi:10.4018/978-1-4666-4153-2.ch082

Williams, A. J. (2013). The role of emerging technologies in developing and sustaining diverse suppliers in competitive markets. In J. Lewis, A. Green, & D. Surry (Eds.), *Technology as a tool for diversity leadership: Implementation and future implications* (pp. 95–105). Hershey, PA: IGI Global. doi:10.4018/978-1-4666-2668-3.ch007

Wilson, L., Goh, T. T., & Wang, W. Y. (2012). Big data management challenges in a meteorological organisation. *International Journal of E-Adoption, 4*(2), 1–14. doi:10.4018/jea.2012040101

Wongsritong, K., Kittayaruasiriwat, K., Cheevasuvit, F., Dejhan, K., & Somboonkaew, A. (1998). Contrast enhancement using multipeak histogram equalization with brightness preserving. *Circuit and System, 1998, IEEE APCCAS 1998, the 1998 IEEE Asia-Pacific Conference on*, 455-458. doi:10.1109/APCCAS.1998.743808

Wright, S. (1932). The roles of mutation, inbreeding, crossbreeding, and selection in evolution. *Proceedings of VI International Congress of Genetics*, 356-366.

Wu, R., Ahn, G., & Hu, H. (2012). Towards HIPAA-compliant healthcare systems in cloud computing. *International Journal of Computational Models and Algorithms in Medicine, 3*(2), 1–22. doi:10.4018/jcmam.2012040101

Xanthakis, S., Ellis, C., Skourlas, C., Gall, A. L., & Karapoulios, K. (1992). Application of genetic algorithms to software testing [application des algorithmes génétiques au test des logiciels]. In *Proceedings of the 5th international conference on software engineering* (pp. 625–636). Academic Press.

Xavier, R., Omar, N., & de Castro, L. N. (2011). Bacterial Colony: Information Processing and Computational Behavior. *Proceedings of Third World Congress on Nature and Biologically Inspired Computing*, 439-443. doi:10.1109/NaBIC.2011.6089627

Xiao, J., Wang, M., Wang, L., & Zhu, X. (2013). Design and implementation of C-iLearning: A cloud-based intelligent learning system. *International Journal of Distance Education Technologies*, *11*(3), 79–97. doi:10.4018/jdet.2013070106

Xiao, M., El-Attar, M., Reformat, M., & Miller, J. (2007). Empirical evaluation of optimization algorithms when used in goal-oriented automated test data generation techniques. *Empirical Software Engineering*, *12*(2), 183–239. doi:10.1007/s10664-006-9026-0

Xie, T., Tillmann, N., de Halleux, J., & Schulte, W. (2008). Method-sequence exploration for automated unit testing of object-oriented programs. *Proc. workshop on state-space exploration for automated testing (sseat 2008)*.

Xing, B., & Gao, W. (2014). Overview of Computational Intelligence. In *Computational Intelligence in Remanufacturing* (pp. 18–36). Hershey, PA: Information Science Reference. doi:10.4018/978-1-4666-4908-8.ch002

Xing, B., & Gao, W. (2014). Post-Disassembly Part-Machine Clustering Using Artificial Neural Networks and Ant Colony Systems. In *Computational Intelligence in Remanufacturing* (pp. 135–150). Hershey, PA: Information Science Reference. doi:10.4018/978-1-4666-4908-8.ch008

Xing, R., Wang, Z., & Peterson, R. L. (2011). Redefining the information technology in the 21st century. *International Journal of Strategic Information Technology and Applications*, *2*(1), 1–10. doi:10.4018/jsita.2011010101

Xue, B., Zhang, M., & Browne, W. N. (2013). Particle swarm optimization for feature selection in classification: A multi-objective approach. *IEEE Transactions on Cybernetics*, *43*(6), 1656–1671. doi:10.1109/TSMCB.2012.2227469 PMID:24273143

Xue, S., Tang, H., & Zhou, J. (2009). Identification of Structural Systems Using Particle Swarm Optimization. *Journal of Asian Architecture and Building Engineering*, *8*(2), 517–524. doi:10.3130/jaabe.8.517

Xu, L., Huang, D., Tsai, W., & Atkinson, R. K. (2012). V-lab: A mobile, cloud-based virtual laboratory platform for hands-on networking courses. *International Journal of Cyber Behavior, Psychology and Learning*, *2*(3), 73–85. doi:10.4018/ijcbpl.2012070106

Xu, Y., & Mao, S. (2014). Mobile cloud media: State of the art and outlook. In J. Rodrigues, K. Lin, & J. Lloret (Eds.), *Mobile networks and cloud computing convergence for progressive services and applications* (pp. 18–38). Hershey, PA: IGI Global. doi:10.4018/978-1-4666-4781-7.ch002

Xu, Z., Yan, B., & Zou, Y. (2013). Beyond hadoop: Recent directions in data computing for internet services. In S. Aljawarneh (Ed.), *Cloud computing advancements in design, implementation, and technologies* (pp. 49–66). Hershey, PA: IGI Global. doi:10.4018/978-1-4666-1879-4.ch004

Yanamadala, S., Morrison, D., Curtin, C., McDonald, K., & Hernandez-Boussard, T. (2016). Electronic health records and quality of care: An observational study modeling impact on mortality, readmissions, and complications. *Medicine, 95*(19), e3332. doi:10.1097/MD.0000000000003332 PMID:27175631

Yang, D. X. (2012). QoS-oriented service computing: Bringing SOA into cloud environment. In X. Liu & Y. Li (Eds.), *Advanced design approaches to emerging software systems: Principles, methodologies and tools* (pp. 274–296). Hershey, PA: IGI Global. doi:10.4018/978-1-60960-735-7.ch013

Yang, H., Huff, S. L., & Tate, M. (2013). Managing the cloud for information systems agility. In A. Bento & A. Aggarwal (Eds.), *Cloud computing service and deployment models: Layers and management* (pp. 70–93). Hershey, PA: IGI Global. doi:10.4018/978-1-4666-2187-9.ch004

Yang, M., Kuo, C., & Ych, Y. (2011). Dynamic rightsizing with quality-controlled algorithms in virtualization environments. *International Journal of Grid and High Performance Computing, 3*(2), 29–43. doi:10.4018/jghpc.2011040103

Yang, X. (2012). QoS-oriented service computing: Bringing SOA into cloud environment. In *Grid and cloud computing: Concepts, methodologies, tools and applications* (pp. 1621–1643). Hershey, PA: IGI Global. doi:10.4018/978-1-4666-0879-5.ch706

Yang, Y., Chen, J., & Hu, H. (2012). The convergence between cloud computing and cable TV. *International Journal of Technology Diffusion, 3*(2), 1–11. doi:10.4018/jtd.2012040101

Yan, Z. (2014). Trust management in mobile cloud computing. In *Trust management in mobile environments: Autonomic and usable models* (pp. 54–93). Hershey, PA: IGI Global. doi:10.4018/978-1-4666-4765-7.ch004

Yassein, M. O., Khamayseh, Y. M., & Hatamleh, A. M. (2013). Intelligent randomize round robin for cloud computing. *International Journal of Cloud Applications and Computing, 3*(1), 27–33. doi:10.4018/ijcac.2013010103

Yau, S. S., An, H. G., & Buduru, A. B. (2012). An approach to data confidentiality protection in cloud environments. *International Journal of Web Services Research, 9*(3), 67–83. doi:10.4018/jwsr.2012070104

Yavuz, M. C., Sahin, F., Arnavut, Z., & Uluyol, O. (2006), Generating and Exploiting Bayesian Networks for Fault Diagnosis in Airplane Engines, *Proceedings of the IEEE International Conference on Granular Computing*, 250-255. doi:10.1109/GRC.2006.1635792

Yin, P.-Y. (2004). A Discrete Particle Swarm Algorithm for Optimal Polygonal Approximation of Digital Curves J. *Vis. Comm. Image R., 15*(2), 241–260. doi:10.1016/j.jvcir.2003.12.001

Yosuf, M. S. (2010). *Nonlinear Predictive Control Using Particle Swarm Optimization: Application to Power Systems. Hidelberg, Germany: VDM Verlag Dr.* Müller.

Young, P. C. (2011). *Recursive Estimation and Time Series Analysis* (2nd ed.). Springer-Verlag. doi:10.1007/978-3-642-21981-8

Yuan, D., Lewandowski, C., & Zhong, J. (2012). Developing a private cloud based IP telephony laboratory and curriculum. In L. Chao (Ed.), *Cloud computing for teaching and learning: Strategies for design and implementation* (pp. 126–145). Hershey, PA: IGI Global. doi:10.4018/978-1-4666-0957-0.ch009

Yusoff, N., Sporea, I., & Grüning, A. (2012). Neural Networks in Cognitive Science: An Introduction. In P. Lio & D. Verma (Eds.), *Biologically Inspired Networking and Sensing: Algorithms and Architectures* (pp. 58–83). Hershey, PA: Medical Information Science Reference. doi:10.4018/978-1-61350-092-7.ch004

Yu, T. (2001). Hierachical processing for evolving recursive and modular programs using higher order functions and lambda abstractions. *Genetic Programming and Evolvable Machines, 2*(4), 345–380. doi:10.1023/A:1012926821302

Yuvaraj, M. (2014). Cloud libraries: Issues and challenges. In S. Dhamdhere (Ed.), *Cloud computing and virtualization technologies in libraries* (pp. 316–338). Hershey, PA: IGI Global. doi:10.4018/978-1-4666-4631-5.ch018

Yu, W. D., Adiga, A. S., Rao, S., & Panakkel, M. J. (2012). A SOA based system development methodology for cloud computing environment: Using uhealthcare as practice. *International Journal of E-Health and Medical Communications, 3*(4), 42–63. doi:10.4018/jehmc.2012100104

Yu, W. D., & Bhagwat, R. (2011). Modeling emergency and telemedicine heath support system: A service oriented architecture approach using cloud computing. *International Journal of E-Health and Medical Communications, 2*(3), 63–88. doi:10.4018/jehmc.2011070104

Yu, W. D., & Bhagwat, R. (2013). Modeling emergency and telemedicine health support system: A service oriented architecture approach using cloud computing. In J. Rodrigues (Ed.), *Digital advances in medicine, e-health, and communication technologies* (pp. 187–213). Hershey, PA: IGI Global. doi:10.4018/978-1-4666-2794-9.ch011

Yu, X., & Gen, M. (2010). *Introduction to evolutionary algorithms.* Springer Science & Business Media. doi:10.1007/978-1-84996-129-5

Zakaria, M. Z., Jamaluddin, H., Ahmad, R., & Loghmanian, S. M. (2010). Multiobjective Evolutionary Algorithm Approach in Modeling Discrete-Time Multivariable Dynamics Systems. In *Second International Conference on Computational Intelligence, Modelling and Simulation* (pp. 65-70). Bali: Academic Press. doi:10.1109/CIMSiM.2010.55

Zaman, M., Simmers, C. A., & Anandarajan, M. (2013). Using an ethical framework to examine linkages between "going green" in research practices and information and communication technologies. In B. Medlin (Ed.), *Integrations of technology utilization and social dynamics in organizations* (pp. 243–262). Hershey, PA: IGI Global. doi:10.4018/978-1-4666-1948-7.ch015

Zapata, B. C., & Alemán, J. L. (2013). Security risks in cloud computing: An analysis of the main vulnerabilities. In D. Rosado, D. Mellado, E. Fernandez-Medina, & M. Piattini (Eds.), *Security engineering for cloud computing: Approaches and tools* (pp. 55–71). Hershey, PA: IGI Global. doi:10.4018/978-1-4666-2125-1.ch004

Zapata, B. C., & Alemán, J. L. (2014). Security risks in cloud computing: An analysis of the main vulnerabilities. In *Software design and development: Concepts, methodologies, tools, and applications* (pp. 936–952). Hershey, PA: IGI Global. doi:10.4018/978-1-4666-4301-7.ch045

Zardari, S., Faniyi, F., & Bahsoon, R. (2013). Using obstacles for systematically modeling, analysing, and mitigating risks in cloud adoption. In I. Mistrik, A. Tang, R. Bahsoon, & J. Stafford (Eds.), *Aligning enterprise, system, and software architectures* (pp. 275–296). Hershey, PA: IGI Global. doi:10.4018/978-1-4666-2199-2.ch014

Zech, P., Kalb, P., Felderer, M., & Breu, R. (2013). Threatening the cloud: Securing services and data by continuous, model-driven negative security testing. In S. Tilley & T. Parveen (Eds.), *Software testing in the cloud: Perspectives on an emerging discipline* (pp. 280–304). Hershey, PA: IGI Global. doi:10.4018/978-1-4666-2536-5.ch013

Zeng, X. (2016). The impacts of electronic health record implementation on the health care workforce. *NCMJ*, *77*(2), 112–114. doi:10.18043/ncm.77.2.112 PMID:26961833

Zhang, F., Cao, J., Cai, H., & Wu, C. (2011). Provisioning virtual resources adaptively in elastic compute cloud platforms. *International Journal of Web Services Research*, *8*(3), 54–69. doi:10.4018/jwsr.2011070103

Zhang, G., Li, C., Xue, S., Liu, Y., Zhang, Y., & Xing, C. (2012). A new electronic commerce architecture in the cloud. *Journal of Electronic Commerce in Organizations*, *10*(4), 42–56. doi:10.4018/jeco.2012100104

Zhang, J., Yao, J., Chen, S., & Levy, D. (2011). Facilitating biodefense research with mobile-cloud computing. *International Journal of Systems and Service-Oriented Engineering*, *2*(3), 18–31. doi:10.4018/jssoe.2011070102

Zhang, J., Yao, J., Chen, S., & Levy, D. (2013). Facilitating biodefense research with mobile-cloud computing. In D. Chiu (Ed.), *Mobile and web innovations in systems and service-oriented engineering* (pp. 318–332). Hershey, PA: IGI Global. doi:10.4018/978-1-4666-2470-2.ch017

Zhang, Y. Q., Fraser, M. D., Gagliano, R. A., & Kandel, A. (2000). Granular neural networks for numerical-linguistic data fusion and knowledge discovery. *IEEE Transactions on Neural Networks*, *11*(3), 658–667. doi:10.1109/72.846737 PMID:18249793

Zheng, S., Chen, F., Yang, H., & Li, J. (2013). An approach to evolving legacy software system into cloud computing environment. In X. Yang & L. Liu (Eds.), *Principles, methodologies, and service-oriented approaches for cloud computing* (pp. 207–229). Hershey, PA: IGI Global. doi:10.4018/978-1-4666-2854-0.ch009

Zhou, J., Athukorala, K., Gilman, E., Riekki, J., & Ylianttila, M. (2012). Cloud architecture for dynamic service composition. *International Journal of Grid and High Performance Computing*, *4*(2), 17–31. doi:10.4018/jghpc.2012040102

Zuo, C., Chen, Q. & Sui, X. (2013). Range limited Bi-Histogram Equalization for image contrast enhancement. *Optik, 124*, 425-431.

Zuo, Y., & Kita, E. (2012). Stock Price Forecast Using Bayesian Network. *Expert Systems with Applications*, *39*(8), 6729–6737. doi:10.1016/j.eswa.2011.12.035

About the Contributors

Mehdi Khosrow-Pour, D.B.A., received his Doctorate in Business Administration from the Nova Southeastern University (Florida, USA). Dr. Khosrow-Pour taught undergraduate and graduate information system courses at the Pennsylvania State University – Harrisburg for almost 20 years. He is currently Executive Editor at IGI Global (www.igi-global.com). He also serves as Executive Director of the Information Resources Management Association (IRMA) (www.irma-international. org), and Executive Director of the World Forgotten Children Foundation (www. world-forgotten-children.org). He is the author/ editor of more than 50 books in information technology management. He is also the Editor-in-Chief of the Journal of Global Information Management, International Journal of Open Source Software and Processes, International Journal of Green Computing, International Journal of Digital Library Systems, International Journal of E-Entrepreneurship and Innovation, International Journal of Natural Computing Research, International Journal of Art, Culture and Design Technologies, International Journal of Signs and Semiotic Systems, and International Journal of Disease Control and Containment for Sustainability, and has authored more than 50 articles published in various conference proceedings and scholarly journals.

* * *

Celso Pascoli Bottura received the B.S degree in Aeronautical Engineering from the Aeronautical Institute of Technology - ITA (São José dos Campos, SP, Brazil) in 1962, the M.S. degree in Engineering from Purdue University (West Lafayette, In, USA) in 1964 and the PhD. Degree in Electrical Engineering from the State University of Campinas - UNICAMP (Campinas, SP, Brazil), in 1973. He is a retired full Professor of the School of Electrical and Computer Engineering of UNICAMP, where he still works as a Volunteer Collaborator Professor. He has professional experiences on power electronics, control of electrical machines, multivariable identification, estimation and control, dynamic games and multi-agent control, state space computational data modeling and intelligent control, intelligent geometric observers and controllers. He is a former President of the Brazilian Society of Automatics (SBA).

Cindy Vanessa Carmona Cadavid received her B.S. degree in Control Engineer from Universidad Nacional de Colombia in 2013, and a M.Sc. degree with emphasis in Automation at the Universidad Pontificia Bolivariana – Medellín in 2017. During 2014 - 2015 she was a Young Researcher at the Universidad Nacional de Colombia funded by "Fondo Nacional de Financiamiento para la Ciencia, la Tecnología y la Innovación Francisco José de Caldas – COLCIENCIAS". At that time, she focused on controllers tuning using genetic algorithms. Nowadays, she is working on the design of communication infrastructure for remotely operated vehicles (ROV). Her research interests include underwater communications; design, analysis, and control of dynamic systems; and controllers tuning methods.

Sanjoy Das completed his BE degree from the Regional Engineering College, Durgapur, ME degree from the Bengal Engineering College (Deemed Univ.), and Howrah, PhD from the Bengal Engineering and Science University, Shibpur. Currently, he is working as an Associate Professor in Department of Engineering and Technological Studies, University of Kalyani. His research interests are tribology and optimisation techniques.

Krishna Gopal Dhal completed his B.Tech and M. Tech from Kalyani Government Engineering College. Currently he is working as Assistant Professor in Department of Computer Science & Application in Midnapore College (Autonomous). His research interests are image Processing and Nature inspired Metaheuristics.

Mateus Giesbrecht was born in Campinas, SP, Brazil in March 6th 1984. Received the B.S. degree in electrical engineering from the State University of Campinas – UNICAMP (Campinas, SP, Brazil), in 2006, the M.S. degree in electrical engineering, automation in 2007 and the Ph.D. degree in electrical engineering, automation in 2013 at the same institution. He worked for ten years as electrical engineer responsible by the design of synchronous generators at Andritz Hydro. Now is a Professor at the School of Electrical and Computer Engineering from the State University of Campinas. His research interests includes electric machines design, electric machines parameters identification, synchronous machines, multivariable identification, dynamic systems modeling, time series realization and natural computing.

Xueyuan Guo is the Ph.D. candidate of the Research Institute of Structural Engineering and Disaster Reduction at Tongji University. She completed the study in the four-year civil engineering undergraduate program discipline, Engineering Disaster Prevention and Risk Assessment, and obtained B.S. from College of Civil Engineering at Tongji University (Shanghai, China) in June, 2016. At the same year, she entered this university as the Ph.D. student. She won the National Scholarship for Ph.D. students in 2016. Her supervisor is Dr. Hesheng Tang at Tongji University. Her research interests include uncertainty analysis, damage prognosis, fatigue mechanics, and system health monitoring.

Jesús-Antonio Hernández-Riveros is an Electrical Engineer from Universidad Nacional de Colombia, M.Sc. and Doctorate graduated with honors at the University of Coruña, Spain. Currently, he is Professor at the Department of Electrical Energy and Automatics at Facultad de Minas (Faculty of Engineering), National University of Colombia. Among his research topics are computational intelligence in engineering, modeling and identification of multidomain systems, sustainable engineering and new control methods for energy efficiency.

Ekaterina Kldiashvili holds a MSc in Biology – Cell and Molecular Biology and a Ph.D. in Histology, Cytology and Embryology from the Tbilisi State University. Ekaterina works as the Executive Director of Georgian Telemedicine Union (Association), manages projects funded by Rustaveli National Science Foundation and 700 for Science, the whole activity of the Georgian Telemedicine Union (Association) and also the creation of eHealth network in Georgia. She is academic staff of the New Vision University (Associate Professor 2013-2016; Professor since 2016); Ekaterina Kldiashvili was the Principal Investigator of NATO Networking Infrastructure and BSEC projects, participant of COST Action IC0604 (Telepathology Network in Europe: EURO-TELEPATH, (2007-2011). Ekaterina is certified specialist of laboratory medicine with an experience to set up, develop and manage clinical laboratories ("NeoClinic", 2009-2010; "NeoLab" - 2010-2012; "TestDiagnostics" - 2013-2014; Center of Molecular Pathology and Early Diagnostics of the Ltd "New Vision University Hospital" - 2015), prepare and realize (in-person and online) educational courses on actual topics of laboratory medicine (14 CME programs, 2006-2008). She is leading PhD program in medicine in New Vision University. Ekaterina was trained in cytological diagnosis of malignant tumors at the Department of Oncology of the Tbilisi State Medical Academy (2002, Tbilisi, Georgia) and Gynecological Cytology Diagnostics by application of the Liquid Based Cytology Method at the company "HOLOGIC" (2014, Rome, Italy). She presented the activity and projects of the Georgian Telemedicine Union (Association) at Med-e-Tel (2004, 2005, 2006, 2008, 2010), Telemedicine Week 2005 (Institute of Tropical Medicine, Antwerp, Belgium), II International Seminar on Telemedicine (Ukraine, 2006), Telemedicine Conference in South Africa (2006), 2nd International Conference and Exhibition on Pathology (2013, USA), The 2014 Pathology Congress (2014, UK), Pathology 2015 (UK). Ekaterina Kldiashvili is author of about 35 articles, 2 chapters and editor of the book.

Goran Klepac, Ph.D., works as a head of Stretegic unit in Sector of credit risk in Raiffeisenbank Austria d.d., Croatia. In several universities in Croatia, he lectures subjects in domain of data mining, predictive analytics, decision support system, banking risk, risk evaluation models, expert system, database marketing and business intelligence. As a team leader, he successfully finished many data mining projects in different domains like retail, finance, insurance, hospitality, telecommunications, and productions. He is an author/coauthor of several books published in Croatian and English in domain of data mining.

Ana Filipa Nogueira graduated in Computer Science Engineering in 2007 and received the M.Sc. degree in 2011, both at the Polytechnic Institute of Leiria, Portugal. Currently, she works as a Project Manager on the IT department of a multinational e-commerce company. She is also a Ph.D. student of the Doctoral Program in Information Science and Technology, at University of Coimbra and a member of the Centre for Informatics and Systems of the University of Coimbra (CISUC), Portugal. Her current main research interest focuses in the concepts related to Software Maintainability, Software Reliability and Software Testing.

Leandro Nunes de Castro has a B.Sc. in Electrical Engineering from the Federal University of Goias, an M.Sc. in Electrical Engineering from Unicamp, a Ph.D. in Computer Engineering from Unicamp and an MBA in Strategic Business Management from the Catholic University of Santos. He was a Research Associate at the University of Kent at Canterbury from 2011 to 2002, a Research Fellow at Unicamp from 2002 to 2006, a Visiting Lecturer at the University Technology Malaysia in September 2005 and a Visiting Researcher at the University of Salamanca in 2014. He is currently a Professor at the Graduate Program in Electrical Engineering and Computing at the Mackenzie University, where he founded and lead the Natural Computing and Machine Learning Laboratory (LCoN). He is acknowledged by the Brazilian Research Council as a leading researcher in Computer Science, and was recognized in 2011 as one of the most cited authors in Computer Science from the country. His main research lines are Natural Computing and Machine Learning, emphasizing Artificial Immune Systems, Neural Networks, Swarm Intelligence, Evolutionary Algorithms and real-world applications. He was the founder and Chief

Editor of the International Journal of Natural Computing Research and member of the committee of several conferences. He has eight books published, from among four were written and the other three organized, and has published over 220 paper scientific papers.

Rodrigo Pasti has a degree in Computer Engineering from the São Francisco University (2004), M.Sc. in Computer Science from the Catholic University of Santos (2007), and Ph.D. in Computer Engineering form the Faculty of Electrical and Computer Engineering (FEEC) at the State University of Campinas (Unicamp). He is currently a postdoctoral research at the Natural Computing Laboratory (LCoN) of the Graduate Program in Electrical Engineering of Mackenzie University. His main areas of research are Artificial Intelligence, Machine Learning, Data Mining, Computational Forensics, Optimization, Operations Research and Natural Computing. Along these years of academic experience, he published several papers in conferences and journals, served as a reviewer of numerous publications, and he was a Professor at the Pontifical Catholic University of Campinas in 2012, where he lectured the courses of Artificial Intelligence and Natural Computing. The latter was a pioneering initiative in Brazil for undergraduate courses. Currently, he has been working not only on academic initiatives, but also bringing these to the productive sector, through projects with public and private institutions.

Alexandre Alberto Politi received her MS in Electrical Engineering and Computing from Mackenzie Presbyterian University in 2017. He is a researcher at the Laboratory of Natural Computing and Machine Learning at the Mackenzie Presbyterian University. He has articles published in the area of Natural Computing, data mining and optimization.

Swarnajit Ray completed his BTech from the Narula Institute of Technology and MTech from the Kalyani Government Engineering College, West Bengal, India. Currently he is working as an Software Engineer in JBMatrix Technology Pvt. Ltd., India. His research interests are Digital image processing and Medical imaging.

José Ribeiro is an Adjunct Professor at the Polytechnic Institute of Leiria, Portugal. He was awarded the PhD degree by the University of Extremadura, Spain; and the MSc and BSc degrees by the University of Coimbra, Portugal. His research focuses on Software Testing and Evolutionary Algorithms, with an emphasis on Object-Oriented Evolutionary Testing. Research interests: Search-Based Software Engineering, Evolutionary Testing, Genetic Programming, Systems Integration.

Mandira Sen completed her BTech from the Academy of Technology and MTech from the Kalyani Government Engineering College, West Bengal,India.Currently she is working as an Assistant Systems Engineer in TATA consultancy services,kolkata. Her research interests are digital image processing and medical imaging.

Hesheng Tang is the Associate Professor of the Research Institute of Structural Engineering and Disaster Reduction at Tongji University. He obtained B.S. in Applied Geophysics from Ocean University of China, M.S. in Solid Mechanics from Tongji University. Since he obtained Ph.D. in Engineering Mechanics from the Tongji University in 2002, he has been working in this university. He worked as a visiting scholar at Kyoto University and Kinki University during 2003-2005 and 2006-2007. His research interests include Bio-inspired intelligence commutating, inverse problems and parameter estimation, system health monitoring, optimal design of structural systems with uncertainty, fatigue mechanics, robust control and identification of dynamic systems with uncertainty.

Jorge Humberto Urrea Quintero received his BS degree in Control Engineer from Universidad Nacional de Colombia in 2013 and his M.Sc. in Electrical Engineer from Universidad de Antioquia in 2017. In 2013 he was awarded as Prominent Bachelor Student by Alcaldía de Medellín. Actually, he is working on his Ph.D. degree in Chemical Engineering at Universidad de Antioquia. His main research interests include the control of large-scale and complex systems, controllers tuning methods, applied mathematics and energy efficiency. His current research projects are related with the modeling and control of multi-scale systems.

Fernando J. Von Zuben received his Dr.E.E. degree from the University of Campinas (Unicamp), Campinas, SP, Brazil, in 1996. He is currently a Full Professor at the Department of Computer Engineering and Industrial Automation, School of Electrical and Computer Engineering, University of Campinas (Unicamp). The main topics of his research are computational intelligence, bioinspired computing, multivariate data analysis, and machine learning. He coordinates open-ended research projects in these topics, tackling real-world problems in the areas of information technology, decision-making, pattern recognition, and discrete and continuous optimization. He has concluded the supervision of more than 40 Master and Ph.D. students, and has published more than 70 full research papers and more than 220 conference papers. Fernando J. Von Zuben is IEEE Senior Member.

Lijun Xie received the B.S. degree in engineering mechanics from the Central South University, Changsha, China, in 2011, and the M.S. in civil engineering from the Tongji University, Shanghai, China, in 2014. She has been studying at Keio University, Tokyo, Japan, since 2014 with financial support from Japanese Government. She obtained the M.S. in space and environment design engineering from the Keio University in 2016, and she is currently pursuing PhD program there. She was selected as research assistant in the Global Environmental Systems Leaders (GESL) Program of Keio University in 2015, and supported by the GESL Program she studied twice, three months and six months, at Columbia University as visiting scholar. Her research interests include civil structural health monitoring, damage assessment, system identification, and uncertainty analysis.

Songtao Xue is the Professor of Department of Architecture in Tohoku Institute of Technology. He obtained B.S. in Solid Mechanics from Tongji University, Shanghai, China, in 1985. He was awarded Monbukagakusho Scholarship from Japanese Government and obtained the M.S. and Ph.D. in Architecture Engineering from Tohoku University in 1989 and 1991. He worked as a Teaching Assistant in Architecture Faculty of Engineering, Tohoku University from 1991 to1995 and became Associate Professor one year later. He worked for Tongji University as a Professor in 1996. His research interests include Civil engineering, civil structural system health monitoring and seismic design for structures.

Mário Zenha-Rela is a Tenured Assistant Professor at the Informatics Engineering Department of the University of Coimbra in Portugal. His research interests lie at the confluence of Dependable and Secure Computing with the Human Aspects of Software Engineering. Mario has participated in several national and international research and industry projects, either as coordinator, collaborator or external consultant. He was Adjunct Teaching Professor at Carnegie-Mellon University (USA) from 2008 to 2013 and served as an external expert for the European Commission during the 7th Framework Programme (FP7).

Index

A

adaptive radiation 129, 145-147, 152-153, 161

B

Bayesian Networks 76, 78-80, 82, 86-89, 91, 100, 197
biogeographic computation 127, 130, 134-136, 139, 155-156
Biogeography 127-131, 156, 161
Biogeograpic Processes 161

C

causality 127, 129, 135, 145-146, 153, 161
chaotic sequence 115-116, 122, 126
cloud computing 238, 240-242, 251, 256
CLPSO algorithm 53-54, 56-57, 60
Computing Technology 261
control parameters 112, 168, 208-209

D

data mining 77, 79-81, 91, 93-98

E

ecosystems 127, 129-131, 134-136, 139-140, 145-146, 152-153, 155-156
E-Health 261
E-Learning 261
entropy 109, 111-112, 118-119, 122, 145-146, 152-153

Evolutionary

Evolutionary algorithms 3, 78, 81, 163, 167, 196, 208-209
Evolutionary computation 52, 74
Evolutionary Testing 162-165, 169, 171, 173, 181

G

Gamut Problem 126
genetic algorithm 4-5, 52-53, 74, 163, 167, 212
Global Optimization 52, 74, 196, 208-209

H

health care 254
heuristic algorithm 22, 25, 75, 196-197
histopathological image enhancement 108
Hue 119, 126

I

image enhancement 108, 112, 114, 119, 126
immuno-inspired algorithms 1, 6, 20-21, 23, 26
Information and Communication Technologies (ICT) 239, 261
Information in Ecosystem 161
information processing 127-128, 135-136
Internet 239-241, 251, 255, 261

L

LQR 195-199, 214, 220-224, 226, 231-233

M

MAGO 195-199, 208-215, 218-219, 224, 226-228, 230-233
medical information system 238-239, 242-243, 251-252, 256-257
metaheuristic algorithms 114-115
metamodel 127, 129-130, 135-138, 140, 145, 156, 161
multi-level thresholding 108, 111
multivariable system identification 1, 15, 21-22

N

Natural Computing 128
neural network 81

O

Object-Orientation 165

P

parameter estimation 52, 60
particle swarm 1, 5, 51-55, 61, 75-76, 78-81, 83, 86-89, 92-93, 100, 114, 182
particle swarm optimization 1, 5, 51-52, 76, 78-81, 83, 86-89, 92-93, 100, 114, 182
PID TUNING 220, 226, 232
premature convergence 51, 53, 69, 75, 116
PSO algorithm 54, 56, 68-69, 78, 81-82, 89-91, 100

R

relation 7, 11, 13-16, 18, 65-66, 82, 88, 91, 98, 131, 137, 139-140, 149, 161, 211

S

Search-Based Software Engineering 162
segmentation 79, 94-96, 98, 108, 110-112, 122, 126
Simulated Annealing 52, 75, 163
simulation 51, 53-54, 60-63, 67-69, 224, 231
Software Testing 163, 165-166, 169
Stochastic Optimization 74-75
structural system 51, 54, 59
swarm intelligence 52, 54
system identification 1-7, 9, 13, 15, 19, 21-22, 25, 46-47, 51-52, 59, 75

T

Telemedicine 241-242, 261
time variant system identification 3, 6, 9, 19, 21-22, 25

W

World Wide Web 240, 261

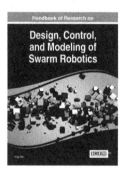

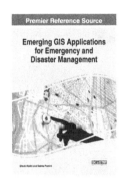